Christine Hodgins.
2/77

The Manse,
Blaina,
Gwent.

Collected Writings of
JOHN MURRAY

Collected Writings of
JOHN MURRAY

PROFESSOR OF SYSTEMATIC THEOLOGY
WESTMINSTER THEOLOGICAL SEMINARY
PHILADELPHIA, PENNSYLVANIA
1937–1966

Volume one
THE CLAIMS OF TRUTH

The Banner of Truth Trust

THE BANNER OF TRUTH TRUST
3 Murrayfield Road, Edinburgh EH12 6EL
PO Box 621 Carlisle, Pennsylvania 17013, USA

© 1976 Valerie Murray

This collection first published Volume 1 1976
ISBN 0 85151 241 0

Printed in Great Britain by
W & J Mackay Limited, Chatham

The claims of truth are paramount. That is why Westminster Theological Seminary was founded. As members of the Faculty we should not be here if it were not for the claims of truth upon us.

But the battle of the faith is oftentimes focused in the inward travail of soul which the claims of truth demand. There are so many temptations to allow the claims of truth to become secondary.

Mental laziness is one of these temptations. We have become accustomed to a certain pattern of thought and conduct. It may be surrounded by the halo of sanctity derived from an established family, social or ecclesiastical tradition, and we are not willing to bring this pattern or conviction to the test of those criteria which the truth demands. Or perhaps after persuasion to the contrary by the evidence of truth, we are not willing to let truth have its way, just because it means a breach with the convenient and the conventional.

The temptation may come in the opposite way. Convenience or opportunity may dictate the renunciation of former conviction, and the renouncing is dictated by convenience rather than by the claims of truth. We must beware of that temptation also.

*John Murray, a fragment
found among his papers.*

Contents

Contents

HISTORICAL

ISSUES IN THE CONTEMPORARY WORLD

Preface

PRIOR to John Murray's death on May 8, 1975 the present publishers had put tentative proposals to him for the contents of a volume of his Collected Writings, and these proposals, with some recommended improvements, he had accepted. It was to be a volume containing substantial theological material, some hitherto unpublished and some which had appeared in former years in *The Westminster Theological Journal*. In the event this first volume differs greatly from what was then envisaged, for after his death the opportunity occurred to examine all the manuscripts of lectures, addresses and sermons which he left in his study at Badbea, his birth place and family home in Sutherland, Scotland.

John Murray rarely proposed any of his own work for publication and it was therefore not surprising to find among his papers not a little material which will be of permanent value to the church of Christ, although he had not seen fit to call attention to it. For the most part this was carefully written in his firm, clear hand, with occasional articles or sermons in typescript. The scope of his *Collected Writings* has thus been enlarged by the introduction of many more articles and addresses than were known to the publishers when their proposal was originally discussed with the author.

This first volume now contains a wide range of shorter articles and addresses, originally prepared not so much for ministers and theological students as for Christians in general. None of these has previously appeared in book form and together they present an aspect of his ministry which may not be familiar to those who have only seen the major volumes[1] which came from his pen. Professor Murray was best known in the English-speaking world for the ability and scholarship with which, unmoved by contemporary fashions, he exegeted Scripture and presented Christian doctrine as one who was in spiritual succession to the leading Reformed expositors of earlier generations.

But like the greatest of his predecessors John Murray was more than a theologian. It was as a preacher that he was first known in his native Scottish Highlands, and when he first appeared in print—especially in the columns of *The Presbyterian Guardian* after its inception in 1935—it was as a pungent and, in the best sense, popular writer. He had more than one mode of treating a subject, believing, with Charles Hodge, that the same truth in one form is milk, in another form strong meat. As Hodge writes on 1 Corinthians 3:2: '"Christ", says Calvin, "is milk for babes, and strong meat for men". Every doctrine which can be taught to theologians is taught to children. We teach a child that God is a Spirit, everywhere present and knowing all things; and he understands it. We tell him that Christ is God and man in two distinct natures and one person for ever. This to the child is milk, but it contains food for angels. The truth expressed in these propositions may be expanded indefinitely, and furnish nourishment for the highest intellects to eternity. The difference between milk and strong meat, according to this view, is simply the difference between the more or less perfect development of the things taught.'

John Murray's writings exemplify this difference. Although in later years he concentrated much of his thought in lectures or writings designed principally for those who handle 'meat', he also continued to prepare addresses for a wider audience. This volume, then, is an attempt to present some of the salient features of his thinking in a form which can be prized by all Christian readers. And it is not thought alone which will be found here. As he observes in these pages when speaking of Calvin, the best Christian teaching will advance piety as well as learning, it will give theology 'shot through with the warmth of ardent devotion'. There is much of that element in this volume.

The material here selected for inclusion was produced between the

[1] Foremost among these are *Redemption: Accomplished and Applied*, 1955; *Principles of Conduct*, 1957; and *Commentary on the Epistle to the Romans*, vol 1, 1959; vol 2, 1965.

years 1935 and 1973. Where an article has already appeared in a journal or as a published lecture we have (when known to us) stated this in a footnote. At least seven pieces come from the pages of *The Presbyterian Guardian*. But a considerable portion of the contents has not hitherto appeared in print. A number of subjects which are handled are treated by the author in greater fulness elsewhere, either in volumes already published, or in material which will be issued later in these *Collected Writings*. For example, the theme of his address on 'The Sanctity of the Moral Law' given in 1935 came to its full expression in his much later work, *Principles of Conduct*: Aspects of Biblical Ethics, 1957. Nonetheless his shorter treatments of themes to which he was to give recurring attention are of great value; they are concise and easily-read statements and they often show the contemporary spiritual application of the subject in question. At the same time it should be added that this first volume also contains his thinking on such subjects as gospel preaching, the Lord's Day, and Christian education, which are either not treated or only handled briefly elsewhere in his writings.

I am deeply indebted to Mrs. Valerie Murray of Badbea, Bonar Bridge, Scotland for what I have considered to be the sacred privilege of examining the manuscripts which her husband left. Such was the precision with which he worked that very little indeed has been required in the way of editing. The responsibility for the selection and arrangement of the material in these *Collected Writings* has been that of the present writer.

It should, perhaps, be pointed out that in quoting Scripture, John Murray not only uses the Authorised Version and the American Standard Version of 1901, but he may also render the original in his own words. This diversity was not accidental. If, for example, he considered, on a point of detail, that the ASV follows a better attested variant reading, he quotes from it. Again, when, on occasions, he was concerned to convey the original more exactly than either of these versions, the reader may find a rendering which is unusual—for example, he prefers 'form of a servant' to 'the form of a servant' in quoting from Philippians 2:7 (cf. p. 180). The exactness with which he thus employs the witness of Scripture is a striking illustration of what he considered to be our chief obligation in all Christian testimony.

Preface

It is anticipated that these *Collected Writings* will run to at least four volumes. An index will be provided in the final volume.

Gratitude is due to Mr. S. M. Houghton for his assistance at every stage in the preparation of these volumes, and to Professors Paul Woolley and John Skilton of Westminster Theological Seminary for the advice and encouragement they have so readily provided. Doctors Arthur W. Kuschke Jr, Librarian of Westminster Seminary, and David Freeman of Holiday, Florida, have graciously provided copies of some articles and material by John Murray which would not otherwise have been available to us. Thanks are also due to John J. Mitchell, Editor of *The Presbyterian Guardian*, for permission to reprint material first published in that journal, and to John Vander Ploeg, Editor of *The Outlook* for the same privilege granted with respect to the articles entitled 'The Atonement and the Free Offer of the Gospel'.

Finally, the publishers would express thankfulness for the response to a fund which was opened after John Murray's death to aid the widest possible circulation of these *Collected Writings*. This fund, which remains open, has been generously supported by many who believe that God will be pleased to honour his servant's work in days yet to come.

All that John Murray wrote was intended to promote 'the obedience of faith'. To that end his one concern was to expound the Word of God. As he wrote in 1964, in the conclusion of the Preface to the second volume of his *Commentary on the Epistle to the Romans*, 'It is the voice of the eternal God we hear in Scripture and his glory is revealed. When the day will dawn and the day star arise in our hearts, we shall find no discrepancy between the witness of Holy Scripture and the glory then manifested'. For him that is now true. For us who read these pages a concern he once expressed about his writings remains relevant: it was 'that by God's grace what is accordant with Scripture will elicit the response of faith and conviction'.

IAIN MURRAY
Edinburgh, September 1976

xiv

The Holy Scriptures

1

The Study of the Bible[1]

I TAKE it for granted that we all believe the Bible to be the Word of God, the only infallible rule of faith and practice. I take it for granted that we all read the Bible with regularity. What I am going to plead for, however, is concentrated, sustained, devoted study of the Bible, the kind of study that is not fulfilled by the perfunctory reading of some passages each day. The set periods of family worship are not, of course, by any means to be disparaged. This is a highly necessary and most fruitful exercise. The influence for good exerted by honouring God's Word in this way is incalculable for all concerned. Indeed, the minimal use of the Bible in this way has often left an indelible impression for good. And furthermore, the set periods of family worship may become the occasions for very concentrated and systematic study of the Bible.

But what I am going to stress is the necessity for diligent and persevering searching of the Scriptures; study whereby we shall turn and turn again the pages of Scripture; the study of prolonged thought and meditation by which our hearts and minds may become soaked with the truth of the Bible and by which the deepest springs of thought, feeling and action may be stirred and directed; the study by which the Word of God will grip us, bind us, hold us, pull us, drive us, raise us up from the dunghill, bring us down from our high conceits and make us its bondservants in all of thought, life and conduct.

The Word of God is a great deep; the commandment is exceeding broad; and so we cannot by merely occasional, hurried and perfunctory use of it understand its meaning and power.

[1] From *The Presbyterian Guardian*, February 25, 1945.

Sustained and diligent study of the Bible is indispensable for several reasons. I am going to mention three of these.

1. The Bible is God's Word, the revealed counsel of God. It is possible for us to develop a certain kind of familiarity with the Bible so that we fail to appreciate the marvel of God's favour and mercy and wisdom in giving it to us. We need to stop and consider what hopeless darkness, misery and confusion would be ours if we did not possess the Bible. We would be without God and without hope in the world, endlessly stumbling over our own vain imaginings with respect to God, with respect to his will for us and with respect to our own nature, origin and destiny. The Bible is the infallible revelation to us of the truth regarding God himself, regarding the world in which we live and regarding ourselves. It reveals God's mind and will for us; it declares the way of salvation; it discloses the knowledge that is eternal life. The secrets of God's mind and purpose, secrets which eye hath not seen nor ear heard, have been laid open to us, the things that concern God's glory, and our highest interests against all the issues of life and death, of time and eternity.

If Winston Churchill wrote a book disclosing to us in his own masterly style a great many of the secrets with respect to this war, secrets which for various reasons must now be concealed, I suppose that we would all be impatient until we should be able to read it. Very likely we would devour its contents. But how trivial in comparison are the secrets hidden in Churchill's mind! The eternal God, of whose plan all history is the unfolding, has let us in on the secrets of his mind and purpose. The mystery hid from ages and generations, the things which prophets and righteous men desired to see but did not see, God has revealed to us upon whom the ends of the ages have come. He has not spoken in secret, in a dark place of the earth. His will is made known to all nations for the obedience of faith.

If we truly appreciate the mystery of God's grace and wisdom, we shall study the Bible as one who has found great spoil. The very nature and content of the Bible as God's Word will compel our most earnest application to it.

2. We must study the Bible with all diligence and persistence if we are really to know and understand its truth. It is perfectly true and an

unspeakable mercy that a certain simplicity characterizes the Bible. We cannot read it with some measure of intelligent attention without getting its great central message. The things necessary to be known, believed and observed for salvation are clearly propounded in Scripture, and he that runs may read. But no Christian should be satisfied with the bare minimum of knowledge necessary for salvation. It is, indeed, to be lamented that the life of many earnest Christians is based upon a fragmentary, piecemeal knowledge of Scripture teaching. Their knowledge is what may be called 'block-knowledge', consisting of a series of rather loosely related and disconnected items, and in their thinking these items are not brought into any coherent or co-ordinated relation to one another.

The Bible revelation should never be compared to a pile of blocks, even should we think of these as blocks of the finest granite, well-shaped and masterfully hewn, arranged in the most symmetrical order. The Bible is an organism; its unity is organic. It is not a compilation of isolated and unrelated divine oracles. The Bible is something that grew over a period of some fifteen centuries. It grew by a process of divine revelation and inspiration. At sundry times and in divers manners God progressively revealed himself and his will until in the fulness of time God sent forth his Son who is the brightness of his glory and the express image of his person.

Our knowledge of the Bible, if it is to be really adequate, must be knowledge of the Bible as it is, and must reflect this organic character, not knowledge of the piecemeal or block variety but knowledge of the vital organic unity that belongs to the Bible. We must understand that the whole Bible stands together and that the fibres of organic connection run through the whole Bible connecting one part with every other part and every one truth with every other truth.

When we appreciate this feature of Scripture and as we engage in concentrated study of one passage, our minds will course back and forth through the whole Bible along the lines which connect that passage with the rest of Scripture, lines which illumine for us the meaning of that particular passage and show the closely-knit organic unity of the whole of Scripture. It is in this way that the Bible will consist for us not in a string of texts to be used simply at random and on what we deem the appropriate occasions, but rather in an organic unit that throbs with life. Each detail of our knowledge and faith will find its place in a body of knowledge that has the same coherent, systematic and closely organized character. What might appear to us to be rather incidental and unimportant details will, on sounder and more intelligent reflection, become replete with meaning. Genesis 50:1, for example, will not be simply an incident to be read and slurred over. There we read that when Jacob died 'Joseph fell upon his father's face, and wept upon him, and kissed him.' It might appear that this is but an interesting example of oriental sentimentalism, scarcely worthy of the maturity and restraint that should characterize strong and self-controlled men. Indeed, there are people who think that it is not a mark of Christian grace to show sorrow and tears at the death of our loved ones. They would aver that Christian character will be emotionally unmoved in such situations. Well, such an attitude may be magnificent stoicism but it is not Christianity. When we read Genesis 50:1 with true insight, we shall see that it is in line with the example of our Lord when he wept at the grave of Lazarus, and in line with the devout emotion of the New Testament saints. 'And devout men carried Stephen to his burial and made great lamentation over him' (Acts 8:2). Joseph's conduct now was in complete harmony with that virile integrity and competence of which his whole life is so conspicuous an example.

3. Painstaking study of the Bible is indispensable to our own thought and practice. Life is very complex and we are constantly beset with baffling questions. New situations daily confront us. If the situations are not entirely new, old situations take on new colour and new settings. We need to know anew what is the right thing to think and what is the right thing to do. If we are to meet these situations, we must be armed with the sword of the Spirit which is the Word of God, and we must be equipped with such knowledge of the Word that we shall derive from it the needed direction and strength.

Indolence is one of our greatest temptations. We are in constant danger of becoming static in our thinking. Perhaps we have a well-rounded and competent knowledge of the Christian faith. Perhaps we have learned the Shorter Catechism or the Heidelberg Catechism. Perchance we have digested some good textbook in theology. All of this is excellent. I know of no compendium of Christian truth that is more excellent than the Shorter Catechism, and what an inestimable reservoir of truth we possess if our memories are stored with and our minds established in the masterly definitions of that treasure of Christian literature! The blessings for the kingdom of God accruing from such catechetical knowledge are incalculable, and the day of judgment alone will declare them all. We do well to peruse our great catechisms and creeds and textbooks and not be carried away by the pedagogical mush to which we are in these days subjected.

But if we rely upon such a reservoir of knowledge we are in a dangerous and slippery position. Thought and life are too complex to be adequately met by any such reservoir. The means God has provided for every exigency that may arise is the Word of God itself. The demand of the multiform situations in which we are placed in our thinking and in our life are met only by the multiform wisdom deposited in the holy Scriptures. However much assistance we may derive from formulations and expositions of Scripture truth—and it is not only impoverishing but God-dishonouring to disparage and neglect these—yet, after all, the Bible is the only *sufficient* rule of faith and life as well as the only infallible rule. We must betake ourselves anew, day by day, with humble and submissive minds to the law and to the testimony so that our minds may be illumined, replenished, refreshed, renewed and re-invigorated by the pure light that shines in the pages of God's inerrant Word. 'Let the word of Christ dwell in you richly in all wisdom.'

We may be loyal to a certain tradition, let us even say a good tradition, and yet be quite petrified and superstitious in our loyalty, if we have no higher norm or appeal than the traditions of the fathers. Our devotion to a tradition is wholesome only when we recognize in that tradition, not the authority of the fathers, but the authority of God's Word. Apart from the recognition of divine authority, all our religious devotion is abomination in the sight of God. It is to the Thessalonians that Paul wrote, 'Prove all things; hold fast that which is good.' And we can find added meaning in the exhortation when we read of the Bereans that they were 'more noble than those in Thessalonica, in that they received the word with all readiness of mind, and searched the scriptures daily, whether those things were so' (Acts 17:11). Hence the necessity of constant grounding of our convictions, of our devotion and of our conduct in the Word of God.

It was Jesus who said, 'Ye shall know the truth, and the truth shall make you free' (John 8:32). The truth is the perfect law of liberty and God's Word is truth. It might seem to us that law and liberty are incoherent. For law binds and liberty makes free. But if we know anything of God's way we know that the free men of Christ Jesus are the bondservants of Christ. The liberty wherewith Christ makes his people free is the freedom that is constituted by and consists in bondservice to God's Word.

In all our study and application of the Word of God, we must appreciate a divinely-fixed co-ordination. It is that of the Word of God and the Spirit of God. 'Where the Spirit of the Lord is, there is liberty.' God has not left us to our own resources in the study of his Word. There is the never-failing promise and the ever-present ministry of the Holy Spirit. He is the author of the Word and it is his peculiar prerogative to illumine the Scripture and to seal its truth upon our hearts. These are the two pillars of faith and life—the whole organism of Scripture revelation and the promise of the Spirit to guide us into all the truth. The Spirit honours and seals his own Word, and the Word assures us that 'if ye then, being evil, know how to give good gifts unto your children, how much more shall the heavenly Father give the Holy Spirit to them that ask him?'

2

The Infallibility of Scripture[1]

SCRIPTURE as the Word of God has many attributes. But no one of these is more precious to the believer than infallibility. This attribute assures him of its stability and it imparts to him that certitude by which alone he can be steadfast in the faith once for all delivered to the saints. The doctrine of infallibility rests upon proper grounds and only as we examine these grounds can we properly understand its meaning and assess its significance.

THE WARRANT

When we say that Scripture is infallible, on what ground or by what authority do we make this confession? When we ask the question, we should realize how momentous is the confession. In this world in which sin and misery abound, in which error is rampant, in which it is so difficult to discover the truth about any complex situation, that there should be an entity in the form of a collection of documents of which we predicate infallibility is a fact with staggering implications. And so, when we ask the question of warrant, we are asking a question of the greatest moment. The authority must be as ultimate as the proposition is stupendous.

We say Scripture is infallible not because we can prove it to be infallible. The impossibility of proof lies on the face of Scripture. For example, how could we prove that the first chapter of Genesis is substantially true, not to speak of its being infallible? This chapter deals

[1] An address given to students belonging to The Inter-Varsity Fellowship (now Universities and Colleges Christian Fellowship), probably c. 1960.

with the origin of created realities, and what collateral or independent evidence do we possess regarding the action by which created entities began to be? We must not depreciate science. But science has to deal with existing realities, not with that which was antecedent to created existence. Or again, if we think of the third chapter of Genesis, who can prove that the events there recorded are true, or that it provides us with an infallible account of what is alleged to have occurred?

It is, of course, necessary to take account of what is our province and duty. It is our obligation to defend Scripture against allegations of error and contradiction. We can often show from the data of Scripture that the Scripture is consistent with itself. And we can also show that its representations are not contradicted by data derived from other authentic sources of information. Oftentimes, though we may not be able to demonstrate the harmony of Scripture, we are able to show that there is no necessary contradiction. There is ample place and scope for this type of defence in order to meet on the basis of all the data provided for us the charges which doubt and unbelief bring against Scripture.

But the main point of interest now is that when we thus defend the Scripture we do not thereby prove its infallibility. We are indeed vindicating the authenticity of Scripture, authenticity without which it would be futile to maintain its infallibility. But we do not thereby prove its infallibility. For one thing there are areas of Scripture, and these the most important, in connection with which we are not able to engage even in the aforementioned type of defence or vindication. How could we prove that when Christ died upon the cross he expiated the sins of a countless number of lost men? How are we to prove that Christ after his ascension entered into the holy places at the right hand of the Majesty in the heavens? It can be demonstrated that the Scripture so teaches but not that these things are true.

Thus, on the question of warrant for the proposition that Scripture is infallible, what are we to say? The only ground is the witness of Scripture to itself, to its own origin, character, and authority.

This may seem an illegitimate way of supporting the proposition at issue. Are we not begging the question? We are seeking for the ground of the proposition that Scripture is infallible. And then we say: we believe this because the Scripture says so, which, in turn, assumes that we are to accept the verdict of Scripture. If we accept this verdict, we imply that its verdict is true, and not only so, but *infallibly true* if the verdict is to support the declaration that Scripture is infallible. This is the situation and we must frankly confess it to be so. It can be no otherwise in the situation that belongs to us in God's providential grace.

THE UNIQUENESS OF SCRIPTURE

Let us try to assess the situation in which we are placed. Apart from the Scriptures and the knowledge derived from them, we today would be in complete darkness respecting the content of our Christian faith. We must not deceive ourselves as to the darkness and confusion that would be ours if there were no Bible. We depend upon the message of Scripture for every tenet of our faith, for every ray of redemptive light that illumines our minds, and for every ray of hope against the issues of time and eternity. Christianity for us today without the Bible is something inconceivable.

We are not presuming to limit God. He could have brought the revelation of his redemptive will by other means than that of Scripture. But the issue now is not what God could have done if he had so pleased. The issue is what he has done. It is the *de facto* situation of God's providential ordering. And the upshot is that Scripture occupies an absolutely unique position. The case is not simply that Scripture is indispensable. Much else besides Scripture is indispensable in our actual situation. There is the witness of the church, there is the Christian tradition, and there is the mass of Christian literature. The fact is that Scripture as an entity, as a phenomenon, if you will, is absolutely unique. We are deceiving ourselves and refusing to face reality if we think that we can maintain even the most attenuated Christian belief or hope without presupposing and acknowledging that absolute uniqueness belonging to Scripture as a collection of written documents. It is this absolute uniqueness that must be taken into account when we speak of accepting its verdict.

It may be objected: does not the foregoing position impinge upon what is central in our faith? Is not Christ, the Son of God incarnate, crucified, risen, exalted, and coming again the Christian faith? Might it not even be objected that this emphasis gives to Scripture the place of God?

Of course, the Scripture is not God and to give Scripture the place of God would be idolatry. Of course, Christ is Christianity and saving relation to him as Lord and Saviour is the only hope of lost men.

But the absolute uniqueness of Scripture is not impaired. Scripture is unique, not because it takes the place of God, nor the place of Christ, but because of its relationship to God, to Christ, and to the Holy Spirit. It is unique because it is the only way whereby we come into relationship to God in the redemptive revelation of his grace, and the only way whereby Christ in the uniqueness that belongs to him as the Son of God incarnate, as the crucified, risen, and ascended Redeemer, comes within the orbit of our knowledge, faith, experience, and hope. We have no encounter with God, with Christ, and with the Holy Spirit in terms of saving and redeeming grace apart from Scripture. It is the only revelation to *us* of God's redemptive will. That is its uniqueness.

Here then is the conclusion proceeding from its uniqueness, its incomparable singularity in the situation that is ours in God's providence. If we do not accept its verdict respecting its own character or quality, we have no warrant to accept its verdict respecting anything else. If its witness respecting itself is not authentic, then by what warrant may we accept its witness on other matters? By reason of what Scripture is and means in the whole compass of Christian faith and hope we are shut up to what Scripture teaches respecting its origin, character, and authority.

THE WITNESS OF SCRIPTURE

What is this witness? Certain passages are of particular relevance. Paul says, 'All scripture is God-breathed' (2 Tim. 3:16), and Peter, 'For prophecy was not brought of old time by the will of man, but as borne by the Holy Spirit men spoke from God' (2 Pet. 1:21). In both passages it is the divine authorship and the character resulting therefrom that are emphasized. Scripture is in view in both passages. Even in 2 Pet. 1:21 this is apparent from the preceding verse which defines 'prophecy' as 'prophecy of scripture', or, as we might say, inscripturated prophecy. These two texts have closer relationship to one another than we might be disposed to think. For in the usage of Scripture the Word of God, the breath of God, and the Spirit of God are closely related. And when Paul says 'all scripture is God-breathed', he is saying nothing less than that all Scripture is God's speech, God's voice invested with all the authority and power belonging to his utterance. Peter explains how what is given through the agency of men can be God's speech—'as borne by the Holy Spirit men spoke from God'.

We think also of the words of our Lord: 'Till heaven and earth pass one jot or one tittle shall in no wise pass from the law, till all be fulfilled' (Matt. 5:18); 'the scripture cannot be broken' (John 10:35). In both passages it is the inviolability of Scripture that is asserted.

There are not only these express passages. There is a mass of witness derived from appeal to Scripture in ways that imply its finality, its divine authority, and its equivalence to God's word or speech. For our Lord, 'Scripture says' is equivalent to 'God says'. And Paul, when referring to the body of Scripture committed to Israel, can speak of it as 'the oracles of God' (Rom. 3:2).

Here then we have the verdict of Scripture. To avow any lower estimate is to impugn the witness of our Lord himself and that is to assail the dependability and veracity of him who is the truth (John 14:6). And it is also to impugn the reliability of the Holy Spirit who is also the truth as well as the Spirit of truth (1 John 5:6; John 16:13). If we reject the witness of both to the character of that upon which we must rely for our knowledge of the whole content of faith and hope, then we have no foundation of veracity on which to rest. It was the foundation of all faith, confidence, and certitude that the apostle appealed to when he said, 'Let God be true, but every man a liar' (Rom. 3:4). It is significant that he forthwith corroborated this truth by appeal to Scripture.

THE CONTEXT OF THIS WITNESS

The doctrine of the infallibility of Scripture is derived from the witness of Scripture. It is equally necessary to bear in mind that this witness is to be understood in the context of Scripture as a whole. Any doctrine severed from the total structure of revelation is out of focus. It is necessary to insist on this for two reasons.

First, it is possible to give formal confession to the infallibility of Scripture and yet belie this confession in dealing with it. The dogma of infallibility implies that Scripture is itself the revelatory Word of God, that it is the living and authoritative voice or speech of God. Unless we are arrested by that Word and summoned by it into his presence, unless we bow in reverence before that Word and accord to it the finality that belongs to it as God's oracular utterance, then our confession is only formal.

Second, unless we assess infallibility in the light of the data with which Scripture provides us, we shall be liable to judge infallibility by criteria to which Scripture does not conform. This is one of the most effective ways of undermining biblical infallibility.

The inspiration of Scripture involves verbal inspiration. If it did not carry with it the inspiration of the words, it would not be inspiration at all. Words are the media of communication. It is nothing less than verbal inspiration that Paul affirms when he says in 1 Corinthians 2:13, 'combining spiritual things with spiritual'. He is speaking of truths taught by the Spirit, as the preceding clauses indicate. But when we say 'words' we mean words in relationship, in grammatical and syntactical relationship, first of all, then in the broader contextual relationship, and last of all in relation to the whole content and structure of revelation as deposited in Scripture. They are words with the meaning which Scripture, interpreted in the light of Scripture, determines. They are Spirit-inspired words in the sense in which they were intended by the Holy Spirit. This is to say that the sense and intent of Scripture is Scripture and not the meaning we may arbitrarily impose upon it.

When the Scripture uses anthropomorphic terms with reference to God and his actions, we must interpret accordingly and not predicate of God the limitations which belong to us men. When Scripture conveys truth to us by the mode of apocalyptic vision, we cannot find the truth signified in the details of the vision literalised. If Scripture uses the language of common usage and experience or observation, we are not to accuse it of error because it does not use the language of a particular science, language which few could understand and which becomes obsolete with the passing phases of scientific advancement. The

Scripture does not make itself ridiculous by conforming to what pedants might require.

There are numerous considerations that must be taken into account derived from the study of Scripture data. And it is a capital mistake to think that the criteria of infallibility are those that must conform to our preconceived notions or to our arbitrarily adopted norms.

CONCLUSION

The doctrine of infallibility is not peripheral. What is at stake is the character of the witness which the Scripture provides for the whole compass of our faith. It is concerned with the nature of the only revelation which we possess respecting God's will for our salvation, the only revelation by which we are brought into saving encounter with him who is God manifest in the flesh, the only revelation by which we may be introduced into that fellowship which is eternal life, and the only revelation by which we may be guided in that pilgrimage to the city which hath the foundations, whose builder and maker is God. In a word the interests involved are those of faith, love, and hope.

3

The Finality and Sufficiency
of Scripture

In the Westminster Confession of Faith the finality of Scripture is expressed in these terms: 'The Old Testament in Hebrew . . . and the New Testament in Greek . . . , being immediately inspired by God, and by his singular care and providence kept pure in all ages, are therefore authentical; so as, in all controversies of religion, the church is finally to appeal unto them' (Chap. I, section viii). 'The supreme Judge, by which all controversies of religion are to be determined, and all decrees of councils, opinions of ancient writers, doctrines of men, and private spirits, are to be examined and in whose sentence we are to rest, can be no other but the Holy Spirit speaking in the Scripture' (Chap. I, section x). This statement of the case is oriented admittedly to the refutation of Rome's appeal to tradition and the voice of the church on the one hand, and to the fanatical claim to special revelation by means of mystical inner light on the other. These divergent positions are still with us and the finality of Scripture as conceived of and formulated by the Westminster Assembly more than three centuries ago is still relevant and worthy of careful examination.

There is one clause in this formulation sometimes misunderstood and mis-applied. It is the clause 'the Holy Spirit speaking in the Scripture'. This does not refer to the internal testimony of 'the Holy Spirit bearing witness by and with the Word in our hearts'. With this the Confession had dealt in section v, which is concerned with the agency by which 'our full persuasion and assurance of the infallible truth and divine authority', of Scripture are induced. But in section x the Confession is dealing with the Scripture as canon, and uses the expression 'the

Holy Spirit speaking in the Scripture' to remind us that Scripture is not a dead word but the living and abiding speech of the Holy Spirit. The Reformers needed to emphasize this quality of Scripture in order to offset the plea of Rome that a living voice is necessary for the faith and guidance of the Church and also to meet the same argument of enthusiasts for the inner voice of the Spirit in the believer. The Confession had earlier in section vi enunciated the sufficiency of Scripture. In section x it is the correlative quality, the finality, that is reflected on, but formulated with a finesse of expression that is of relevance for us today in a context that the divines of the Assembly could not have anticipated.

As we read a great deal of the theological output of the present day, the output that claims the greatest amount of attention, we find that one of its most striking features is the well-nigh total absence of any attempt to expound or be regulated in thought by the Scripture itself. This is because the regulative principle of the Reformation, especially of its Reformed exponents, has been abandoned, and with it, by necessity, the finality of Scripture. No one has been given more attention in the last two years than John A. T. Robinson, Bishop of Woolwich, and perhaps no one has been given as much. We are shocked, no doubt, when we read *Honest to God* and *The New Reformation?*, and we wonder how far removed from the whole biblical framework of thought and feeling a bishop of the Church of England can be. While we may be in sympathy with Dr. Robinson in his devastating criticism, for example, of the colossus of organizational structure found in so many denominations and particularly in his own, while we must agree that the professing church has failed to meet the situation of a secularized generation, and while we may admire his courage in exposing the sterility of a church that has lived on its fat and the fat is running out, yet we cannot but be appalled by the complete disparity between the basic patterns of his thought and those that Scripture would dictate and create. All of this lies on the face of the books I have mentioned.

But perhaps we should not be surprised. Our surprise arises, I fear, from our failure to assess the significance of what has been going on for a hundred years or more within the Protestant camp. We are suddenly awakened by the outspokenness of John Woolwich. But all of this and more is implicit in seeds sown long before we were born, when the axe was laid at the root of the tree in the denial of the veracity of Scripture. Incipient denials may take decades to work out their consequences and bear their bitterest fruit. But the fruit is now being borne, and we can see it not only in the realm of doctrine and faith but in the staggering proportions of moral disintegration.

When we speak of the sufficiency and finality of Scripture, we must, first of all, assess what Scripture is. There is no validity in the claim to finality unless the high estimate involved in finality is grounded in our conception of what Scripture is. It is here that we must appreciate the significance of inscripturation. For when we speak of Scripture we refer to what is written and, therefore, to inscripturated word as distinguished from word communicated by other means. The finality of Scripture has for us a distinctive import because of the place we occupy in the history of God's unfolding redemptive will. There is a term that is much in use, *Heilsgeschichte*, salvation history. I want to make use of that concept in its true and proper application. It is all-important in our theme.

There were periods in the history of God's redemptive revelation when the finality of Scripture had no meaning. There was no inscripturated revelatory Word. God's mind and will were communicated and transmitted by other methods. Even when revelation began to be committed to writing and was therefore to some extent inscripturated, there were centuries of redemptive history in which the finality of Scripture did not have for the church the precise import it has for us today. Undoubtedly there was a finality to what had been written. This is evident in the finality which our Lord himself attached to what was written. 'It is written' and 'Thus saith the Scripture' were for him the formulae of irrefutable appeal. And yet his own teaching was, in terms of his own claims, invested with a finality. 'Heaven and earth shall pass away, but my words shall not pass away'. And beyond what he had taught them he gave to his disciples the assurance that, when the Holy Spirit as the Spirit of truth would come, he would guide them into all truth, and that it was, therefore, expedient that he himself should depart in order that he might send the Spirit unto them for this purpose.

It is apparent that revelation was not complete even with the advent of the Lord of glory himself. And so when he ascended on high there was not to extant Scripture the finality of which we speak now, the reason being that the revelatory process was still in operation. Unless we believe that revelation is still in process as it was in the days of the prophets, in the days of our Lord, and in the days of the apostles subsequent to our Lord's ascension, then Scripture occupies for us an exclusive place and performs an exclusive function as the only extant mode of revelation. It is granted by those with whom we are particularly concerned in this address that Scripture does not continue to be written, that it is a closed canon. Once this is admitted, then we must entertain, what our opponents are not willing to grant, namely, that conception of Scripture taught and pre-supposed by our Lord and his apostles, and insist that it is this conception that must be applied to the whole canon of Scripture. Since we no longer have prophets, since we do not have our Lord with us as he was with the disciples, and since we do not have new organs of revelation as in apostolic times, Scripture in its total extent, according to the conception entertained by our Lord and his apostles, is the only revelation of the mind and will of God available to us. This is what the finality of Scripture means for us; it is the only extant revelatory Word of God.

There is a position pleaded with a good deal of plausibility and with vehement insistence, that this view of Scripture incarcerates and petrifies the Word of God, particularly that it deprives revelation of its personal character and thus of the personal encounter which revelation involves. The argument is that Christ is the incarnate Word, that he is the revelation of God, and that he is the centrum of Scripture itself. Scripture is the medium of encounter with him, and only in him is God manifest. All that is claimed for the centrality of Christ we not only admit but unreservedly proclaim. But with all this emphasis, and even more respecting the uniqueness of Christ in the history of revelation and redemption, can we fail to discern the place of Scripture in the revelation that Christ is, and in the encounter with him? It is only in and through Scripture that we have any knowledge of or contact with him who is the image of the invisible God. As in the days of his flesh the disciples had no understanding of Jesus, or faith in him apart from his spoken word, so we are wholly dependent upon their witness,

witness indeed anticipated and foreshadowed in the Old Testament, but embodied and inscripturated in the New. Without Scripture we are excluded completely from the knowledge, faith, and fellowship of him who is the effulgence of the Father's glory and the transcript of his being, as destitute of the Word of life as the disciples would have been if Jesus had not disclosed himself through his spoken word; and not only from the knowledge, faith and fellowship of the Son, but also from the knowledge and fellowship of the Father and the Spirit.

Our dependence upon Scripture is total. Without it we are bereft of revelatory Word from God, from the counsel of God 'respecting all things necessary for his own glory, man's salvation, faith and life.' Thus when the church or any of its spokesmen fails to accord to Scripture this eminence, and fails to make it the only rule of faith and life, then the kind of affront offered to Father, Son and Holy Spirit is that of substituting the wisdom of man for the wisdom of God, and human invention for divine institution. As we read the literature that claims the admiration of so many, we discern the tragedy of Satanic deception that can be indicted as no less than apostasy from the simplicity that is unto Christ. And this is apparent not only in the overt divergences from and denials of the witness of Scripture, but also in the confused conglomeration of ideas and proposals, confused and self-contradictory to some extent because of the attempt to fuse a modicum of Christian tradition with what is derived from the fountains of unbelief.

The finality of Scripture, if it has any meaning, demands that those who profess commitment to Christ and the church in its collective capacity, direct all thought, activity, and objective by this Word as the revelation to us of God's mind and will.

There is no gainsaying the fact that the situation in which we are placed today is one of peculiar gravity. There is, as the spokesmen of heterodoxy are constantly reminding us, the intense secularism of the man of today. To this mentality the supernaturalness of the gospel and of the revelation that embodies the gospel is wholly irrelevant. The leading writers of the Protestant fold are doing us the service of dinning this into our ears, and we may not close our ears to the thunder. They have, to a large extent, analysed this modern framework of thought and attitude in a way that we must reckon with in our witness to the gospel. It is, however, as we are confronted with this mentality that we must appreciate with renewed confidence the implications of the finality of Scripture and the correlative doctrine of its sufficiency. It is the challenge of the secularized mind, the technologically conditioned mind, and the supposed irrelevance to this outlook of the gospel as historically understood, that have constrained the leading exponents of today's Protestantism to reconstruct the gospel so that it will be relevant. This is the capital sin of our generation. Taking their starting point from the modern man's mentality they have revised the gospel to meet the dilemma in which the church has found itself in the face of wholesale indifference and hostility. But the question for us is: how are we, holding to the sufficiency and finality of Scripture, going to meet the secularism, or whatever else the attitude may be, of this modern man?

Here, I believe, we have too often made the mistake of not taking seriously the doctrine we profess. If Scripture is the inscripturated revelation of the gospel and of God's mind and will, if it is the only revelation of this character that we possess, then it is this revelation in all its fulness, richness, wisdom, and power that must be applied to man in whatever religious, moral, mental situation he is to be found. It is because we have not esteemed and prized the perfection of Scripture and its finality, that we have resorted to other techniques, expedients, and methods of dealing with the dilemma that confronts us all if we are alive to the needs of this hour. Some of us may have relied upon our heritage, our tradition, and may have been content with the reiteration of certain traditional formulae prescribed for us by our forefathers in a noble tradition, and with the reproduction of patterns eminently appropriate and fruitful in past generations. I do not say but signal blessing from God attends such a ministry. God blesses inadequate witness in the sovereignty of his grace. Some, on the other hand, may be so enamoured of modernity, that without abandoning a basically sound proclamation of the gospel, they have nonetheless been to such an extent influenced by the flabbiness of present-day thinking that witness to the whole counsel of God has suffered at the points of both breadth and depth. Again, I do not say that God does not bless such witness though it be impoverished and to some extent compromising.

But what I do say, and with all due emphasis, is that both are failing to bring to faithful expression the finality and sufficiency of Scripture. Let us learn from our tradition, let us prize our heritage, let us enter into other men's labours; but let us also know that it is not the tradition of the past, not a precious heritage, and not the labours of the fathers, that are to serve this generation and this hour, but the Word of the living and abiding God deposited for us in Holy Scripture, and this Word as ministered by the church. And we must bring forth from its inexhaustible treasures, in exposition, proclamation, and application— application to every sphere of life—what is the wisdom and power of God for man in this age in all the particularity of his need, as for man in every age. There will then be commanding relevance, for it will be the message from God in the unction and power of the Spirit, not de- rived *from* the modern mentality, but declared *to* the modern mentality in all the desperateness of its anxiety and misery.

Likewise, let us not refuse any of the parcels of enlightenment on many aspects of truth which even this confused generation may bring us. But let us beware of the controlling framework of modern thinking lest its patterns and presuppositions become our own, and then, before we know it, we are carried away by a current of thought and attitude that makes the sufficiency and finality of Scripture not only extraneous but alien to our way of thinking. Sadly enough this is what has taken place so often, and there comes to be no basic affinity between the faith entertained and proclaimed, on the one hand, and that which the im- plications of the sufficiency and finality of Scripture demand and con- strain, on the other.

Let us reassess the significance of *Scripture* as the Word of God and let us come to a deeper appreciation of the deposit of revelation God in his grace and wisdom has given unto us as the living Word of God, sharper than any two-edged sword, and let us know and experience its power in its sufficiency for every exigency of our individual and collec- tive need, until the day dawn and the day-star arise in our hearts. 'All scripture is given by inspiration of God and is profitable for doctrine, for reproof, for correction, for the instruction which is in righteousness, that the man of God may be perfect, thoroughly furnished unto every good work' (2 Tim. 3:16).

4

The Unity of the
Old and New Testaments[1]

THERE are certain texts that are familiar or at least ought to be. They teach us the place in history occupied by the New Testament or, more precisely, the new covenant economy (Gal. 4:4; Heb. 9:26; 1 Cor. 10:11). The New Testament era is 'the fulness of the time', 'the consummation of the ages', 'the ends of the ages', the consummating era of this world's history. Correlative with this characterization is 'the last days' (Acts 2:17; Heb. 1:2; 1 John 2:18). These began with the coming of Christ: So the world period is the last days.

This implies ages of this world's history that were not the last days; they were prior, preparatory, anticipatory. The last days are characterized by two comings, notable, unprecedented, indeed astounding— the coming into the world of the Son of God and the Spirit of God. In order to accentuate the marvel of these comings we must say that God came into the world, first in the person of the Son and then in the person of the Holy Spirit. They came by radically different modes and for different functions. But both are spoken of as comings and they are both epochal events. These comings not only introduce and characterize the last days; they create or constitute them.

Nothing in the history of the world could be comparably significant, and that is why the era is invested with such momentous finality so as to be the fulness of the time, the consummation of the ages.

These comings are not to be conceived of as continuous with and an extension of creation, as if the revelation given in creation required

1 From the author's notes of an address given to the Christian Union of the University of Dundee, 1970.

these comings in order to perfect it and put the cope stone upon it. They are both related to and the provisions of grace for the exigencies created by sin. In a word, they are redemptive, reparatory, restorative in character. The revelation involved is always redemptively conditioned, redemptively revelatory and revelationally redemptive.

In the nature of the case the Old Testament pointed forward; the New realized and fulfilled. But in a true sense, as will be shown later, the realities which give character and such momentous significance to the New Testament are those that give meaning to the Old Testament. In this sense the Old Testament revelation is derived from and based upon realities that transpired in the New, realities summed up in the coming of the Son and of the Holy Spirit. The New embodies the archetypal, heavenly, transcendent realities that validate and explain the Old Testament revelation and the corresponding acts of redemptive grace. This can also be stated in reverse.

With this perspective in view we see the unity. And nothing demonstrates the unity more than to observe how the pivotal events connected with the coming of the Son and of the Spirit are anticipated and disclosed in the Old Testament.

The great miracle of history is the coming of the Son of God. He came by becoming man, by taking human nature into union with his divine person. The result was that *he* was both God and man, God in uncurtailed Godhood, in the fulness of divine being and attributes, and man in the integrity of human nature with all its sinless infirmities and limitations, uniting in one person infinitude and finitude, the uncreated and the created. This is the great mystery of history. And since Christianity is the central and commanding fact of history, it is the mystery of Christianity, 'the mystery of godliness' (1 Tim. 3:16). So unique is this fact that we might well think that disclosure would have to wait for the fulfilment. But astounding is the fact that the Old Testament furnishes the elements, and we read: 'Unto us a child is born, unto us a son is given' *etc* (Isa. 9:6). Again: 'There shall come a shoot out of the stock of Jesse' (Isa. 11:1).

Observe the precision. When the Son of God came into the world, it was not as Adam without genealogy. He was made of a woman and of a particular line—'made of the seed of David' (Rom. 1:3). Hence

Isaiah writes 'a child is born', "a shoot out of the stock of Jesse'. In his incarnation there is genetic continuity with the human race.

Yet, though made of the woman and of the seed of David, he did not come by ordinary generation. He was begotten by the Holy Spirit (Matt. 1:20, 21; Luke 1:26–35). The Old Testament announces this (Isa. 7:14). And so Matthew: 'And so all this was done that it might be fulfilled which was spoken of the Lord by the prophet, saying, Behold a virgin shall be with child, and shall bring forth a son' (1:22, 23).

When the Son of God came, the first signal event in his introduction to Israel was his baptism by John. There are two outstanding features as a result—the witness of the Father and enduement with the Holy Spirit. 'This is my beloved Son, in whom I am well pleased' (Matt. 3:17). And Jesus 'saw the Spirit of God descending like a dove, and lighting upon him' (Matt. 3:16). Both have their counterpart in the Old Testament (Psalm 2:7; Isa. 42:1; 11:2; 61:1).

When we take account of Jesus' character, he was meek and lowly in heart. Probably this prompted John the Baptist's question (Matt. 11:3) and Jesus' reply is corroborative (11:4–6). The prophets did not fail to disclose this (Isa. 42:1–7; Psalm 72:2–4).

But we must hasten to the climactic events of Jesus' commission— death upon the cross and resurrection. No passage in Scripture is more replete with delineation than Isaiah 52:13–53:12. Note the personage, the Lord's action, the Servant's action, the spectacle, the reason, the triumphal sequel.

With reference to the cross there is the relation to the powers of darkness (John 12:31; Col. 2:15; Heb. 2:14; 1 John 3:8). The first promise is in these terms (Gen. 3:15).

The resurrection of Christ is clearly a theme of the Old Testament (Psalms 16:10, 11; 68:18).

The events of New Testament realization, as noted, afford validity and meaning to the Old Testament. They not only validate and explain; they are the ground and warrant for the revelatory and redemptive events of the Old Testament period. This can be seen in the first re- demptive promise (Gen. 3:15). We have a particularly striking illus- tration in Matt. 2:15: 'Out of Egypt have I called my son'. In Hosea 11:1 (cf. Numb. 24:8) this refers to the emancipation of Israel from

Egypt. But in Matthew 2:15 it is applied to Christ and it is easy to allege that this is an example of unwarranted application of Old Testament passages to New Testament events particularly characteristic of Matthew. But it is Matthew, as other New Testament writers, who has the perspective of organic relationship and dependence. The deliverance of Israel from Egypt found its validation, basis, and reason in what was fulfilled in Christ. So the calling of Christ out of Egypt has the primacy as archetype, though not historical priority. In other words, the type is derived from the archetype or antitype. Hence not only the propriety but necessity of finding in Hosea 11:1 the archetype that gave warrant to the redemption of Israel from Egypt.

In this perspective, therefore, we must view both Testaments. The unity is one of organic interdependence and derivation. The Old Testament has no meaning except as it is related to the realities that give character to and create the New Testament era as the fulness of time, the consummation of the ages.

Jesus Christ

5

The Redeemer of God's Elect[1]

In the whole compass of Christian literature, apart from sacred Scripture, the Shorter Catechism holds a unique position. It is the most perfect document of its kind that the Christian church has produced. To assess a document in this way is to pay it a very extraordinary tribute.

In giving such an estimate of the Shorter Catechism we are not saying that it is perfect; it is a human document and is therefore not inspired or infallible. Of all literature only the Word of God is perfect, and it is perfect because it is the Word of God, the only infallible rule of faith and practice.

Furthermore, we must not forget that other works of human authorship provide us with fuller, and in this respect more adequate and serviceable, expositions of the Word of God. The Shorter Catechism is a catechism, and a small catechism at that; there are numerous needs which the Shorter Catechism does not fulfil and was not intended to supply.

But there is no other document of its kind that presents the truth of the Christian faith with such precision of statement, such brevity of expression, such balanced proportion, such rhythmical stylistic quality, and such theological adequacy. This is just saying that there is no other document of human composition that packs into so few words such an excellent summary of the truth respecting God and his holy will revealed to us in the Scriptures of the Old and New Testaments. Any one who has perused it with some Christian intelligence must be persuaded that it is *par excellence* a masterpiece of human thought and

1 From *The Presbyterian Guardian*, November 10, 1947.

labour, a masterpiece, too, in those things that concern man's chief end —'to glorify God, and to enjoy him for ever.' What loss has been sustained by those who in their tender years have not been disciplined in its instruction, and in their maturer years have not been fortified with the truth it so effectively inculcates, words of ours cannot calculate.

THE MYSTERY OF THE INCARNATION

There is one answer in the Shorter Catechism that for many years has impressed the present writer as an unexcelled example of precision, brevity, adequacy and completeness. It is the answer to the question, 'Who is the Redeemer of God's elect?' The answer runs as follows: 'The only Redeemer of God's elect is the Lord Jesus Christ, who being the eternal Son of God, became man, and so was, and continueth to be God and man, in two distinct natures, and one person, for ever.' The very punctuation should be observed.

Any one who reads the New Testament with the humility of believing devotion and therefore with the reverence begotten of faith must be overcome again and again with the mystery that surrounds the person and work of the Lord and Saviour Jesus Christ. As understanding expands and as reverent inquiry seeks to push further and deeper there grows upon the believer the marvel of the Saviour's person and work. In reading the four Gospels, for example, one comes increasingly to appreciate the repeated expressions of wonderment on the part of those who were the eyewitnesses of the manifestation of Christ's glory. A deep chord of intelligent acquiescence is struck in the believing reader's breast as ever and anon he comes across the exclamations and acclaims of astonishment. 'What manner of man is this, that even the winds and the sea obey him!' 'And the multitudes marvelled, saying, It was never so seen in Israel.' 'And they were astonished at his doctrine: for he taught them as one that had authority, and not as the scribes.'

Jesus was indeed man. But he was also truly God. All the marks of humanity! And no less the insignia of deity! What a stupendous and incomparable conjuncture! It was never so seen in Israel. No wonder that at the very beginning of the Christian era Satan should have hurled his darts at the mystery of godliness, and in one way or another have done his utmost to destroy the faith of this Jesus. Sometimes he secured instruments to deny the reality of the Lord's humanity and sometimes to assail the reality of his deity. By hook or by crook Satan sought to destroy the faith of the church in that which constituted the mystery and the offence of Christ the incarnate Son of God. It is no wonder that the Church struggled through centuries of conflict and controversy to preserve the precious truth and to state it in the most precise and definite terms available. It is with profound gratitude to God that we should remember the issue to which these centuries of struggle came in 451 A.D. when at Chalcedon an ecumenical council was able to arrive at a statement of the faith that fixed and conserved the precious truth regarding the person of Christ, that he was truly God and truly man in one person.

In the answer from the Shorter Catechism, quoted above, this cornerstone of the Christian faith is expressed in language which a child can memorize, in language that is unexcelled in its well-balanced emphasis, and in terms that adequately guard and declare the great mystery.

ETERNAL SON OF GOD

At the outset it should be observed that the person here spoken of is called the eternal Son of God. This means that he was eternally God's Son. He did not become the Son of God. There is a Sonship, therefore, that belongs to this person quite irrespective of his becoming man. There are some people who think that the title 'Son' applies to Christ only because he became man, so that, though he was God before he became man, yet it was when he became man that he assumed the title 'Son'. This view might seem to be in the interests of guarding the full deity of Christ and his equality with the Father. It is, however, an unscriptural tenet, and it really impairs the evidence which the Scripture presents for the full deity of Christ and for his distinct personality.

If we should deny that the Lord Jesus Christ was eternally the Son of God, then we should have to deny that the Father was eternally Father. For if the first person is eternal Father, it is necessary that there be a Son of whom he is the eternal Father. And this means that the second person must be eternally the Son of the first person. Again, it is in this way that the distinction between the Father and the Son is maintained. It is also very important to notice that, if we deny that the Son was eternally the Son, then we do grave prejudice to the greatness of God's love in sending Christ into the world. The Scripture magnifies the love of God by showing that it was none other than his own well-beloved and only-begotten Son that the Father sent. He must then have been sent as the Son and not simply to be the Son. It is the greatness of such a gift that advertises the greatness of the Father's love.

We thus see how precious a truth the Shorter Catechism guarded and confessed when it prefixed the word 'eternal' to the title 'Son of God'.

Another very significant word in this answer of the Catechism is the simple word 'being'. This is what we call a present participle. And how important tenses are when we are dealing with divine truth! This participle means that the Lord Jesus was not only the eternal Son of God but that he continued to be such when he became man. There was no interruption of or interference with the eternal Sonship when he became man. And again we have a striking example of care and precision when, in addition, it is stated or, at least, implied that his continuing to be God is the corollary of his being the eternal Son of God. The one is co-ordinate with and inseparable from the other.

We are very liable to think that the title 'Son of God' suggests that the second person of the Trinity is in some way or other less than the Father. How can the Lord Jesus Christ, we are disposed to say, be both God and the Son of God? Does not the latter title indicate inferiority rather than equality? It is here that the Catechism shows its faithfulness to Scripture teaching. It is a signal feature of Scripture that, instead of representing the eternal Sonship of the second person as inconsistent with his Godhood and his equality with the Father, it rather teaches that the eternal Sonship implies or carries with it the Godhood of Christ. We have a good example in John 5:18: 'Therefore the Jews sought the more to kill him, because he not only had broken the sabbath, but said also that God was his Father, making himself equal with God.' The Jews quite properly interpreted Jesus' claim that God was his Father as tantamount to 'making himself equal with God.' That the Jews were right in this inference is shown by the fact that Jesus does not repudiate their inference but rather proceeds to vindicate his claim and to support the inference, namely, that he was equal with God.

Hence the Catechism shows a fine perception that the eternal Sonship and the Godhood of Christ are necessarily co-ordinate, and that since he was and continued to be the eternal Son he also was and continued to be God.

HE BECAME MAN

The Lord Jesus Christ, however, became man. How he became man is stated in the Catechism in the answer to the succeeding question. But in the answer with which we are now concerned it is simply stated that he became man. We come now to a very important distinction. It is the distinction between the two words 'being' and 'became'. 'Being' indicates what the Lord Jesus Christ was eternally; he did not *become* the eternal Son of God. But he did *become* man. How important again are tenses! His being as man was something that happened; it began to be. Since it was something that had a beginning it was, therefore, a temporal, historical event. Beginning to be can never be separated from time, for time and beginning belong together. So the Lord Jesus Christ became something which he previously was not. The Catechism by the simplest of terms and distinctions propounds the most mysterious of all happenings, the truth with which our holy faith stands or falls, to wit, the historical reality of the incarnation of the Son of God.

It was man that the Lord Jesus Christ became, not the appearance of man, not superman, not even deified man, but really man with a true body and a reasonable soul. And as a result of what he became he was man. It is not as if he united himself to another man, not as if he, a divine person, became conjoined to another who was a human person. It was he, a divine person, who himself became man, so that as truly as he was the eternal Son of God so truly was he also man. The Catechism was jealous to say precisely this, for its framers knew the Scripture teaching that he was both God and man in one person. They were faithful to John 1:14 and many other texts—'the Word became flesh'.

It might appear to us that Christ's becoming man required in some way or other a transmutation of what he previously and eternally was, a metamorphosis whereby his deity would be reduced or curtailed to the measure of humanity. So men have, in effect, taught. Or it might be thought that there was in some mysterious way a merging of the divine and the human and no longer undiluted deity or unchanged humanity. This has been the tendency of much speculation. But the beauty and adequacy of the concluding statements of the answer of the Catechism appear—'and so, was and continueth to be God and man, in two distinct natures, and one person, for ever'.

If there had been some kind of transfer of human properties to the divine nature, then the Lord Jesus Christ would have ceased to be truly God. If there had been some kind of transfer of divine properties to the human nature he would not have been truly man. In the one case he would no longer be the eternal Son of God and equal with God. In the other case he would not be of one flesh with us, made in the likeness of sinful flesh, clothed with our nature and the High Priest endued with a feeling of our infirmities, tempted in all points like as we are, yet without sin. Hence the preciousness of the statement, 'two distinct natures, and one person, for ever'.

GOD AND MAN—FOR EVER

A word must be said about the expression, 'for ever'. It might be plausibly protested: surely Christ is not now, in his glorified state, man; in any case, surely he will not be man for evermore! Or, it might be said, did not Jesus' exaltation mean, at least, the deification of his human nature? It is true that Jesus was exalted in his human nature. He was exalted in human nature far above all principality and power and might and dominion, and given the name that is above every name, that at the name of Jesus every knee should bow and every tongue confess that Jesus Christ is Lord, to the glory of God the Father. It is in human nature that he sits at the right hand of God. And it is also true that by his exaltation his human nature was endowed with the qualities that fit it for and are appropriate to that transcendent realm and the specific functions which are peculiar to that glorified state. But it must be noted that it is in human nature he is exalted and, although his human nature is fitted for the supernal realm of resurrection life and activity, yet his human nature is not endowed with qualities that are proper to any other nature than the human. It is surely significant that, when Christ will come the second time, God will judge the world in righteousness by *the man* whom he hath ordained (Acts 17:31). Jesus will come in human nature to judge the world. And the truly human character of the nature in which Christ is exalted is intimated in such a statement as, 'who shall change the body of our humiliation to be conformed to the body of his glory' (Phil. 3:21). Jesus' body in the exalted state is no more divine than will that of the saints be when they will be resurrected in glory. The saints will indeed be conformed to the body of Christ's glory and that will mean a glorious transformation. But the glory of it all resides in the fact that the transformation will consist in conformity to the resurrection glory of that same human nature in which the Lord of glory suffered and died. To deny the integrity of our Lord's human nature as truly and properly human in his exalted and glorified state is to overthrow what is nothing less than the pivot of Christian hope— 'then we which are alive and remain shall be caught up together with them in the clouds, to meet the Lord in the air: and so shall we ever be with the Lord' (1 Thess. 4:17). 'God and man, in two distinct natures, and one person, for ever'!

6

The Death of Christ

OUR familiarity with the fact that Jesus died, indeed the fact that his death is central to the Christian faith, is liable to obscure the astounding character of this event. Death is the wages of sin and it does not cease to be such in the case of Christ. If it is the wages of sin, how could death be applicable to him, how could it be predicable of him? He was holy, harmless, undefiled, and separate from sinners. He was the only person born of a woman who was without sin and, although there were two humans, not made of a woman, who were without sin, they did not continue without sin. He alone of all humans was without sin and continued so to be. He could protest: 'Who is he that convicteth me of sin?', and say: 'The prince of this world cometh, but he hath nothing in me'. So in the death of Christ we encounter an absolute abnormality. In all other cases men and women deserve to die. He did not deserve to die. Yet he died. What is the reason?

But there is something, perhaps more astounding. This arises from who he was. He was the eternal and only-begotten Son of God and for that reason equal with God the Father in respect of Godhood, of divine identity. He, the Word, eternally pre-existing, eternally with God, and eternally God, became flesh. He was the eternal life with the Father and in him was life. So death was not only the contradiction of what he was as human. It was the contradiction of all that he was as God. This is the astounding feature of Christ's death. He died. But death in his case was the contradiction of all that he was as divine and human, as God-man. This, therefore, points up the absolute uniqueness, the unprecedented, unparalleled character of his death. And it points up the urgency of the question: why?

This leads us to another aspect of the question. Jesus' death was not only unique for what he was as God without subtraction—holy, holy, holy, Lord God of hosts—, as man without blemish or spot. It was unique because of the way in which he died. No other died as he died. How can this be? All others die because forces other than their own wrest life from them and sever the bond uniting body and spirit. Not so Jesus on the accursed tree. He was indeed crucified by others; he did not crucify himself. His enemies killed the Prince of life; he did not kill himself. But when he died, he dismissed his spirit, he laid down his life, he in the exercise of his own agency and by authority given severed the bond. Did he not say: 'No man taketh it from me, but I lay it down of myself. I have authority to lay it down, and I have authority to take it again: this commandment have I received from my Father' (John 10:18)?

The uniqueness and the necessity for his death reside in the fact that all that Jesus did he performed in terms of obedience. When Paul says that Jesus was 'obedient unto death, even the death of the cross', he does not mean that he was obedient up to the point of death, but obedient to the extent of yielding up his life and dismissing his spirit in death. Death was the climactic requirement of his obedience.

Now this thought of obedience points us to the whole explanation of the astounding event of Christ's death. We have asked the question: why did Jesus die if, of all who died, he alone deserved not to die? Why should he have to embrace what was the contradiction of all that he was as God and man? Here is the reason. Obedience was his obedience to the Father, and obedience implies commission, and commission implies mission.

Here is the marvel of grace and love. Death is the wages of sin and therefore Jesus' death pertained to sin. Nothing is more basic or central than this little expression 'for sin'. 'What the law could not do in that it was weak through the flesh, God sending his own Son in the likeness of sinful flesh and for sin condemned sin in the flesh' (Rom. 8:3). 'When the fulness of the time was come, God sent forth his Son' (Gal. 4:4).

If God the Father sent his own Son 'for sin', we must appreciate at the outset what this involved. Sin is complex in its *nature* and in its *consequences*. And if the Father sent his Son for sin, he sent him to deal with sin in all the gravity of its complexity as to nature and consequence. He sent him to make an end of sin by bearing it. It is necessary to stress this fact that Jesus *bore* the sins of his people. As implied in what has been said, that death is the wages of sin, and as will be unfolded presently, Jesus bore the penalty of sin, the whole penal judgment of God upon the sin he vicariously bore. But we are not doing justice to the teaching of Scripture, nor to the reality of Christ's sin-bearing, if we restrict our thought or definition to that of bearing the penalty of sin. The Scripture is very clear in its statements. He bore our sins. He made purgation of sins. The Lord laid on him the iniquities of us all. Paul is very confident of this all-important fact when he uses an expression that surpasses all others: 'Him who knew no sin, he (*i.e.* the Father) made to be sin for us' (2 Cor. 5:21). The fact is that the Lord Jesus came not only into the closest relation to *sinful humanity* that it was possible for him to come without becoming himself sinful, but he also came into the closest relation to *sin* that it was possible for him to come without thereby becoming himself sinful. And the apostle, bringing both into conjunction, reminds us that only one who was himself sinless could be made sin so that we might be made the righteousness of God in him. If Jesus did not bear sin, he could not have dealt with its penal consequence, and the enduring of its consequence would have contradicted the dictates of heavenly propriety if he had not borne the sin which made the consequence a necessity.

There is also, however, the liability or consequence of sin and it is manifold. Jesus came to save and, therefore, dealt with the whole entail of sin. This is the significance of those diverse categories in terms of which the Bible interprets for us the atoning death of Christ. It views the death of Christ as sacrifice, as propitiation, as reconciliation, and as redemption. These are all conditioned in their precise character by the various ways in which the entail of sin is to be viewed.

Sin involves guilt and the death of Christ as sacrifice is the provision for our guilt. Sin evokes the wrath of God and propitiation is that which propitiates the wrath of God. Sin alienates us from God and reconciliation is directed to that exigency arising from sin. Sin consigns us to bondage, bondage to sin itself and to Satan. Redemption is the provision for this bondage, the death of Christ is our ransom.

There is one all-important aspect of the virtue proceeding from the death of Christ that it would be a capital error to overlook. It is the destruction of death itself. We may properly designate this the triumphal aspect and there are two facets.

The first of these facets is brought strikingly to our attention in Hebrews 2:14, 15 where we are told that Jesus through death brought to nought him that had the power of death, that is the devil, and delivered them who were all their lifetime subject to bondage. The bearing of Christ's work upon the devil is elsewhere brought to our attention (cf. John 12:31; Col. 2:15; 1 John 3:8; Gen. 3:14, 15). But in Hebrews 2:14 it is the deliverance wrought by bringing destruction to bear upon the archenemy as the one who had the power of death.

The second of these facets is the bringing to nought of death itself (cf. 2 Tim. 1:10). It is a question: how can death be considered as brought to nought when death is still executed upon the people of God? There are several considerations.

1. In Jesus himself there is the complete victory over death. 'In that he died he died unto sin once . . . death hath no more dominion over him' (Rom. 6:9, 10). He became dead but he is living for evermore. He is the living one, the firstbegotten from the dead. He is the only one risen from the dead who dies no more.

2. He has taken the sting out of death for all his own. The sting of death is sin. In union with Christ and in the virtue of expiation and remission the sting is removed. They are delivered from the bondage of death's dread, and they can say that to depart and to be with Christ is far better.

3. The final victory will be achieved in the resurrection (cf. 1 Cor. 15:54–58). They will then be partakers to the fullest extent of the resurrection life which Christ achieved. 'The last enemy, death, will be destroyed.'

7

The Living Saviour[1]

1. *Jesus Doing and Teaching* 'The former treatise I made, O Theophilus, concerning all that Jesus began both to do and teach . . .' Acts 1:1.

It has been said that Jesus came not to preach the gospel but to do something so that there would be a gospel to preach. This is a false antithesis. Jesus came to do both. And the text brings this forcefully to our attention—'both to do and teach'.

Luke is the writer of the book of Acts and refers to his Gospel as 'the former treatise'. The most significant feature of this reference is that the Gospel, in distinction from the Acts, is concerned with what Jesus began to do and teach. So what Luke records in the present treatise is what Jesus *continued* to do and teach. The Gospel of Luke closes with the ascension of Christ into heaven; the book of Acts is therefore concerned with the doing and teaching of Christ from his exalted glory. It is proper to emphasize and glory in the finished work of Christ. The central message of the gospel is that Christ was once offered to bear the sins of many and that when once for all he purged sins he sat down on the right hand of the Majesty on high. But prejudice is done to the work of Christ and to our faith in him when we overlook or even fail to emphasize the continued ministry of Christ in both doing and teaching. He is ever active in the exercise of his prophetic, priestly, and kingly offices.

The fact that Jesus continued to teach after his ascension is of paramount importance for the authority of Christ in the teaching of the apostles and in the books of the New Testament. Prior to his ascension

[1] Notes of an address on Acts 1:1–3, delivered at the Leicester Ministers Conference, England, in April 1965.

Christ's teaching was directly by word of mouth. But afterwards he taught by a different mode. He taught by the ministry of appointed witnesses and inspired writers. The New Testament, all of which was written after Jesus' ascension, is not one whit less the teaching of our Lord than that delivered verbally during the days of his flesh. How utterly false it is to set up a contrast between the authority of Jesus' spoken words and the authority of the New Testament as Scripture. The latter is the teaching of Christ given in his own appointed way after his ascension.

We are reminded of Jesus' word to the disciples: 'I have yet many things to say unto you, but ye cannot bear them now. Howbeit when he, the Spirit of truth, is come he will guide you into all truth' (John 16:12, 13). It is from his own lips the certification of Luke's statement in our text. The guiding of the Holy Spirit into all truth does not suspend Jesus' own speaking. 'I have yet many things to say unto you.' But he says these things through the Holy Spirit and thus there is the seal of both divine persons, the Son and the Spirit. Let us prize with the ardour of our whole soul what Jesus continues to do, and teach. He is the living, acting, and teaching Lord.

2. *Apostolic Commission* 'Concerning all that Jesus began both to do and teach, until the day in which he was received up, after that he through the Holy Spirit had given commandments unto the apostles whom he had chosen . . .' Acts 1:1–2.

The unique place belonging to the apostles is an all-important feature of the New Testament institution. The authority they exercised they did not arrogate to themselves. They were chosen by Christ, appointed to this office, and invested with power for the execution of its functions (cf. Matt. 16:19; Luke 22:29, 30; 24:48, 49; John 20:23; Acts 1:8). It is to be observed that our Lord himself, prior to his departure from this world, made this choice and investiture. The text, in accord with other passages, draws this to our attention. He was not taken up until 'he had given commandments unto the apostles whom he had chosen'. As in the institution of baptism and the Lord's supper, the Head of the church acted directly in the appointment of his delegated representatives and, hence, there can be no disjunction of Christ's own authority and the authority he vested in the apostles.

The text, however, mentions something that we would not expect, something that might seem unnecessary and out of place. Jesus had earlier told his disciples to tarry at Jerusalem until they would be endued with power from on high (Luke 24:49) and on this same occasion he told them to wait for the promise of the Father (Acts 1:4, 5). But the striking fact mentioned in the text is that while Jesus was still with them and gave the apostles commandments, he did so 'through the Holy Spirit'. We are thus advised in a striking way of the truth so often reflected on in the New Testament, the close interdependence that obtained between our Saviour and the Holy Spirit. It is an example of the co-operation of all three persons of the Godhead in the economy of salvation. Jesus did nothing apart from the Father (cf. John 5:17, 19). And neither did he do anything apart from the Holy Spirit. It was by the Spirit he was begotten in the womb of Mary (Luke 1:35). He was baptized with the Holy Spirit at his baptism by John (Matt. 3:16). It was by the Spirit he was led into the wilderness to be tempted of the devil (Matt. 4:1; Mark 1:12; Luke 4:1). It was in the power of the Spirit he returned into Galilee (Luke 4:14). By the Spirit he cast out demons (Matt. 12:28). In the Holy Spirit he rejoiced and thanked the Father (Luke 10:21). Through the eternal Spirit Jesus offered himself on the cross (Heb. 9:14). The Holy Spirit was active in the resurrection (cf. Rom. 1:4; 8:11). According to our text the agency of the Holy Spirit is present in Jesus' commissioning of the apostles. Their commission is not only exercised by the authority of Christ and in the power of the Spirit; it was bestowed by the action of both. Herein likewise resides its sanctity.

3. *Jesus Presented Alive* 'The apostles whom he had chosen: to whom he also showed himself alive after his passion by many proofs, appearing unto them by the space of forty days, and speaking the things concerning the kingdom of God:' Acts 1:2-3.

When Jesus rose from the dead he did not show himself to all the people but to 'witnesses chosen before of God' (Acts 10:41). We might have thought otherwise, that he would have met the challenge of the chief priests, scribes, and elders (cf. Matt. 27:41, 42) by demonstrating something greater than to have come down from the cross, namely, resurrection after three days in the tomb. But it was not so. Divine wisdom dictated a different mode of demonstration. Luke is careful to observe this and underlines again the place of the apostles in witnessing to the certainty of the resurrection. To them he presented himself alive; they received the convincing, infallible proofs. It is necessary to bear in mind that there is no such thing as brute facts. Facts belong to a context and as evidence they must be properly interpreted. The chosen witnesses were able to evaluate the evidence and receive it for what it was, convincing proof. So incontestable were Jesus' appearances as the living one who became dead but lived again (cf. Rev. 1:18) that no alibi was possible. The constancy and boldness with which the apostles bore witness to the resurrection (cf. Acts 1:21; 2:31; 4:2, 33; 17:18; 1 Cor. 15:4; 1 Pet. 1:3) certify to us the conviction they entertained and the significance they recognized as belonging to it.

The form of expression Luke uses should be noted: Jesus 'presented himself alive'. It was the same Jesus the apostles knew as having suffered on the cross, as having died, and as the One who had been buried. The identity and continuity are significantly stressed. The transformation undergone by the resurrection is sufficiently marked by the emphasis placed upon 'alive'. But it was the same person in the same body in which he suffered. Here again, in what is perhaps an unsuspecting way, testimony is given to the only doctrine of which the New Testament knows anything. It is that Jesus came from the tomb of Joseph in that body that had been laid there. It was a physical resurrection in accord with Jesus' own word to his disciples: 'Why are ye troubled? and why do thoughts arise in your hearts? Behold my hands and my feet, that it is I myself: handle me, and see; for a spirit hath not flesh and bones as ye see me have' (Luke 24:38, 39). Yes, the living Saviour, alive for evermore, is the same Jesus who suffered and died. We cannot know him as the living One in any other identity. And we cannot know him in his vicarious suffering and death on our behalf in any other identity than that defined by his resurrection and the endless life that is his by the great event of the first Lord's day.

8

The Heavenly,
Priestly Activity of Christ[1]

IT was in pursuance of his priestly office that Christ offered himself a
sacrifice to God upon the cross. 'Every high priest taken from among
men is ordained on behalf of men in things pertaining to God, in order
that he may offer both gifts and sacrifices for sins' (Heb. 5:1). And since
every high priest is thus ordained 'it was necessary that this one also have
something which he might offer' (Heb. 8:3). The sacrifice he offered
was none other than himself—'he offered himself without spot to God'
(Heb. 9:14). That this priestly function is not continued in the heavens is
the unambiguous witness of the New Testament and particularly of this
same epistle. 'Who needs not daily, as those high priests, to offer up
sacrifices, first for his own sins and then for the people's: for this he did
once for all when he offered up himself' (Heb. 7:27). 'Through his own
blood he entered in once for all into the holies, having obtained eternal
redemption' (Heb. 9:12). 'Nor that he should offer himself often, as the
high priest enters into the holies every year with blood of others, for
then must he often have suffered from the foundation of the world. But
now once in the consummation of the ages hath he been made manifest
for the putting away of sin by the sacrifice of himself' (Heb. 9:25, 26).

But that he does not discontinue his priestly office and function is
equally patent. That Jesus is a priest for ever after the order of Melchizedek is the refrain of this epistle. 'Thou art a priest for ever after the
order of Melchizedek' (Heb. 7:21). 'But this one because he continueth
ever has the priesthood unchangeable' (inviolable) (Heb. 7:24). There

[1] The Campbell Morgan Bible Lecture for 1958, delivered in Westminster Chapel,
London, on June 18 of that year.

must therefore be a high priestly activity perpetually carried on by Jesus in the heavenlies, in what this writer calls 'the right hand of the throne of the Majesty in the heavens' (Heb. 8:1). And so the question arises: what is this high priestly activity in the heavenlies? It is usually spoken of as intercession. That it includes intercession is beyond question. Paul, delineating for us the pivotal events of Jesus' accomplishment, is careful to remind us that co-ordinate with the death, resurrection, and session of Christ at the right hand of God is the fact that 'he also makes intercession for us' (Rom. 8:34). And in the epistle to the Hebrews we read: 'Wherefore he is able to save also to the uttermost those who come to God through him, seeing he ever lives to make intercession for them' (Heb. 7:25). It is a mistake, however, to conceive of Christ's heavenly priestly activity as consisting merely in intercession.

In the epistle to the Hebrews we also read that Christ is entered into heaven itself, 'now to be made manifest in the presence of God for us' (Heb. 9:24). Our attention is here drawn to a representative mediatory office, exercised in the presence of God at the right hand of the throne of the Majesty in the heavens, which embraces much more than the making of intercession. Again, the confidence enjoined upon us by which we may draw near in full assurance of faith is not only inspired by the faith that a new and living way has been consecrated by the blood of Christ, but also by the assurance of Christ's continued priestly rule over the house of God. 'Having, therefore, brethren, boldness to enter into the holiest by the blood of Jesus . . . and having a high priest over the house of God, let us draw near with a true heart in full assurance of faith' (Heb. 10:19–22). Furthermore, we note in this same epistle the extent to which the sympathy of the exalted Christ is related to his priestly activity or springs from his priestly rôle. 'Wherefore it behoved him to be made like to his brethren in all things, in order that he might be a merciful and faithful high priest in things pertaining to God, to the end that he might make propitiation for the sins of the people. For in that he himself hath suffered being tempted, he is able to succour those who are being tempted' (Heb. 2:17, 18). 'Seeing then that we have a great high priest who is passed into the heavens, Jesus the Son of God, let us hold fast our confession. For we have not an high priest who cannot sympathize with our infirmities, but was tempted in all things by way of likeness, without sin' (Heb. 4:14, 15).

There is not only this multiformity of aspect derived from the epistle to the Hebrews but there is confirmation and addition supplied by other New Testament data. In Johannine usage the term that closely corresponds to the terms used in the epistle to the Hebrews is that of *paraclete*—'We have an advocate with the Father, Jesus Christ the righteous' (1 John 2:1). The *paraclete* is the person who is called to help, to plead, to comfort, to support. So Jesus in heaven is the pleader, the helper, the comforter of those who come to God through him. That this must be referred to the priestly activity of the Saviour is surely borne out by the analogy of the teaching in the epistle to the Hebrews, particularly that Jesus appears in the presence of God for us and dispenses succour in his capacity as the high priest, touched with a feeling of our infirmities. It is also borne out by the fact that the heavenly advocacy is in 1 John 2, as in Hebrews 2:17, 18, directly related to the propitiation which Jesus Christ the righteous one has performed and which he ever continues to be. So the activity as *paraclete* should most suitably be viewed as pre-eminently priestly activity based upon his finished priestly action in making propitiation.

These considerations provide the basis for a broader concept of Christ's high priestly activity in heaven than that involved in intercession. But there are considerations which open up a still wider perspective. In the epistle to the Hebrews Christ is represented as high priest over the house of God, and it is put beyond question that it is as the apostle and high priest of our confession, faithful to him who appointed him, as Moses was faithful in all his house, that Christ as Son exercises the rule over his own house. There is an administration exercised over the house of God, and the writer forthwith proceeds to identify this house as the people of God who hold fast the confidence and the rejoicing of the hope steadfast unto the end (Heb. 3:1-6). When we correlate this with the teaching of Peter to the effect that believers are built up a spiritual house for a holy priesthood (1 Peter 2:5), we can scarcely doubt that the church of God on earth is viewed as the house over which Christ exercises the rule and administration as the high priest of our confession. The church on earth as the body of Christ is the sphere of his activity in his capacity as high priest at the right hand of God. To use the symbolism of the book of Revelation, it is as the high priest that he walks in the midst of the seven golden candlesticks and in that capacity he addresses the seven churches in Asia. The epistles to the seven churches are, therefore, examples of the way in which, as a Son over his own house and as our apostle and high priest, he administers this heavenly office. Truly Christ executes his kingly office as head over all things to his body the church. But Christ is a priest upon his throne, and we must not allow the consideration of his kingly office to eclipse that aspect of Christ's heavenly activity with which we are now concerned. There is here an inter-permeation of the various offices. What we are concerned with now is to recognize that his specifically high priestly ministrations are more operative and pervasive in the church upon earth than we are frequently disposed to appreciate. And when his specifically priestly function is duly appreciated, new perspectives are opened up in the interpretation of the activity of our exalted Lord. The definition of the office of high priest that he is 'ordained for men in things pertaining to God' (Heb. 5:1), is brought to bear upon the continued high priestly activity of the Redeemer. His continued activity has a Godward reference as truly as did his finished priestly offering. This adds new richness to our conception of the relation he sustains to his people and enhances our understanding of the significance for us, as individual believers and as members of the body which is the church, of the activity which Christ in heaven continues to exercise in reference to God on behalf of those whom he has purchased with his blood.

There is another consideration, derived also from the epistle to the Hebrews, that gives the broadest possible scope to Jesus' high priestly activity. It is the fact that Jesus as high priest is the surety and mediator of the new and better covenant. The new covenant is contrasted with the Mosaic. Just as the high priest of our profession is counted worthy of more glory than Moses because he is the Son over his own house, so his pre-eminence over Moses consists also in the fact that he is the surety of a new and better covenant. 'And inasmuch as not without an oath . . . by so much the more did Jesus become the surety of a better covenant' (Heb. 7:20, 22). And the oath was, 'thou art a priest for ever' (vs. 21; cf. 9:15). The new covenant brings to its consummation the communion which is at the heart of all covenant disclosure from Abraham onwards, 'I will be your God, and ye shall be my people'. Redemptive grace reaches its zenith in the full and final realization of this promise. And if Christ as priest after the order of Melchizedek is the mediator and surety of the new covenant as the everlasting covenant, this means that his priestly function is operative in the consummating action which will bring to final and perfect fruition the redemptive counsel of God. The ever-active priestly activity of Christ is thus brought into relation with the consummation of redemption, just as it is his priestly function of making propitiation which ensured by its once-for-all transcendent efficacy and perfection that redemption would be consummated. In other words, the priestly activity of the Redeemer is central in the whole redemptive process. It is because he is a priest for ever after the order of Melchizedek that redemption in its Old Testament adumbration had saving effectiveness, that redemption in its objective accomplishment has meaning, and that redemption in its consummation will be achieved.

The heavenly high priesthood of Christ means, therefore, that Christ appears in the presence of God at the right hand of the throne of the Majesty in the heavens to present himself as the perfected high priest to plead on the basis of what he has accomplished the fulfilment of all the promises, the bestowment of all the benefits, and enduement with all the graces secured and ratified by his own high priestly offering. This is a ministry directed to the Father. This it is pre-eminently. The Godward reference is primary here as it is also in the once-for-all priestly offering. But it is also a ministry on behalf of men. As directed to the Father it has no relevance except as he is appointed for men in things pertaining to God (cf. Heb. 5:1). But since it is a ministry on behalf of men, it is also a ministry which reaches *to* men in that it involves the administration of the house of God upon earth and the ministration of succour to the people of God in all their temptations and tribulations.

There are two aspects of this high priestly activity on which we may reflect as they bear directly upon the succour and comfort afforded to the people of God on earth.

I. THE SYMPATHY OF CHRIST

This is reflected on expressly in the two texts already referred to (Hebrews 2:17, 18; 4:14, 15). These texts make it clear that this sympathy is derived from the experience of suffering, trial, and temptation which Christ endured during his humiliation. This exemplifies what appears all along the line of his high priestly functions; the heavenly exercise of this office is based upon the accomplishments of his earthly ministry in the days of his flesh. In this instance the particular aspect of the earthly ministry upon which the heavenly is based is that of the sufferings and temptations to which he was subjected while on earth. This requires us to take a much more expansive view of the earthly accomplishment which provides the basis for his heavenly priestly activity. The work once for all accomplished upon earth reached its climax and finds its focal point in the death upon the cross. The whole course of obedience moved to its climactic demand and fulfilment in the yielding up of his life in death. I say climactic fulfilment though not terminal fulfilment. For his resurrection from the dead, insofar as Jesus was active in the resurrection, was an integral element of his messianic commission and obedience. The death on the cross it was, however, that placed the resources of obedience under the most exacting demand. Likewise his sufferings reached their most demanding expression in those of Gethsemane and Calvary. Yet his obedience, sufferings, and temptations covered the whole course of his humiliation. And it is the experience derived from these sufferings and temptations that equips him with fellow-feeling or sympathy so that he is able to support and succour his own people in their sufferings and temptations. His earthly undertaking, therefore, was not only that he should offer himself once for all as a sacrifice, not only that he should have learned obedience through sufferings so as to be able in obedience to fulfil the climactic demand of his commission, but also that he might be fully equipped with the fellow-feeling requisite to the discharge of his priestly ministry of succour. We need to appreciate the continuity and inter-dependence of our Lord's earthly and heavenly ministries. For we are too ready to construe the exaltation of Christ and the ministry which he performs in the state of his exalted glory in disjunction from the state of humiliation. Or, to look at this from another angle, we are prone to emphasize the once-for-allness of his earthly accomplishment to such an extent that we fail to take account of the unity and continuity of the earthly and heavenly aspects of his high priestly function. This is but another way of recognizing the reality of our Lord's human nature in heaven, and that it is in human nature that the Son of God in heaven exercises his heavenly priesthood. Once we say human nature, we must remember that his human nature in heaven cannot be conceived of apart from the progressive developments which characterized that human nature on earth and which condition the state of consciousness, feeling, and will of that human nature in heaven.

To view the heavenly sympathy of our Lord from the aspect of our existential need, how indispensable to comfort and to perseverance in faith, to know that in all the temptations of this life we have a sympathiser, and helper, and comforter in the person of him from whom we must conceal nothing, who feels with us in every weakness and temptation, and knows exactly what our situation physical, psychological, moral, and spiritual is! And this he knows because he himself was tempted, like as we are, without sin. That he who has this feeling with us in temptation appears in the presence of God for us and is our advocate with the Father invests his sympathy and help with an efficacy that is nothing less than *omnipotent compassion*.

We sometimes entertain difficulty with the fact of Jesus' sinlessness in this connection. How can he have sympathy with us when there is the total discrepancy between our situation and his, both in the state of humiliation and exaltation. But when we pursue the subject a little more carefully we find that it is the fact that he was tempted without sin, without sin as antecedent, concomitant, or consequent, that charges his fellow-feeling with unique virtue and consolation. In our relationship to our fellowmen, do we receive much help or comfort from the person who, as respects weakness and sin, is in the same position as we are ourselves? Misery likes company and it may be that we receive some comfort from the fact that others are as weak and sinful and miserable as we are ourselves. But this is a sinister kind of comfort and it is not godly consolation. On the other hand, how great is the uplift we receive when one who is immeasurably above and beyond us in sanctification helps and succours us from the similarity of his own experience with the same temptation! How much more then when Jesus Christ the righteous, who was holy, harmless, undefiled, and separate from sinners, affords us sympathy derived from his own experience of suffering and temptation. The fact that he lends this succour from the presence of the Father enhances the marvel of its exercise. And the thought that we in the stresses and conflicts associated with the body of our humiliation are objects of the solicitude and compassion of him who sits at the right hand of the throne of the Majesty in the heavens, and who dispenses from the reservoir of his knowledge and experience consolation, fellow-feeling, and strength, injects into our fainting hearts the confidence of his invincible grace. How devastating to the faith which is the anchor of the soul both sure and steadfast, entering within the veil, and how lacking in appreciation of the existential demands of the believer's situation, is any conception of the Redeemer which does not take account of the reality of his human nature in heaven and of the reservoir of sympathy stored up in that human nature because the great high priest of our profession was tempted in all points like as we are and learned obedience from the things which he suffered! Any conception that robs our Lord of the reality and continuity of his human nature and experience is but a form of docetism which deprives the Saviour and our faith of what is indispensable to both.

II. THE INTERCESSION OF CHRIST

Whether the idea denoted by the term translated as 'intercession' is more inclusive than that of intercession, nevertheless it must include intercession. This is apparent from Romans 8:26, 27. For there the term refers undoubtedly to the intercession of the Holy Spirit. And it would be necessary to include that same notion in Romans 8:34. In Acts 25:24 a closely related idea is present. No more appropriate import could belong to the term in Hebrews 7:25. Hence we shall have to reckon with a heavenly intercession of Christ on the basis of Romans 8:34 and Hebrews 7:25, and possibly Isaiah 53:12.

We could readily encounter difficulty in entertaining the doctrine of a heavenly intercession on the part of the exalted Lord. There is some plausibility to the argument that petition, though appropriate while Jesus was upon earth as a necessity of his humiliation and of his being made in all things like unto his brethren, would be neither necessary nor fitting in his exalted state. There are various angles from which the apparent incongruity could be viewed. Is not Jesus given all authority in heaven and in earth as Head over all things to his body the church and therefore in possession of all the resources for the perfecting of the church and of all the grace to be bestowed upon its members? Is he not the Lord of the Spirit and does he not himself send forth the Holy Spirit as the advocate and comforter of the people of God upon earth? Would it not be inconsistent with his own sovereignty to exercise a function which implies dependence and subordination? And does it not detract from the high exaltation bestowed upon him to suppose that he must resort to the Father in the capacity of mediator and intercessor?

Or to view the question from another angle, is it not a reflection upon the knowledge, love, and beneficence of the Father to suppose that solicitation on the part of Christ is necessary to the bestowments of grace of which the Father is the agent? Did not Jesus say while on earth, 'In that day ye shall ask in my name, and I do not say that I will pray the Father for you; for the Father himself loveth you' (John 16:26)? So the notion of heavenly intercession could be placed in a light that would seem dishonouring to both the Father and the Son.

These objections point up the necessity of avoiding assumptions and conceptions that are divorced from the data of revelation, or at least the necessity of taking all the data of revelation into account when we think of Jesus' heavenly ministry. If we are disposed to think along the lines of these objections it is because we are ready to indulge in abstract thinking, and we betray a pattern of thought that is alien to the concreteness and diversity of the biblical witness. The biblical witness is to the effect that there is an economy of redemption and we must not discount the relations which the persons of the Godhead sustain to one another in terms of that economy. The process of redemption is not yet consummated, and, because so, the arrangements of that economy are still in operation. It is in terms of the fulfilment on the part of the three persons of the Godhead of their respective and distinguishing functions that the process of redemption progresses to its consummation. If we do not make allowance for, indeed thankfully entertain, the specific and distinguishing operations of the persons of the Godhead in the progressive realization of the counsel of salvation, then we are doing something dangerously akin to the demythologizing which relegates to the realm of myth the integral elements of our holy faith. It is not difficult to discover in the frame of mind which is inhospitable to the idea of the intercession of Christ the same tendency which eliminates the concreteness and factuality of the past historical in the once-for-all accomplishments of redemption. There is an indestructible relationship between the economical arrangement whereby Jesus intercedes with the Father in heaven and the concrete facts of Jesus' humiliation as the servant of the Father. If it was not dishonouring to the Father to send his own Son into this world, it is not dishonouring for the Father to act now in the progressive realization of his saving counsel through a mediation which the Son exercises through the mode of intercession. Divine exigencies required that redemption should have been wrought through mediation of the Son, and it only enhances our view of the knowledge, love, and beneficence of the Father to discover the economy in terms of which he brought to fruition the designs of his love. And, as far as the exaltation of Christ is concerned and the sovereignty he exercises by reason of that exaltation, we must not forget that it is an economical exaltation. It is one awarded to him because he took the form of a servant and was obedient unto death, even the death of the cross. And if it is an economical exaltation, it is an exaltation that does not suspend economical arrangements. There is a continuity between that phase of the process of redemption which is complete and the phase that is still unfolding itself. It is a patent fact written in the boldest fashion on the New Testament witness that the mediation of Christ is not suspended and the intercession is but one concrete aspect of that mediation.

That Jesus directed petition to the Father while he was on earth is apparent. To Peter he said, 'I have prayed for thee that thy faith fail not' (Luke 22:32). 'Father, forgive them, for they know not what they do' (Luke 23:34). The fullest recorded example is the high priestly prayer of John 17. John 17 is not exclusively intercession, that is to say, petition on behalf of others. For Jesus there prays on his own behalf as well—'glorify thou me with thine own self, with the glory which I had with thee before the world was' (vs. 5; cf. vs. 1). But it is to a large extent intercession. The intercession exemplified in John 17 was an essential part of his messianic undertaking and the appropriate expression of his concern for the fulfilment of his Father's will respecting his own. These recorded intercessions of our Lord in the days of his flesh provide us with some index to the content of his intercession at the right hand of God. It is unreasonable to suppose that such petitions as the following have ceased to have relevance. 'I pray not that thou shouldest take them out of the world, but that thou shouldest keep them from the evil one' (vs. 15). 'Father, that which thou hast given to me, I will that where I am they also may be with me, in order that they may behold my glory which thou hast given to me' (vs. 24). Petitions more appropriate to the need of the people of God in the world could not be conceived of, and these surely indicate the lines along which the heavenly intercession proceeds. Another example is provided by John 14:16. 'And I will pray the Father, and he will give to you another comforter that he may be with you for ever.' The giving of the Spirit refers specifically to Pentecost and the abiding presence of the Holy Spirit with the people of God as a result of Pentecost. The prayer directed to the Father in reference to this event can scarcely be excluded from the heavenly intercession; it was subsequent to the ascension that the Holy Spirit was given. The most natural interpretation is that Jesus is referring to petition directed to the Father after his departure from this world. By good inference, therefore, from some of the recorded intercessions we may gather something of the direction which the heavenly intercession follows.

But in those *contexts* where the heavenly intercession is mentioned there is an indication of the type of intercession which Jesus offers. In Romans 8:34 the context is one in which the people of God are contemplated as being challenged by their adversaries. At least the apostle is adducing those considerations which provide the answer to any charge which may be laid against them. 'Who shall lay a charge against the elect of God? It is God that justifies: Who is he who condemns? It is Christ Jesus who died, yea rather is risen, who is at the right hand of God, who also makes intercession for us' (Rom. 8:33, 34). Whether the four data with reference to Christ—his death, resurrection, exalted state, and intercession—are the answer to the question, 'who is he who condemns?', which precedes, or to the question 'who shall separate us from the love of Christ?', which follows, it is obvious that the intercession of Christ is co-ordinated with the death, resurrection, and exalted

54

glory as that which ensures the vindication, on the one alternative, or the security, on the other alternative, of the people of God. And this means that the active and abiding intercession of Christ is engaged with the permanency of the bond that unites the people of God to Christ in the efficacy of his death, in the power of his resurrection, and in the security of his exalted glory. The intercession is appealed to here for the purpose of assuring believers that there is an abiding concern on the part of the exalted Lord with the conflicts and trials which beset the people of God, and that this concern expresses itself in prayer on their behalf, that none of the assaults upon them will be successful in sundering the bond that unites them to him, and that they will be more than conquerors in every engagement with their adversaries. In a word, it is intercession directed to every exigency of their warfare and therefore to the supply of grace for every need.

Likewise in Hebrews 7:24, 25, the thought is clearly to the effect that Christ is able to save to the uttermost because he has an unchangeable priesthood and ever lives to make intercession. 'But because he abides for ever, he has the priesthood unchangeable: Wherefore he is able to save also to the uttermost them that draw nigh to God through him, seeing he ever lives to make intercession for them.' The intercession is mentioned more specifically as that which ensures salvation to the uttermost. The idea of saving to the uttermost is very inclusive, and implies salvation to the full extent, salvation complete and perfect. The inference is inescapable that the intercession of Christ brings within its scope all that is necessary to salvation in the fullest extent of its consummated perfection. This is to say that the intercession covers the whole range of what is requisite to, and of what is realized in, the eschatological salvation. The intercession of Christ is interposed to meet every need of the believer. No grace bestowed, no blessing enjoyed, no benefit received can be removed from the scope of the intercession, and the intercession is the guarantee that every exigency will be met by its efficacy. The security of salvation is bound up with his intercession, and outside of his intercession we must say that there is no salvation.

When we are thinking of the saving grace which is embraced in the scope of Christ's heavenly intercession, the intercession of Christ must be severely restricted to those who are the heirs of salvation. Jesus' intercession is always availing. 'I know that thou hearest me always' (John 11:42). It would wreck the meaning of intercession on Jesus' part to suppose that he was ever denied what was the subject of his petition to the Father. The efficacy of Jesus' intercession includes, of course, those who are still unbelievers but who are among the elect. This appears in his high priestly prayer of John 17. 'Not for these only do I ask, but also for those who believe on me through their word; that they all may be one; even as thou, Father, art in me and I in thee, that they also may be in us, in order that the world may believe that thou hast sent me' (vss. 20, 21). The intercession of which we have examples and which is referred to in Romans 8:34 and Hebrews 7:25 is strictly within the realm of saving efficacy. The objects are the heirs of salvation.

This fact is correlative with another feature that bears closely upon the efficacy of our Lord's intercession. It is that of the unity and co-extensiveness of his high priestly accomplishments and activities. The intercessory aspect of the priestly function must never be divorced from the propitiatory. The intercession is based upon the atonement. In the two passages where intercession is expressly mentioned, this correlation and dependence are clearly implied. 'It is Christ that died . . . who also makes intercession for us' (Rom. 8:34). And the context of Hebrews 7:25, specifically verses 26, 27, indicates this relationship. It was such a priest who was needed, the writer proceeds to say, who could offer himself once-for-all as a sacrifice (vs. 27). And the close parallel thought in Hebrews 9:24, that he is made manifest in the presence of God for us, is related directly to the fact that he purified the holies with better sacrifices than those of the Levitical antitypes, and that once in the consummation of the ages he was manifested to put away sin by the sacrifice of himself (vss. 23, 26).

There are two inferences that are unavoidable.

1. It would violate the implications of the unity of his priestly functions to give to the propitiatory a more inclusive extent, as respects its redemptive efficacy, than is given to the intercession. The security which is, on all accounts, bound up with the intercession is a security which must likewise inhere in the propitiation. Otherwise the intercession would not extend as far as the high priestly offering provided for, and there would be an area of accomplishment which the pro-

pitiation embraced that would not be covered by the intercession.

I am well aware that questions arise at this point respecting the privileges and opportunities accruing from the death of Christ for those who are not themselves the heirs of salvation, and therefore privileges and opportunities that are comprised in the design of the death of Christ. This is the question of the relation of the death of Christ to the gifts which fall into the category of what we call common grace. It is within the mediatorial dominion which Christ exercises as the reward of his once-for-all high priestly accomplishment that this common grace is dispensed, and the grace dispensed must sustain a relationship to his redemptive work. We must remember, however, that common grace by its very nature is non-saving grace and therefore does not fall within the sphere of that security of which we are now speaking, nor is it to be defined in terms of that which propitiation, as propitiation, contemplates. And we do not have warrant from Scripture to include within what is called *intercession* on Christ's part that which falls within the non-saving grace which those who are not the heirs of salvation enjoy in this life. But, even if certain considerations arising from the universality of Christ's dominion and from the organic relations which the operations of non-saving grace sustain to the fulfilment of God's redemptive design, required us to bring the operations of common grace within the compass of Christ's intercession in some way or other, we must remember that such intercession cannot extend beyond the efficacy and effect of non-saving grace. The *intercession* that is brought to our attention in these passages is intercession which cannot be reduced to lower terms than the efficacy of saving grace.

2. The heavenly intercession is a messianic function just as truly as was his propitiatory offering. It is therefore conducted in pursuance of the economy of salvation. It belongs to that arrangement designed by the love, grace, and wisdom of God. As in the propitiation itself, there is no place for the notion that the Father is won over to clemency and grace by inducements which the Son brings to bear upon him. Just as the propitiation is the provision of the Father's love, so must we say that the intercession is also. All messianic appointment and investiture has its origin, by way of eminence, in the Father's love. The intercession is simply one element or aspect of that provision which God in love and

9

The Atonement and the Free Offer
of the Gospel[1]

I

JESUS after his resurrection said to his disciples that 'repentance unto remission of sins should be preached in his name unto all the nations' (Luke 24:47). On the eve of his ascension he gave the mandate, 'Go ye therefore and make disciples of all the nations, baptizing them in the name of the Father, and of the Son, and of the Holy Spirit' (Matt. 28:19). Here is the world-wide mission committed first of all to the apostles but permanently assigned to the church and to be continued to the end of the age (cf. 28:20). It is the mission of gospel proclamation with its necessary attendants of discipling and teaching and baptism construed as a necessary part of the process of discipling.

The gospel is the proclamation of good tidings, good tidings from God, good tidings of what God has done, good tidings of what he has promised to do. The passion of missions is quenched when we lose sight of the grandeur of the evangel. It is to a lost world the gospel is sent. To a world lost in sin and misery is proclaimed the marvel of God's love and grace, the tidings of salvation, salvation full and free, salvation that could not be greater, because it is salvation in him who is himself the wisdom, power, and righteousness of God. It is when the sense of the gravity of sin, as offence, defilement, guilt, bondage, and misery takes hold of our minds that we grasp the significance of Jesus' word, 're-pentance unto remission of sins unto all the nations'. All partitions are broken down, the valleys have been exalted, the mountains made low,

1 Reprinted from *The Torch and Trumpet* (now *The Outlook*), Grand Rapids, March, May–June, and November, 1965.

and the rough places smooth. There is no longer Jew nor Gentile, male nor female, bond nor free. The glory of the Lord has been revealed, and all flesh shall see it together.

Repentance may seem a harsh word; it means radical change. But it is redolent of the gospel; it is unto the remission of sins. And remission bespeaks the heart of the good tidings. We have redemption through Jesus' blood, 'the forgiveness of our trespasses, according to the riches of his grace' (Eph. 1:7). Good tidings without radical revolution would only confirm the world's sin and misery. That the proclamation should be in Jesus' name is the certification that release bears the Saviour's signature.

'Unto all the nations' bespeaks universality. And since repentance is redolent of the gospel, the universality of the demand for repentance implies the universal overture of grace. To think otherwise would abstract repentance from the grace to which it is directed in the word of Jesus; it is repentance unto the remission of sins. No word in Scripture is more unambiguous on this score than Paul's word on the Areopagus. 'The times of ignorance therefore God overlooked; but now he commandeth men that they should all everywhere repent' (Acts 17:30). Terms could not be more unrestrictive than 'all everywhere.' That it is the *demand* for repentance to all men everywhere underlines the urgency of the appeal. But it also advertises the universal overture of grace. In the forefront is the radical change in God's administration. 'In the generations gone by [God] suffered all the nations to walk in their own ways' (Acts 14:16). This is the meaning when Paul says: 'the times of ignorance therefore God overlooked'. But *now*, because the middle wall of partition has been broken down (cf. Eph. 2:14), he commands men that they should all everywhere repent. For the reason already stated this is the full and unrestricted offer of the gospel to all men. Those who deny the free overture of grace must rob the demand for repentance of its gospel implications. Denial dismembers Jesus' word, 'repentance unto remission of sins' and it contradicts the plain import of Paul's 'all everywhere'. The doctrine of the universal overture of mercy is supported by much biblical evidence. It is not necessary to adduce this evidence. Luke 24:27 in conjunction with Acts 17:30 puts the propriety and necessity beyond all question.

We may not overlook the context in which Jesus' word, 'that repentance unto remission of sins should be preached in his name unto all the nations', appears. It is preceded by 'Thus it is written, that Christ should suffer and rise from the dead on the third day.' It cannot be doubted that the suffering and resurrection of Christ are represented as the events that open the way and provide the ground for the proclamation of the evangel to all nations. The suffering and resurrection are the pivotal events of redemption according to Jesus' own witness elsewhere (cf. *e.g.,* Luke 24:26; John 10:17, 18). In the present instance these events are said to have their fruitage in the preaching of the gospel to all the nations. The same line of thought underlies Matthew 28:18, 19. The disciples are commanded to make disciples of all nations because 'all authority in heaven and in earth' had been committed to Christ. But the investment with this authority is the reward of his completed task which reached its climax on the cross (cf. John 17:2, 4, 5; Phil 2:8, 9).

When our Lord referred to his suffering as that which prepared for the preaching of repentance to all nations, he must be alluding to the redemptive implications of his suffering. That the suffering is viewed as that unto death is implied in the rising *from the dead* on the third day. In other words, he must have in view the suffering that was climaxed on Calvary when he laid down his life. This he interprets for us elsewhere as giving his life a ransom for many (Matt. 20:28; Mark 10:45). No word in Scripture is more significant for the interpretation of the suffering unto death of our Saviour. His death was vicarious ransom; it is redemptive. This is but to say that what we often speak of as the atonement is that which laid the ground for the preaching of repentance to all the nations; atonement, of course, in conjunction with its necessary sequel, the resurrection. We thus see that the universal demand for repentance and the unrestricted overture of grace involved must be grounded, according to our Lord's own express teaching, in the atonement. Hence the *whole* doctrine of the atonement bears directly upon the missionary task of the church. And this is so for the simple reason that the mission of the church is that which it pursues in obedience to Christ's commission, and this commission is grounded in his suffering unto death and rising again on the third day.

It is an obvious truth that without the atonement there would be no gospel to preach. But our interest now is not this general proposition. It is something more specific. There are two considerations. First, it is of particular interest to observe that our Lord himself enunciated this connection in his parting commission to the disciples.[1] And, second, it is the relation of his redemptive death and resurrection to the *world-wide* proclamation of the gospel that is brought to the forefront, world-wide in distinction from the restriction that obtained prior to the fulfilment of these redemptive events. There must be, therefore, a certain universalism belonging to the redemptive events that lays the basis for and warrants the universal proclamation. In other words, the extension in proclamation cannot be divorced from the question of extent. And it might seem, as many have maintained, that the universal overture presupposes universal atonement.

THE LOVE OF GOD AS THE SOURCE

The atonement in none of its aspects can be properly viewed apart from the love of God as the source from which it springs. The Scripture clearly expresses this relationship. 'For God so loved the world that he gave his only-begotten Son' (John 3:16). 'But God commends his own love toward us, that while we were yet sinners Christ died for us' (Rom. 5:8). 'In this is love, not that we loved God, but that he loved us and sent his Son a propitiation for our sins' (1 John 4:10). Thus it is not only the extent of the atonement that is thrust into the foreground by the world-wide overture of grace but also the character and extent of the love of God of which the atonement is the expression and provision. There are, therefore, the two questions which the free and unrestricted overture of grace makes unavoidable, the extent of the atonement and the love of God.

When we speak of the atonement we must always have in view the categories in terms of which the Scripture defines what we have come to speak of inclusively as the atonement, namely obedience, sacrifice (expiation), propitiation, reconciliation, and redemption. The question of extent is bound up with that of nature. For the question is: for whom

---

[1] We find the same conjunction in John 12:24, 31–33, words of Jesus spoken on the occasion of his being informed of the request of certain Greeks who came to worship at the feast.

did Christ *vicariously* render the obedience, offer sacrifice, and make propitiation? Whom did he reconcile to God and redeem by his blood? The Scripture often uses brief formulae such as he 'died for us', he 'died for the ungodly', he 'died for the unjust', he 'died for our sins' or simply he 'died for sins'. The meaning of 'died for' must be derived from the categories already mentioned. Hence the extent of 'died for' cannot be any more limited or more inclusive than that of the categories, and so the question may also be stated in the terms: for whom did Christ die?

The topic is sometimes spoken of as the design of the atonement. In the discussion the term 'design' is frequently the appropriate and convenient term. But there is also an advantage in the term 'extent'; it has a denotative quality and serves to point up the crux of the question: who are embraced in that which the atonement actually accomplished? For whom were obedience, sacrifice, propitiation, reconciliation, and redemption designed? In this question the categories must not only be understood in the specific character belonging to each but also as correlative with and interpenetrative of one another. We may not ask or discuss the question in terms of one, but of all in their mutual relationships.

Many benefits accrue to the non-elect from the redemptive work of Christ. There is more than one consideration to establish this proposition. Many blessings are dispensed to men indiscriminately because God is fulfilling his redemptive purpose in the world. Much in the way of order, equity, benevolence, and mercy is the fruit of the gospel, and the gospel is God's redemptive revelation centred in the gift of his Son. Believers are enjoined to 'do good to all men' (Gal. 6:10) and compliance has a beneficent result. But their identity as believers proceeds from redemption. Again, it is by virtue of what Christ has done that there is a gospel of salvation proclaimed to all without distinction. Are we to say that the unrestricted overture of grace is not grace to those to whom it comes? Furthermore, we must remember that all the good dispensed to this world is dispensed within the mediatorial dominion of Christ. He is given all authority in heaven and in earth and he is head over all things. But he is given this dominion as the reward of his obedience unto death (cf. Phil. 2:8, 9), and his obedience unto death is but one way of characterizing what we mean by the atonement. Thus all the good showered on this world, dispensed by Christ in the exercise of his exalted lordship, is related to the death of Christ and accrues to man in one way or another from the death of Christ. If so, it was designed to accrue from the death of Christ. Since many of these blessings fall short of salvation and are enjoyed by many who never become the possessors of salvation, we must say that the design of Christ's death is more inclusive than the blessings that belong specifically to the atonement. This is to say that even the non-elect are embraced in the design of the atonement in respect of those blessings falling short of salvation which they enjoy in this life. This is equivalent to saying that the atonement sustains this reference to the non-elect and it would not be improper to say that, in respect of what is entailed for the non-elect, Christ died for them.

We have in the Scripture itself an indication of this kind of reference and of the sanctifying effect it involves in some cases. In Hebrews 10:29 we read: 'Of how much sorer punishment, think ye, shall he be accounted worthy, who hath trodden under foot the Son of God, and hath counted the blood of the covenant wherewith he was sanctified an unholy thing, and hath done despite unto the Spirit of grace?' The person in view we must regard as one who has abandoned his Christian profession and for whom 'there remaineth no more sacrifice for sins, but a certain fearful expectation of judgment' (Heb. 10:26, 27). It is the person described in Hebrews 6:4, 5 in terms of the transforming effects experienced but who falls away and cannot be renewed unto repentance. In 2 Peter 2:20–22 the same person is described as having 'escaped the defilements of the world', as having 'known the way of righteousness', but as having turned back and returned as the dog to his vomit or the sow to wallowing in the mire. This is—terrible to contemplate!—the apostate. Our particular interest now is that he is represented as sanctified in the blood of Christ. Whatever may be the particular complexion of the sanctification in view, there can be no question but that it is derived from the blood of Christ and, if so, it was designed to accrue from the blood of Christ. The benefit was only temporary and greater guilt devolves upon the person from the fact that he participated in it and then came to count the blood by which it was conveyed an unholy thing. But, nevertheless, it was a benefit the blood of Christ procured, and procured for him. We must say that, to that extent Jesus shed his blood for his benefit. Other passages are probably in the same category. But this one suffices to show that there are benefits accruing from the death of Christ for those who finally perish. And in view of this we may say that in respect of these benefits Christ may be said to have died for those who are the beneficiaries. In any case it is incontrovertible that even those who perish are the partakers of numberless benefits that are the fruits of Christ's death and that, therefore, Christ's death sustains to them this beneficial reference, a beneficial reference, however, that does not extend beyond this life.

THE LOVE OF GOD AND THE NON-ELECT

These considerations require us to return to the question of God's love, for it is the fountain from which Christ's death flows. The question is: must we also say that the love of God has likewise a reference to the non-elect?

It should not be questioned that benefits bestowed on the ungodly are the expression of God's kindness. This is clearly implied in passages that deal with the gifts of God's general providence. When Jesus instructed his disciples to love their enemies, to pray for those who persecuted them, to do good to those who hated them, and to bless those who cursed them (Matt. 5:44; Luke 6:27, 28), the underlying reason and incentive is stated expressly to be, 'Ye shall therefore be perfect as your heavenly Father is perfect' (Matt. 5:48) and 'be ye merciful as your Father is merciful' (Luke 6:36). In a word, they must be like their heavenly Father.[1] Examples are given of their Father's beneficence. 'He makes his sun to rise upon the evil and the good, and sends rain upon just and unjust' (Matt. 5:45). There are two characterizations of God given. 'He is kind to the unthankful and to the evil' (Luke 6:35) and he

---

[1] It is to be observed that the Fatherhood of God referred to in these passages is not extended beyond the disciples. There is no warrant for the inference that the Fatherhood is as general and inclusive as the gifts bestowed. It is, however, the person who sustains to the disciples the fatherly relation who dispenses his favours to men indiscriminately.

is merciful' (Luke 6:36).[1] The implication of the latter is that he is merciful to the unthankful and evil as well as kind. It cannot then be disputed that such benefits as are exemplified in sunshine and rain, bestowed upon the ungodly, flow from God's kindness and mercy. It is because he is kind and merciful that he dispenses these benefits to his enemies. He is beneficent because he is benevolent.

We have a similar observation in Acts 14:16, 17 to the effect that even in the generations gone by, when God suffered all the nations to walk in their own ways (cf. Acts 17:30), 'yet he left not himself without witness, in that he did good and gave . . . from heaven rains and fruitful seasons'. Applying the analogy of our Lord's own teaching in the passages quoted above, we must say that the goodness done, as expressly stated, proceeded from the goodness by which God must be characterized. He is good even to those abandoned to ungodliness, and his beneficence in rains and fruitful seasons bore witness to his goodness. Thus we have the kindness, mercy, and goodness of God exercised toward the ungodly.

In the Matthaean and Lucan passages the reason urged for the exercise of kindness and mercy on the part of the disciples is that God is kind and merciful. The conduct of the disciples is to be patterned after God's action, their disposition after God's disposition. They are in this way to be 'sons of the Most High' (Luke 6:35), sons of their 'Father who is in heaven' (Matt 5:45). The inclusiveness of this pattern is seen when Jesus says, 'Ye shall therefore be perfect as your heavenly Father is perfect' (Matt. 5:48). Are we not, therefore, required to extend the characterizations beyond kindness, mercy, and goodness?

On three distinct occasions in these passages we have the exhortation 'love your enemies' (Matt. 5:44; Luke 6:27, 35). Must we not then say that the love entertained by the disciples is likewise to be patterned after the love of God, and in this case, as the contexts require, the love of God for the ungodly, the unthankful, and the evil? It might be argued that not all of the injunctions presuppose a corresponding disposition in God. For example, 'love your enemies' is conjoined with 'pray for them that persecute you' (Matt. 5:44) and 'pray for them that despitefully use you' (Luke 6:28). Since it is God the Father who is specifically in view as the

---

[1] The term rendered 'merciful' has in it the note of compassion.

heavenly Father, we cannot say that God the Father prays. Christ prayed and still intercedes at God's right hand as the Advocate with the Father and the Holy Spirit makes intercession for the saints (Rom. 8:26, 27). But there is an obvious incongruity in predicating prayer of God the Father. Other expressions could also be pleaded to give apparent support to the thesis that for all the injunctions we must not seek an analogy in the disposition and action of God the Father—'to him that smiteth thee on the one cheek, offer also the other; and from him that taketh away thy cloak withhold not thy coat also' (Luke 6:29; cf. vs. 30 and Matt. 5:47).

Into all the questions that arise in connection with such arguments or objections it would be distracting to enter. Suffice it to say that what underlies prayer for our enemies is benevolence and what underlies the other exhortations quoted and cited is the same disposition and companion virtues. This disposition must be exercised in ways that are relevant to *our* life in this world. But it has its analogue in God and comes to expression *in his case* in ways relevant to his providence of which concrete examples are given in Matthew 5:45 (cf. Acts 14:17). Obviously there is difference between the sphere of our life and that of God's government. Yet our virtues are patterned after God's own perfections. And this is surely true of the pre-eminent virtue, love. It would be impossible to make such a disjunction between God's kindness and mercy, on the one hand, which are expressly stated to be the pattern of our conduct, and love, on the other, with the result that, while kindness and mercy to the ungodly are predicated of God, yet love is not. In both passages love has the priority in exhortation and the character of God has primacy as the pattern by which we are to be directed. Are we to say that the love of God is to be excluded from the divine pattern while kindness and mercy are to be included? This would be exegetical violence amounting to monstrosity. We need but read the passages to see the impossibility of such interpretation. 'Love your enemies . . . that ye may be sons of your Father who is in heaven' (Matt. 5:44, 45). 'Love your enemies . . . and ye shall be sons of the Most High' (Luke 6:35). If anything exhibits this sonship it is love. But it is so because of its conformity to the character of God and therefore his character in respect of love. Consequently the love of God, specifically the love of the Father as the person who is the Father of the disciples, must be brought within the scope of the dispositions which find expression in the benefits dispensed indiscriminately to mankind and of which even the non-elect are participants in this life. If this is so with reference to the gifts of ordinary providence, how much more certainly must this be the case in the bestowments of an immensely higher order, namely, those that accrue from the gospel and its world-wide proclamation.

There are many biblical passages bearing upon God's overtures of grace to men that carry this implication.[1] It is not necessary to expand this study in order to adduce this evidence. The foregoing exposition is sufficient to show that there is a love in God that goes forth to lost men and is manifested in the manifold blessings which all men without distinction enjoy, a love in which non-elect persons are embraced, and a love that comes to its highest expression in the entreaties, overtures, and demands of gospel proclamation.

THE DIFFERENCE IN THE BENEFITS

We have found that there are included in the design of the atonement benefits which accrue to the non-elect. The fruits of the atonement enjoyed by some non-elect persons are defined in very lofty terms. Non-elect are said to have been sanctified in the blood of Christ, to have tasted the good word of God and the powers of the age to come, to have escaped the pollutions of the world through the knowledge of the Lord and Saviour, and to have known the way of righteousness (cf. Heb. 6:4, 5; 10:29; 2 Pet. 2:20, 21). In this sense, therefore, we may say that Christ died for non-elect persons. It must, however, be marked with equal emphasis that these fruits or benefits all fall short of salvation, even though in some cases the terms used to characterize them are such as could properly be used to describe a true state of salvation. These non-elect persons, however reforming may have been the influences exerted upon them and however uplifting their experiences, come short of the benefits accruing from the atonement, which the truly and finally saved enjoy. It is, therefore, apparent that the atonement has an entirely

[1] Cf. *The Free Offer of the Gospel* by John Murray and Ned B. Stonehouse, Phillipsburg, n.d., pp. 5–25; R. B. Kuiper: *For Whom Did Christ Die?*, Grand Rapids, 1959, pp. 89–100.

different reference to the elect from that which it sustains to the non-elect on the highest level of their experience. It is this radical differentiation that must be fully appreciated and guarded; it belongs to the crux of the question respecting the extent of the atonement. The difference can be stated bluntly to be that the non-elect do not participate in the benefits *of* the atonement and the elect do. The non-elect enjoy many benefits that accrue *from* the atonement but they do not partake of the *atonement*.

It is here that the precise *meaning* of the categories is bound up strictly with the extent. The non-elect are not partakers of the obedience of Christ, nor of the expiation Christ accomplished by his sacrifice, nor of the propitiation, reconciliation, and redemption Christ wrought. If they are not the partakers, they were not designed by God to be the partakers and, consequently, they are not included among those for whom the atonement, in its specific character as defined by the categories, was designed. This is but to say that it is limited in its extent. The atonement was designed for those, and for those only, who are ultimately the beneficiaries of what it is in its proper connotation. And likewise, when we think of Christ's 'dying for' in the substitutionary terms which are its proper import, we must say that he did not die for those who never become the beneficiaries of that substitution; he did not 'die for' the non-elect. For it is one thing to say that the non-elect are the recipients of many benefits that accrue from Christ's death, it is something entirely different to say that they are the partakers or were intended to be the partakers of the vicarious substitution which 'died for' properly connotes. To sum up, there is radical differentiation between the benefits accruing from Christ's death for the non-elect and the benefits accruing for the elect, and it is the latter that belong to the atonement in its biblical definition.

THE DIFFERENCE IN THE LOVE OF GOD

We also found that the love of God is exercised towards and is manifested to men indiscriminately, that the non-elect come within the ambit not only of God's beneficence but of the love, kindness, and mercy expressed in that beneficence. But here again we must take account of differentiation within the love of God no less than the differentiation within the benefits accruing from the death of Christ. It must be said from the outset that there is differentiation in the love of God.[1]

It is not necessary now to summon all the evidence establishing the pregnant import of 'foreknew' in Romans 8:29.[2] 'Foreknew' has undoubtedly cognitive and volitive ingredients. But it is impossible to suppress the emotive quality and, therefore, the ingredient of love belongs to the definition of what is denoted. That this love is differentiating lies on the face of the text. It is co-extensive with predestination: 'for whom he foreknew, he also predestinated to be conformed to the image of his Son.' And predestination is co-extensive with calling, justification, and glorification (vs. 30). The restrictive scope is indicated also by the appeal to election in verse 33: 'Who shall lay anything to the charge of God's elect?' The apostle in verse 29 is analysing the purpose spoken of in verse 28 and is, therefore, enunciating in the use of the word 'foreknew' what is ultimate in God's saving counsel. The differentiation is incontestable. The love as embraced in 'foreknew' is exercised towards those, and those only, who are the heirs of a salvation measuring to no lower dimensions than conformity to the image of God's Son and glorification. It is love with such *character* that it issues in the salvation of its objects and could not be universalized without positing the restoration of all.

Ephesians 1:5 is parallel to Romans 8:29. But here is explicitly expressed the fact that predestination is impelled by love: 'in love having predestinated us unto adoption.' It is because God loved that he predestinated. So, again, it is impossible to think of this love as exercised toward those not predestinated to adoption. The love impelling to predestination is of such a *character* that the determinate issue in adoption

---

[1] 'But this universal love should be always so conceived as to leave room for the fact that God, for sovereign reasons, has not chosen to bestow upon its objects that higher love which not merely desires, but purposes and works out the salvation of some . . . Neither this indiscriminate goodness in the sphere of nature, however, nor the collective love which embraces the world as an organism, nor the love of compassion which God retains for every lost sinner, should be confounded with that fourth and highest form of the divine affection which the Saviour everywhere appropriates to the disciples.' Geerhardus Vos: 'The Scriptural Doctrine of the Love of God' in *The Presbyterian and Reformed Review*, January, 1902, pp. 22f.; cf. also R. B. Kuiper: *op. cit.*, pp. 68f.

[2] Cf., by the writer, *The Epistle to the Romans*, Vol. I, Grand Rapids, 1959, *ad loc.*

flows from it; everything hangs on the qualitative distinctiveness of the love involved. The parallelism in verses 4 and 5 adds force to the particularism of both the love and its issue. Verse 4 speaks of election in Christ before the foundation of the world as directed to the end that the elect should be holy and without blemish, verse 5 of love as directed to adoption. The distinguishing quality of the love corresponds to the distinguishing quality of the election.

In Ephesians 2:4 God's 'great love' is set forth as the reason for quickening together with Christ and raising up with him. These terms in themselves refer to what is efficaciously saving and the context allows for no other reference. The 'great love' cannot be universalized; it is that which impels to the efficacious actions and cannot have an extent broader than those embraced in the actions specified. The same kind of relationship obtains between the 'great love' and the saving actions as obtains between love and predestination in Ephesians 1:5 and, again, the quality of the love must be as distinctive as the saving acts which are its result.

Other passages are corroborative of the foregoing conclusions. In Colossians 3:12—'elect of God, holy and beloved'—it is apparent that 'beloved' stands in apposition to 'elect of God' and cannot be given wider denotation. Likewise, in 1 Thessalonians 1:4 'beloved of God' is within the orbit of 'election'. In 2 Thessalonians 2:13 'beloved of the Lord' cannot be given broader scope than those identified as those whom 'God chose from the beginning unto salvation in sanctification of the Spirit and belief of the truth' (cf. 2 Thess. 2:16). In Jude 1 the 'beloved in God the Father' are those 'kept for Jesus Christ'. And in Hebrews 12:6 we are given the assurance that 'whom the Lord loves he chastens, and scourges every son whom he receives', a chastening directed to life and righteousness (cf. vss. 9, 11). In 1 John 3:1 we have another reference to the greatness of God's love (cf. Eph. 2:4). Here it is not a love indiscriminately exercised; it is the love of the Father *bestowed* in being called children of God and is, therefore, defined or, at least, characterized by that gift. The marvel consists in the status it constitutes and its specificity is certified by the apex of privilege the status involves. The differentiation is illustrated by what John adds: 'For this cause the world knoweth us not because it knew him not.'

The distinguishing character of this love of God, especially in the earlier passages dealt with, is borne out by the permanence and security correlative with it. The bond which Paul unfolds for us in its various aspects in Romans 8:28–34 is one that finds its focus, as also its origin, in 'the love of God, which is in Christ Jesus our Lord' (vs. 39). And so he gives the challenge: 'Who shall separate us from the love of Christ?' (vs. 35) and concludes that nothing 'shall be able to separate us from the love of God'. The embrace of this love is the guarantee of glorification, conformity to the image of God's Son. It is love so potent, so irresistible, so enduring, that nothing can dissolve its grasp or defeat its redeeming, preserving, and glorifying purpose.[1]

We must distinguish between the love of pure benevolence and that of complacency. The former is the love of sovereign good pleasure constrained not by virtuous qualities in the object but by sovereign grace. The latter is the love drawn out by commendable character. Since we are now dealing with differentiation in the love of God, it is not out of place to make mention of God's love of complacency and adduce a few passages that reflect upon it. Our Lord said to his disciples: 'He that hath my commandments and keepeth them, he it is that loveth me; and he that loveth me shall be loved of my Father, and I will love him and will manifest myself to him. . . . If any one love me, he will keep my word, and my Father will love him' (John 14:21, 23; cf. 16:26, 27).[2] Here is love that is premised upon love to Christ on the part of men and the keeping of Christ's commandments. It is a love drawn out and circumscribed by this condition in men and thus exists only where this condition is present. It is a love constrained by that which reflects God's own perfection. It has this distinct quality and we might venture to describe it to this extent that it is the love of approbation and responsive delight. It is love that reciprocates. The love in men that elicits it is the fruit of God's grace and a transcript of his glory.

[1] It is not necessary to expand this study by adducing the copious evidence of God's discriminating love in the Old Testament. The following passages in respect of the word 'know' bear on the face of them the differentiation which is involved: Gen. 18:19; Exod. 2:25; Psalm 1:6; Jer. 1:5; Hos. 13:5; Amos 3:2; and in respect of the word 'love': Deut. 4:37; 7:8, 13; 10:15; 23:5; 1 Kings 10:9; 2 Chron. 9:8; Jer. 31:3; Hos. 11:1; 14:4; Mal. 1:2. For treatment of this subject cf. Geerhardus Vos: *op. cit.*, pp. 6ff.

[2] 1 Cor. 8:3 may be in the same category.

DISCLOSURE OF THIS LOVE IN THE GOSPEL OFFER

We must now return to the question: how does this differentiation in the love of God apply to the love of which the atonement is the expression? Earlier in the discussion we found that the blessings of which even the non-elect are participants come within the design of the atoning work of Christ[1] and that these benefits are an expression of the love, kindness, and mercy of God. We cannot avoid the inference that the atonement is the expression of this kind of love. In other words, we may not exclude from that love of which the atonement is the provision this general love of God to lost mankind. And in the proclamation of the gospel and the presentation of the free overtures of grace to men indiscriminately it would not be proper to withhold the implications. No truth may be suppressed. So neither may this one. In the gospel offer far more is entailed than the disclosure of this love with which we are now dealing.[2] But it is not unimportant that this love should be brought to bear upon the appeal to men. Rejection of the gospel offers insult to the love, kindness, and mercy that the overture of grace necessarily betokens, and the wooing appeals of that love should be pressed home upon lost and perishing men.

But, again, as in the differentiation that must be maintained in the *reference* of the atonement, so here likewise we must recognize the differentiation in respect of the *love expressed* in the atonement. The elect, as shown above, are the objects of a love that is not exercised to the non-elect. The elect are partakers *of* the atonement; the non-elect are not. The differentiating love is that which ensures for the elect that they will be partakers of the atonement. The atonement expresses that love and is the provision for the realization of the purpose that flows from it. Once we recognize the differentiating love and the whole gamut of consequences emanating from it, then this love is the only love adequate to explain the atonement, and apart from this love the atonement in its specific character cannot be properly construed. We cannot interpret the atonement outside the inter-trinitarian counsel of salvation.[3] Jesus said:

[1] Cf. R. B. Kuiper: *op. cit.,* pp. 78f.

[2] This will be dealt with later on in these studies.

[3] I have used this designation to denote what has often been called the covenant of redemption.

'For I am come down from heaven, not to do mine own will, but the will of him that sent me. And this is the will of him that sent me, that of all that which he hath given me I should lose nothing, but should raise it up at the last day' (John 6:38, 39).

II

It is not my purpose in these studies to deal with all the biblical evidence in support of the doctrine of definite or limited atonement. But there are some passages that are particularly relevant to the differentiations that have been propounded earlier and also show how the expiatory death of Christ is restricted to those who are the partakers of that expiation.

1. JOHN 10:10–29.

The teaching of our Lord in this instance requires more analysis than is sometimes given in the debate concerned with the extent of the atonement.

At the outset it should be noted that by the metaphors of 'sheep' and 'shepherd' Jesus is speaking of the distinctive relation he sustains to certain persons and they sustain to him. They are those whom he knows and who know him (vs. 14), those who know his voice and follow him (vs. 27), those to whom he gives eternal and unloseable life (vs. 28), those for whom he lays down his life (vs. 15). On the other hand, there are those who are not in this category; they are not of his sheep (vs. 26), and this is stated to be the reason why they do not believe. The distinction, therefore, between sheep and those who are not does not reside merely in the fact that some believe and some do not. The difference in the relationship to Christ has its basis in something more ultimate than the empirical fact of believing and not believing.

There is also another facet of Jesus' teaching in this passage pointing to this more ultimate factor. He said: 'And other sheep I have which are not of this fold: them also I must bring, and they will hear my voice, and there will be one flock, one shepherd' (vs. 16). These had not yet believed; they had not yet heard his voice; they had not yet been brought. But they are, nevertheless, sheep and are not in the category of verse 26. They will one day be brought and hear Jesus' voice and come to follow him. It is obvious that the 'sheep' are not merely those marked out by the response of faith. They are those determined as such and, therefore, appointed to be brought, to hear Jesus' voice, and to follow him. There is the differentiation of being counted among the sheep and from this differentiation the afore-mentioned results accrue.

We are specially interested now in the design or extent of the laying down of Jesus' life (vs. 15). The following considerations are to be observed:

1. *The Purpose of Jesus' Coming.* Jesus' words are: 'I came that they might have life and have it abundantly. I am the good shepherd. The good shepherd lays down his life for the sheep (vss. 10, 11). The life of which he speaks must embrace and find its consummation in the resurrection life of John 6:39, the indestructible life of verses 28, 29. The purpose for which Jesus came into the world is thus plainly asserted to be the giving of this life to the sheep and it is inconceivable that the purpose for which he came was frustrated or could be frustrated. The sheep will be given this life not only in its essential character but in its abundant realization (cf. vs. 10). To think otherwise would mean that Jesus failed in the execution of the Father's will (cf. John 6:38, 39), and this is an impossible hypothesis.

2. *The Means of Achieving this Purpose.* The means is unmistakably the giving of his life. This is apparent from verses 11, 15, 17, 18. This formula of laying down his life for the sheep, used repeatedly in this discourse, can have no lesser import than the giving of his life as a ransom (Matt. 20:28; Mark 10:45). It is of redemptive blood-shedding, of substitutionary sacrifice Jesus is speaking. More inclusively, *the laying down of his life for* must be understood in terms of all the categories in which Scripture interprets the atonement and is, therefore, equivalent to the statement that Jesus made atonement for the sheep.

We must reckon with the correlativity of the design and the means. Our Lord came that the sheep might have life in the fulness and security enunciated in John 6:39; 10:10, 28, 29. The design, as already demonstrated, cannot fail of accomplishment. But the means can no less fail of achieving its purpose than can the design for which he came and to which the giving of his life is subordinate. This is but to say that the laying down of life is efficacious to the design of giving life to the sheep and, therefore, ensures for them this life in the abundance which Jesus defines for us in this passage. The inescapable conclusion is that the substitutionary sacrifice ensures the eternal life of all who are in this category of 'sheep'.

3. *The Exclusiveness of both Design and Means.* There is distinction between the sheep and those not sheep, as noted above, and Jesus does not say that he laid down his life for those who were not of his sheep. It is not simply the absence of such a statement, however, that must be taken into account; it is that such a proposition would be impossible in view of the relationship between the giving of his life and the design, between the giving of his life and the securing of eternal life for those who are partakers of it.

It is to be admitted that, logically speaking, the *mere proposition* that Jesus laid down his life for the sheep does not carry with it the implication that he gave his life for no others. All that the proposition *of itself* would involve is that the sheep were included in those for whom he gave his life. But others in other categories might also be included. It is not, however, the mere proposition that we find in this passage. Jesus tells us the purpose for which he came into the world, he states the means whereby that purpose is realized, he assures us of the issue involved for those on whose behalf he gave his life, and he restricts the giving of his life to those who are sheep as distinguished from those outside this category. So interrelated are all the elements of his teaching that any one proposition cannot be abstracted and dealt with in isolation. It would be impossible in terms of the *logic* of the total teaching not to include in the 'sheep' all those who are partakers of eternal life and are embraced in the substitutionary sacrifice that ensures this life. To take the formula 'laying down his life for' out of the relationship in which it occurs and apply it to those who finally perish is to make a disjunction that Jesus' own teaching forbids.

II. EPHESIANS 5:25–27.

This second passage is closely related to the preceding in its implications. There are the following features of Paul's teaching pertinent to our present interest:

1. *The Sacrificial Death.* There can be no question but the clause 'gave himself for it', that is to say for the church (vs. 25), refers to the substitutionary blood-shedding of Christ. Hence any indication given in this passage respecting the extent or design of the atonement is relevant to our subject.

2. *The Love Expressed.* The sacrificial giving is represented as the expression of Christ's love—'Christ loved the church and gave himself for it' (vs. 25). There is here causal relationship between Christ's love and self-giving parallel to the love of the Father and the giving of the Son in John 3:16. There should be no question but that Jesus' love and sacrificial death are correlative and causally so in the order stated. There can be no disjunction.

The love is the love for the church. Differentiation is suggested by the analogy instituted in the text. Husbands are to love their wives even as Christ loved the church. Marital love is human love on the highest level and with its own distinguishing quality; it must not be transferred or duplicated. That it finds its analogue in the love of Christ for the church is the highest sanction and betokens its intensity. In any case the love of Christ referred to here is the love for the church, and we must not place it on any lower level nor predicate of it any lesser quality or intensity. This is the love of which Paul speaks, and its supreme quality is evidenced by Christ's self-giving on behalf of that which is stated to be its object.

3. *The Design of the Sacrifice.* The design is expressly stated to be 'that he might sanctify it' (vs. 26) and 'that it might be holy and without blemish' (vs. 27; cf. also vs. 26). Again, we may not make any disjunction between the self-sacrifice and the design. It is impossible to dissociate 'the giving himself for' in its meaning, purpose, and effect from the results contemplated in the design unless we can conceive of Christ's atoning work as failing of the end for which he gave himself. That which Jesus is said to have loved, by reason of his self-giving, is sanctified and cleansed, presented to himself glorious, holy, and without blemish.

4. *The Exclusiveness of the Sacrifice.* It cannot be said of those who fail to attain this specified goal that Christ loved them and gave himself for them in terms of the love and self-giving envisioned in the text. If we universalize the 'gave himself for', we shall have to universalize the designed effect as well as the love.

It is true here again that, in terms of formal logic, the mere proposition 'Christ loved the church and gave himself for it' does not of itself limit the love and self-giving to the church. But, as in John 10:10–29, we may not make a disjunction in the various elements of the text. If there is another classification embraced in this love and self-giving, then of those embraced in that other category it will have to be said likewise that Christ loved and gave himself for them that he might sanctify them and present them to himself glorious, holy, and without blemish. Paul is, no doubt, thinking of the church concretely as it existed in Ephesus, Philippi, Corinth, and other places. But it is apparent from the passage that, wherever there are those loved in terms of verse 25, there are also the corresponding actions, design, and unfailing results of verses 26, 27.

As we found in the earlier studies there is the love that God bears to the non-elect and we must predicate the same of Christ. We must also say that Christ gave himself with the design of bestowing benefits upon the non-elect. But to this design we cannot give any higher content than the blessings enjoyed by the non-elect in this life and falling short of salvation. Likewise, we cannot accord to the love the quality that characterizes the love for the church and we cannot give to 'gave himself for' the content and meaning of the text (vs. 25). This is to say we cannot construe the atonement in terms of the attenuated meaning and relevance that the death of Christ has for the non-elect. The *atonement* cannot be given a reference or extent that is broader than those who are sanctified and cleansed by the washing of water by the Word.

III. JOHN 3:16.

Certain observations may serve to place this text and its teaching in proper focus:

1. *The Object of the Father's Love.* It is, of course, God the Father specifically who is in view when the text says 'God so loved the world'. Only of the Father could it be said that 'he gave the only begotten Son'. The Father gave, and only of the Father is Christ the only begotten Son. It is of the ultimate fountain of salvation the text speaks and this is the love of the Father.

Our present interest is particularly the object, 'the world'. In the usage of John this term is often used in an ethical or qualitative sense, the world as sinful, estranged and alienated from God, resting under his wrath and curse, the world, indeed, as detestable because it is the contradiction of all that is holy, good, righteous, true, and loving—the contradiction, therefore, of God. It is not the denotative extent that is in view but the character.

When Jesus said to his disciples, 'not as the world giveth give I unto you' (John 14:27), it is not the thought of all men distributively that governs the conception but the world as a system alien to the kingdom of God. Or when he says, 'Now is the judgment of this world: now shall the prince of this world be cast out' (John 12:31; cf. 14:30), it is apparent that he is not reflecting on distributive extent but upon the world as the kingdom of darkness. Again, in this same Gospel, that 'the world' is not used in the sense of all men inclusively is demonstrated by Jesus' word: 'If the world hates you, ye know that it hated me before it hated you' (John 15:18). The disciples are the object of the world's hatred and, therefore, distinguished from the world. In the next verse they are said to be 'not of the world' (vs. 19). Other instances can be adduced to the same effect (John 14:17; 16:11; 1 John 2:15, 16; 3:1, 13; 4:5; 5:4, 19; cf. 1 Cor. 1:20; 3:19; 5:10; Gal. 6:14; Eph. 2:2; James 1:27).

It is this concept, with the complexion appropriate to the total emphasis of the text, that we have every good reason to believe appears in John 3:16. It is what God loved in respect of its character that throws into relief the incomparable and incomprehensible love of God. To find anything else as the governing thought would detract from the emphasis. God loved what is the antithesis of himself; this is its marvel and greatness.

2. *The Intensity of the Love.* The object of God's love exhibits its surpassing greatness. But it is the contrast between the character of the object and the identity of the gift that displays its intensity. God the Father so loved that he gave his only begotten Son, the Son of his bosom, his own Son. He gave him, too, to bear the contradiction which made the world the hateful, despicable thing that it is. Exposition fails to fathom that before which sanctified understanding is affixed with amazement. Love so amazing! We cannot scale its heights nor fathom its depths. Eternity will not exhaust its wonder.

3. *The Security Contemplated.* There is the design of, and the certainty

emanating from, the giving of the only begotten. The design is the salvation of all who believe in Jesus. This design is infallibly achieved. The security is obvious from the terms: 'should not perish but have everlasting life'. This is just as important in its own place as are the preceding features of the text; the design and result are indefectibly secure.

There is, after all, nothing in this text to support what it is frequently supposed to affirm, namely, universal atonement. What it actually says is akin to definite atonement. Something is made infallibly certain and secure—all believers will have eternal life. What definite or limited atonement maintains is that God gave his Son to make something infallibly secure. Though John 3:16 does not state all the truth concerning God's counsel in respect of security, yet what it does express is wholly in line with what the doctrine of limited atonement is jealous to maintain.

John 3:16 must not be severed from 3:17: 'For God sent not his Son into the world to condemn the world, but that the world through him might be saved'. The design stated in verse 17 cannot be interpreted as having less security of achievement or less certainty of attainment than the design of verse 16. This follows from the virtual parallelism of the two verses. More analytically stated, verse 17 enforces and confirms the certainty and indefectibility of the salvation referred to in verse 16, namely, 'that every one that believes in him should not perish but have everlasting life.' But, if we regard 'the world' in verse 16 as denotatively universal, we would have to give 'the world' in verse 17 similarly inclusive denotation, and we would have to paraphrase the clause thus: 'that all men through him might be saved'. This introduces patent incompatibility. It is inconsistent with the limitation specified in the final clause of verse 16 with which it is parallel and it would defeat the security implicit in the clause itself. The only way whereby universalism can be posited in verse 16 and 17 is to assume that all men will believe in Christ and be saved, a position contrary to the teaching of our Lord and a position not adopted by those who have been in the centre of the debate as proponents of universal atonement.

III

UNLIMITED OVERTURES OF GRACE

Our interest in these studies is focused in the free offer of the gospel to all men without distinction. We found that the unrestricted overture of grace is grounded in the atonement and that the *whole* doctrine of the atonement bears upon the missionary task of the Church. If the atonement is limited in its extent and if God did not design that all to whom the gospel comes should be partakers of the reconciliation and redemption that the atonement secured, it might seem that some kind of limitation or restriction must attach itself to that which is indiscriminately offered in the free overture of grace. It might also appear that the differentiating love of God of which the atonement is specifically the expression and provision requires some reserve in the proclamation of the gospel offer.

It is a fact that many, persuaded as they rightly are of the particularism of the plan of salvation and of its various corollaries, have found it difficult to proclaim the full, free, and unrestricted overture of gospel grace. They have laboured under the inhibitions arising from fear that in doing so they would impinge upon the sovereignty of God in his saving purposes and operations. The result is that, though formally assenting to the free offer, they lack freedom in the presentation of its appeal and demand.

It must be said without reserve that there is no limitation or qualification to the *overture* of grace in the gospel proclamation. As there is no restriction to the command that 'all everywhere' should repent (Acts 17:30), so is there none to what is correlative with it. The doctrines of particular election, differentiating love, limited atonement do not erect any fence around the offer in the gospel. No text is more eloquent of the pure sovereignty of both the Father and the Son in the revelation of gospel mystery than the words of our Lord in Matthew 11:25-30: 'Thou hast hid these things from the wise and prudent, and hast revealed them unto babes. Even so, Father: for so it seemed good in thy sight.' Here is the sovereign will and differentiation of the Father. 'He to whomsoever the Son willeth to reveal him.' This is the witness to Jesus' own sovereignty in revealing the Father to men. But the immediate sequel is:

'Come unto me, all ye that labour and are heavy laden.' The lesson is that it is not merely conjunction of differentiating and sovereign will with free overture, but that the free overture comes out from the differentiating sovereignty of both Father and Son. It is on the crest of the wave of divine sovereignty that the unrestricted summons comes to the labouring and heavy laden. This is Jesus' own witness, and it provides the direction in which our thinking on the question at issue must proceed. Any inhibition or reserve in presenting the overtures of grace should no more characterize our proclamation than it characterized the Lord's witness.

What is freely offered in the gospel? The word of Jesus already quoted (Matt. 11:28) gives the answer. It is Christ who is offered. More strictly, *he* offers himself. The whole gamut of redemptive grace is included. Salvation in all of its aspects and in the furthest reaches of glory consummated is the overture. For Christ is the embodiment of all. Those who are his are complete in him and he is made unto them wisdom from God, and righteousness, and sanctification, and redemption. When Christ invites us to himself it is to the possession of himself and therefore of all that defines his identity as Lord and Saviour.

The riches of this overture are not sufficiently expressed, however, unless we also keep in view the implications of union with *Christ*. Jesus said: 'I and the Father are one' (John 10:30); 'Believe me that I am in the Father, and the Father in me' (John 14:11). Union with Christ means also union with the Father (cf. John 17:20–23), a union of inhabitation that is complemented by the embrace of his love (cf. John 14:23). And, likewise, union with Christ means the inhabitation and abiding presence of the Holy Spirit (cf. John 14:16, 17). It is thus union with Father, Son, and Holy Spirit in the particularity that each person sustains to men and in the distinguishing grace that each bestows in the economy of salvation. To nothing less are sinners invited in Christ's overture of himself. If we are insensitive to its surpassing grandeur it is because our minds are blinded by the god of this world (cf. 2 Cor. 4:3, 4).

The corollaries of the foregoing implications of the gospel overture should be apparent.

First, if Christ—and therefore salvation in its fulness and perfection— is offered, the only doctrine of the atonement that will ground and warrant this overture is that of salvation wrought and redemption accomplished. And the only atonement that measures up to such conditions is a definite atonement. In other words, an atonement construed as providing the possibility of salvation or the opportunity of salvation does not supply the basis required for what constitutes the gospel offer. It is not the *opportunity* of salvation that is offered; it is salvation. And it is salvation because Christ is offered and Christ does not invite us to mere opportunity but to himself.

Secondly, it is not the general love of God to all mankind, the love manifested in the gifts of general providence, that is offered to men in the gospel. As we found earlier in these studies, this general love is not to be discounted. It is to be proclaimed and its significance made known to men. The character of God is disclosed therein and all that God is and does is to be declared to his glory. But this love is not the love specifically overtured to men in the gospel. The love presented in the gospel is as specific as is the gospel itself. Since Christ invites men to himself, he invites them to union and communion with himself and with the Father and the Holy Spirit in all the particularity of grace that each person bestows in the economy of salvation. When Christ invites us to himself he invites us to the embrace of his love on the highest level of its exercise and therefore to the love wherewith he loved the church and gave himself for it; the love that passeth knowledge. He invites us to the love of the Father in the intensity manifested on Calvary when he spared not his own Son but delivered him up, and also to the love of complacency of which Jesus spoke: 'If a man love me, he will keep my words: and my Father will love him' (John 14:23). He invites likewise to the love of the Spirit and to the manifold operations of grace that the Spirit's love ensures. We thus see how impoverished would be our conception of the free overture of Christ in the gospel if the appeal were simply to the undifferentiating and general love of God. It is the love of which the accursed tree is the supreme exhibition that invests the free offer of Christ in the gospel with constraining appeal.

Thirdly, it is only in Christ that this love and the riches of grace involved can be known and experienced. To this love Christ invites when he invites sinners to himself. But only those who respond are partakers. It is not therefore a love that may be declared to be the possession of all indiscriminately or, more pointedly stated, to be love in which all are embraced. There are various ways in which this distinction may be stated. Sinners to whom the claims of the gospel come are not asked to believe that God or Christ loves them with this differentiating love. The faith the gospel demands is not belief of the proposition that Christ loves them with this love. The gospel demands that they come to Christ and commit themselves to him. In coming to him they will know *his* embrace and with him they will know his love on the highest plane of its exercise. This way of stating the case is parallel to what is true of election. Sinners do not come to Christ because they first believe that they have been elected. They come to Christ and only then may they believe that they were chosen in Christ before the foundation of the world. The same is true in the matter of the atonement. It cannot be declared to men indiscriminately that, in the proper sense of the term, Christ died for them. The belief of this proposition is not the primary act of faith. Only in commitment to Christ as freely offered may we come to know that he died for our sins unto our redemption. It should be seen that not only are the doctrines of the love of God and of the atonement involved but also a proper conception of the gospel offer and of the faith that responds to it. Christ is offered and faith is first of all commitment to him. It is receiving and resting upon him alone for salvation.

Implicit in what has been said is the doctrine of the *warrant* of faith. The question is: by what authority does a sinner commit himself to Christ for salvation? For a person awakened to the gravity of sin and its ill-desert this is not an academic question. It is the burning question. And what needs to be borne home to this person and to be proclaimed with insistence is that the warrant a sinner has and must have is that which is undiscriminating—the invitation, command, demand, overture, and promise of the gospel. The warrant is not any assurance that Christ has saved him. This would contradict his rightfully entertained conviction. The gospel comes to him as an unsaved sinner and its demand is that he commit himself to Christ in order that he may be saved. What intrudes to justify this entrustment is the all-sufficiency and suitability of the Saviour and the Saviour's own word in the free overture of his grace. And, when we think of the Saviour's surpassing glory and the greatness of the salvation so fully offered, there are not only the invitation and overture to constrain faith but also the claims that make is extreme insult to reject. Faith is not only warranted; rejection it perversity.

It is the word of the reconciliation that is committed to the church, the proclamation of the reconciliation once for all accomplished when 'God was reconciling the world unto himself in Christ' (2 Cor. 5:19). This is the gospel message. The corresponding exhortation addressed to men is 'be ye reconciled to God' (2 Cor. 5:20). And the import of this plea on Christ's behalf is that men should enter into the relation constituted by 'the reconciliation' and appropriate the grace that it establishes and conveys. No office possesses greater dignity and glory than the proclamation of the message and of the plea. For it is as ambassadors on behalf of Christ, and as of God beseeching through them, that the preachers of the evangel pray men to be reconciled to God (cf. 2 Cor. 5:20). All that the atonement means and secures is that of which sinners dead in trespasses and sins are invited to become partakers. And the demand of Christ's commission to his ambassadors is that he, in the integrity of his saviourhood and lordship as prophet, priest, and king, be presented to lost men for their faith, love, and obedience. In this presentation there is no restraint. He cannot be brought too close to men's responsibility and opportunity. Wherever there is faith as slender as one strand of the spider's web, *there* the fulness of redeeming grace is active. 'Him that cometh unto me,' said Jesus, 'I will in no wise case out' (John 6:37).

10

The Advent of Christ[1]

THE fruit of the Spirit is manifold, manifold because the salvation in Christ is manifold. The apostles provide us with examples of this multi-formity (cf. Rom. 12:1–21; Gal. 5:22, 23; Eph. 4:1–32; 2 Pet. 1:5–10). But the grand triad is faith, hope, and love (cf. 1 Cor. 13:13). We are familiar with the centrality of faith (cf. Eph. 2:8). It is basic. And we may not forget the primacy of love (cf. Mark 12:28–31; Rom. 13:10; 1 Cor. 13:13). But have we appreciated the place of hope? No text points up the indispensability of hope more than Romans 8:24: 'We were saved by hope'. Hope does not occupy the place of faith. We were not saved by hope as we are by faith. The meaning is that 'in hope were we saved'. Salvation in possession is characterized by hope, oriented to and conditioned by hope. If we do not have hope we are unsaved (cf. 1 Thess. 4:13b). Among the many evidences of departure from the faith of the gospel is the extent to which assured hope is absent in our generation. Rampant aimlessness and hopelessness are the marks of a perverse and faithless age.

What is the focal point of the Christian hope? What looms highest on the believer's horizon as he looks to the future? There is but one answer; it is the advent of Christ in glory. This is 'the blessed hope', 'the appearing of the glory of the great God and our Saviour Christ Jesus' (Tit. 2:13), when he will 'descend from heaven with a shout, with the voice of the archangel and with the trumpet of God' (1 Thess. 4:16; cf. 1 Cor. 15:52). Just as hope itself has suffered eclipse in our day, so

[1] Four articles reprinted from *The English Churchman*, August 1970.

has the focus of hope. The scepticism of which Peter warned is so largely ours: 'Where is the promise of his coming? for since the fathers fell asleep, all things continue as they were from the beginning of the creation' (2 Pet. 3:4). And even believers are too liable to be influenced by current patterns of thought. Let us be alert to the subtlety of unbelief and to Satan's devices.

Diversity of viewpoint respecting the relation of other events to Christ's advent should never obscure the centrality of faith and hope of the advent itself. The coming in great power and glory is the common property of all faith that is biblically conditioned. It is well to take account of the concreteness of this hope. Too frequently the expectation that the Christian entertains is defective in this respect. It is the bliss of what he calls 'heaven' and may not partake of the definiteness that characterizes the biblical representation. Or his hope may be framed in terms of bliss that awaits the believer when he departs this life and goes to be with Christ in heaven. The bliss of the disembodied state for a child of God is not to be depreciated. To depart and to be with Christ is far better, and to die is gain (cf. Phil. 1:21, 23). To be absent from the body is to be present with the Lord (cf. 2 Cor. 5:8). It is not improper to desire to depart and enter into this rest. And the assurance of going to be with Christ on the eventuality of death must come within the compass of a believer's expectation. But if it is the bliss of the disembodied state that is focal in the hope of a believer, then the perspective of hope has been gravely diverted from the biblical witness. There are two respects, particularly, in which this is true.

First, preoccupation with the disembodied state fails to have prime concern for the honour and glory of Christ. The final phase of his exaltation is waiting for his advent. He is now exalted far above all principality and power and given the name that is above every name (cf. Eph. 1:21; Phil. 2:9). But not all the implications of his lordship have been realized. His reign is still one of conquest and he has not yet put all enemies under his feet. The last enemy, death, has not been destroyed, and to him every knee has not bowed and confessed that he is Lord to the glory of God the Father (cf. 1 Cor. 15:26; Phil. 2:11). He has not yet judged the world and thus executed the final assize to which he is appointed (cf. Matt. 25:31–46; Acts 17:31). The believer's prime jealousy is the glory of Christ and it is apparent how far short we come if his advent with glory is thrust to the periphery of hope and expectation. If we love the Lord we long for and hasten unto his coming. We love his appearing *for his own sake*.

Second, the fault mentioned fails to accord to the resurrection the place it occupies in the salvation of the just. The separation of body and spirit is evil, the result of sin. Hence the termination of this evil is integral to redemption. It is significant that the term 'redemption' should be used to designate the resurrection of the body (cf. Luke 21:28; Rom. 8:23; 1 Cor. 1:30; Eph. 1:14). The hope of immortality in Scripture is not an abstract one, not one for the soul as distinct or in separation from the body, but the immortality that resurrection bestows when this corruptible will put on incorruption and this mortal will put on immortality, and death will be swallowed up in victory (cf. 1 Cor. 15:53, 54). It is then that mortality will be swallowed up of life (cf. Rom. 8:11). This paramount interest of the believer in the consummation of redemption is waiting for Christ's advent. For then the dead will be raised and the living changed (cf. 1 Cor. 15:52). So with the apostle we must say: 'not for that we would be unclothed, but clothed upon, that mortality might be swallowed up of life' (2 Cor. 5:4).

II

The word 'advent' is an appropriate term to identify what we often speak of as 'the second coming'. Though the New Testament does not use this latter designation in so many words, yet the idea is present in Hebrews 9:28 when it says that Christ 'will be manifested a second time without sin for them that look for him unto salvation'. And since Christ came into the world and then ascended into heaven, his coming again to the world can properly be distinguished as his second coming, though in a different manner and for different purposes.

It is significant, however, that, in respect of the term in Greek that corresponds to our word 'advent', the New Testament never speaks of the second advent. It speaks of 'the advent'. This is true also of other terms that are synonymous with the advent as far as event is concerned. This is all the more remarkable when we find Peter using this same term 'advent' with reference to Christ's first coming: 'we have not followed cunningly devised fables when we made known to you the power and coming of our Lord Jesus Christ, but were eye-witnesses of his majesty' (2 Pet. 1:16). We are compelled to ask why New Testament writers, when they refer to the second advent, do not need to specify it as the second but simply as 'the advent' of Christ. One thing we can say is that New Testament believers were so intently occupied with the second coming of Christ, so absorbed were they with the hope it entailed and the consequences involved, that they did not need to characterize it as we do, but spoke and wrote of it as 'the coming' of the Lord. The identity implied in his titles 'the Lord and Saviour Jesus Christ' could not be conceived of apart from his first coming and all that this involved. So, when they spoke of 'the coming', it was the advent in glory that was in view. It is a pertinent and searching question: do we share the outlook that constrained this manner of speech? If not we have diverged from apostolic example.

When Jesus will come he will be manifested in the body. This is the witness of the angels to the disciples on the occasion of the ascension: 'this same Jesus, who is taken up from you into heaven, shall so come in like manner as ye have seen him go into heaven' (Acts 1:11). He will be seen (cf. Heb. 9:28). Our Lord himself emphasized the public, visible character of his advent. When he comes there will be no possibility of mistake or deception. 'For as the lightning comes out from the east and shines unto the west, so will be the coming of the Son of man' (Matt. 24:27). 'Then all the tribes of the earth will mourn, and they will see the Son of man coming on the clouds of heaven with power and great glory' (Matt. 24:30). There is no evidence to support the notion of a secret coming. The 'rapture' of 1 Thessalonians 4:17 is nothing more than the snatching up of believers to meet the Lord in the air, and contains no suggestion of an advent prior to that which is uniformly set forth as the public, visible coming.

Unbelief that does not reckon with the supernatural and momentous character of Christ's advent is ready to scoff at the idea of a coming that will be universally visible. But this particular aspect of universality is consonant with all the other features of the advent and with the finality of its various concomitants. Everything associated with the

Lord's coming is unprecedented and correspondingly stupendous.

The advent will be sudden. Of the day and hour no man knows (cf. Matt. 24:36). Christ repeatedly stressed this aspect (cf. Matt. 24:37–39, 44, 50; 25:13; Luke 21:34, 35; Acts 1:7). And Peter reiterated the Lord's teaching (cf. 2 Peter 3:10). This does not mean that no well-defined events, predicted by Christ and the apostles, will antedate the advent. Our Lord's discourse in Matthew 24 (cf. Mark 13; Luke 21) delineates for us a history of events that will transpire. But at the same time our Lord urged his disciples to watch because they knew not the time of his coming. The events predicted to occur required faith as to their occurrence. But this conviction required by faith in the Lord's veracity did not obviate the necessity of watching and waiting for the advent. We must recognize the compatibility of these two attitudes. Otherwise we cannot interpret aright Christ's own teaching nor be guided by its import.

It is all-important that we today confront ourselves with the implications for faith and hope of the sustained witness of the New Testament respecting the advent. Much is being written and spoken of the need for relevance and the plea is that the gospel message must be adjusted to the supposedly scientific world-view of modern man. And modern man, it is claimed, is impervious, by reason of his scientifically conditioned conceptions, to the whole notion of such an intervention in and finale to world history as the advent of Christ in glory demands. This assessment of modern man is true in some cases. In other cases it is nonsense. For in numberless instances men and women are not so oriented in their thinking as the contention would assume. But, in any case, if anything is integral to the New Testament, to the witness of our Lord, and to apostolic Christianity, it is the faith, as also the hope, that world history is moving to the grand climax of the believer's assurance and expectation, the return of the exalted Saviour, the Lord of glory, to terminate this age and usher in the age to come, a return in all the majesty that is his as King of kings and Lord of lords. An adjustment of the gospel that discards this tenet of faith and hope is an abandonment of Christianity, and the proponents of it ought to have the candour to acknowledge that the relevance for which they contend is not a version of the Christian faith but its contradiction.

III

There are other terms to designate the coming of Christ in glory besides the term appropriately rendered 'advent', such as 'revelation', 'appearing', 'the end', 'the day of the Lord', 'the end of the age'. Though these terms designate the same event or complex of events bound up with Christ's coming, they are not exactly synonyms. They specify different facets of Christ's advent or events coincident with it and flowing from it. 'Revelation' (cf. 1 Cor. 1:7; 2 Thess. 1:7; 1 Pet. 1:7; 4:13) and 'appearing' (cf. 2 Thess. 2:8; 1 Tim. 6:14; 2 Tim. 4:8; Tit. 2:13) signify the manifestation Christ's advent involves. 'The end' (cf. 1 Cor. 1:8; 15:24; 1 Pet. 4:7) and 'the end of the age' (cf. Matt. 13:39, 40, 49; 24:3; 28:20) express the consummating character or consequence of the advent in terminating the present age and introducing the age to come. 'The day of the Lord' (cf. 2 Pet. 3:10) points to the momentous nature of the advent.

Many have regarded these terms, or at least some of them, as separate events in the unfolding of the eschatological plan of God. Those who hold this construction are to be accorded all due respect. But the present writer does not believe it to be tenable. Thorough examination would require extended discussion. But brief analysis of a few passages will serve as an index to what more copious exposition will, I believe, demonstrate.

In 1 Corinthians 1:7, 8 we find three of the terms mentioned above— 'the revelation of our Lord Jesus Christ', 'the end', and 'the day of our Lord Jesus Christ'. Here 'the revelation' is said to be that for which believers are waiting, and as they wait Christ will also confirm them unto 'the end'. The force of 'also' is not to suggest that 'the end' is something distinct from and posterior to 'the revelation'. The 'also' goes with the verb 'confirm', not with 'the end'. So the intent is to stress what Christ will do right on to that event for which believers wait. The accent in verse 8 falls on the faithfulness of Christ, as in verse 9 on the Father's faithfulness. Then again 'blameless in the day of the Lord Jesus Christ' informs us of the effect of Christ's confirming grace, and stands in apposition to 'confirm you unto the end'. Furthermore, it would be incongruous to think of confirmation as necessary beyond the day when believers are presented blameless. And that day, according to the uniform witness of the New Testament, is the day of Christ's advent when the dead will be raised and the living changed (cf. 1 Thess. 4:16, 17; 1 Cor. 15:52). The terminus or goal of keeping, preserving, confirming grace, as also of watching, waiting, striving on the part of the believer, is the advent of Christ in glory. It becomes impossible, therefore, in such a passage as this to regard 'the revelation', 'the end' and 'the day of the Lord' as separable events. They are simply different designations of the climactic event which constitutes the pole star of believers' expectation. The passage is particularly significant as indicating Paul's view of the place of 'the end' in the complex of events bound up with Christ's coming (cf. 1 Cor. 15:24; 2 Cor. 1:13).

In 1 Corinthians 15:23, 24 there are several reasons for maintaining that the 'coming' (advent) of verse 23 and 'the end' of verse 24 are coincident. But one of these, probably the most cogent, may be mentioned. In verses 24–26 it is apparent that the final subjugation of all enemies including death, the last enemy, is coincident with 'the end'. For it is expressly stated that at the end Christ delivers over the kingdom to God, and this occurs because he will have put all enemies under his feet. But in verses 53–55 the victory over death is said to occur when the corruptible will put on incorruption and the mortal immortality. This is at the resurrection of the just (cf. vss. 50–52). And the resurrection is at Christ's advent (cf. vs. 23). If the victory over death—'death has been swallowed up in victory' (vs. 54)—is achieved at and by the resurrection to life at Christ's advent, it is impossible to think that the subjugation of death (vss. 25, 26) is something different, and a victory to be secured much later in the programme of events. No terms could be stronger to express subjugation and destruction than 'death has been swallowed up in victory' (vs. 54). Thus if the victory over death is at 'the end' (vss. 24–26) and also at the resurrection and advent (vss. 23, 53–55), 'the end' and the 'advent' must be together and in immediate conjunction.

One other passage may be briefly alluded to. It is 2 Peter 3:4–13. In verse 4 the advent of Christ is distinctly in view in the taunt of unbelief: 'where is the promise of his coming?' With this mockery Peter proceeds to deal in the subsequent verses. In verse 10 he says: 'But the day of the Lord will come as a thief'. He is giving emphatic contradiction to the unbelief referred to in verse 4. 'The day of the Lord' cannot be but another designation of 'the advent' (vs. 4). Otherwise the certainty for which Peter is pleading would not be asserted. It should also be noted that the destruction of the present heavens and earth by consuming fire (cf. vs. 12) is coincident not simply with the day of the Lord but with its coming (vs. 10). So the consummatory act for this world's history is brought into conjunction with the advent of Christ.

When this closely-knit unity is recognized, there is a profound interest bound up with it. The advent of Christ is the focal point of the Christian hope. This coming, however, can never be viewed in abstraction from all it embraces for the believer—resurrection from the dead, the body of humiliation conformed to the body of Christ's glory, the glorification with Christ, the obtaining of an incorruptible inheritance, the being ever with the Lord, complete conformity to the image of Christ as God's Son. Implicit in all of these is the consummation. To dissociate the advent from the consummation of all things is to interfere with the purity of the eschatological hope. Can we reasonably conceive of all that is involved for the believer in Christ's coming as falling short of the consummated order of the age to come, the new heavens and the new earth and creation itself delivered from the bondage of corruption into the liberty of the glory of the children of God (cf. Rom. 8:19–22; 2 Pet. 3:13)?

IV

In the preceding article it was maintained that the advent of Christ will be consummatory. There are a few implications worthy of special attention.

The first is that the period of time in which we live is 'the last days' (cf. Acts 2:17; 2 Tim. 3:1; Heb. 1:2; James 5:3; 1 Pet. 1:20; 2 Pet. 3:3; 1 John 2:18), 'the consummation of the ages' (Heb. 9:26), 'the ends of the ages' (1 Cor. 10:11). This means, as the foregoing passages will show, that the whole period between Christ's first advent and the second is the closing era of this world's history. There are no data given to us to determine its length. Already nearly two thousand years have elapsed. However long this era may be, it is the last time and so we are advised that the two advents of Christ are the determinative events of history. In God's plan all history is oriented to the incarnation of the Son of God and to his manifestation in glory at the end of the age. The lessons for us are numerous. But one is of paramount importance. Life here and now that is not conditioned by faith in Jesus' first coming and oriented to the hope of his second is godless and hopeless. And the imminence of our Lord's return (cf. Rom. 13:12; James 5:8; 1 Pet. 4:7) is simply that the next great epochal event, correlative with the other pivotal events of redemptive accomplishment, is our Lord's advent in glory. This is the index to its finality.

A second feature related to the consummatory nature of the advent is the judgment. No scripture is weighted with more solemnity than our Lord's description in Matthew 25:31–46. The location of the judgment delineated for us here should be observed. There can be no question but that the advent is in view in Matthew 24:37–44. Then we have a series of parables to enforce the various lessons pertinent to the coming, particularly those of faithfulness and readiness. There is no hint of transition to anything other than the advent when we read: 'When the Son of man shall come in his glory and all the angels with him, then will he sit upon the throne of his glory' (Matt. 25:31). All the terms point to the advent as the event in view. When he says that 'before him will be gathered all the nations', usage elsewhere shows that 'all the nations' is but a way of denoting all mankind. It is the note of universality that is expressed. We have this same note in other passages (cf. Rom. 2:5–16; 2 Thess. 1:5–10).

The judgment is charged with solemnity. Then all things will be made manifest in their true character. This is why it is called 'the day' (cf. Rom. 13:11; 1 Cor. 3:13; 1 Thess. 5:4; Heb. 10:25; 2 Pet. 1:19). All darkness and obscurity will be dispelled and every man's work will be made manifest. But there is also the grandeur of this event. The whole panorama of history will then be placed in the pure light of God's judgment and adjudicated with perfect equity. Nothing will be left at loose ends. What a dismal prospect the future would offer if this were not the case! God will bring every work into judgment, with every secret thing whether good or bad (cf. Eccl. 12:14; 2 Cor. 5:10). Recoil from this thought on the part of Christians discloses more concern for what they consider to be their own comfort than for the glory of God.

Universal judgment belongs to God's sovereignty and to the perfect equity that characterizes it.

God will judge the world by 'the man whom he has ordained' (Acts 17:31). That Christ will execute the judgment is filled with consolation for the people of God. The solemnity will not for them be retracted. It will rather lend its glory to their joy that their Saviour's honour and lordship will be fully demonstrated and vindicated and their inheritance dispensed by the King (cf. Matt. 25:34, 40). And nothing will accentuate the chagrin of Christ rejecters more than that he whose overtures of grace they refused will then say: 'Depart from me, ye cursed' (Matt. 25:41).

A third feature related to the consummatory nature of the advent is the deliverance of the creation 'from the bondage of corruption into the liberty of the glory of the children of God' (Rom. 8:21). The redemption wrought by Christ is of cosmic proportions; it extends to the material creation. Redemption from sin includes deliverance from its curse. And since the curse extended to the creation (cf. Gen. 3:17; Rom. 8:20), the completeness of redemption involves the removal of creation's curse. This is a necessary ingredient of the believer's hope and exemplifies again the concreteness of this hope. The focus of hope is the bodily return of the Lord, a return that brings with it the redemption of the body. It is a resurrection hope. The final abode is not one unrelated to the creation, but the renovated creation without the least trace of sin's curse. In Peter's words: 'Nevertheless we, according to his promise, look for new heavens and a new earth, wherein dwelleth righteousness' (2 Pet. 3:13).

Westminster Theological Seminary and its Testimony

11

The Banner of Westminster Seminary[1]

ON the cover of the official magazine of the church in which I was reared in Scotland, there was always quoted the text from Psalm 60, 'Thou hast given a banner to them that fear thee, that it may be displayed because of the truth'.

We are meeting tonight on the occasion of the fifteenth annual commencement of Westminster Theological Seminary. It may well be said in connection with Westminster Seminary, 'Thou hast given a banner to them that fear thee, that it may be displayed because of the truth'.

Westminster Seminary was founded in 1929. The half decade in which that year falls was a critical one in the history of Presbyterian churches in the North American continent and elsewhere. The Seminary came into existence as a result of the crisis that overtook the Presbyterian Church in the U.S.A. in 1929, namely, the reorganization of Princeton Theological Seminary by action of the general assembly of that year. That action was, however, but the registering of the tragic state of affairs that existed in the Presbyterian Church in the U.S.A. In 1924 this state of affairs was signalized by the signing of what is known as the Auburn Affirmation in which 1293 ministers of that denomination attached their signatures to a document that denied outright the doctrine of Biblical inerrancy, and also denied the necessity of belief in the virgin birth of our Lord, his substitutionary atonement, his bodily resurrection and the supernatural character of his miracles, for the

[1] Address delivered at the Alumni Banquet held on the occasion of Westminster's Fifteenth Annual Commencement and published in *The Presbyterian Guardian*, July 10, 1944.

ordination and good standing of ministers in the Presbyterian Church in the U.S.A. This fact, together with the fact that not one of these signers had ever been disciplined for such avowal, shows the lamentable decline from the true faith in the denomination concerned.

It was not merely in the Presbyterian Church in the U.S.A. that such decline had been taking place. In the year 1925 the United Presbyterian Church of North America completed its adoption of what is known as the Confessional Statement. That Statement shows that the United Presbyterian Church had decisively departed from its historic creedal position, had adopted a position whereby the gateway was opened to doctrinal laxity, and that such laxity was officially protected by the provision that forbearance in love was to be exercised toward any brethren who might not be able fully to subscribe to the Standards of the church.

In that same year, 1925, a great spiritual calamity occurred in the church history of Canada. It was in that year that the union of the Methodist, Congregational and Presbyterian churches was consummated. By this union a large proportion of the Presbyterian Church in Canada abandoned the historic Presbyterian witness and entered into a communion that had as its basis a confession acceptable to the overwhelming majority of Methodists and Congregationalists in that Dominion.

At the outset I made reference to a detail that concerned Scotland. In 1929 there took place in that country the union of the Church of Scotland and the United Free Church of Scotland. As things had come to be in these two churches by 1929, I do not suppose that any great doctrinal issue was at stake in this union. But the union of 1929 showed the extent to which declension had taken place in both of these churches in the preceding years. These two Churches, comprising the large majority of nominal Presbyterians in Scotland, could in 1929 unite on a basis that involved for ministers no more stringent a confession than to believe in one God—Father, Son and Holy Spirit; to believe the Word of God, which is contained in the Scriptures of the Old and New Testaments, to be the supreme rule of faith and life; and to believe the fundamental doctrines of the Christian faith contained in the Westminster Confession of Faith. The fundamental doctrines of the Christian faith remain undefined and what the import of subscription to the Confession means is not in the least clarified by the opaque statement that the united Church 'holds as its subordinate standard the Westminster Confession of Faith, recognising liberty of opinion on such points of doctrine as do not enter into the substance of the Faith'. This union brought into clear focus the abandonment of the historic Reformed and even evangelical confession.

These are simply a few of the facts which evince that the founding of Westminster Seminary in 1929 was no mere coincidence. The Seminary came into being at a time when the very things for which it was established and to which it stands committed, the very things for which it raised and unfurled a banner, were being repudiated by large sections of the Reformed churches in North America and in Europe. It would be more accurate to say that Westminster Seminary raised a banner for the whole counsel of God when concrete events had made it more than apparent that Reformed churches throughout the world had laid in the dust that same banner, defaced, soiled and tattered. When the enemy came in like a flood, God in his abundant mercy and sovereign providence raised up a standard against him.

It is true, of course, that Westminster Seminary came into existence upon the occasion and particularly for the reason of widespread defection in the Presbyterian Church in the U.S.A., and its more immediate purpose was to provide training for the future ministers of that denomination. But two facts must not be forgotten.

The first is that Princeton Seminary, the downfall of which was the reason for the founding of Westminster, had been during its history a nursery for the training of ministers of many denominations. Princeton opened its doors to students of various churches and for this reason the contribution that Princeton Seminary made to catholic Christianity was incalculable. Westminster Seminary was not to be any less hospitable. And the history of fifteen years has demonstrated both its appeal and its generosity in this regard.

The second fact is the general ecclesiastical situation at the time Westminster opened its doors and ever since. In view of the widespread defection both of churches and theological schools throughout the world, young men looking towards the gospel ministry and seeking the training that would fit them for service in their own denominations found in Westminster Seminary the kind of institution that met this need. We must recognize what is a fact of God's providence, that God raised Westminster Seminary to train men for the great work and battle of the faith in a great variety of denominations.

For what does Westminster Seminary stand? It stands for the whole counsel of God, for unswerving fidelity to that permanent and unchanging deposit of truth embodied in the Scriptures of the Old and New Testaments and for the consistent application of that truth to the whole of life. It exists to maintain this truth, to set forth the grounds of belief in it as the Word of God, the only infallible rule of faith and practice, to defend this truth and to be the instrument of blazing forth that truth to the whole world. It stands, as Dr. John Duncan was wont to say in other connections, for the truth that is according to godliness and for the godliness that is according to truth.

We who are closely associated with Westminster Seminary have to confess that we have come far too short of our profession and aim. Indeed, when we think of our own sins and shortcomings, we are amazed that God in his displeasure has not wrenched this banner out of our hands and given it to others more worthy than we. We marvel that God has not removed his candlestick out of our midst.

But surely the facts show that he has not done so. In his abundant mercy he has borne with our sins and faults. I do not think it is presumption to say, and to say it to God's praise, that the banner has not been folded up and laid in the dust. We have not raised it aloft as we should have done, we have not unfurled it as we should. But it has not been lowered or furled.

God has brought Westminster to the kingdom for such a time as this. May I plead that by our prayers, by our labours, by our support and by our promotion we may stand in the place where God has caused our feet to stand, that in these difficult and perilous days there may not be retreat or recession, but that now and in the days to come, against every assault upon and evasion of the whole counsel of God, with persistent and aggressive display of the banner of God's glory and truth, to the establishment of true faith and to the promotion of truly sanctified life, with steadfastness and zeal born of divine commission and compulsion,

Westminster Seminary may go on to greater fidelity and usefulness in the kingdom of our Lord and Saviour Jesus Christ.

'We wrestle not against flesh and blood, but against principalities, against powers, against the rulers of the darkness of this world, against spiritual wickedness in high places' (Eph. 6:12). We shall often cringe before the assaults of sin and Satan. But let us not forget that Christ is King upon the holy hill of Zion, that he has all authority in heaven and in earth. To him has been given the promise, 'I shall give thee the heathen for thine inheritance, and the uttermost parts of the earth for thy possession' (Psalm 2:8). He must reign until all his enemies will be made his footstool. Let us be warned and encouraged—warned when we falter or fail, encouraged when by God's sufficient grace we seek to raise and unfurl the banner of truth, that he who is King on God's holy hill will one day cast all error and deceit into the pit of eternal dismay and will vindicate to the glory of God and to the everlasting joy of all his people the very counsel which it is our responsibility and privilege now to display.

12

Greeting to Entering Students, 1944[1]

IN the name of the Faculty of Westminster Theological Seminary it is my duty and privilege now to welcome to the fellowship and work of the Seminary the members of the incoming class. On behalf of the Faculty I therefore extend to you cordial congratulation and welcome.

The purpose of Westminster Seminary is to form men for the gospel ministry. 'It is to provide an adequate supply and succession of able and faithful ministers of the New Testament; workmen that *need not to be ashamed*, being qualified *rightly to divide the word of truth*.' This Seminary indeed offers its facilities to those properly qualified to make use of them who desire theological training even though they may not have declared their intention to become ministers of the gospel. A theological training is a great asset in other departments of life and this Seminary is glad to open its doors to men who earnestly desire a theological equipment even though they have no intention to become official ministers of the Word. Nevertheless the Seminary's purpose is to form men for the gospel ministry.

I take it that all of you who are entering this Seminary today are enrolling for the purpose of preparing for the gospel ministry. Unless you are exempt from the draft regulations on some other ground, and I am not aware that any of you are, the reason why in the circumstances you are able to be here is that you are *bona fide* aspirants for the gospel ministry.

It may have appeared to you that theological study in the quiet of

[1] Because of World War II the Seminary ran a summer session in 1944. This was the opening address, given on June 30.

these halls and of this campus is remote from the most practical contribution which you could render in the exigencies of this present time. Unless for some physical reason you are ineligible for military service I hope you have felt something of the urge to enlist in the services of your country in the present emergency. Indeed I hope you have felt that urge in a very potent way. I hope you have found it very difficult to take advantage of the opportunities and privileges that are now being given you when so many of your fellow-countrymen have to face the hardship and peril of the field of battle, and face these perils and endure so many hardships for the protection of the many privileges that are now yours. If perchance you have not weighed these considerations, then I hardly think your decision to follow the course upon which you have embarked is worthy of your privilege and of the task that lies ahead of you.

What I mean is simply this, that I hope it has been hard for you to come here, and hard for the very reason that it offers you an immunity from the hard, bitter and painful ordeal through which many of your fellow-countrymen of your age are being called upon to experience at the present time.

Why then do we welcome you to Westminster? On the assumption that yours has been a painful decision. Why do we congratulate you? We do so for this reason. You have come here, we trust, because of divine compulsion. You believe that you have been called by God to prepare yourselves for the gospel ministry. You are under the compulsion of a divine call to the greatest vocation upon earth. Under that compulsion you are here to serve the King of kings and Lord of lords. In a very peculiar and pre-eminent sense you are here as good soldiers of Jesus Christ, and as such you are performing the highest service to God, and to Caesar. You are performing, even to your country, to the United Nations, yes, to the world, the highest ministry that can be rendered. For you are preparing yourselves in pursuance of a divine call for the ministry of that Word without which the whole world perishes in sin, in misery and death. You are training for the most militant service in that kingdom that is an everlasting kingdom and in that dominion which shall not be destroyed. Militant service, indeed, for we wrestle not against flesh and blood, but against principalities, against powers, against the world rulers of this darkness, against the spiritual hosts of wickedness in high places.

All of this lays upon you an exacting obligation. You are being spared many of the bitter hardships through which so many of your contemporaries are called upon to pass. But you are embarking upon a course that entails hardships of which the most of your contemporaries have not even dreamed. The discipline of the theological curriculum is arduous and oftentimes painful. Sometimes you may be tempted to think that the routine of class-work and the time-consuming energy expended on details are not relevant to or promotive of the great vocation to which you are called. Sometimes a feeling of bewilderment and confusion may overtake you, especially in the early stages of your course of study. You may not be able to see unity or correlation or purpose in the various parts of your work. Sometimes the gigantic nature of the field of study and of the task that lies ahead of you will give you an overwhelming sense of your inadequacy and it may appear hopeless for you to continue on that long journey of sweat and travail and perhaps tears that leads to the goal of intelligent and effective ministry.

If you are ever caught in the grip of these temptations I would urge you to patience and perseverance. Do the little bit of work that falls to your hand day by day. Do it faithfully and diligently. In this sphere of human endeavour and divine vocation we are pedestrians. We cannot fly to the mountain tops. We must climb by the steep and thorny path. We may try to fly. But our attempt will end in disaster. There are no runways or landing strips on these majestic peaks. Even if we do survive a crash landing, we shall soon have to come down and we shall come down with the ignominy of folly on our brow.

The faculty of Westminster Seminary invites you to a fellowship of labour but also reminds you of the divine promise, 'My grace is sufficient for thee, for my strength is made perfect in weakness.' 'Every man shall receive his own reward according to his own labour.' 'Whatsoever ye do, do it heartily as to the Lord and not unto men, knowing that of the Lord ye shall receive the reward of the inheritance, for ye serve the Lord Christ.'

13

Charge to Edmund P. Clowney[1]

My dear friend and colleague, my esteem for your person and my high estimate of the qualifications you bring to the discharge of the Chair in which you have now been installed, make it very difficult for me to perform this assignment of giving you the charge. I am also aware that you are more sensitive than I could be to the demands of your office and to your complete dependence upon the grace of God for the fulfilment of these demands. To give you a charge then would seem superfluous and even presumptuous. But since I have been asked to do this I deeply appreciate the privilege, and in giving you the charge perhaps the chief result will be the recognition on our part of the harmony that exists between us respecting the aims to be realized in the conduct of the department now more fully committed to your charge.

1. First I would remind you that the responsibilities devolving upon you, arduous though they be, are at the same time unspeakable privileges. To the extent to which the responsibilities are arduous, to the same extent the privileges are magnified.

The proclamation of the gospel is the greatest vocation upon earth. The heralds of the gospel are the ambassadors of Christ, the King of kings and Lord of lords. Your task is pre-eminently to train men for this ministry. The task is overwhelming. But you are called to it, and grace is always according to need. And you are but Christ's chosen vessel into which at each step of your responsible undertaking he will pour from the plenitude of his wisdom, knowledge, grace, and power

[1] Given on October 22, 1963, when Dr. Clowney was installed as Professor of Practical Theology.

for the supply of all that is necessary for the fulfilment of your vocation.

2. Second, I would charge you to humility, humility for several reasons. You, like all of us, are still sinful. May you always be imbued with the broken spirit and the contrite heart, and before the vision of God's majesty say with the prophet, 'Woe is me for I am undone. I am a man of unclean lips, and I dwell among a people of unclean lips, for mine eyes have seen the King, the Lord of hosts'. You, like all of us, are not sufficient for any of these things. Be increasingly aware of your dependence upon God's grace. Particularly would I now stress your dependence upon the Holy Spirit. For though your task is very largely concerned with the communication of the gospel, communication is never effective to the accomplishment of the gospel's purpose without the demonstration and power of the Holy Spirit.

3. Your department is that of practical theology. The bane of much that goes under this title is the divorce of practics from theology. You are well aware of this evil and you have determined to counteract it. But it may not be out of place to put you in remembrance. Practical theology is principally systematic theology brought to practical expression and application. And this means the whole counsel of God brought to bear upon every sphere of life, and particularly upon every phase of the life and witness of the church. He would be a poor theologian indeed who would be unaware of, or indifferent to, the practical application of God's revealed counsel. But likewise, and perhaps more tragically, he would be a poor exponent of practical theology who did not know the theology of which practics is the application. I charge you to make it your concern to be the instrument of inflaming men with zeal for the proclamation of the whole counsel of God and of doing so with that passion and power without which preaching fails to do honour to the magnitude of its task and the glory of its message.

4. Your work is concerned with homiletics, the exposition and effective presentation of the Word of God. I charge you to continue to press home, as you have done in the past, the necessity of discovering, unfolding, and applying the particularities of each text or portion of God's Word. Few things are more distressing to the discerning, and more impoverishing to the church, than for a preacher to say much that is scriptural, indeed altogether scriptural, and yet miss the specific message

of the text with which he deals. It is by the richness and multiformity of God's revealed counsel that the church will grow up into the measure of the stature of the fulness of Christ, and the witness of the church will be to all the spheres of life and to all the obligations of men.

5. I charge you to concentration upon the discipline to the professorship of which you have been inaugurated. There are temptations to dissipate time and energy in devotion to other worthy tasks. But the only way of retaining and increasing the proficiency your installation expects is by concentrating on the tasks of the particular discipline which is your field of labour and by making all other activities contribute to your greater effectiveness in the field of practical theology.

May you long be spared to fulfil this high vocation in Westminster Theological Seminary, a Seminary devoted, as few are, to the maintenance and proclamation of the whole counsel of God!

14

Greeting to Entering Students, 1966[1]

In the name of the Faculty of Westminster Theological Seminary it is now my privilege to welcome to the fellowship and work of the Seminary the members of the incoming class. In doing so it is appropriate that I should say something about the position which the Seminary maintains and the purpose it seeks to promote. The position and purpose are set forth in the charter. But it is well summed up in five words you will find on the seal, derived from the words of Paul to the elders of the Church at Ephesus, 'the whole counsel of God' (Acts 20:27). The Seminary is founded upon the whole counsel of God and its aim is the understanding and proclamation of this counsel.

When we speak of the whole counsel of God as both position and aim, we do not mean that we claim to know it all. None of us and not all of us together know the whole counsel of God. It will take eternity to explore the riches of truth God has revealed in his Word, and then we shall not have plumbed all its depths, nor shall we have scaled all its heights.

We do not mean the hidden counsel of God. The unrevealed will of God is a profound abyss and we do not presume to know what is hid in the mind and will of God. We are mindful that the hidden things belong to the Lord our God and the things that are revealed belong unto us.

There are three things that we do mean.

1. We do have in the Scriptures the revealed counsel of God, and the

[1] Given on September 14, three months before he laid down his work at the Seminary on December 15, 1966.

110

whole of the counsel God in his wisdom and grace has been pleased to impart to us men until the consummation of all things. We do not accede to the pronouncement of the Second Vatican Council proclaimed on Nov. 18, 1965: 'Consequently it is not from Sacred Scripture alone that the Church draws her certainty about everything which has been revealed. Therefore both Sacred Tradition and Sacred Scripture are to be accepted and venerated with the same sense of loyalty and reverence.'[1] We know no antithesis between Christ as the Word, as the brightness of God's glory and the express image of his being, as the image of the invisible God, on the one hand, and the plenary inspiration, authority, perfection, and finality of the Scripture, on the other. It is just because of what Christ supremely and astoundingly is that Scripture possesses its authority and finality. The Old Testament is the inscripturation of that revelation which was the prelude to, and given in anticipation of, Christ's coming. And the New Testament is the inscripturation of that revelation of which Christ is the embodiment. And it is because Scripture is the deposit of God's revealed will that we have any knowledge of or access to Christ in his identity as the Word made flesh.

2. At Westminster the whole curriculum of study is directed to the proper understanding and application of this counsel of God. Among members of the Faculty there is a distinctly marked harmony of conviction and purpose. We have disagreements on details of interpretation and application. As individuals, and as a unit, we have not attained to perfection of understanding or of practice. We are still sinful. We come lamentably short of willing to do the Saviour's will and, therefore, correspondingly short in knowing the doctrine. But by God's grace we believe there is a system of truth in Scripture, that this system is one, and we believe it to be of God as the truth revealed to us for our faith and prescribing for us the way of life. When we agree on what the Scripture teaches and demands, then that is a finality.

3. Expediency is not the policy that regulates the witness or behaviour of the Seminary. It would sometimes be to our apparent advantage to suppress certain aspects of truth, to soft-pedal on matters that evoke the dissent or even provoke the ire of many people. Many of the positions maintained are unpopular and we lose support. Sometimes we are

1 *The Teaching of the Second Vatican Council*, ed. G. Baum, p. 353.

15

Edward J. Young: An Appreciation[1]

On Wednesday, the 14th of February (1968), Edward J. Young, Professor of Old Testament at Westminster Theological Seminary, Philadelphia, Pa., U.S.A. was called hence to be with the Lord. The end of his earthly pilgrimage by a heart attack came unexpectedly. The church of God on earth has lost one of its most devoted ornaments and the cause of Reformed scholarship one of its most erudite and consecrated exponents. It was an inestimable privilege to have been closely associated with Dr. Young for some thirty years as a colleague at Westminster Seminary. In the last four years before retirement from my work at the Seminary I was deeply impressed by the evidence my friend gave of the maturing fruit of the Spirit. But little did I think that he was being rapidly prepared for the immediate presence of the Saviour whom he loved and whose glory he delighted to proclaim. We had all expected many more years of his devoted labour.

Edward J. Young adorned his Christian profession. So many were the virtues making up this adornment that it is difficult to single out any for special appreciation. But his humility was so conspicuous that no one could fail to mark it. For those who knew him more intimately his circumspect consistency was no less evident. Unassuming and reluctant to make his own voice heard, he was always ready to speak out when the honour of Christ and the claims of truth demanded it. He burned with holy jealousy for the integrity of God's Word and for the maintenance of the whole counsel of God.

1 Written shortly after Dr. Young's death in 1968. Dr. Young, who reached his sixtieth birthday on November 29, 1967, had been professor of Old Testament at Westminster since 1936.

Dr. Young was an untiring worker. His literary output was prodigious. Those acquainted with his many contributions to Old Testament studies soon discovered the thoroughness of his preparation and the breadth of his scholarship. His linguistic talent was phenomenal. He was master of Hebrew and Aramaic, and with the Semitic languages bearing upon Old Testament studies he was thoroughly conversant. But not only were the ancient tongues his province. He read with ease a great variety of modern languages and thus no significant phase of Old Testament study escaped his notice or failed to receive his assessment. His greatest undertaking was a three-volume commentary on the Book of Isaiah. The first volume appeared in 1965, the second is apparently about to be issued.[1] How far advanced was the work on the third volume I am unable to say. No one living today surpassed Dr. Young in reliable, well-informed, and well-considered judgment on questions related to the Old Testament.

The distinction for which, above all others, Dr. Young should be commended and remembered as a scholar is the reverence he entertained for Scripture as the Word of God. To the defence of the Bible as such, and to its exposition as the living Word of the living God, he devoted all his talents and energies. Destructive criticism of the Scripture he resisted to the utmost. The Bible, he believed, was revelation from God, always relevant, and by the Holy Spirit sealed in our hearts to be what it intrinsically is, the inerrant Word of God. That this was the controlling factor in Dr. Young's thinking is evident in all his writings, and the devotion it implied and produced is demonstrated in what may be regarded as his more devotional volumes. He knew nothing of the antithesis between devotion to the Lord and devotion to the Bible. He revered the Bible because he revered the Author. And he revered and served the God of Scripture because he was captive to Scripture as revelatory Word.

The influence exerted by Edward J. Young will continue through the many books and articles that came from his pen. Supreme wisdom and love ordained his removal from our midst. Before the Lord's sovereign will we must bow in humble resignation and also with gratitude upon

[1] It was published in 1969 (William B. Eerdmans) and the third volume, the manuscript of which Dr. Young had completed shortly before his death—appeared in 1972.

every remembrance of the Saviour's grace in and to our departed friend. 'Blessed are the dead which die in the Lord from henceforth: Yea, saith the Spirit, that they may rest from their labours; and their works do follow them' (Rev. 14:13).

The Gospel and its Proclamation

16

The Grace of God

THE term 'grace' has various shades of meaning in the Scripture. When it speaks of the grace of God, what is in view most frequently is the favour of God. It is not always unmerited favour. Of Jesus it is said that 'he increased in wisdom and stature, and in favour with God and man' (Luke 2:52). But, generally, sinful men are in view as the objects of God's favour and then it is always unmerited favour. This is brought out very clearly when we read, 'Now to him that worketh is the reward not reckoned of grace, but of debt' (Rom. 4:4); 'And if by grace, then it is no more of works: otherwise grace is no more grace' (Rom. 11:6). Grace is here placed in sharp contrast with what is earned and therefore with all merit. Grace is undeserved favour and if any constraint is placed upon God, arising from worthiness on our part, whether it be of thought or word or action, then it is no longer grace.

We cannot think of sinners as merely undeserving; they are also ill-deserving. The grace of God to sinners is, therefore, not simply un-merited favour; it is also favour shown to the ill-deserving, indeed to the hell-deserving. When Paul says, 'justified freely by his grace through the redemption that is in Christ Jesus' (Rom. 3:24), the grace in view must be understood on the background of the judgment of God referred to in verse 19—'that every mouth may be stopped, and all the world may become guilty before God'. It is guilty men, and therefore hell-deserving men, that the justifying grace of God contemplates.

It is from this primary meaning of the word 'grace' that various other meanings are derived. The grace of God can refer to the gracious influences which are brought to bear upon men (cf. Luke 2:40; Acts 4:33; 2 Cor. 12:9). It can refer to the state of grace into which men are introduced (cf. Rom. 5:2). It can refer to the gifts bestowed and to the virtues generated (cf. Rom. 12:3, 6; 2 Cor. 8:7). But so closely related are these shades of meaning, and so dependent are they upon the primary import, that it is often difficult to be certain what particular thought is being expressed. We are always pointed back to the disposition of favour, of loving kindness in God as the source, and as that which gives character to all grace in exercise.

SALVATION BY GRACE

The grace of God comes to its richest expression in redemption and salvation. How plainly this is set forth in Paul's well-known word, 'By grace are ye saved through faith; and that not of yourselves: it is the gift of God' (Eph. 2:8)! When he says 'and that not of yourselves', he is reminding us of the true nature of grace, that its whole urge and explanation reside in God. It may be easy to give formal assent to this text. Every evangelical Christian will do so. But how ready we are to shy away from its implications! In reality we deny the truth here asserted when we introduce at any point in the whole span and process of salvation a decisive autonomy on the part of man. If salvation at any point is contingent upon some contribution which man himself makes, then at that point it is *of ourselves*, and to that extent it is not of grace. Paul's definition 'and that not of yourselves' is thereby effaced and the true nature of grace is denied.

THE CROSS OF CHRIST

The marvel of God's grace is pre-eminently displayed in the cross of Christ. It was by the will of the Father he was given and sent. It was by his own will that Christ came. He was sent to save and he came to save. The only alternative was that the whole human race should perish (cf. John 3:16; Matt. 1:21). Jesus alone is the captain of salvation. No one but he wrought redemption, no one but he made expiation, propitiation, and reconciliation for sin. How blasphemous would be the thought that we men had any part in this grand accomplishment! 'Now once in the end of the world hath he appeared to put away sin by the sacrifice of himself' (Heb. 9:26). It is as we view the solitary uniqueness of Christ's cross, the magnitude of the grace it exhibits, and its complete effectiveness unto salvation, that we learn the riches of God's 'grace in his kindness toward us through Christ Jesus' (Eph. 2:7). And it is here the insult we offer to God's grace appears when we try to condition its character or operation by some ingredient of our making. It is this perspective of God's great love when we were dead in sins that evokes Paul's word, 'by grace are ye saved'.

ELECTION OF GRACE

The span of salvation has its origin in election before the foundation of the world. And election is of grace (Rom. 11:5). Too often Christians have sought to intrude human decision as the explanation of the distinction which election requires. God elects, it is said, those whom he foresees will believe, and thus man's choice determines God's choice. If this is the true account of election, then we should have to say that what we *ourselves* decide determines election. In that event Ephesians 2:8 cannot apply to election, for here Paul says 'and that not of yourselves', and the grace of election would have to be of an entirely different character. But how impossible! If election is of grace (Rom. 11:5), it must be of the same grace defined in Ephesians 2:8, and therefore in no respect of *ourselves*, but wholly the gift of God. Besides, it is *salvation by grace through faith* that is the gift of God and so faith itself is of grace and not something that resides in human autonomy. The faith which God foresees is the fruit and not the root of electing grace.

Grace demands humility, the humility that constrains us to be willing debtors all along the line of salvation from its fount in election to its consummation in glory. Salvation is of the Lord, and it is only of him if it is all of him. This is the doctrine of grace and it is its glory.

JUSTIFICATION BY GRACE

It was the discovery of the grace of God that signalized the Protestant Reformation. The movement was focused in the uncovering of the great truth which Rome had buried beneath a pile of superstition, the doctrine of justification by faith alone and of grace alone. It was this same truth that Paul identified with the gospel, and it was the denial of it that elicited the severest denunciation we find in the New Testament. 'But though we, or an angel from heaven, preach any other gospel unto you than that which we have preached unto you, let him be accursed. As we said before, so say I now again, If any man preach any other gospel unto you than that ye have received, let him be accursed' (Gal. 1:8, 9). When later on he says, 'Christ is become of no effect unto you, whosoever of you are justified by the law; ye are fallen from grace' (Gal. 5:4), the thought is not that of falling away from a state of grace but rather that, if, to any extent, we look to our own works for justification, then we have abandoned grace altogether. Grace does not comport with any human contribution. If grace is in operation, if it has any place, it must have the whole place, it must be exclusively operative. If we are justified to any degree by works of law, we are debtors to do the whole law (cf. Gal. 5:3) and justification must be wholly of law.

Here again we have the same principle exemplified and confirmed: grace knows no human contribution. If of grace, then it is wholly and exclusively of grace. Since salvation is of grace, it is all of grace. Human autonomy is excluded at every point as decisively as at the point of justification.

SANCTIFICATION

Sanctification begins by union with Christ. There is a once-for-all breach with sin in its power, love, and defilement. By union with Christ believers partake of the virtue of Jesus' death and the power of his resurrection. In that Christ died to sin he died to sin once for all (Rom. 6:10). So believers died to sin and they live in newness of life (Rom. 6:2, 5). The unmixed grace of this release is apparent from the fact that it was by God's effectual call they were ushered into union and fellowship with Christ and therefore into the participation of his death and resurrection (1 Cor. 1:9).

Sanctification is also progressive until it is completed in glorification. It might appear that in this process there is the convergence of grace and works. We are to work out our own salvation with fear and trembling (Phil. 2:12). This activity on the part of believers must not be denied. Our whole personality in its diverse aspects and activities is enlisted in the doing of God's good pleasure. But this doing means no suspension of grace. The apostle goes on to say, 'for it is God which worketh in you both to will and to do of his good pleasure' (Phil. 2:13). Our willing and doing are altogether of God's working and therefore of grace. And this operative grace of God is not only the cause but also the urge and incentive to our activity for his good pleasure.

SOVEREIGN GRACE

The sovereignty of grace is implicit in its nature. If grace excludes the constraint of human merit, if its whole constraint and explanation reside in God, it must be of his free good pleasure. It is well to note the emphasis which the Scripture places upon this fact of sovereign will. When it speaks of the riches of God's grace (Eph. 1:7) and of what will redound 'to the praise of the glory of his grace' (Eph. 1:6), it is then that we find the reiterated reference to 'the good pleasure of his will' (Eph. 1:5), to 'the mystery of his will, according to his good pleasure' (Eph. 1:9), and to 'the purpose of him who worketh all things according to the counsel of his will' (Eph. 1:11). To dissociate grace in its source, progress, or fruition from pure sovereignty of will is to annul not only its character but also that by which its exercise is conditioned. And Paul's teaching here is the reproduction of our Lord's—'even so, Father: for so it seemed good in thy sight' (Matt. 11:26).

The mansions of glory will eternally resound with the praise of God's grace. It is not the minimum of salvation that the saints will enjoy but salvation the highest conceivable. No higher destiny could be appointed for them than to be glorified with Christ and conformed to the image of God's own Son (Rom. 8:17, 29). Nothing but sovereign grace at the zenith of its counsel and exercise could explain such glory. For it must be placed against the desert that is ours, the blackness of darkness forever. The contrast God's grace alone can explain.

17

The Message of Evangelism[1]

THE word 'evangelism' has generally been understood to apply to the propagation of the gospel among the unsaved. In dealing, however, with the obligation that rests upon the church of Christ to witness to the gospel it does not appear that the various activities of the church that may properly be embraced in the work of evangelism have exclusive reference to those who are reckoned, in the judgment of the church, as without God and without hope in the world. Particularly is this true when it is remembered that many believers in Christ have so inadequate a knowledge of the gospel, and so impoverished a conception of the Christian life, that a considerable part of the work of the church, properly regarded as evangelism, must needs have as its aim the instruction and edification of such believers. The evangelism that the true church of Christ undertakes must therefore contemplate the bringing of the gospel in its full import and demands to those who, though believers, are nevertheless the victims of ignorance, unfaithfulness and compromising associations.

This report, however, in accordance with what is believed to be the intent of the Ninth General Assembly, will deal in the main with the message of evangelism as the message of the gospel to the lost.

[1] A report by the Committee on Local Evangelism sent to the ministers and sessions of the Orthodox Presbyterian Church and considered at the Eleventh General Assembly of that Church. It was written by John Murray who was Secretary of the Committee. Other reports prepared by different members of the same Committee, were on: 'The Prerequisites of Evangelism', 'Preparation for the Evangelistic Meeting', 'Personal Work', and 'Intensive Survey Work'.

THE WHOLE COUNSEL OF GOD

The message of evangelism is the whole counsel of God as revealed in his Word, the Scriptures of the Old and New Testaments. Too often this commonplace statement is not accepted or, if accepted, not appreciated or followed. The cause of evangelism has been greatly prejudiced and hindered by the supposition, far too prevalent, that for the lost the message has to be restricted to the central elements of the gospel, namely, sin, redemption by the blood of Christ, and the demand for faith and repentance. It is true that evangelism should always keep in the forefront of its message the central and elementary principles of the gospel. But two facts must be borne in mind:

1. The Scripture pattern will not support the conclusion that the central message of the gospel is the exclusive content of the message of evangelism, and

2. the central message itself cannot properly be presented or understood except as it is presented in the context of the whole counsel of God.

Paul's message to the Athenians reached its conclusion in the declaration that God commands men that they should all everywhere repent. But that conclusion was prefaced by appeal to God as the creator of all, to God as the Lord of heaven and earth, to the self-sufficiency and spirituality of God and to God as the Lord of all nations, and Paul's appeal for repentance was oriented to God's final judgment. It can be seen then that the declared orbit within which Paul delivered the gospel of repentance was the orbit defined by the doctrine of God as the absolutely self-sufficient and spiritual God, Creator and Lord of heaven and earth, and that the termini of the history within which the message of repentance is given are creation at the beginning and judgment at the end.

When it is said that the whole counsel of God is the message of evangelism this should not be understood to mean that the whole counsel of God can be compassed in each message. Nor is it to be understood as meaning that sound judgment and wisdom are not to be used to the fullest extent in the selection of the topics to be presented at particular times and in the devising of the manner in which they are to be presented. The message of God's counsel is multiform and the particular needs of men are varied. The message should, therefore, always be adapted to the peculiar need and condition of the persons concerned and great care should be exercised that the truths presented and the manner of presentation should be chosen and framed so as to make the most direct and effective impact upon those who are the recipients of the message. Great care and sometimes exacting labour are required in the interest of ensuring, as far as possible, that the inopportuneness of the time chosen for the presentation of a particular message and the inappropriateness of the manner adopted do not become the occasion for a distorted understanding on the part of the persons to whom the message is given, just as alertness and faithfulness are equally required to ensure that the appropriate opportunity for the presentation of a particular message is not lost by indolence and weakness on the part of the evangelist. It frequently happens that the evangelist has to refrain from the presentation of certain truths until the proper foundation is laid in the minds of the persons concerned by the understanding and acceptance of other truths. And it just as frequently happens that to refrain from imparting the necessary instruction at a particular time imperils the success and the fruitage of the evangelist's work.

There is need, therefore, for the greatest wisdom in dealing with the numerous diversities that exist among the subjects of evangelism, diversities of tradition, of education, of temperament, of religious knowledge and conviction, of social standing, and even of vocation.

But admitting all of these reservations and taking all care that they be duly applied, it must, nevertheless, be maintained that there is no part of the revelation of Scripture that is not the fit subject for the message of evangelism. This proposition will be illustrated by a few examples.

EXAMPLES

1. *Election*. It might be supposed that the doctrine of election could not properly be incorporated into an evangelistic message or, at least, could not properly be the topic of an evangelistic message. This is a grievous mistake. It is true that only believers have any right to regard themselves as elect of God and only they can derive from the truth of election covenant assurance and comfort. But the doctrine of election, when properly conceived and handled, has the closest bearing upon the lost. It may be used in arousing the lost from lethargy and indifference. Election

implies non-election. It concerns the ultimate destinies of men and to that question the lost cannot afford to be indifferent. The truth of election may thus be used to bring the unsaved to the most earnest solicitude concerning their salvation, and when thus awakened to concern, it provides them with the understanding of the ground upon which they may entertain hope with respect to the grace of salvation as it applies to them.

God's sovereign election is the one source of the only salvation there is for lost men. It was in pursuance of God's electing love that God sent his Son into the world. It was in pursuance of electing love that Jesus died upon the cross, was raised from the dead and sat down at the right hand of God. The nature of the salvation offered to lost men in the gospel can not be abstracted from that purpose of grace in pursuance of which salvation was wrought and in subordination to which it is being constantly applied. Therefore the salvation offered to the lost, the salvation presented to their need and demanding the response of their faith, is salvation determined in its very character by election.

Election is the only source of the salvation presented in the gospel. As such it is calculated to bring hope to the perishing. For in election there is the assurance that God loved sinners from eternity, that he loved sinners with such invincible love that he did not spare his own Son but delivered him up for them. The evangelist should show this truth to be aglow with hope for those who, under the conviction of sin, are tempted to believe that so grievous are their sins that God could not love them and save them. Election shows the character of God's love, that it is love for the lost, that it is sovereign love, not love determined by the degrees of sinnership but by the mere good pleasure of God and therefore not in the least incompatible with the sinnership and hell-deservedness of those who are its objects. It should be apparent how close a bearing election has upon the most urgent demands of a practical evangelism.

2. *Limited Atonement.* It is often argued that the doctrine of definite or limited atonement is quite foreign and even inimical to the interests of evangelism. For how, it may be plausibly protested, can salvation be freely offered to the lost and its claims pressed upon them if salvation has been procured only for a limited number? Proper analysis of the salvation offered to lost men will show, however, that only on the basis of a

definite atonement can full salvation be offered to lost men. True evangelism must ever bear in mind that it is not the mere possibility of salvation, nor simply provision for salvation, that is offered freely in the gospel. It is rather *salvation* full, perfect and free. For it is Christ in all the glory of his person as Saviour and Redeemer, and in all the perfection of his finished work, who is offered to sinners in the gospel. This glory and this perfection that reside in Christ as Saviour have come to reside in him only by virtue of what he has done in his capacity as the captain of salvation. And what he has done in this capacity is not that he made the salvation of all men possible, nor that he made provision for the salvation of all, but rather that he wrought and purchased redemption. It is salvation with such completeness and perfection that is presented to lost men in the full, free and unfettered call of the gospel. But only on the basis of a limited atonement could such salvation and redemption be wrought, and only on the basis of a limited atonement can such salvation be offered. We should not then be loathe to make known to lost men the real nature of the extent of the atonement. For bound up with a limited extent is the real nature of the salvation and of the Christ offered. If we universalize the extent of the atonement we must limit its efficacy, and when we limit its efficacy it is an impoverished and trun- cated salvation that the ministers of evangelism have to offer. Just as we mutilate the salvation offered, so do we empty our message of the irresistible appeal that the proclamation of a full and perfect salvation provides. Evangelism thereby not only proves itself unfaithful to the fulness of the gospel but also robs itself of that which is indispensable to its effectiveness, namely, the recognition on the part of men of the claim, privilege and opportunity that the full and free offer of Christ entails.

3. *Total Depravity*. The doctrine of total depravity and inability must not be compromised and avoided in the conduct of evangelism. It is true that any emphasis upon this doctrine appears quite inappropriate in dealing with the unsaved. For the assertion of human inability seems to cut the nerve of any motive to that exercise of faith and repentance which is the demand of the gospel message, and it may very plausibly be contended that evangelism should not prejudice the urgent demand for faith by proclaiming human inability. It is also true that men have

oftentimes shielded themselves against the claims and demands of the gospel by pleading the subterfuge of their own inability.

It must be recognized, however, that human inability does not remove responsibility, and neither does the abuse of inability, arising from the perversity inherent in human depravity, provide us with any valid reason for deceiving men with respect to the real nature of their moral and spiritual condition or for withholding from them the truth with respect to the consequences of that condition.

But, to speak more positively, it is the self-sufficiency that proceeds from failure to appreciate our complete spiritual bankruptcy and impotence that is the greatest obstacle to that contrition of heart that alone creates the state of mind requisite to the appropriation of the gospel of grace. Evangelism must produce, by God's grace and the operations of the Spirit, a deep sense of helplessness in the minds of those evangelized. Without conviction of sin there will never be acceptance of the gospel. It is the preaching of man's total depravity and inability manifested in the overt transgression of God's law that is calculated to induce this sense of sin, of helplessness and of need. And so this doctrine of depravity and inability is not only necessary as belonging to the whole counsel of God but is also one of the most fruitful elements of that counsel in promoting the interests of wholesome and effective evangelism.

PARTICULAR REQUISITES OF THE MESSAGE

I. *The Conviction of Sin.* The most formidable barrier to effective evangelism in any generation, and particularly accentuated in ours, is self-sufficiency and self-righteousness. It was the witness of our Lord himself that the whole need not a physician but they that are sick. One of the primary tasks of the evangelist, therefore, is to bring the demands of law and gospel to bear upon the consciences of men so that they may be convinced of the reality of the condemnation to which they are subject, of the reality of their separation from God, and of the certainty of eternal doom apart from the gospel of redeeming grace.

One of the most appalling defects of much present-day evangelism is the absence of any consistent and sustained emphasis upon the holiness, justice and authority of God. This defect is illustrated very concretely in the failure to proclaim and apply the binding authority and sanction of

God's law, summarily comprehended in the ten commandments. It is as these commandments are brought to bear upon the hearts and lives of men that the effect referred to by the apostle Paul is produced, 'I was alive without the law once, but when the commandment came, sin revived and I died' (Rom. 7:9); 'Verily I had not known lust except the law had said, Thou shalt not covet' (Rom. 7:7). This conviction is an invariable result of faithful proclamation of the binding claims and sanctions of the law of God and we must not deceive ourselves by thinking that the sophistication of which modern philosophy has made men the victims in any way abrogates the divinely established rule that by the law is the knowledge of sin. Only the sharp arrows of God's commandments can pierce the heart of the King's enemies and only these can lay low the self-sufficiency of human pride.

A conspicuous defect, closely co-ordinate with the foregoing, is the absence of warning and of condemnation in evangelistic effort. The naturalistic temper of our age, united with its callousness, makes the doctrine of hell peculiarly uncongenial. It is more often the subject of crude jest than it is of solemn warning or foreboding. The supposed politeness of modern etiquette has too often succeeded in creating the sentiment that any serious reference to hell and damnation is not accordant with the canons of good taste. These evils have in many cases ensnared even the orthodox.

But hell is an unspeakable reality and, if evangelism is to march on its way, it must by God's grace produce that sense of condemnation complexioned by the apprehension of perdition as the due reward of sin. For it is in the anguish of such a sense of condemnation, in the anguish of a conscience that stings with the apprehension of the wrath and curse of God, that the gospel of God's free grace becomes as cold water to a thirsty soul and as good news from a far country.

2. *The Free Offer of the Gospel.* As pertinent to this subject there are in particular two evils that have to be avoided. The first is the presentation of the gospel with an Arminian complexion or on an Arminian basis. A very considerable part of the evangelism that has been conducted for several decades, if not for the last two centuries, has been of an Arminian character. This type of evangelism proceeds on the assumptions that Christ died to save all men or, at least, to make provision for the salva-

tion of all men, and that all men have by natural retention or by gracious restoration the ability to believe in Christ. The overtures of grace in the gospel are therefore presented on the assumption that God has done his utmost in this matter of salvation and that now it is left to men in the exercise of their own autonomous will to accept Christ. The really decisive factor in the matter of salvation, now that Christ has died and is freely offered to men, is held to be the autonomous decision and action on the part of men themselves.

It must be admitted that this construction of the gospel and of man's responsibility and opportunity has many appealing and plausible features. In favour of it might seem to be the fact that it has produced mighty results. Indeed it has seemed to many that this is the only feasible way in which to present the claims of Christ and the appeal for faith. Being the predominant form of evangelism in many parts, people of Reformed persuasion have readily fallen into line with this type of evangelistic effort.

Oftentimes as an accompaniment of this conception of the message and of the response to the message there has been fostered a certain type of high-pressure appeal and of emotional excitement that is scarcely compatible with the sobriety and dignity that ought to characterize the preaching of the gospel, and scarcely consistent with the deliberateness and intelligence appropriate to the exercise of faith in Christ as Saviour and Lord.

The second evil is that of hyper-Calvinism. Those thoroughly convinced of the error of Arminian anthropology and soteriology have quite properly reacted from the type of evangelism that is the characteristic expression of it. But deep persuasion of the particularism of the plan of salvation, and revulsion from Arminian evangelism, have sometimes been the occasion for the abandonment of evangelism altogether or, at least, for the denial of the full and free offer of the gospel to lost men. If this reaction does not go to the length of theoretically denying the free offer of the gospel, it nevertheless manifests itself in a conspicuous awkwardness and lack of spontaneity in the preaching of the free offer. Reaction from the error of Arminian doctrine and methods, together with persuasion of man's total inability and God's absolute predestination, have rendered many unable to understand or work out in practice the complete congruity of man's inability and of consistent particularism in the plan of salvation with the full, free and unfettered offer of Christ to lost sinners, and they have also been unable to appreciate the congruity of man's inability and God's predestination with the necessity for the most urgent and passionate appeal for the exercise of faith and repentance.

The only proper path for true evangelism is the path that lies between these two extremes. Evangelism must understand that election and the particularism of the whole process of redemption puts no fence around the free offer of Christ in the gospel. Neither does human inability and the necessity of efficacious grace in any way circumscribe the offer of a free and full salvation to those who are dead in trespasses and sins. And the responsibility, privilege and opportunity of lost men as they are confronted by the external call of the gospel are not in the least curtailed by the fact that efficacious grace is indispensable to the saving exercise of such responsibility and to the saving embrace of the privilege and opportunity.

3. *Human Need and Responsibility*. In earlier parts of this report on the message of evangelism, stress has been laid upon the necessity of intelligent evangelism. But evangelism must also be zealous and persistent. The zeal of evangelism must find its origin in the recognition of the gravity of sin and of its consequences. Sin is directed against God's glory and majesty and it has its consequence in alienation from him. Lost men are therefore in desperate need of the gospel. Apart from the faith of the gospel the only outlook for man is the blackness of darkness for ever, eternal destruction from the presence of the Lord and from the glory of his power. These facts impart an irresistible urgency to the task of evangelism and require that urgent demand be characteristic of the delivery of the message. This is to say that the message of evangelism can never be presented as if it were simply a reasonable hypothesis or probability, attested as good and useful by the witness of experience. It must rather be presented as the only alternative, as the absolute truth which must not be rejected except at the peril of eternal death. It must be presented as unescapable finality that there is none other name given under heaven among men whereby we must be saved but the name of Jesus. And so faith and repentance must be urged upon men as not only good and useful resorts but as imperative demands and duties.

The responsibility of men as they are presented with the claims and overtures of the gospel springs not only from the gravity of their need but also from the glory and perfection of God's gracious provision in Christ. Evangelism must impress upon those who are the subjects of it the heinousness of the sin involved in the rejection of such unspeakable grace. To reject the gospel is to offer insult to the supreme revelation of God's glory. It is the claims of God's glory, as that glory reaches the zenith of its disclosure in the person and work of him who is the image of the invisible God, that cause to rest upon men so stupendous a responsibility. 'This is the condemnation, that light is come into the world, and men loved darkness rather than light, because their deeds were evil' (John 3:19).

4. *Christ Crucified and Risen.* Evangelism must always be jealous to make Christ as the crucified and risen Redeemer the sum and substance of its message. The example of the apostle is final and conclusive in this respect. 'For the Jews require a sign, and the Greeks seek after wisdom: but we preach Christ crucified, unto the Jews a stumblingblock, and unto the Greeks foolishness; but unto them which are called, both Jews and Greeks, Christ the power of God, and the wisdom of God' (1 Cor. 1:22–24). 'And I, brethren, when I came to you, came not with excellency of speech or of wisdom, declaring unto you the testimony of God. For I determined not to know anything among you, save Jesus Christ and him crucified' (1 Cor. 2:1, 2).

It is doubtless true that the recording of Christian experience has its proper place in Christian testimony, and the record of the experience which is the fruit of God's saving grace has often exercised a powerful influence for good upon the ungodly. It is also true that a godly life is an indispensable element in our witness to the power of the gospel. But evangelism has been ensnared by the subtlety of Satan when it regards the witness of Christian experience as that which constitutes testimony to Christ. Too often an egocentric interest and emphasis, very plausibly bearing the appearance of doing honour to Christ, has nevertheless grievously perverted the true witness of evangelism. We must ever be faithful to the import of the apostle's word, 'For we preach not ourselves, but Christ Jesus the Lord; and ourselves your servants for Jesus' sake' (2 Cor. 4:5).

The preaching of Christ is the preaching of Christ crucified. Christ is not truly preached unless there is the offence that is to Jews a stumbling-block and to Greeks foolishness. This offence that inheres in the cross lays evangelism open to the temptation to eliminate or tone down that which appears to imperil the success of evangelistic effort, the temptation to withhold, at least at the outset, the very kernel of the gospel of grace. This is fatal dishonour to Christ, and nothing more successfully ensures that the gospel we preach is not the gospel but the wisdom of men. It is the cross of Christ as the exalted Lord that embodies the supreme revelation of the justice, love and grace of God, and to eliminate or tone down the offence of the cross is to preach another than the God and Father of our Lord Jesus Christ, and it is to fall under the condemnation of the inspired apostle who, after having testified that the Lord Jesus Christ 'gave himself for our sins, that he might deliver us from this present evil world, according to the will of God and our Father' (Gal. 1:4), also wrote, 'But though we, or an angel from heaven, preach any other gospel unto you than that which we have preached unto you, let him be accursed, . . . For do I now persuade men or God? or do I seek to please men? for if I yet pleased men, I should not be the servant of Christ' (Gal. 1:8, 10).

18

The Propagation of the
Reformed Faith in New England[1]

'THE harvest truly is plenteous but the labourers are few; pray ye therefore the Lord of the harvest that he will send forth labourers into his harvest.' How fitting are these words of our Lord to the situation that has now for long existed in New England! The currents of unbelief and indifference have left in their wake spiritual devastation. The multitudes are scattered abroad as sheep not having a shepherd. They are destitute of the ministry of that gospel which is the only power of God unto salvation.

It is the burden of this great need in the field that was once the home of the godly pilgrim fathers who there sought refuge from hierarchical tyranny, that constrained a small group of men to form, less than a year ago, 'The Committee for the Propagation of the Reformed Faith in New England'. The purpose was to launch humbly, yet in confident reliance upon divine grace, upon the task of sending men imbued with intelligent devotion to the gospel into these needy fields.

The result was that during the course of last summer and early fall nine men were sent to this work. The number of weeks for each man ranged from sixteen to four. The average number of weeks for each was eleven. And in addition, during the course of the winter to the date of writing, two men have laboured continuously on the field.

As regards personnel, all of the men who worked either in the course of the summer and fall or throughout the winter have been graduates or students of Westminster Theological Seminary in Philadelphia.

The fruits of these endeavours have been in a signal sense gratifying.

1 *The Presbyterian Guardian*, April 24, 1937.

To the Committee one of the most gratifying features was the self-sacrificing devotion and enthusiasm of the men and, to the men themselves as well as to the Committee, the evidence given of the Lord's hand and blessing upon their labours.

Now, as our session at Westminster Seminary is drawing to a close, we are making plans for summer work to begin not later than May 15th, and to continue to the end of September. We are hoping that, in addition to the two men who are already on the field, we shall be able to place at least ten men from among our graduates and students. Various circuits are being arranged so that with the aid of automobile or bicycle each man may be able to cover a fairly wide area and thus have as many as four or five preaching stations at which services and Bible classes may be conducted either on the Lord's day or on week days. Much attention will also be devoted to house visitation. By the arrangement of these circuits and by the provision on the part of the committee or of the men themselves of adequate means of transportation, one man will be able to cover four or five times the territory that one man covered last year, and that without any necessary diminishing of attention to each particular town or village.

It will have been noticed that the phrase, 'Reformed Faith', appears in the title of this Committee. There is nothing for which the Committee exists other than that which is comprehended in that phrase. It is for the propagation of the Reformed Faith, and that means simply the propagation of the whole counsel of God as revealed in his holy Word, the whole counsel of God as it respects faith and life. Its purpose is the evangelism which is not only consistent with the Reformed Faith but the necessary expression of it wherever it really exists as the controlling thought of the mind and passion of the heart. It is evangelism in pursuance of the Lord's command, 'Go ye, therefore, and disciple all the nations.'

In these times there is much evangelism that is clap-trap, much so-called evangelism that does not have the gospel, and much also of evangelism that, though evangelical in its general spirit and result, is not true to the whole counsel of God. It is the aim of this Committee to foster and further evangelism that will not be dependent upon the sensational for its appeal or success, but evangelism grounded in the conviction of the absolute sovereignty and efficacy of the grace of God, evangelism among the degraded and ignorant, the indifferent and hostile, that does not fear to declare the whole counsel of God and to proffer to men lost and dead in sin the full and free salvation that is in Jesus Christ our Lord. It is confident evangelism because, though not given in the persuasive words of human wisdom, it depends for its efficacy upon the demonstration of the Spirit and of power. And thus the faith of men will come to rest not upon the wisdom of men but in the power of God.

We are conscious of weakness. We know something of the infirmities of others because we are conscious of our own. But grace overcomes infirmity. And most gladly, therefore, will we rather glory in our infirmities that the power of Christ may rest upon us.

We are hoping this summer to send ten, perhaps fifteen, men. We trust that the needs of these men will be met, for 'the earth is the Lord's and the fulness thereof'. We wish we had sufficient funds and men so that we could send a hundred. Even then we should only be touching the fringe of the need in this greatly unevangelized field. A great door and effectual is opened unto us. We pray for consecration in ourselves. We pray for the same in the men who will be sent, and for the baptism of the Spirit upon them. May they in true apostolic fashion turn that world upside down. But we also with deep earnestness solicit your prayers and interest. Precious seed has already been sown and, we believe, will be sown. And may we not remind you as well as ourselves that 'he that goeth forth and weepeth, bearing precious seed, shall doubtless come again with rejoicing bringing his sheaves with him' (Ps. 126:6).

The members of the Committee are the Rev. W. P. Green, 1626 Columbia Road, South Boston, Mass., *Treasurer*; the Rev. John Skilton, 371 Congress Street, Portland, Maine, *Secretary*; the Rev. David Freeman, 429 Wellesley Road, Philadelphia, Pennsylvania, *Vice-Chairman*; and the present writer, of Westminster Theological Seminary, Philadelphia, Pennsylvania, *Chairman*. Such gifts as have been received for the work have gone in their entirety to the support of the missionaries. Committee members have themselves borne all the incidental expenses, and have given their services without charge. This same policy and method will continue to be pursued.

19

The Power of the Holy Spirit

Jesus said to his disciples on the eve of his ascension: 'Ye shall receive power when the Holy Spirit is come upon you' (Acts 1:8). Earlier than this, on his appearance to the disciples on the resurrection day, 'he breathed on them and said, Receive ye the Holy Spirit' (John 20:22). How we are to interpret this action in reference to the charge of Acts 1:4 and the promise of Acts 1:8 may be a moot question. As there were stages in Jesus' own endowment with power, so the same thought of progression may be applied in this instance to the disciples. Or John 20:22 may be simply in anticipation of Acts 1:4, 8. But in any case John 20:22 does not in the least interfere with the momentous event referred to in Acts 1:4, 8. With many other sayings the promise of Acts 1:8 witnesses to the significance of Pentecost. Pentecost was a once-for-all event to be co-ordinated with the death, resurrection, and ascension of Christ. The particular phenomena with which it was accompanied and certified were phenomena that are to be regarded as peculiar to the event. Then the Holy Spirit came in the fulness of his grace and power in world-wide activity for the fulfilment of the promise given to Abraham (Gen. 22:18) and that given to Christ (Psalm 2:8), in fulfilment of the world-wide redemptive design and accomplishment. There was the coming of the Son by a distinctive mode and for a distinct undertaking. There is also the coming of the Holy Spirit by a distinctive mode and for a distinctive function.

We must not forget it. This is the age of Pentecost. Let us not overlook Acts 1:8b; 'Ye shall be my witnesses' etc. This is why we have the gospel. It is because the utmost part of the earth has come within the scope of the Holy Spirit's activity.

Our particular interest now is the *power* of the Holy Spirit. There are several aspects from which this may be viewed.

I.   THE SOURCE OF FAITH

In this connection we think particularly of 1 Cor. 2:4, 5; 1 Thess. 1:5; 2:13; 1 John 2:20, 21, 27. When Paul says that faith is in the power of God (ἐν δυνάμει Θεοῦ), he is surely implying that faith is elicited by and rests upon the power of God. But this power is surely specified in the preceding verse as 'the demonstration of the Spirit and of power', and he is thinking of that attendant influence of the Holy Spirit in virtue of which the Word was effectual at Corinth. Although Paul is thinking of the power attending his ministry, we must also think of that power as that by which the Word of the gospel was registered in the hearts of believers as the truth of God. In other words, the power was the certification of divinity and it was power so compulsive that it constrained faith. The thought is very similar in 1 Thess. 1:5: 'Our gospel came not unto you in word only, but also in power and in the Holy Spirit and much assurance'. Again the apostle is reflecting on the attendant influence and on the confidence with which the gospel was proclaimed. But we must regard the assurance created in the Thessalonians as due to the power of the Holy Spirit, because later Paul says that they received the Word 'not as the word of men, but as it truly is, the word of God, which also works effectually in you who believe' (1 Thess. 2:13). This confidence is the theme of John when he refers to the unction of the Holy One by which they know the truth, have no need that any one teach them, for the unction teaches them, and know that no lie is of the truth (1 John 2:20, 21). We must speak of compulsive conviction, irresistible conviction, not because human psychology is violated, but because the Word is certified by the highest conceivable evidence of its veracity. It is divinity attesting divinity and the inevitable result is certitude, full assurance.

This has been called the internal testimony of the Holy Spirit. It has sometimes been construed as illumination whereby our minds are opened and made responsive to the evidence the Word contains of its divine origin, character, and authority. This it is. But it is also more. It is demonstration, certification the Holy Spirit supplies. Just as the Holy

Spirit himself is the earnest of the inheritance, so in this case the Holy Spirit, actively operative in his demonstration, is himself the seal of the veracity and divinity of the Word.

II. SOURCE OF EFFECTUAL PROCLAMATION

From what we have found in the power of the Spirit as the source of faith, it follows that proclamation, in order to be effectual unto salvation, must be accompanied by the power of the Spirit. But there are particular considerations more strictly relevant to this aspect of the subject.

1. *Dependence.* This is but the application within this sphere of the general principle that in the economy of salvation all is of grace. A great deal is being said today about the art of communication and, without question, communication of the gospel to a world whose patterns of thought are so alien is one of the most challenging tasks confronting the church. But with all that may properly be conceived and applied in developing the art, how dismally we fail in communication if we overlook the fact that in the last analysis communication is dependent upon a grace we cannot command and cannot pour into the channels of our ingenuity! It constrains us to prostrate ourselves and recognize: 'Except the Lord build the house they labour in vain that build it'. Here we need an attitude that will pervade our thought—the sense of dependence. How deceitful is art destitute of the Spirit (cf. 1 Cor. 2:4)!

2. *Cultivation of the Means.* It is dishonour to the Spirit if we do not recognize and acknowledge our complete dependence upon his grace. But no less dishonouring is it when we allow our sense of dependence to be an excuse for sloth. As in other areas, divine sovereignty never eliminates human responsibility, and the co-ordination is such that those most persuaded of God's sovereignty are the persons who are most diligent in the exercises that come within the sphere of human responsibility. When we think of the power of the Holy Spirit as that by which the Word is certified and made effectual, correlative with this persuasion will be the blood, sweat, toil, and tears of devoted and sustained study of that Word to which the Spirit adds certification. We must bear in mind again that the power is attendant in proclamation and therefore in the preparation that is antecedent. The Word is explored as the Word of

God sealed by the Spirit, and the attendant power is indispensable to effectual preparation as well as to the subsequent proclamation. If we are sensitive, discerning, and zealous, we soon discover in ourselves and in the ministrations of others the absence of what is the channel of the Holy Spirit's power. The product of the Holy Spirit's revelation, and the power by which it is certified as his product, always go together. And if we neglect this conjunction our supposed reliance on the power of the Holy Spirit is mockery. The conjunction is the lesson of Jesus' word: 'It is the Spirit who quickens' *etc.* (John 6:63).

It would be improper to omit the necessity of prayer as the complement of our dependence and of our proclamation, an exercise that demands intense application of heart, mind, and will. It is likewise the channel. 'Before they call, I will answer' *etc.* (Isa. 65:24).

III. SOURCE OF ENCOURAGEMENT

The proclamation of the gospel encounters many circumstances replete with what tends to discouragement. Every faithful minister of the Word knows the temptations that arise as he is confronted with unresponsiveness, coldness, and indifference and, most particularly, with unfaithfulness on the part of those who have professed faith in the gospel. All of this drives home the lesson of our helplessness in the conflict with human depravity; and the two considerations that meet the situation are, first, the gospel as the power of God unto salvation and, second, the sealing power of the Holy Spirit. These are mutually complementary. And what needs to be stressed at this point of our study is the confidence we may and must entertain that, as Christ promised his own presence to the end of the age in the discipling of all the nations (Matt. 28:18–20), so the Holy Spirit abides in and with the church as the Spirit of Pentecost, convicting the world of sin, of righteousness, and of judgment, and disclosing to men the glories of the Redeemer. We must remember the great truth of John 3:8 in respect of sovereignty but also in respect of efficacy. 'If ye being evil' *etc.* (Luke 11:13). Our confidence should be as unbounded as our dependence is complete. Our desires and intercessions should be as extensive as the promises of God (Gen. 22:18; Psalm 2:8), and as extensive as the commission to disciple all the nations. Defeatism and discouragement are the hall marks of unbelief and the counsel of the

20

Some Necessary Emphases
in Preaching[1]

IN speaking to you on this subject I am not posing as an authority on preaching or on practical theology. Neither am I supposing that I am a good example of the virtues I am going to plead. In this, as in other matters, we preach not ourselves. Sometimes one can properly bring to the attention of others the very defects of which he is deeply conscious in his own life and witness. If we are alert to the needs of our own souls and to the needs of the souls of others, we become sensitive to the defects from which pulpit ministrations suffer and by reason of which the effectiveness of the pulpit and the witness to Christ are impaired. There are many emphases which fall into this category. I have selected only a few.

I. THE MINISTRY OF JUDGMENT
By this is meant particularly the proclamation of the judgment of God upon sin. There is, of course, no preaching of the gospel, even in the broadest evangelical sense, that does not involve some proclamation of this judgment. But we are thinking now, not of what is indispensable by way of minimum, but of what is demanded by way of proper emphasis. And what I have observed as conspicuously minimal in the preaching of evangelical and even reformed Churches is the proclamation of the demands and sanctions of the law of God. To put it bluntly, it is the lack of the enunciation with power, earnestness, and passion of the demands and terrors of God's law.

[1] An address given to the Alumni of Westminster Theological Seminary at the annual homecoming on February 19, 1952.

I am well aware that the plea for such preaching can be readily dismissed with a shrug of the shoulder, and perhaps also with some self-complacency, by saying that such an emphasis is simply legalism and not congruous with the grace of the gospel. But if we pursue our analysis but a little we shall discover that such a reply is only an alibi to evade the force of a very serious and searching charge. The emphasis upon the demands and sanctions of the law of God is only another way of asserting the demands and sanctions of God's holiness. What is now being pleaded is nothing more or less than that which is the complement of our recognition of God's majesty. In the realm of religious exercise the heart of our reformed faith is the profound apprehension of God's majesty; and that is just saying, the profound apprehension of his holiness. Who will say that such is legalism? It is the soul of Christian piety.

When emphasis upon the demands and sanctions of God's law is neglected, there are grave consequences for the propagation of the gospel itself. And when I say 'propagation' I am thinking not merely in terms of extension but also of intension.

1. When the proclamation of God's law is neglected, the significance of the gospel is correspondingly reduced in our presentation and in the apprehension of men. The gospel is the gospel of salvation, and salvation is, first of all, salvation from sin in its guilt, defilement, and power. If our emphasis on the judgment of God upon sin is minimal, correspondingly minimal will be our esteem of salvation and of the Saviour. One sometimes wonders whether the faith in Christ which is demanded of men in the presentation of the claims of Christ can have any real content in view of the beggarly conception of the gravity of sin which is presented as its presupposition and concomitant. Faith in Christ does not arise in a vacuum. It arises in the context of conviction of sin and it is to the creation of that conviction that the ministry of judgment ministers. 'By the law is the knowledge of sin.' Has the apostle Paul become obsolete or is his witness becoming obsolescent? 'I was alive without the law once: but when the commandment came, sin revived, and I died' (Rom. 7:9). 'Nay, I had not known sin, but by the law: for I had not known lust, except the law had said, Thou shalt not covet' (Rom. 7:7). What we need to recognize is that faith in Christ is not simply a fine thing, not simply a good thing, but that it is indispensable. The

gospel is an indispensable message for sinners lost to God, lost to his fellowship, lost to his love, and lost to his glory. It is this note that will impart to the message of the gospel and to the demand for faith and repentance the urgency that is consonant with the desperate situation for which the gospel is the one and only provision. Our age needs the ministry that will make men tremble before the awful majesty and holiness of God and in the conviction of the reality of his holy wrath.

2. If we fix attention upon the thought of guilt we can perhaps bring into sharper focus the necessity of the proclamation of judgment. The consciousness of guilt has suffered eclipse in the context of modern Christianity. It is easy to see, however, that when guilt is pushed into the background and the sense of guilt becomes well-nigh extinct, the grand article of the gospel becomes correspondingly meaningless. What is this grand article, the grand article of grace? If our minds do not immediately supply the answer, it is because we ourselves have become infected with the stupor so characteristic of our generation. It is, of course, the article of justification by grace through faith. The appreciation of that article, and the appreciation of the gospel as it is epitomised in that article, takes its inception from the consciousness of guilt. There is an amazing and distressing paucity of the agonizing question which is, after all, the basic religious question: how can a man be just with God? And there is likewise, and inevitably as a consequence, a paucity of the exultant joy which comes with the realization of complete and irrevocable justification by free grace through faith. The root from which all such impoverishment proceeds is the absence from our thinking and from our preaching of the divine judgment upon sin. Without the ministry of judgment and condemnation the foundation is not laid in the conviction which gives meaning and appeal to the gospel of free and sovereign grace.

II. THE FREE OFFER OF THE GOSPEL

In the circles in which most of us live and conduct our ministry there is no controversy regarding the fact of the free offer of the gospel to all men. There may be, however, an assent to this tenet and even a vigorous defence of it in the polemics of ecclesiastical and theological controversy, and at the same time an almost complete absence of this great truth in the actual presentation of the gospel. Sometimes the reason for this is as follows. Many who have come to this Seminary have come from backgrounds which were imbued with Arminian sentiment and the free offer of the gospel with which they have been conversant is after the Arminian pattern and based upon Arminian premises. By the grace of God, the teaching given in this Seminary has weaned them from the Arminian system of thought and practice. They have been constrained to adopt a consistently biblical position. In a word, they have become Calvinists and thus they have had to abandon Arminian patterns of thought and Arminian modes of expression as well as practices which have received their inspiration from Arminian theology. The Arminian way of presenting the free offer of the gospel they have been compelled to relinquish. But, too frequently I fear, they have not been able to make the proper adjustment in their thinking so as to be able to present the full offer of the gospel with freedom and spontaneity. Somehow or other they have begun to fear that the full, free, and unfettered overture of Christ in the gospel to all men without distinction, and the pressing upon men lost and dead in sin the claims and demands of that free overture, would impinge upon other truths such as sovereign election, definite atonement, and efficacious grace. Consequently, while indeed avowing the *doctrine* of the free offer, they have not been successful in bringing it to bear upon men with spontaneity and without any reserve. This is a grave failure. And the failure gathers the proportions of tragedy when we remember that if it is the reformed faith that has given the most consistent expression to the whole counsel of God, then it is only on the basis of the reformed conception of salvation and of grace, of Christ and of his work, that a full, free, and unfettered overture of Christ can be presented. It is only with the definiteness and particularism which characterizes our reformed faith that Christ can be presented in all his fulness and freeness as a Saviour. It is a grave sin against Christ and his gospel not to realize that it is precisely the definiteness of the redemption which he accomplished that grounds and validates the fulness and freeness with which he is offered to all men in the unrestricted overtures of his grace. And if we have any reserve or lack of spontaneity in offering Christ to lost men and in presenting the claims which inhere in the glory of his person and the perfection of his finished work, then it is because we have a distorted conception of the relation which the sovereignty of God sustains to the free offer of Christ in the gospel. It is on the crest of the wave of the divine sovereignty that the full and free overtures of God's grace in Christ break upon the shores of lost humanity.

But not only so. If we fail to appreciate what the free offer of the gospel is, and if we fail to present this free offer with freedom and spontaneity, with passion and urgency, then we are not only doing dishonour to Christ and his glory but we are also choking those who are the candidates of saving faith. It is only in reference to the full and free overture of Christ in the gospel that a true conception of faith in Christ can be entertained. To put it otherwise, it is only when Christ is presented to lost men in the full and free overture of his grace that true faith can be elicited. What is the primary act of faith? It is not the acceptance of certain propositions, although it cannot exist apart from the belief of the propositions of the gospel. Faith is essentially an entrustment to Christ as Lord and Saviour. It is self-commitment to him. It is not the belief that we have been saved, not even the belief that Christ died for us, but the commitment of ourselves to Christ as unsaved, lost, helpless, and undone *in order that we may be saved*. This is the specific character of that act of faith whereby we respond to the free overture of Christ in the gospel. With this act of faith there is one thing that is congruous, and one thing only that provides its proper warrant. It is the presentation of Christ in his fulness and freeness as the all-sufficient, all-suitable, and perfect Saviour. Faith is the engagement of person to person, the engagement of a lost sinner to Christ, in the commitment of faith. How can there be such engagement and entrustment except as lost and helpless sinners are confronted with the Saviour. And they are confronted with him in the full, free, and unfettered overture which he makes of himself in the gospel of his grace.

III. SELF-EXAMINATION

The duty of self-examination relates itself particularly to baptized and communicant members of the church. In connection with this subject there is admittedly the danger of morbid introspection. There are true Christians who are so much given to what is called the 'experimental' in religion that they feed to a very large extent upon their own experience.

This type of piety can become nauseating. When analysed it is seen to be dishonouring to Christ and detrimental to true religion. It is true that piety produces experience, and the deeper the piety the deeper and richer will be the experience. But the point to be stressed is that piety does not feed on experience. Piety feeds on Christ, on his truth, on the mysteries of God's revelation, and on the promises which are all yea and amen in Christ. And wholesome piety recoils from the experientialism which makes human experience the centre of interest and preoccupation. Yet the danger of experientialism does not eliminate the necessity or rightness of self-examination. It is necessary for several reasons.

1. We must never take our own salvation for granted. God by his grace may have made us the partakers of his saving grace long before we were able intelligently to understand the meaning of salvation. God regenerates many in infancy. And such have not known what it is to have been without God and without hope in the world. From their earliest years they have enjoyed the nurture of the Lord. But the salvation they possess they must never take for granted. If they are to entertain the assurance and joy of salvation it is by examining and proving the grounds of their faith and hope.

There are many Christians who have entered into the possession of salvation through well-defined experience in the years of intelligence and understanding. They can never forget the process and they are able to give an intelligent account of it. Even such must not take their salvation for granted. The assurance of salvation does not rest upon a past experience, however closely related that experience may be to the grounds upon which the assurance properly rests. For such Christians, also, the grounds of faith and hope must be honestly examined.

2. We are not indulging in unwarranted censorship when we say that the church of Christ has too frequently been characterized by a form of godliness that denies its power, and that the Christianity of too many who profess the Christian faith is little more than, if as much as, enrolment in a society. This evil is not one by which we are unaffected; it is not one outside the pale of our responsibility and witness. Is it not apparent that we are imperilling the eternal well-being of men and women if we do not confront them with the necessity of making their calling and election sure? Just as we must be honest with ourselves, so

we must strive to cultivate honesty in others. We do not examine men and women to find out what the condition of their hearts is. But we must inculcate the necessity of their examining themselves, to the end that they may prove themselves and know themselves as the blood-bought possession of Christ. Our situation has not made any less relevant the word of the apostle to the church at Corinth: 'Examine yourselves, whether ye be in the faith; prove your own selves. Know ye not your own selves, how that Jesus Christ is in you, except ye be reprobates?' (2 Cor. 13:5).

3. It is not sufficient that members of the church should be true believers and be heirs of eternal life. It is also necessary that they be self-consciously and intelligently so. The apostles were aware of this need in their day. 'These things have I written unto you that believe on the name of the Son of God, that ye may know that ye have eternal life' (1 John 5:13). 'Wherefore the rather, brethren, give diligence to make your calling and election sure: for if ye do these things, ye shall never fall' (2 Pet. 1:10). The low ethical and spiritual plane on which true Christians often live finds its explanation in the failure to bring within explicit consciousness the status that belongs to them by God's grace in Christ and the hope of the promise in the gospel.

IV. THE HIGH DEMANDS OF THE CHRISTIAN VOCATION

It is apparent that this emphasis is closely co-ordinate with the duty of self-examination. But the evil which this emphasis is intended to correct is an evil which often exists among those who are self-consciously and intelligently true believers in Christ. It is prevalent among such because they have an attenuated notion of what the Christian vocation is.

The vocation with which believers are called is a high, holy, and heavenly vocation in its origin, character, and destiny. It is very easy to reduce the criteria by which this vocation is to be judged. It is easy to reduce them to a few negations, negations respecting things which in themselves are in the category of indifferent things. It should be understood, of course, that the Christian vocation has its negations. It is necessary to remind ourselves that most of the ten commandments were given in negative form. The ethic which has no place for the negative is not Christian any more than is the doctrine which has no place for polemic denial. 'Thou shalt not' is written large on the portals to Christian fellowship. But we must remember that the Christian vocation does not consist simply in negatives. It does not consist at all in the negatives of human imposition and invention. And it does not consist merely in the negatives of divine prescription. The Christian vocation is one of positive virtue, and believers should be so occupied with the practice and love of virtue that the negations will be expelled by the expulsive power of that preoccupation. It is to nothing less than conformity with the image of Christ that the Christian faith calls us. Christianity as possession is not simply an experience of salvation in the past, not simply a status once for all bestowed; it is a vocation to be fulfilled. And, if we are earnestly and intelligently and self-consciously imbued with an appreciation of what this entails, we shall not rest until we attain to the prize of the high calling of God in Christ Jesus. As ministers of Christ it will be our aim to present every man perfect in Christ Jesus, that all may come in the unity of the faith and of the knowledge of the Son of God unto a perfect man, to the measure of the stature of the fulness of Christ.

CONCLUSION

These emphases which I have been pleading have a progressive unity. The first is directed to the end of inducing that conviction of sin which is the prerequisite of faith, the second to the eliciting of faith itself as an act of commitment to the proferred Saviour, the third to the end of making believers self-consciously so, and the fourth to the end of cultivating the duties and virtues of the high and holy and heavenly vocation. What I have had in view is the revival of those emphases which by God's blessing may be instrumental in building up the church of Christ and establishing it in the self-conscious intelligent exercise of those fruits which are the fruits of the Spirit. May our ministry be directed by zeal for the glory of God and the honour of Christ. When zeal for Christ's honour is paramount, then we must have zeal for the integrity of the church which is his body. And we shall inculcate the inspired witness: 'And beside this, giving all diligence, add to your faith virtue; and to virtue knowledge; and to knowledge temperance; and to temperance patience; and to patience godliness; and to godliness brotherly kindness; and to brotherly kindness charity. For if these things be in you and abound, they make you that ye shall neither be barren nor unfruitful in the knowledge of our Lord Jesus Christ' (2 Pet. 1:5–8).

21

Co-operation in Evangelism[1]

THE question with which we are concerned in this article is whether evangelicals may properly co-operate with modernists in the actual conduct of evangelism. When we say 'properly', we mean whether it is in accord with the revealed will of God as set forth for us in Holy Scripture. It is a question that is seriously debated by both evangelicals and modernists, though the criteria by which modernists seek to determine the question are admittedly different from those of the evangelicals.

For the latter, by and large at least, the question is focused in the relevance of certain biblical injunctions such as, 'have no fellowship with the unfruitful works of darkness' (Eph. 5:11), 'be ye not unequally yoked together with unbelievers' (2 Cor. 6:14), and 'if there come any unto you, and bring not this doctrine, receive him not into your house, neither bid him God speed' (2 John 10). Obviously, if this kind of co-operation falls within the scope of such prohibitions, then *for the evangelical* this should be an end of all debate. Within the evangelical camp it is precisely this question that has been ardently debated back and forth.

THE EVANGELICAL'S BELIEF

An evangelical is committed to certain well-defined positions regarding the Christian faith. He is a trinitarian and believes that there are three persons in the Godhead, the Father, the Son, and the Holy Spirit.

[1] *The Bible Times*, vol viii, Number 5, published by the Japan Mission of the Independent Board for Presbyterian Foreign Missions, editor John M. L. Young.

He says without equivocation that there is one God, that the Father is God, the Son is God, and the Holy Spirit is God, and that these three are distinct persons, as B. B. Warfield so simply stated the doctrine.

The evangelical also believes that the Scriptures of the Old and New Testaments are the infallible Word of God written, inerrantly inspired of the Holy Spirit, the only infallible rule of faith and life. This latter belief is becoming increasingly the distinguishing mark of the evangelical as over against modernism, not because this belief of itself makes one an evangelical, but because, in terms of our present-day situation, a person begins to move away from his evangelical moorings whenever he is ready to abandon this position and because it is at this point that the attack on evangelical belief is most sharply drawn.

The evangelical believes that the eternal Son of God became man by being supernaturally begotten by the Holy Spirit in the womb of the virgin Mary and was born of her without human fatherhood. The Son of God came into this world by this means in order to save men from sin and for this reason he shed his blood upon the accursed tree as a substitutionary sacrifice. He rose from the dead on the third day in that body that had been crucified and laid in the tomb of Joseph. After forty days he ascended up to heaven and was highly exalted, reigns from heaven as head over all things until he will have subdued all enemies, and will return again personally, visibly, and gloriously to judge living and dead.

The evangelical believes that all men are lost and dead in sin, that there is salvation in none other name but that of Jesus, and that apart from regeneration by the Holy Spirit and faith in Christ Jesus men are irretrievably lost. He believes in heaven and hell as places of eternal bliss and eternal woe respectively and that these are the two final abodes of mankind. Evangelism, therefore, for the evangelical, is the proclamation of the gospel of Christ to lost men in order that they may be saved. He must proclaim this gospel with the urgency which the gravity of the issues of life and death demands. Evangelism is supported by the fact that Christ is offered freely to all without distinction and that God commands men that they should all everywhere repent.

This summary does not cover the whole field of evangelical belief.

But it indicates what the identity of an evangelical is. If a professed Christian does not entertain the type of belief which the foregoing summary represents, then he is not an evangelical.

The term 'modernist' is flexible enough to include much diversity of belief. Indeed it is this flexibility that may be said to mark out and differentiate modernism. The modernist is exactly the person who, professing to be Christian, is not characterized by the well-defined and articulate viewpoint or system of belief which the foregoing portrayal of evangelicalism represents. He does not avow that viewpoint; it is not his faith. The more intelligently self-conscious he is the more he frankly disavows it. Even when he is simply non-committal he is still modernist. For the evangelical is never agnostic on what belongs to the Christian faith; he is positively assertive, and unequivocal confession is a distinguishing mark of his identity.

THE MODERNIST'S UNBELIEF

We may instance some examples of the modernist's disbelief. He is quite opposed to the doctrine of Holy Scripture which the evangelical holds. Indeed this is the point at which he most vehemently and perhaps scornfully disagrees. He is not willing to accede to the doctrine of eternal perdition. Faith respecting the virgin birth of our Lord is not essential to what he considers to be the doctrine of the incarnation. Substitutionary atonement in the sense so precious to the evangelical does not condition the faith in Christ which he professes.

The modernist cannot be hospitable to the exclusiveness of the Christian faith which excludes all hope for men who are outside the pale of the gospel revelation and for that reason his evangelistic interest cannot be impassioned by the fervour and urgency which belief in the lost condition of men must generate. It is apparent, therefore, that the belief or lack of belief of the modernist defines an entirely different pattern from that of the evangelical. Radically different conceptions of the Christian faith are involved in these opposing views and the modernist is alert enough to recognize that divergence. He recoils at those very points which constitute the essence of the evangelical's faith.

First and foremost there is a different conception of God. The God of the evangelical is a God who, consistently with his perfections, will consign men to everlasting perdition. The God and Father of our Lord Jesus Christ is such a God. Our Lord Jesus himself said so. The modernist says he cannot believe in such a God, that this belief is incompatible with what he believes to be the God of love. It is surely apparent, therefore, that the God of the evangelical is not the God of the modernist. For, after all, the God in whom we believe and whom we worship is not the vocables by which he is designated but the God with respect to whom we entertain certain conceptions.

We can use all the titles by which God is named in Holy Scripture, but unless we entertain the proper conception of the God thus designated we are not believing in or worshipping him. We may honour him with our lips and our hearts be far from him. There must be truth in the inward parts. And since the modernist openly disavows conceptions of God which are integral to the faith of the evangelical, they do not worship the same God. It is not man's prerogative to search the heart of another. But here we are not dealing with what is *hidden* in the heart but with concrete, open confession which we are in a position to evaluate and must evaluate. Otherwise all discrimination is at an end.

Again, let us think of Christ. The evangelical believes that Christ vicariously bore upon the cross the penalty due to our sins, that he satisfied the justice of God and propitiated his wrath, that God the Father delivered up his own Son to the damnation which our sins deserved. The faith which the evangelical reposes in Christ and which changes his whole outlook for time and for eternity is conditioned by this view of Calvary. Take away substitutionary atonement in the sense defined and the evangelical cannot rest in Christ for salvation. But the modernist cannot accept that view of Calvary. Indeed he may recoil from it. In any case, he will insist that Christian faith, or *the* Christian faith, is not tied to that conception of the cross. Is it not obvious, therefore, that on the most cardinal question of faith in Christ there is radical difference and that the Christ of the one is basically different from that of the other?

Let us think also of Holy Scripture. The difference here is concerned with our view of revelation from God as it comes into concrete and practical relation to us. Nothing affects our religion all along the line of its activity more intimately than our view of revelation. Revelation is the source and norm of all thinking of God, of Christ, of salvation, of vocation, and of destiny. If the modernist's view of revelation as it comes into relevant relation to us is so different that he cannot accept the Bible to be what the evangelical so jealously regards it, then divergence appears not only at specific points of belief but in connection with that which determines and conditions all belief within the realm of faith and worship. That which gives direction to all thinking and believing is conceived of in radically divergent ways.

We thus see how impossible it is to bridge the gulf that divides between the two brands of belief with which we are dealing. It is only by suppression or compromise of conviction that the cleavage can be discounted. And this is honest neither for the evangelical nor for the modernist. The differences are not peripheral—any candid appraisal shows that they are concerned with what is central in faith and worship. Even though modernists do not always carry to logical conclusions the basic assumptions of their position and sometimes espouse tenets which have no warrant on other than evangelical premises, premises which they disavow and even combat, yet the basic assumptions always persist and come to vocal expression at cardinal points of belief and confession. Their world of thought is alien to that of evangelical conviction.

THE ISSUES INVOLVED

When we address ourselves to the question of co-operation in evangelism, it is to evade the implications of the foregoing analysis to overlook the fundamental differences. The conception of God is radically divergent for it concerns nothing less basic than what belongs to God as justice and love. The conception of Christ is radically divergent for it concerns nothing less than the doctrine of his cross as well as the mode of his incarnation. The conception of revelation is radically divergent, and so the difference concerns that which gives character to all that falls within the compass of faith and devotion. Shall we say then that such apostolic injunctions as those of 2 Cor. 6:14–18 and 2 John 10, 11 have no relevance? Are we to say that they have no bearing upon fellowship in evangelism?

It needs no argument that evangelism is one of the most sacred functions assigned to the church of Christ. It is not the whole work of preaching but it is a large part of it. Evangelism is the proclamation of the message of the gospel. And in no detail of the church's function and commission is it more important to maintain purity of witness and of fellowship. All evangelicals would surely agree that we could not possibly, without the most tragic betrayal of Christ, co-operate with Mohammedans or Hindus in promoting evangelism. The antithesis is so blatant that the suggestion is absurd. 'What communion hath light with darkness?' (2 Cor. 6:14). The relevance of Paul's challenge is immediately clear.

Vehement opposition will be offered to the relevance of such an illustration. Admittedly modernists, in terms of our discussion, are not Mohammedans or Hindus. It is also clear that Paul in the passage from which we have just quoted is dealing with pagan idolatry. 'What agreement hath the temple of God with idols?' (vs. 16). We must not by any means overlook the specific context in which these injunctions occur or the situation that the apostle has in view. But that the teaching of Paul does not apply to the situation with which we are now dealing is not to be hastily concluded.

We must bear in mind that, if the principle which underlies the apostle's injunctions is relevant to our situation, then we cannot escape their application, however different may be the circumstances. That is the implication of the relevance of Scripture as the infallible rule of faith and practice. It is obvious that Paul could not have had Mohammedanism in mind when he wrote the second epistle to Corinth. But it is equally obvious, at least to every evangelical, that 2 Cor. 6:14–18 applies to this kind of fellowship with Mohammedans just as surely as to the unbelievers whom Paul had distinctly in view.

As respects the question we are discussing, we may not forget the radical cleavage that divides evangelicals and modernists. We found radically divergent conceptions of the Christian faith. The God of the evangelical is not the God of the modernist. The Christ of the evangelical is not the Christ of the modernist. Revelation, as the source and norm of all faith and worship, is conceived of in radically different ways. There cannot be a residual common basis of faith and worship for the simple reason that the conceptions which are central to both faith and worship are so radically divergent.

It is this impasse that the evangelical must reckon with. For it is precisely that kind of impasse that dictated the inspired severities of 2 Cor. 6:14–18. If we plead that this passage is not applicable to the question at issue, it is only because we have failed to discern the grave issues at stake in the gulf that divides between evangelical faith and modernist unbelief.

DID PAUL CO-OPERATE?

We have good reason to believe that the heresy which disturbed the churches of Galatia was far from being characterized by many of the errors which distinguish present-day modernism. The Judaisers were undoubtedly professed Christians. And the evidence would indicate that they did not controvert Paul's gospel on many of its most precious tenets. For Paul did not find occasion in his epistle to defend many of the articles of the Christian faith which he propounds elsewhere. But because the Judaisers had perverted the grand article of justification by grace through faith he pronounced his *anathema*.

He called this perversion 'another gospel, which is not another' and added, 'But though we, or an angel from heaven, preach any other gospel unto you than that which we have preached unto you, let him be accursed. As we said before, so say I now again, If any man preach any other gospel unto you than that ye have received, let him be accursed' (Gal. 1:7–9). No imprecation could be stronger than that of *anathema*. Are we to suppose that Paul would have co-operated with these perverters of the gospel of Christ in promoting evangelism? The suggestion is inconceivable. He could allow for no obscuration of the issues at stake. To the core of his being he was convinced that the perversion took the crown from the Redeemer's head and was aimed at the damnation of perishing souls. 'Christ is become of no effect unto you, whosoever of you are justified by the law; ye are fallen from grace' (Gal. 5:4).

Are the issues at stake in the modernist controversy of less moment? Strange blindness has overtaken us if we think so. And we have little of Paul's passion left. The Judaising heresy struck at the heart of the gospel. Consequently Paul's intolerance. Modernism gives us a new version of Christianity and that is worse than perversion. May we then co-operate with modernists in one of the most sacred functions committed to Christ's church? The thought is intolerable.

ARE JOHN'S INJUNCTIONS RELEVANT?

Or let us think for a moment with the disciple whom Jesus loved. John had written that 'many false prophets are gone out into the world (1 John 4:1). And 'to the elect lady and her children' (2 John 1) he writes, 'Whosoever transgresseth (or goeth before), and abideth not in the doctrine of Christ, hath not God' (2 John 9). There is incisiveness and decisiveness. Perhaps we don't like it. But John had learned the mind of his Lord. And so he continues, 'If there come any unto you, and bring not this doctrine, receive him not into your house, neither bid him God speed: for he that biddeth him God speed is partaker of his evil deeds' (2 John 10, 11).

The modernism with which we are confronted today may not take precisely the same form as the denial which John had specifically in view. But that the modernist's denials go counter to the doctrine of Christ is just as evident. John's word must therefore be relevant and regulative in our context. There is a stringency about John's prohibition that goes further than anything with which we are now concerned—we are not to receive the exponent of false doctrine into our house. How much less may we enter into partnership and fellowship in promoting the gospel? To participate with him or to join hands with him in that which is most sacred goes right in the teeth of John's interdict. If there is one thing that comes under John's ban it is *co-operation*. For then we would not only be extending to him the kind of hospitality which John condemns but we would be publicly entering into partnership in the promoting of the faith and, in terms of John's verdict, become partakers of his evil deeds.

This latter assessment is significant. It is not only the gross works of the flesh that can be characterized as evil deeds. The promulgation of false doctrine falls under that indictment. John calls the teaching of deceivers an iniquitous work. We dare not obscure the antithesis to the doctrine of Christ by extending to the proponent of this evil the hospitality and greeting which are the tokens of Christian fellowship. The word of Paul has the same import: 'have no fellowship with the unfruitful works of darkness, but rather reprove them' (Eph. 5:11). After all, John and Paul are one when doctrine that strikes at the pivots of our faith is the issue. It is not only the doctrine that is to be condemned: co-operation with its emissaries is unthinkable.

PREACH TO ALL, CO-OPERATE WITH BELIEVERS ONLY

The gospel is to be preached to all men irrespective of creed. The evangelical must seize every opportunity to bear witness to the faith in its purity and power. If, for example, a modernist minister invites the evangelical to preach and makes available certain facilities to this end, the evangelical may not decline the invitation simply on the ground that the request comes from one who is a modernist any more than may he decline a similar invitation from a Mohammedan.

Or if a group of modernists in concert with one another extend such an invitation, the evangelical may not decline to preach the gospel in compliance with such a request simply on the ground that the invitation comes from, and the opportunity is offered by, such an organization. The evangelical must indeed preach the gospel in its integrity and purity *and preach it in its direct bearing upon the unbelief of which the same modernists are the exponents*. Otherwise he is unfaithful to his evangelical witness— preaching must be negative as well as positive.

But the point now is that no principle of fidelity to Christ need be compromised by preaching the evangel under these circumstances. Paul did not compromise in the midst of the Areopagus when he preached the gospel in answer to the invitation, 'May we know what this new teaching is, which is spoken by thee?' (Acts 17:19). It may indeed be the case that in a certain situation, because of other conditions and circumstances, the evangelical would be required to decline. He might judge that more prejudice would be done to the witness of the gospel and to his own witness by acceptance. Into these conditions and circumstances it is not necessary to enter. Suffice it to say that the source from which the invitation comes does not of itself require the evangelical to decline the invitation. Fidelity to Christ and to his commission may demand acceptance.

This does not, however, annul the thesis of this article, namely, that evangelicals may not co-operate with modernists in promoting the gospel, nor even co-operate in sponsoring an evangelistic undertaking. The reason is that then partnership or fellowship with the exponents of unbelief comes into being and it is this co-operation that the Scripture forbids. The distinction is not one so finely spun that it may be alleged to be one without a difference. There is a wide gulf of difference between preaching the gospel at the invitation of modernists, on the one hand, and entering into partnership with modernists for the promotion of the gospel, on the other. It is in principle the distinction between preaching the gospel to Mohammedans at their invitation and co-operating with Mohammedans in sponsoring and promoting gospel proclamation. In the latter case there is the *partnership* which the Bible condemns; in the former there is but the proclamation of the gospel to all, and this the commission of Christ requires.

GOD'S REVEALED WILL VERSUS THE PRAGMATIC TEST

It is sometimes urged as an argument in favour of the co-operation and mixed sponsorship which this article controverts that the signal blessing of God has been witnessed in evangelistic enterprises where this kind of co-operation has been practised. There are a few observations which should be borne in mind. First of all, God is sovereign and at times fulfils his holy purposes of grace through the medium of actions which are in direct contravention of his revealed will. The crucifixion of our Lord is the supreme example. The arch-crime of human history is not relieved of its extreme wickedness by the fact that in this same event of the accursed tree God fulfilled his supreme purpose of love and grace for lost men (cf. Acts. 2:23; 4:27, 28). What God does in the overruling movements of his providence is not the rule by which we may determine what is right for us.

Secondly, God blesses his own Word, and he often blesses it when it is proclaimed under auspices which do not have the approval of his revealed will. It is not ours to limit God in the exercise of his gracious sovereignty. But he has limited us by his revealed will. Beyond that revealed will we may never act, nor in contravention of it.

Thirdly, Paul the apostle could rejoice when Christ was preached even of envy and strife and faction and pretence. He rejoiced because Christ was proclaimed. And surely he had respect to the saving effects which would follow from such proclamation. The gospel is not negated as to its character or power by the wrong motives or intentions of those who proclaim it. But this does not condone or justify these motives. In the like manner we are not to condone the *method* by which Christ may be proclaimed simply because the gospel is proclaimed and saving fruits accrue therefrom. We may, like Paul, rejoice that Christ is preached and yet must severely condemn the auspices under which this proclamation takes place.

The upshot is, therefore, that our thought is to be regulated by the revealed will of God. Whenever we relinquish this criterion and attempt to judge what is well-pleasing to God by results, then we have made pragmatism our rule. This is the way of darkness and not of light. In no sphere of our activity must the principle that God's *revealed* will is the rule for us be guarded and applied with greater jealousy than in those sacred functions which are ours by the commission of the Saviour.

The Christian Life

22

Worship

WHEN we are thinking of worship we must distinguish between the generic and the specific. The generic is the devotion we owe to God in the whole of life. God is sovereign, he is Lord, having sovereignty over us and propriety in us, and therefore in all that we do we owe subjection to him, devotion to his revealed will, obedience to his commandments. There is no area of life where the injunction does not apply: 'Whether therefore ye eat, or drink, or whatsoever ye do, do all to the glory of God' (1 Cor. 10:31). In view of the lordship of Christ as Mediator all of life comes under his dominion. 'Whatsoever ye do, do it heartily, as unto the Lord, and not unto men, knowing that of the Lord ye shall receive the reward of the inheritance: for ye serve the Lord Christ' (Col. 3:23, 24).

The specific is the exercise of worship in the specialized sense— prayer, thanksgiving, reading the Word, preaching, singing God's praises, administering the sacraments. Some of these may be exercised in private, all of them in the public worship of God, which is God's instituted communal worship in the assembly of the saints. There are exercises of worship that should be attached to other functions or may be properly attached to other functions. Food is sanctified by the Word of God and prayer, and in partaking of food we ought to ask God's blessing. But a meal is not a part of the instituted worship in the assemblies of the saints. Compare also marriage, the burial of the dead, the convening of political assemblies *etc.*

1. *Assembly*. Perhaps the most explicit passage in the New Testament is Hebrews 10:24, 25: 'Let us consider one another to provoke unto love

and good works; not forsaking the assembling of ourselves together, as the custom of some is, but exhorting one another; and so much the more as ye see the day approaching'. There is clear reference to this assembling in such passages as 1 Cor. 11:17, 18; 14:26; James 2:2. Indeed the word for 'church' in the New Testament means 'assembly'. It is not so much the called-out ones as the called-together ones, going back to the Old Testament assembly before the glory of God's self-manifestation at Sinai. This notion of assembly is closely related to the doctrine of the church as the body of Christ. The assembly for worship is one of the principal ways of giving expression to the unity of the Spirit in the bond of peace, and to the communion of the saints with one another in the oneness of Christ's body.

2. *The Object of Worship.* God alone is to be worshipped. It is with this word that our Lord resisted one of Satan's temptations: 'Thou shalt worship the Lord thy God and him only shalt thou serve.' When we come together it is to worship God. Everything else really rests upon this. Whatever we may do, in worship, if it is not directed to the worship of God, no matter how decorous and embellished our exercises may be, then it is not worship. If we go to the house of God simply because it is custom or to fill up a quota of exercises, then we are not worshipping God. There are numberless ways in which in the exercises of instituted worship we may desecrate worship. All exercises must be directed by, and contribute to, the worship of God.

The only God is the triune God. New Testament believers did not worship another God than the God of the Old Testament. But New Testament believers worshipped the true God in the full light of the revelation God gave of himself in the incarnation of the Son and the coming of the Spirit at Pentecost. This is the astounding feature of the worship of the saints that, without any consciousness of breach or discontinuity, the one God of worship was now conceived of as Father, Son, and Holy Spirit. 'Giving diligence to keep the unity of the Spirit in the bond of peace. There is one body and one Spirit, even as ye were called in one hope of your calling; one Lord, one faith, one baptism, one God and Father of all, who is over all, and through all, and in all' (Eph. 4:3–6; cf. 1 Cor. 8:6). This comes to particular forms in the worship of Christ. In the Old Testament a characteristic way of expressing the worship of the true God was to call upon the name of the Lord. The mark of New Testament believers is that they call upon the name of the Lord Jesus (cf. 1 Cor. 1:2). Note the salutations and benedictions of Scripture and Jesus' institution of baptism.

3. *The Attitude of Worship*: Reverence and Simplicity. You have no doubt heard that adoration is an element of worship. It is not so much an element as the attitude that must permeate all the elements or exercises of worship. Adoration springs from the apprehension of God's majesty, and where this is, there must be reverence, that is, godly fear. Here again much of our worship falls under the charge of irreverence and therefore under condemnation. There is a place in life for jollity and jollification. But how alien to the worship of God would this be in the sanctuary. God is 'the King of kings, and Lord of lords, who only hath immortality, dwelling in light unapproachable, whom no man hath seen, nor can see.' (1 Tim. 6:15, 16.) The King eternal, immortal, invisible, the only God (1 Tim. 1:17)!

With respect to simplicity, there is a marked contrast to be observed between the worship of the Old Testament and that of the New. The centre of the worship of the Old Testament was the tabernacle and later the temple. The worship was characterized by elaborate ritual associated particularly with the various offerings.

There is ritual in the New Testament—baptism and the Lord's Supper. But even these have a simplicity that marks the contrast. It is one of the marks of decadence that the liturgical movement is so prevalent in Protestant Churches. As we study the New Testament we observe that prayer, singing God's praises, preaching the Word, reading the Word, the administration of the sacraments, are the elements.

4. *The Mode of Worship*. How are we to worship God? 'Wherewith shall I come before the Lord, and bow myself before the high God?' (Micah 6:6). This is the question of the regulative principle of worship. How can I know that what I bring is acceptable to him? Worship consists of the offering of 'spiritual sacrifices acceptable to God by Jesus Christ'. This will surely not be questioned. So the matter of supreme concern is: What is acceptable? What is dictated and directed by the Holy Spirit?

The question is really that of 'Spiritual worship', worship authorized by the Holy Spirit, constrained by the Holy Spirit, offered in the Holy

Spirit. And so we must ask: Where does the Holy Spirit give us direction respecting that which he approves and leads us to render?

The answer is: only in the Scripture as the Word which he has inspired. This simply means that for all the modes and elements of worship there must be authorization from the Word of God.

The Reformed principle is that the acceptable way of worshipping God is instituted by himself, and so limited by his revealed will that he may not be worshipped in any other way than that prescribed in the Holy Scripture, that what is not commanded is forbidden. This is in contrast with the view that what is not forbidden is permitted.

There are some texts in the New Testament that bear directly on this question: Mark 7:7, 8; John 4:24; Col. 2:20-23; 1 Peter 2:5.

In the Orthodox Presbyterian Church there is general agreement on this. But in application it is not observed. Psalms[1]

[1] The above address has been printed from the author's incomplete notes. The concluding reference, where the manuscript breaks off, concerns his conviction that the Psalter, being the divinely appointed manual of praise, should be used exclusively in congregational praise. With William Young he submitted to the O.P.C. General Assembly a Minority Report on this subject and this was printed in the *Minutes of the Fourteenth General Assembly*, 1947, 58-66.

23

Christian Doctrine and Life

THERE would be no dispute among evangelicals that the atoning death of Christ is at the centre of the Christian faith. No doubt some would say that it is the central tenet of the faith. I refrain from saying so because the resurrection of Christ is equally important. The death and resurrection are the pivotal events of redemptive accomplishment and they may never be separated. Yet the death of Christ in its vicarious significance is at the centre and no event is more central.

It is worthy of note that some of the most characteristic definitions of Christ's atoning accomplishment are given in appeals to believers to practise the most elementary virtues of their heavenly vocation. In the teaching of our Lord himself no statement of his is more significant than Matt. 20:28; Mark 10:45: 'For even the Son of man came not to be ministered unto but to minister and to give his life a ransom for many'. But have we observed the context in which this word was spoken 'Whosoever would be great among you, let him be your minister, and whosoever would be chief, let him be your servant' (Mark 10:43, 44). It is to enforce that lesson that he appeals to his own example of supreme self-sacrifice in giving his life a ransom. Apostolic teaching follows the same pattern. Paul, for example, says: 'For ye know the grace of our Lord Jesus Christ, that though he was rich, for your sake he became poor in order that ye by his poverty might be made rich' (2 Cor. 8:9). But again the context is one in which the apostle is pleading the grace of Christian liberality. 'I speak, not by commandment, but by occasion of the forwardness of others, and to prove the sincerity of your love' (2 Cor. 8:8). And our Lord's self-impoverishment is adduced to press home this grace on the part of believers. No passage in Paul is more replete with meaning relevant to our Lord's incomparable self-humiliation than Philippians 2:6–8. But what is the lesson being enjoined? 'Look not every man on his own things, but every man also on the things of others' (Phil. 2:4). It is unselfish regard for the well-being of others, and so 'let this mind be in you which was also in Christ Jesus' (vs. 5). It is likewise with Peter. We are familiar with the word: 'Who his own self bore our sins in his body upon the tree' (1 Pet. 2:24). But Peter is exhorting to patient endurance of suffering, and the Saviour's example is the seal of necessity. 'For even Christ suffered for us, leaving us an example, that ye should follow his steps' (1 Pet. 2:21).

All of this does not mean that we follow Christ in performing his vocation, that we participate in his unique and peculiar work. It is, rather, that in the vocation that was exclusively his, he is our supreme example in the vocation that belongs to us. And the great lesson for our present interest is that there is a direct connection between the most sacred truths of our faith and the most elementary duties of our Christian calling. The great truth of the atonement, than which nothing is more central, is the incentive to humble, devoted, self-sacrificing service in the kingdom of God. These texts are sufficient to show that doctrine and practice are integrally related, and that practice exemplifying our faith is drawn from the spring of doctrine.

We may tarry for a few moments longer on the death of Christ. The foregoing passages have shown that there is a straight line of connection between the death of Christ and elementary virtues of the Christian life. But now we may deal more specifically with an aspect of the death of Christ intimately related to the Christian life in which the understanding of this aspect is indispensable to its application. The death of Christ is set forth in two respects—his death for us and our death in him. We may focus attention upon Romans 6:2–6. Believers died with Christ; they have been planted together in the likeness of his death. The point now is that the recognition of that truth, of that relationship to the death of Christ, is necessary to the proper effect in our lives. Paul says: 'Know ye not that as many of us as were baptized into Christ Jesus were baptized into his death?' (Rom. 6:3), and this in reference to the question: 'How shall we who have died to sin live any longer therein?' (vs. 2).

We must now pass on to other aspects of doctrine. The Christian life is one of godliness; it is a living godly in Christ Jesus. It is a life conducted in the fear of God, and fear understood in the sense of reverential awe. What is the practical effect? It is the sense of God's all-pervasive presence and of our dependence upon him. It is the sense of his incomparable majesty. The doctrine of God underlies all this. It is our conception of God, and conception framed in terms of the glory that is his. And this is none other than the doctrine of God. How should we fear him other than in terms of who he is and what he is. This is but the doctrine of his being, perfections, relations, and will.

This leads inevitably to the doctrine of the Trinity. The Christian faith is necessarily trinitarian. However basic and important is our conception of God in his oneness and transcendent majesty, if this conception is not framed in terms of Father, Son, and Holy Spirit, then our conception of God is not Christian. The apostle Paul points this up eloquently when dealing with the antithesis offered by idolatry. The answer to idolatry is indeed that there is one God. But this is not all. So Paul replies: 'But to us there is one God, the Father, of whom are all things, and we unto him; and one Lord Jesus Christ, through whom are all things, and we through him' (1 Cor. 8:6). Cf. Eph. 4:4–6. But the teaching of the apostles in this respect does not surpass that of our Lord himself. We are too liable to overlook the fact that, when Jesus deals with faith in himself, there is sustained emphasis upon the identity in which faith is directed to him, the identity as the sent of the Father. 'He that believeth in me believes not in me but on him who sent me' (John 12:44; cf. 17:3, 8). In a word, the faith in Jesus unto life is one that is conditioned by the differentiation involved in the distinction between the Father and the Son.

There are two phases of doctrine embraced in this conception:

1. There is the intrinsic distinction. If it is a conception of *God*, then the distinction is not one that came to be. It is essential, intrinsic, and eternal; in other words, it is the doctrine that there is one God; the Father is God, the Son is God, the Holy Spirit is God; these three are distinct persons.

2. There are the distinguishing prerogatives, functions, actions, and relations of the three persons in the economy of salvation. We have no

adequate understanding of the salvation that is ours except as we think of the Father as designing redemption, of the Son as the Redeemer, and of the Holy Spirit by way of eminence as the Sanctifier. Thinking specific-ally of the Christian life, have we considered that the ultimate norm of behaviour is the pattern of the Father's character. 'Ye shall be perfect, as your heavenly Father is perfect' (Matt. 5:48). It is likewise God the Father who is in Peter's purview when he writes: 'But as he who called you is holy, be ye also holy in all manner of life, because it is written, be ye holy, for I am holy' (1 Pet. 1:15, 16). Again, there is nothing invested with higher sanction or greater relevance in life than the example of Christ in his identity as the God-man who has given us 'an example that we should follow his steps' (1 Pet. 2:21). The goal for the believer, foreordained of God the Father, is that we should be con-formed to the image of the Son (cf. Rom. 8:29). And Christ is made unto us, not only wisdom and righteousness, but sanctification also. Of the Holy Spirit likewise we read: 'If ye by the Spirit put to death the deeds of the body ye shall live' (Rom. 8:13). It is therefore obvious that the life of holiness is dependent upon our appreciation of the distinguish-ing relations sustained to the three persons of the Godhead, and this is but to say the doctrine of the inter-trinitarian relations in the economy of salvation. So when we think of the fear of God as the soul of godli-ness, and of godliness as the conditioning attitude of the Christian life, it is only as that fear is concretized and particularized in terms of response appropriate to each person of the Godhead, that it is relieved of vague-ness and abstractness, and therefore relieved of what makes it meaning-less and impractical.

There is one other doctrine woven into the texture of Christian life that cannot be omitted. If the fear of God is the conditioning feature of the Christian, the description correlative with this is that the believer is a 'man of God'. The aim of the man of God is that he be perfect, thoroughly furnished unto every good work. Surely this is incontestable. But what is it that supplies this furnishment? 'All scripture is given by inspiration of God.' And note its uses.

Two observations: (1) The use of Scripture for doctrine is as indis-pensable to the equipment of the man of God as its use for reproof and correction and instruction. (2) Scripture is used to this end only in the character defined; it is God-breathed. This is the doctrine of Scripture. So not only is Scripture the source of doctrine directed to the furnishing of the man of God, but it is Scripture as God-breathed and in that quality that serves these purposes indispensable to Christian life.

24

The Christian Ethic

THE Christian ethic is concerned with the manner of life or behaviour consonant with the Christian faith. The Christian faith is distinctive and the Christian ethic is correspondingly distinctive. The Christian is a new creation, a new man, and the old man has been crucified. Peter draws our attention to this when he writes: 'not with corruptible things, silver and gold, were ye redeemed from your vain manner of life received by tradition from your fathers, but with the precious blood of Christ' (1 Peter 1:18, 19). The newness is not only certified by the ransom price as that which secured it, but also by the effectual call, the call of God the Father, through which the new life has been actually created. And so Peter also writes in the same context: 'As obedient children, not fashioning yourselves according to the former lusts in your ignorance, but as he who called you is holy, be ye also holy in all manner of life' (1 Peter 1:14, 15). These are particularly the guarantees and the bonds of the new manner of life—redemption by Christ's blood and the call of the Father, the one the supreme cost of emancipation and the other the act by which the emancipation is registered in our experience. And these two are intimately related, because the call is into union with Christ, by which we are planted together in the likeness of his death and resurrection; and as Christ was raised from the dead by the glory of the Father so we also come to walk in newness of life (cf. Rom. 6:4, 5; Eph. 4:1). There is a new pattern, a new kind of conformity, eloquently expressed by way of antithesis when Paul says: 'Be not conformed to this world (be not fashioned to this age) but be ye transformed by the renewing of your mind' (Rom. 12:2).

Now what is this new manner of life? How is it characterized? If it is conformity, conformity to what? It must have its criteria, its marks, its distinguishing features, and it must have content that has respect to life, to the whole of life, and therefore as concrete and practical as life itself. Life is not ethereal mysticism; it is existential.

There is no consideration more basic and important than that it is life patterned after the character of God himself. 'Ye shall be perfect as your heavenly Father is perfect' (Matt. 5:48). Man's definition consists in this, that he was made in the image of God. 'And God said, Let us make men in our image, after our likeness' (Gen. 1:26). And the new life in Christ is defined as 'having put off the old man with his affections and lusts, and having put on the new man who is being renewed unto knowledge after the image of him who created him' (Col. 3:10; cf. Eph. 4:24). It is true that this concept of likeness to God must be guarded; it is not absolute. For there is a sense in which to aspire after likeness to God is the epitome of sin. This the tempter knew well when he seduced Eve with the plea: 'Ye shall be as God, knowing good and evil' (Gen. 3:5). In view of the radical distinction, revelation specifying the respects in which likeness to God constitutes the pattern of human behaviour is indispensable. Otherwise confusion would be unavoidable. So we must ask: What are the lines of demarcation and differentiation; what are the criteria? What are the norms that define the way of life patterned after God's own character?

The answer that would appear to be the obvious and only answer is that since Christ is the image of the invisible God, the effulgence of his glory and the express image of his being, since he could say himself, 'He that hath seen me hath seen the Father' (John 14:9), the example of Christ is the pattern for us, and as such it is ultimate and exclusive. It is not to be denied that our Lord pleaded the sanction and norm of his example, and nothing could be invested with a higher sanction for us than the example of him who, as the man Christ Jesus, was holy, harmless, undefiled, and separate from sinners, who could say that he always did those things that pleased the Father. But however relevant the example of our Lord is, and necessarily so, there are two observations:

1. The relevance to us of our Lord's example has to be strictly guarded just as likeness to God has to be guarded. If this is not done we fall into the same error of failure to distinguish between the respects in

which the attempt at likeness would be iniquity and the respects in which likeness is required. There are respects in which we may not and could not make our Lord's conduct an example for us. His identity as God-man was unique. His offices and prerogatives were unique. His task as Saviour was unique. The faith he demanded in himself, and the obedience he claimed from his disciples, were such as belong to none else. So the application to ourselves requires radical differentiation. In other words, the *example* that our Lord supplies is severely restricted by reason of the uniqueness that pertained to him in respect of his person, office, commission, prerogative, and task. It is scarcely necessary to observe how glib and superficial is the ethic that is content to say: What would Jesus do?

2. Our Lord himself, as well as Scripture in its total witness, makes appeal to other norms that prescribe behaviour. Stated inclusively, the norm of behaviour is the revealed will of God, and the whole of Scripture is the revealed will of God for the regulation of thought and conduct well-pleasing to him (cf. 2 Tim. 3:16, 17). But because of the situation that exists today in thought and practice it is particularly relevant and necessary to focus attention upon the law of God in the more restrictive sense of the law of commandments. This, of course, is paramount in any case as we think of Christian behaviour. But our present-day situation makes the principles involved of the most urgent concern.

The law of God guards the distinction so germane to the basic obligation, namely, likeness to God. For the law of God is the will of God *for us*. This is why every depreciation of the law of God leads to the adoption of patterns that impinge upon God's unique prerogatives in the glory that belongs to him alone. There is one lawgiver. When we forget this, or even suppress its truth, we arrogate to ourselves the presumption of being our own lawgivers, and we become the victims of human imposture in the denial of divine obligation and the deprivation of God-given rights. But when the sanctity of God's law is maintained and we reverence him in the prerogative that is his as the one lawgiver, then the likeness to God demanded by our creation in his image and by the new creation in Christ is realized. The law bears the imprint of God's character as his character is normative for us. It is

God's character coming to expression for the regulation of thought and conduct consonant with his glory. It is the transcript of his glory.

The law of God is both negative and positive. No one factor has been more prejudicial to the Christian ethic in the home, the church and society, than contempt for the negatives of God's law. The argument often advanced is that in ethical nurture we must be positive, that negatives are psychologically harmful and not conducive to the development of character. It is true that the Christian ethic does not consist in negation, that virtue cannot be defined as an accumulation of 'don'ts'. The biblical ethic aims at proving what is the good, and acceptable, and perfect will of God. But to depreciate the negatives is to become unrealistic. If there were no sin or liability to sin, there would be no need of prohibition. Why did God give a prohibition to Adam in his state of integrity (Gen. 2:17)? Only because there was the liability to sin, a liability that became actuality in the eating of the forbidden fruit. Why are eight of the ten commandments expressly in negative form? That forbidden has, of course, its counterpart in a requirement. But they are enunciated in terms of the forbidden. The reason is the reality and pervasiveness of sin. God's law is realistic; it takes account of sin and therefore of the fact that if we are to bear the fruit of virtue there must be the negation of vice. When our Lord defined the condition of entrance into the kingdom of God he emphasized the need for purification as well as the positive communication. So he said 'born of water'. Because so much of ethical theory and of pedagogy has not faced up to the realism of our human situation it has failed tragically to cope with the ills of society. So let us appreciate the grand realism of 'Thou shalt not'.

It is well to tarry a little longer on this aspect of the Christian ethic, and we have to reflect for a moment on Paul's injunction: 'Abstain from every appearance of evil' (1 Thess. 5:22). Regrettably the misunderstanding of this text has obscured its meaning. It has been interpreted to mean abstinence from what appears to be evil, abstinence from what people may judge to be evil. There is a prohibitionism that legislates in things not wrong in themselves, and piety has been construed to a large extent as consisting in these abstinences. This prohibitionism has done great damage to the ethics of Christian behaviour. Paul deals with its pernicious demands in 1 Tim. 4:1–5. It is apostasy from the faith, the propaganda of seducing spirits, and the doctrines of demons.

What Paul says is: 'Abstain from every form of evil'. And here is the absolute prohibition of the Christian ethic, a prohibition with no reservation or exception. There is no situation in which God has placed us in which we can plead the necessity of wrongdoing. It may cost us our life to abstain from wrong. But this is the glory of devotion to Christ. 'He that loseth his life for my sake, the same shall save it' (Luke 9:24).

In dealing with the positive in God's law it is necessary to take full account of the primacy of love (cf. Matt. 22:37–40; Rom. 13:10). It is 'the royal law' (James 2:8). There are several observations:

1. Love is primary because only by love can the commandments be fulfilled. Love is emotive, motive, impulsive, and expulsive. It is emotive in that it constrains affection for its object, motive because it is the spring of action, impulsive because it impels to action, expulsive in that it expels what is alien to the interests of its object. We know only too well what a grievous burden is formal compliance with commandments when there is no love. Why is labour so distasteful, why so much heartlessness, and with heartlessness deterioration in quality and the mark of dishonesty on the product? It is because there is no love. Most tragic of all is the evidence of this in the highest of vocations and the discharge of the most sacred functions. The apostle reminds us: 'Though I speak with the tongues of men and of angels, and have not charity, I am become as sounding brass or a tinkling cymbal. And though I have the gift of prophecy . . . and though I have all faith so that I could remove mountains, and have not charity, I am nothing. And though I bestow all my goods to feed the poor, and though I give my body to be burned, and have not charity it profiteth me nothing' (1 Cor. 13:1–3).

2. Co-ordinate with the primacy of love is the *priority* in love. The order our Lord enunciated is of paramount importance. Love to God is first. If we do not observe the first, we cannot keep the second. Preoccupation today with inter-human relations is failing dismally in respect of good relations of the most elementary kind. Why? Because the priority in love is neglected. Why so much revolt against authority? Why is the sanctity of life so lamentably disregarded and, as an instance, the prevalence of abortion a shocking scandal for every sensitive soul? Why is the

sanctity of sex so desecrated and the sanctuary reserved for the marital relation subjected to wholesale invasion? Why has truth fallen in the street and equity cannot enter? It is because the sanction of the commandments as the ordinances of God has ceased to command human relations, and the reason for that is the absence of love to God. We have dragged God down to our level and have forgotten the incomparable in love—love to God with all the heart, and soul, and mind.

3. Love and commandments are correlative. Our Lord did not say that love takes the place of law or that love is the distillation of the law. What he did say was that on these two commandments hang all the law and the prophets. If the law hangs on love, it is not dispensed with. That on which something hangs serves no purpose and has no meaning apart from that which hangs on it. And if love is the fulfilment of the law, it is the fulfilment of the *law* and the fulfilment of the law exemplified by Paul in the context (Rom. 13:8, 9). Love does not devise the norms of its exercise nor the ways of expression. Love is not a self-directing principle. If love were its own monitor, it is easy to imagine the resulting desecrations. An unwed couple are deeply in love with each other. They may both have ardent sex desire and such is natural and normal. They are alone together. It is natural that they should give expression to their mutual love and satisfy their sex impulses by the sex act. This is what love itself would dictate. There is, however, the prohibitive ordinance, 'flee fornication'. Because love is not informed, regulated, and sanctified by the ordinance of God, the sexual trespass is to such an extent the order of our day, and we encounter the sexual filth that rots our society, and its stench rises to high heaven. The ethic that condones sexual intercourse outside the bond of matrimony is degrading love to the level of lust and justifying a perversion of the God-implanted sex impulse.

Examples could be multiplied of the way in which love divorced from regulative ordinances can be used not only to excuse but to justify all the ills that gnaw at the root of that integrity which the law of God demands and inculcates, and which it is the purpose of the gospel to create, nourish, and perfect.

To conclude our study and to enforce now more particularly the regulative authority of commandments in their positive application, it is necessary to appeal to that sanction than which there is none more sacred and ultimate. In dealing with the Christian ethic there would be a lamentable hiatus if we did not adduce the example of our Lord himself, his example in that which invests the keeping of commandments with the highest relevance and sanction. It is the fact that he defined the purpose of his coming into the world in terms of fulfilment of the Father's commandments. And not only did he define the purpose in such terms, but also the discharge of his commission in all its details, including the climactic requirement, in the same way.

Our Lord expressed this in general terms as doing the Father's will. 'My meat is to do the will of him who sent me and to finish his work' (John 4:34). 'I can of myself do nothing: as I hear I judge, and my judgment is just, because I seek not my own will but the will of him who sent me' (John 5:30). 'I am come down from heaven not to do my own will but the will of him who sent me' (John 6:38). In the agony of Gethsemane he prayed, 'O my Father, if it is possible, let this cup pass from me; yet not as I will but as thou wilt . . . O my Father, if this cannot pass except I drink it, thy will be done' (Matt. 26:39, 42). But he also becomes more specific in the language of commandment. 'I have not spoken of myself, but the Father who sent me, he gave me a commandment what I should say and what I should speak. And I know that his commandment is life everlasting. What things therefore I speak, as the Father said unto me, so I speak' (John 12:49, 50). 'If ye keep my commandments ye shall abide in my love, even as I have kept my Father's commandments and abide in his love' (John 15:10). And then the pivotal events of accomplishment are fulfilled in pursuance of the Father's commandment: 'Therefore doth my Father love me' *etc.* (John 10:17, 18). The inclusiveness is apparent, but is also expressly stated in respect of word and deed: 'I do nothing of myself, but as my Father has taught me I speak these things' (John 8:28).

It is in this perspective that we must interpret those passages which describe the work of the Redeemer as obedience, and obedience, be it remembered, in his capacity of Servant. When the apostle writes that our Lord took form of a Servant and 'became obedient unto death, even the death of the cross' (Phil. 2:8), he is describing the whole course of Jesus' self-humiliation as one of obedience until it reached its climax in the death upon the cross. And in the Epistle to the Hebrews we are told that Jesus, 'though he was a Son, yet learned obedience from the things he suffered' (Heb. 5:8). By this process he was constituted perfect as the captain and author of salvation (cf. Heb. 2:10; 5:9). Hence there is no more basic aspect in the fulfilment of the Father's commission than that of obedience.

The keeping of commandments and obedience are thus witnessed to by our Lord and the inspired writers as defining his character and conduct. These, of course, go together. They are definitive of each other. If they describe what was most characteristic in the case of our Lord, they constitute what is most relevant to us by way of example. The upshot is that if Jesus has given us an example that we should follow his steps, and, if the Christian ethic is thus to be defined, then that which most necessarily characterizes the Christian manner of life and behaviour is obedience to the commandments of God. It is significant that the obedience of Christ and that of believers should be brought into close juxtaposition when we read in Hebrews 5:8, 9: 'Though he was a Son, yet learned he obedience . . . all them that obey him'.

Do we recoil from the notion of obedience, of law observance, of keeping commandments? Is it alien to our way of thinking? If so, then our Lord's way is not our way. That is the issue and it is surpassingly grave. It is the issue of our day and it is aimed at the centre of our holy faith. It is aimed at the Saviour's self-witness and aimed at his supreme example. Anew, therefore, may we appreciate the ethic that is derived from him who said: 'I delight to do thy will, O my God: yea, thy law is within my heart' (Psalm 40:8), and that follows in the train of a psalmist who said: 'O how love I thy law! it is my meditation all the day' (Psalm 119:97), and of an apostle: 'I delight in the law of God after the inward man . . . So then with the mind I myself serve the law of God' (Rom. 7:22, 25).

25

Adorning the Gospel

IN speaking on Adorning the Gospel, or, as the subject may be called, the Manward Expression of Piety, I am convinced of two things:

1. How difficult the subject is!—difficult, not because there is not abundant instruction given in the Bible on adorning the gospel, but because the teaching of Scripture is so copious that it is difficult to know on what to focus attention. Again, when the manward expression is the subject, it is doubly difficult for the reason that, if we truly adorn the gospel, our thought is not absorbed in the manward expression so much as in the necessity of exemplifying the claims of the vocation with which we are called.

2. How far short we come of adorning the gospel! I am convinced that piety is a rare plant. Formal profession is common but piety in the sense of godliness is not.

If we are to express piety there must be piety. We cannot express what does not exist. I am not saying that there may not be witness to the gospel, and witness to its effects, without the piety of the heart. A person may declare the gospel who is himself a stranger to its saving and sanctifying power, and we may not say that this witness is without good effect and useless. And a person may exemplify fruits in outward morality, beneficence, charity, kindness, and not be himself a partaker of the grace of the gospel, or manifest the fruit of the Spirit. The works of unregenerate men may be, as to the matter of them, things which God commands and of good use both to themselves and others.[1]

But if there is to be the expression of piety, there must be piety.

[1] *Westminster Confession of Faith*, cf. XVI, vii.

What is piety? It is godliness. Godliness is God-consciousness, an all-pervasive sense of God's presence. It will mean that never do we think, or speak, or act, without the undergirding sense of God's presence, of his judgment, of our relation to him and his relation to us, of our responsibility to him and dependence upon him. This God-consciousness is spoken of as the fear of God, the profound reverence for his majesty and the dread of his judgments. This fear of God is not something abstract—it is filial reverence springing from a relation that has been constituted by redemption in Christ, justification and forgiveness by his grace, adoption in his love. There is faith, love, gratitude, confidence. In a word, this God-consciousness is conditioned by all the provisions of saving grace as brought to bear upon us in Christ Jesus, and by the distinct relations that we sustain by God's grace to the Father, the Son, and the Holy Spirit.

There is the intimacy constituted by adoption and the sonship created thereby, but never an intimacy that degrades the majesty of God or degenerates into the familiarity that destroys reverence.

Where this godliness exists it cannot but express itself and it will express itself in the following:

1. *Conformity to the revealed will of God.* To speak of godliness apart from the direction proceeding from the only way in which God relates himself to our consciousness is mockery. He relates himself to our consciousness only in revelation. And this is principally for us his Word, the Scripture. This is a commonplace of our faith but not a platitude. It is here that so often our manward expression of piety suffers most of all. The psalmist expresses it thus: 'Thy word have I hid in my heart that I might not sin against thee' (Psa. 119:11). Jesus, in prophetic utterance, says: 'I delight to do thy will, O my God, yea, thy law is within my heart' (Psa. 40:8). Paul expresses it by saying, 'bringing every thought into captivity to the obedience of Christ' (2 Cor. 10:5).

The Word of God is relevant to all of life and therefore to all the relations we sustain to our fellow men. In our human relations, to what extent do we bring the mind, judgment, and will of God to bear upon our viewpoint, our assessment of situations, our conduct? To what extent are our speech, our reactions, our responses theistically conditioned? The whole case of manward expression is focused in this consideration. For it drives us back to the exercises of piety itself—the study of God's Word, meditation, prayer. So there is the constant interaction and interdependence of the exercises of godliness and the manward expression of it.

2. *Obedience to the commandments of God.* Nothing is more prejudicial to the adornment of the gospel and the manward expression of faith than *to be long on profession and short on integrity.* What contradiction! What occasion given to the adversary to speak reproachfully and to blaspheme, if profession is not complemented by the basic elements of morality. Dishonesty, untruth, impurity, grasping, greed, intemperance, loose talk, gossip, slander, irreverent use of the name of God, sacrilegious and salacious humour—they all make profession a travesty of Christian witness.

The snare here is that there are accepted patterns of behaviour prevalent in business, in society, and in the professing church that are the violation of the commands of God. And because they are the accepted patterns they are not reckoned to be wrong and we do not come under reproach when we conform. There, brethren, is the claim and the opportunity for us. It may be as a bombshell. But there is the opportunity for us to interject the biblical ethic. We dishonour Christ when we conform to accepted practice. By well-doing we put to silence the ignorance of foolish men.

Paul says of office-bearers that they must have good report of them that are without.

3. *Meekness.* The world mistakes meekness for weakness. And we are liable to succumb to the world's estimate of strength and fight fire with fire.

Meekness is to be contrasted with retaliation, reviling, vengefulness, backbiting, unholy temper, envy, strife, malice. 'Laying aside all malice, and all guile, and hypocrisies, and envies, and all evil speakings' (1 Pet. 2:1).

Meekness and humility are companionate, just as envy and pride are.

4. *Compassion.* This comprises a group of virtues such as generosity, hospitality, mercy. It has respect to the destitute condition of others and is the expression of love. It means that we identify ourselves with the condition of other people, particularly the poor and the afflicted. 'He

that seeth his brother have need, and shutteth up his bowels of compassion from him, how dwelleth the love of God in him?' (1 John 3:17).

Here we touch upon one of the great evils which in our situation has marred the witness of the church of Christ. The ministry of mercy is one of the arms which Christ has put into the hands of the church for effective witness. It is underlined by the fact that one of the permanent offices in the church of Christ has this ministry as its function.

5. *Cheerfulness.* When we suffer reverse, calamity, affliction, do we behave as if the bottom had fallen out of the universe? Do we show composure, tranquillity, resignation, gratitude, thanksgiving; patience in adversity, gratitude in prosperity, confident assurance respecting the future? Again this touches the heart of godliness. Do we believe in the living God? that the very hairs of our head are all numbered? Let us express this in the day of adversity, not by forced hypocritical smiles which belie our inmost attitude, but by the confident assurance that God reigns and that not a sparrow falls to the ground without his knowledge. Fretful, gnawing, distrusting, unbelieving anxiety is a denial of faith. 'The Lord gave and the Lord hath taken away: blessed be the name of the Lord' (Job 1:21). 'Shall we receive good at the hand of the Lord and shall we not receive evil?' (Job 2:10). 'Be careful for nothing . . . let your requests be made known unto God' (Phil. 4:6).

6. *The Proclamation of the Gospel.* 'Be ready always to give a reason of the hope that is in you with meekness and fear' (1 Peter 3:15).

There are three things that need to be stressed—sincerity, earnestness, urgency. We are never to be self-assertive—that is pride. We are never to have a superiority complex—that is the opposite of meekness! We must never act as if we had in ourselves a reservoir of resources to meet every situation. But let us never be apologetic about the gospel. Let us never have an inferiority complex respecting the gospel, but forthrightness, confidence, arising from the conviction that there is none other name given under heaven among men whereby men must be saved, that it is the power of God unto salvation to every one that believes.

'Thanks be unto God which always causeth us to triumph in Christ' (2 Cor. 2:14).

26

The Guidance of the Holy Spirit

IT is proper to speak of the guidance of the Holy Spirit in the affairs of Christian life and conduct. The question that arises, however, is: How does the Holy Spirit guide and direct the people of God? This is a large and complex question and to deal with it adequately would require extensive and detailed treatment. We may deal with only one aspect of this broad question.

The basic premise upon which we must proceed is that the Word of God in the Scriptures of the Old and New Testaments is the only infallible rule of practice, as it is also the only infallible rule of faith. Complementary to this basic premise is another, namely, that the Word of God is a perfect and sufficient rule of practice. The corollary of this is that we may not look for, depend upon, or demand new revelations of the Spirit. In this respect we are in a different situation from those who lived during the era of revelation and inspiration. During the era, or we should preferably say the eras, of revelation, new revelations of the Spirit were given from time to time in a great variety of situations and for manifold purposes. These revelations were given by direct and supernatural communication to those who were the recipients of them. For that reason they are often called special in order to distinguish them from the revelation which is given in the light of nature and the works of creation and providence. From this consideration, that we must distinguish between the situation in which we are placed and the situation that existed while special revelation was in operation, we derive another premise, namely, that it is contrary to the situation in which God has cast our lot, contrary to the rule under which he has placed us, contrary to the perfection and sufficiency of the Scripture with which he has provided us, and dishonouring to the Holy Spirit, for us to expect or require special revelations to direct us in the affairs of life.

It is possible, however, to admit the validity and necessity of these foregoing premises and yet adopt a position which in reality undermines and defeats their implications. That is to say, we may still fall into the error of thinking that while the Holy Spirit does not provide us with special revelations in the form of words or visions or dreams, yet he may and does provide us with some *direct* feeling or impression or conviction which we are to regard as the Holy Spirit's intimation to us of what his mind and will is in a particular situation. The present writer maintains that this view of the Holy Spirit's guidance amounts, in effect, to the same thing as to believe that the Holy Spirit gives special revelation. And the reason for this conclusion is that we are, in such an event, conceiving of the Holy Spirit as giving us some special and direct communication, be it in the form of feeling, impression, or conviction, a communication or intimation or direction that is not mediated to us through those means which God has ordained for our direction and guidance. In the final analysis this construction or conception of the Holy Spirit's guidance is in the same category as that which holds to direct and special revelation, and that for the reason that it makes little difference whether the intimation is in the form of impression or feeling or conviction or in the form of a verbal communication, if we believe that the experience which we have is a direct and special intimation to us of what the will of God is. The essential point is that we regard the Holy Spirit as giving us guidance by some mode of direct operation and intimation. We are abstracting the operation of the Spirit, in respect of guidance, from the various factors which may properly be regarded as the means through which we are to be guided. Particularly, we abstract the operation of the Spirit from the infallible and sufficient rule of practice with which he has provided us.

It needs to be stressed in this connection that the Word of God is relevant to every situation in which we are placed, and in one way or another bears upon every detail and circumstance of life. This is just saying, in different words, that we are never in a situation in which we are non-moral or which is for us non-moral. The demands of God's law are all-pervasive, and the revelation God has given to us of his will in the Scriptures applies to us in every situation. It is equally necessary to remember that we must rely upon the Holy Spirit to direct and guide us in the understanding and application of God's will as revealed in Scripture, and we must be constantly conscious of our need of the Holy Spirit to apply the Word effectively to us in each situation. The function of the Holy Spirit in such matters is that of illumination as to what the will of the Lord is, and of imparting to us the willingness and strength to do that will.

, It needs also to be recognized that, as we are the subjects of this illumination and are responsive to it, and as the Holy Spirit is operative in us to the doing of God's will, we shall have feelings, impressions, convictions, urges, inhibitions, impulses, burdens, resolutions. Illumination and direction by the Spirit through the Word of God will focus themselves in our consciousness in these ways. We are not automata. And we are finite. We must not think, therefore, that a strong, or overwhelming feeling or impression or conviction, which we may not be able at a particular time to explain to ourselves or others, is necessarily irrational or fanatically mystical. Since we are human and finite and not always able to view all the factors or considerations in their relations to one another, the sum total of these factors and considerations bearing upon a particular situation may focus themselves in our consciousness in what we may describe as a strong feeling or impression. In many cases such a feeling or impression is highly rational and is the only way in which our consciousness, at a particular juncture, can take in or react to a complex manifold of thoroughly proper considerations. In certain instances it may take us a long time to understand the meaning or implications of that impression.

It is here, however, that careful distinction is necessary. The moment we desire or expect or think that a state of our consciousness is the effect of a direct intimation to us of the Holy Spirit's will, or consists in such an intimation and is therefore in the category of special direction from him, then we have given way to the notion of special, direct, detached communication from the Holy Spirit. And this, in respect of its nature, belongs to the same category as belief in special revelation. The only way whereby we can avoid this error is to maintain that the direction and guidance of the Holy Spirit is through the means which he has provided, and that his work is to enable us rightly to interpret and apply the Scripture in the various situations of life, and to enable us to interpret all the factors which enter into each situation in the light of Scripture.

There are two observations to be made in this connection. The first is that the guidance and direction of the Holy Spirit is specific. The guidance which he affords us is in the concrete of our daily lives. The Word of God and the illumination of the Spirit in and through the Word are in the truest sense existential. That is inherent in the belief that the Bible is revelation and that the Holy Spirit constantly seals that revelation in our hearts and minds. The second observation is that our dependence upon an infallible rule and our reliance upon the infallible Spirit do not eliminate all error in judgment or wrong in decision on our part. We are always fallible, imperfect, and sinful. But this doctrine of guidance does eliminate the error of an erroneous criterion. If our criterion or standard of judgment is wrong, then we are deprived of the means whereby our wrong may be corrected. It is one thing to come short in the application of a right rule; it is another to have a wrong rule. It is one thing to limp in the right way; it is another thing to run in the wrong way. In the one case we have a basis for progress; in the other we have not started to make progress.

The notion of guidance by immediate impression, when such an impression is interpreted as the direct intimation of the Holy Spirit to us, distorts our thinking on the question of guidance and stultifies what the apostle prayed for in the case of the believers at Colosse: 'For this cause we also, since the day we heard it, do not cease to pray for you, and to desire that ye might be filled with the knowledge of his will in all wisdom and spiritual understanding; that ye might walk worthy of the Lord unto all pleasing, being fruitful in every good work, and increasing in the knowledge of God' (Col. 1:9, 10). In this connection we need to appreciate the implications for godly living of one of the most familiar texts in the New Testament: 'All Scripture is inspired of God and is profitable for doctrine, for reproof, for correction, for the instruction which is in righteousness, that the man of God may be perfect, thoroughly furnished unto every good work' (2 Tim. 3:16, 17).

The Moral Law
and the Fourth Commandment

27

The Sanctity of the Moral Law[1]

THE history of the Christian Church is to a very great extent the history of controversy between naturalism and supernaturalism, paganism and Christianity. As long as evil persists in the world it cannot be otherwise. It was our Lord who said 'Think not that I am come to send peace on the earth: I came not to send peace but a sword.' It was his inspired apostle who said 'We wrestle not against flesh and blood, but against principalities, against powers, against the rulers of the darkness of this world, against spiritual wickedness in high places.' At no point in history has this controversy been more acute than at the present time.

It is this controversy that brought the 'League of Evangelical Students' into existence, and continues to justify its existence.

It is too readily supposed that this controversy between Christianity and what we at the present time call modernism is exclusively concerned with what we call more specifically doctrine. The modernist very often prides himself on the supposition that he is concerned with life, with the principles of conduct and the making operative of the principles of Jesus in all departments of life, individual, social, ecclesiastical, industrial, and political. His slogan has been that Christianity is life, not doctrine, and he thinks that the orthodox Christian or fundamentalist, as he likes to name him, is concerned simply with the conservation and perpetuation of outworn dogmas of doctrinal belief, a concern which makes orthodoxy in his esteem a cold and lifeless petrification of Christianity.

The orthodox Christian has too often been concessive to this con-

1 An address delivered at the Tenth Annual Convention of the League of Evangelical Students, held February 21 to February 24, 1935 at the Tenth Presbyterian Church, Philadelphia.

tention of his opponent. He has been too concessive when he has tolerated even the suggestion that the difference between him and the modernist is largely confined to the realm of what we call more specifically doctrinal belief. For the attack upon the Christian Faith is not a whit less in the realm of standards of moral obligation, that is of principles of life and conduct, than it is in the realm of what we call doctrine or dogma. The modernist is just as avowed and consistent an exponent of the one attack as of the other.

Perhaps you will permit an illustration drawn from the present-day history of the Presbyterian Church in the U.S.A. Though drawn from this particular denomination, it exemplifies what is prevalent in many other denominations of the Protestant Church. In the Presbyterian Church in the U.S.A. there are approximately 1200 ministers who are signers of what is known as the 'Auburn Affirmation'. This document attacks the Christian faith at its centre. It affirms that the doctrine of Biblical inerrancy is not only not true, but also dangerous, and impairs the supreme authority of the Scriptures for faith and life, and that other doctrines—the virgin birth of our Lord, his vicarious sacrifice to satisfy divine justice, his bodily resurrection and the supernatural character of his miracles—are simply theories which may be held or not, but must not be considered as tests for ordination or good standing in the Church. It is manifestly heretical, and heretical not at the periphery of our faith but at the core, and therefore expressive of what is the antithesis of our Christian religion. It means the existence of another religion within the external unity of the Presbyterian Church, and that is surely a tremendously serious affair. A house divided against itself cannot stand.

But does the seriousness of the Auburn Affirmation confine itself to the realm of what we call doctrinal belief? Oh, not at all! Another aspect of it is equally if not more serious, because in that aspect of it, it evidences departure from the *very principle of truth itself*. These same men have solemnly vowed belief in and adherence to these great verities which they have either denied or branded as mere theories. In justice and truth their continuance in the Presbyterian Church can only last as long as they are faithful to these vows. It is manifest that they are not faithful to these vows. What does this mean? It means simply blatant breach of trust, of the basic principle of honesty, in one word, of truth.

It is tantamount to moral perjury, and that in one of the most sacred relations that exists in this world. Can you say that there is no relation between a man's position in the realm of doctrine and his principles of life and conduct? No; they are one because they concern truth and the sanctity of truth. Truth is one, and it is a moral and psychological impossibility for a man's belief with respect to what constitutes Christianity to be heterodox and his beliefs with respect to what constitutes the norm of Christian life to be orthodox.

The primal necessity is truth in the inward parts, and error with respect to God, Christ, sin and redemption cannot co-exist there with a true standard of moral obligation. Modernism in doctrine and modernism in ethics are ultimately one.

This comes, however, much nearer home. A similar fault exists within the camp that is called by its opponents, fundamentalist. There are, I fear, earnest men, believing men, contending perhaps for some of the central truths of our holy faith, and who with all that is in them are opposed to the type of religion that modernism represents, but who nevertheless appear to be out of sympathy with some of the distinctive doctrines of that communion whose doctrines they may have solemnly vowed to believe and maintain. I am willing to grant that many such have never seriously considered the implications of their position, and perhaps have never had an adequate opportunity to become acquainted with the doctrinal position of their own Church. They are in these respects ignorant, and that ignorance we may with charity allow to be a considerable extenuation of their wrong. But ignorance is no final excuse. In a very serious, indeed, grossly serious way, they are violating the first principle of honesty and truth. Divergence in faith is coupled with a serious delinquency in ethical conduct.

Why has a situation of which I have given a few high-spot instances become so prevalent? Why has the church of God, ordained of God to witness to the truth, become so conspicuous an example of such flagrant dishonesty? Why is it that truth has thus fallen in *her* streets and equity cannot enter?

I venture to say, that while many reasons may be given, no reason can be so justly assigned as the loss of the consciousness of the sanctity of the moral law, and of its implications in truth and justice.

What is moral law? Law frequently sounds to our uninstructed ears as something very primitive, crude, temporary, arbitrary. Antinomian tendencies inherent in our sinful hearts, and given widespread currency in much of what professes to be evangelical teaching, are responsible for this. It is due, however, to complete misunderstanding, or still worse, perversity. Moral law is in the last analysis but the reflection or expression of the moral nature of God. God is holy, just and good, and the law which is also holy, just and good is simply the correlate of the holiness and justice and goodness of God. Man is created in the image of God and the demand, the inescapable postulate of that relation that man sustains to God as responsible and dependent creature, is that he be conformed in the inmost fibre of his moral being and in all the conditions and activities of his person to the moral perfection of God. 'Ye shall be holy, for I am holy.' 'Ye shall be perfect, even as your Father in heaven is perfect.' No rational being can ever be relieved from the obligation to love the Lord our God with all the heart and soul and strength and mind, and his neighbour as himself. Moral law is the moral perfection of God coming to expression for the regulation of life and conduct.

But if this is what moral law essentially is, where is it to be found? What is its content?

It is true that the sense of obligation is engraven upon the moral constitution of man. It is the apostle Paul who says that the Gentiles who have not the law do by nature the things of the law, in that they show the work of the law written in their hearts, their conscience also bearing witness and their thoughts accusing or else excusing them. Man has a conscience and that means that in some vague sense at least he recognizes that there is a distinction between right and wrong.

But the conscience of man though indispensable to the fact and sense of obligation, and though not eradicated by sin, has nevertheless suffered just as much damage by the ruin of sin as does any other function or activity of his being. Man has fallen as a totality, and we must remind the naturalistic moralist that his *conscience* has fallen, as we remind the Arminian that his will has also fallen. Can man by the movements of conscience in relation to the various experiences of life determine what is right and good and holy? Is man's conscience so perfect and accurate a reproduction of God's perfection that it can reveal to us what is in accord with his will? Does it so derive its life-blood from the eternal God that its heart-beat is in perfect accord with his? If I may use the words of James Henley Thornwell, 'In our present fallen condition it is impossible to excogitate a standard of duty which shall be warped by none of our prejudices, distorted by none of our passions, and corrupted by none of our habits. . . . It is only of the law of the Lord as contained in the Scriptures that we can justly say, It is perfect.'[1]

Yes, the conscience of man may give us the dictum that there is a distinction between right and wrong, that it is right to do right and that it is wrong to do wrong, but it cannot tell us what the right is, nor how we are to apply it and fulfil it. The fact is that in the matter of right and wrong we are just as dependent upon special divine revelation as we are in the realm of truth. It is the principle of our Christian faith that we have in Holy Scripture a complete, infallible and sufficient rule of duty and conduct.

This is a very comprehensive proposition. It would be disastrous to tone it down in any way. It is Holy Scripture in all its manifoldness and richness, extent and detail, yet in its compact organic unity, that sets before us the sum of human obligation and the rule of duty. God's Word is a lamp to our feet and a light to our path. There is no circumstance or situation of life in all its variety and detail for which the revelation of God's will in inspired Scripture is not a sufficient guide. We must do nothing to prejudice the principle that the rule of life as well as the rule of faith is the *whole* of Scripture.

But we nevertheless do find in Scripture itself a summing up of the moral standard of which Scripture as a whole is the representation. It should not strike us as strange that it does so. It does very much the same thing in the realm of faith. The inspired writers, sometimes with a conciseness that simply overwhelms us, express in a few pregnant sentences the cardinal basic truths of the scheme of redemption. When we apprehend such brief statements and try to drink them in, we have no sense of confinement; we are not conscious of any prejudice to the principle that the rule of faith is the *whole* of Scripture, from which we are to take nothing and to which we are to add nothing. That summary

1 *Collected Writings*, Vol. II, p. 457.

statement only leads us to a high eminence from which we get a new appreciation of the whole of God's special revelation in the length of it and in the breadth of it.

It is similar with the moral law. It also has its central, cardinal, basic, principles, and our Westminster divines were right when they asked the question, 'Where is the moral law summarily comprehended?', and answered, 'The moral law is summarily comprehended in the ten commandments.'

The statement of such a position is exceedingly distasteful to many phases of modern thought both within and without the evangelical family. It is argued that the conception of an externally revealed and imposed code of duty, norm of right feeling, thought and conduct, is entirely out of accord with the liberty and spontaneity of the Christian life. We are told that conformity to the will of God must come from within, and that therefore any stipulation or prescription from without in the form of well-defined precepts is wholly alien to the spirit of the gospel. It is inconsistent, they say, with the spirit or principle of love: 'Don't speak of law, nor of moral precepts, nor of a code of morals. Speak of the law of love.'

Furthermore we are told that the Christian is not under law but grace. To argue that the moral law binds the conscience of the believing man who has been set free by the grace of the gospel is to abolish, they say, the distinction between the dispensation of law and the dispensation of grace, and thus to enthrall the Christian again in the yoke of bondage.

We should not be forgetful of the elements of truth embodied in such a series of slogans. It is true that the Christian is freed from the dominion of sin, because he has been redeemed by the grace of God. He has not been saved from sin's guilt or sin's thraldom by his own obedience to any law. He has been set free by the precious blood of Christ. It is true on that account that he is not under the law but under grace, in the sense in which Paul in Romans 6:14 meant it.

It is true also that conformity to the will of God must be first a condition of the heart, created by the Spirit's regenerative grace and fostered by his sanctifying presence. Upright conduct can never co-exist with impurity of heart. Mere external and servile conformity to precepts of law does not constitute obedience. Upon none did the anathemas of our

Lord descend with such awful severity as upon the legalistic Pharisees who made clean the outside of the cup and of the platter, but who were within full of malice and hypocrisy, who were like whited sepulchres outwardly beautiful, but within full of dead men's bones and of all uncleanness. Without the inward condition of purity and the inward impulsion of love, obedience is impossible.

But in these watchwords of our modern exponents of the Christian ethic there is also devastating error. We are not saved *by* obedience to the law, but we are saved *unto* it. In their insistence upon love they have placed love in opposition to law. We have just to remind them with well-balanced emphasis that love is the fulfilling of the *law*. It is not love in opposition to law but love fulfilling law. What our modern apostles of love really mean is the very opposite of this: they mean that love fulfils its own dictates, that love not only fulfils, but that it is also the law fulfilled, that love is as it were an autonomous, self-instructing and self-directing principle, that not only impels to the doing of the right but also tells us what the right is. This is certainly not what Paul meant when he said, 'love is the fulfilling of the law.' He tells us not only that love fulfils, but also what the law is which it fulfils. 'Owe no man anything but to love one another, for he who loveth another hath fulfilled the law. For this, Thou shalt not commit adultery, Thou shalt not kill, Thou shalt not steal, Thou shalt not covet: and if there is any other commandment, it is summed up in this word, namely, Thou shalt love thy neighbour as thyself. Love worketh no ill to his neighbour; therefore love is the fulfilling of the law' (Rom. 13:8–10). It is noteworthy that Paul cites four precepts. He reminds us by the brief sentence, 'and if there is any other commandment,' that he does not consider these four as the complete sum of man's duty to man. He has cited four to exemplify his meaning. But what I wish especially to stress is, first, that these four he enumerates are four of the well-known ten commandments. It is in the decalogue that Paul finds the epitome of Moral Law. And second, it is *that* law that love fulfils. *The directing principle of love is objectively revealed statutory commandments, not at all the dictates which it might itself be presumed to excogitate.*

A study of another passage in Paul will yield the same result. This passage is more negative, just as the preceding is more positive. It is

1 Cor. 6:9–11. There Paul is condemning sin—fornication, idolatry, adultery, effeminacy, sodomy, thievery, covetousness, drunkenness, reviling, extortion. They who commit such things shall not inherit the kingdom of God. The most cursory review of these sins will show that the obligatoriness and authority of the ten commandments underlies his whole exhortation and doctrine. Idolatry—the first and second commandments; adultery—the seventh commandment; thievery and extortion—the eighth commandment; reviling—the ninth and perhaps the third; covetousness—the tenth. He has not exhausted the list of sins; elsewhere he mentions others not specifically mentioned here. But he has enumerated enough to evince to us that the underlying presupposition of his thought is, that summarily, at least, the decalogue is the norm by which sin is to be known, as it is also the norm of that righteousness which characterizes the kingdom of God and those who belong to it. He just says in effect what the apostle John says, that 'sin is the transgression of the law.' *Abolish or abrogate law and you deny the reality of sin. Where no law is there is no transgression.*

It might, however, be objected that this principle of love in subordination to law is not as invariable as these two instances might lead us to think. For is not the apostle Paul, for example in the eighth chapter of First Corinthians, to be understood as commending to his readers at Corinth his own example of abstinence in certain circumstances from meat offered to idols, lest their eating of that meat should be a stumbling-block to them that were weak? There is no law against the eating of meat offered to idols, for the apostle contends in this matter for the liberty of the strong and intelligent believer. He knows that no idol is anything in the world and there is no other God but one. The earth is the Lord's and the fulness thereof. And for the man who is aware of that fact and serves the Lord, meat is not contaminated by the fact of its having been offered by another, who is an idolater, to an idol. He may freely eat and give the Lord thanks. Yet there are certain circumstances under which considerations of love to another, and the consideration of the weakness of the conscience of another, constrain him to abstain. Now it might be plausibly argued that here you have love operating in complete abstraction from law, and so love conceived of as an autonomous, self-instructing and self-directing principle.

A merely superficial examination of the passage will expose the fallacy of such an interpretation. The law of God, its sanctity and authority, underlies the whole situation. Why is the intelligent believer enjoined in the circumstance to abstain? Simply and solely because there is the danger of the *sin of idolatry* on the part of the weak brother, the danger of wounding his weak conscience in the eating of meat as offered to an idol. In other words it is the danger of transgression, on the part of the weak believer, of the first commandment, 'Thou shalt have no other gods before me.' Remove that fact from the situation and the whole argument of the apostle is nullified. The law requires that we ourselves abstain from idolatry; but it also requires that we love our neighbour as ourselves, and so when our doing what so far as we ourselves are concerned is a perfectly innocent act becomes, and that to our knowledge, the occasion for the commission of sin on the part of another believer, love to our neighbour as ourselves will impel us to abstain from so unloving and unworthy conduct. It is not, however, love abstracted from law but love operating under the authority and sanctity of that commandment, 'Thou shalt have no other gods before me.'

We have the same result when we examine the teaching of our Lord himself. 'If ye love me ye will keep my commandments.' 'He that hath my commandments and keepeth them, he it is that loveth me.' 'Whosoever shall break one of these least commandments, and shall teach men so, he shall be called the least in the kingdom of heaven: but whosoever shall do and teach them, the same shall be called great in the kingdom of heaven' (John 14:15, 21; Matt. 5:19). He leaves us in no doubt as to what he had in mind by commandments, for he proceeds to give us examples. In the succeeding context of the last quotation he appeals to the sixth and seventh of the decalogue, and asserts in the most emphatic way the penetrating and searching depth and breadth of their application when he says, 'Whosoever is angry with his brother without a cause shall be in danger of the judgment'; 'Whosoever looketh on a woman to lust after her hath committed adultery with her already in his heart' (Matt. 5:22, 28). His teaching with respect to obedience and his denunciation of sin is simply steeped in the permanent authority and inviolable sanctity of the decalogue. Just look at the catalogue of sins he condemns—fornication, thefts, murders, adulteries, covetings, wickedness, deceit, lasciviousness, an evil eye, railing, pride, foolishness, idolatry, false swearing, the obscuration and virtual nullification of the Sabbath institution by the carnal impositions of men—and the ten commandments as the basic norm of righteousness is the lesson which he who runs may read.

On one occasion, when accused by the Pharisees for violation of the tradition of the elders, he exposes their hypocrisy by asking pertinently, 'Why do ye also transgress the commandment of God by your tradition. For God said, Honour thy father and thy mother . . . Ye have made void the law of God because of your tradition' (Matt. 15:3–6).

Yes, with all the emphasis of which I am capable, I do say, that in the denial of the permanent authority and sanctity of the moral law there is a direct thrust at the very centre of our holy faith, for it is a thrust at the veracity and authority of our Lord himself. If we wish to lend speed and force to the widespread attack upon the Christian religion, we need but endorse and support this antinomian propaganda.

It is scarcely necessary to give more instances from the New Testament, but there is one from the Epistle of James which I cannot refrain from quoting. It is James 2:8–12: 'If ye fulfil the royal law according to the Scripture, Thou shalt love thy neighbour as thyself, ye do well: But if ye have respect to persons, ye commit sin, and are convinced of the law as transgressors. For whosoever shall do the whole law, and yet offend in one point, he is guilty of all. For he that said, Do not commit adultery, said also, Do not kill. Now if thou commit no adultery, yet if thou kill, thou art become a transgressor of the law. So speak ye, and so do, as they that shall be judged by the law of liberty.'

The widespread indifference and even antagonism to ethical standards of which we gave a few high-spot instances at the outset has come to be the shame of our Protestant churches, a shame in company with, and just as much as, the shame of our theological heterodoxy. What is to be the remedy? The only remedy is the path of repentance. Repentance must start with change of mind, recognition of the facts, the fact of our shame and the fact of the full-orbed truth of our Christian faith.

Our Christian faith is a body of fact and doctrine. It is not a vague sentiment, some mystical feeling of communion with the unseen. It produces true sentiment and results in communion with the great unseen God, but it is first of all a faith in certain well-defined and un-changeable data of fact and teaching.

But as truly as it is a faith it involves a life. And just as there is the un-changeable and immovable in the realm of what we call faith, so there is the unchangeable and immovable in the norms and principles of life. God does not change; his moral perfections do not change; his moral law does not change. Times change; conditions change; we change. But under and through all there remains man's conscience, man's responsi-bility; and over all there is the unchanging holiness, justice, and authority of God, issuing in the commands that bind man's conscience and, with a divine imperative must regulate his life, in one word, the moral law.

Recognition of this datum of awful sanctity, and republication of it with conviction and authority is the only path of repentance and restoration. As we recognize the awful sanctity that surrounds the law, we shall certainly be crushed with a sense of our own hell-deserving guilt and hopeless inability. We shall certainly be constrained to cry out, 'Woe is me for I am undone.' 'Surely I am more brutish than any man, and I have not the understanding of a man.' (Isa. 6:5; Prov. 30:2). But in that condition there falls upon our ears and into our hearts the sweet news of the gospel, the gospel of a crucified and risen Redeemer and Lord. 'Christ hath redeemed us from the curse of the law, being made a curse for us' (Gal. 3:13). We shall be constrained to come to Calvary.

But when we come to Calvary for the expiation of our guilt and the remission of our sin, it is not to diminish our esteem of that law nor relax our sense of its awful sanctity and binding authority. Oh no! As the brilliant and eloquent James Henley Thornwell spoke and wrote nearly a hundred years ago: 'He that stands beneath the Cross and under-stands the scene dares not sin; not because there is a hell beneath him or an angry God above him, but because Holiness is felt to reign there— the ground on which he treads is sacred, the glory of the Lord encircles him, and, like Moses, he must remove the shoes from his feet. The Cross is a venerable spot. I love to linger around it, not merely that I may read my title to everlasting life, but that I may study the greatness of God. I use the term advisedly. God never appears to be so truly great, so intensely holy, as when, from the pure energy of principle, He gives

Himself, in the person of His Son, to die, rather than that His character should be impugned. Who dares prevaricate with moral distinctions and talk of death as a greater evil than dishonour, when God, the mighty Maker, died rather than that truth or justice should be compromised? Who, at the foot of Calvary, can pronounce sin to be a slight matter?'[1]

When we are possessed by the sense of the authority and sanctity of the moral law, we must come to Calvary if any true and living hope is to be engendered within us. But when we rise from our prostration before the Cross, it is not to find the moral law abrogated, but to find it by the grace of God wrought into the very fibre of the new life in Christ Jesus. If the Cross of Christ does not fulfil in us the passion of righteousness, we have misinterpreted the whole scheme of divine redemption. 'For what the law could not do in that it was weak through the flesh, God, sending his own Son in the likeness of sinful flesh, and for sin, condemned sin in the flesh (Rom. 8:3). Is it that the moral law might cease to bind and regulate? Oh no! But 'that the righteousness of the law might be fulfilled in us, who walk not after the flesh, but after the Spirit.'

[1] *Collected Writings*, Vol. II, pp. 460–1.

28

The Sabbath Institution[1]

THE questions relating to the weekly day of rest and worship are of perennial interest and concern. The circumstances in connection with which these questions arise differ from generation to generation, from family to family, and from person to person. But the basic questions are always the same. Any argument for or against the weekly Sabbath which fails to come to terms with these basic questions is one which misses the point of the debate. This is why a great deal that has been written in the interests of libertinism is a begging of the question, and, sad to say, a good deal written and pleaded in behalf of Sabbath observance has lacked the cogency of divine sanction. The argument for the perpetuity of the Sabbath rest stands or falls with the question of divine institution and obligation. Whatever expediency might dictate, it can never carry the sanction of law and it cannot bind the conscience of man. There is no law of expediency; it changes with circumstance. And what changes with circumstance is not universal and perpetual law. The recognition of this is necessary not only to guard law; it is also necessary to guard liberty. If we once allow expediency to dictate law then we are on the road to tyranny and conscience is no longer captive to the law of God but to the variable fancies of men.

There are three questions that must be dealt with if controversy regarding the Sabbath institution is to be placed in proper focus and if

[1] An address given at Golspie, Sutherland, on August 12, 1953, and subsequently published—'expanded at certain points and abbreviated at others'—by the Lord's Day Observance Society, London.

the perpetuity of this ordinance is to be established. These are the *Obligation*, the *Sanctity*, and the *Observance* of the Sabbath.

THE OBLIGATION

When we assert the obligation of the Sabbath we are not dealing simply with its obligation under the Mosaic economy. It is the question of its perpetual obligation; it is the question of the relevance to us of the institution which was defined for those of the Mosaic economy in the fourth commandment. What are the facts which indicate that it is of permanent application?

1. *The Sabbath was instituted at creation* (Gen. 2:2, 3). It belongs, therefore, to the order of things which God established for man at the beginning. It is relevant quite apart from sin and the need of redemption. In this respect it is like the institutions of labour (Gen. 2:15), of marriage (Gen. 2:24, 25), and of fruitfulness (Gen. 1:28). The Sabbath institution was given to man as man, for the good of man as man, and extended to man the assurance and promise that his labour would issue in a Sabbath rest similar to the rest of God himself. The Sabbath is a creation ordinance and does not derive its validity or its necessity or its sanction, in the first instance, from any exigencies arising from sin, nor from any of the provisions of redemptive grace. When sin entered, the circumstances under which the Sabbath rest was to be observed were altered just as in the case of these other institutions. The forces of redemptive grace were now indispensable to their proper discharge. But the entrance of sin did not abrogate the Sabbath institution any more than it abrogated the institutions of labour, marriage, and fruitfulness. The depravity arising from sin did not make in any way irrelevant or unnecessary the obligations emanating from these divine institutions. In a word, sin does not abrogate creation ordinances and redemption does not make superfluous their obligation and fulfilment.

2. *The Sabbath rests upon the divine example* (Gen. 2:2). This is expressly stated in the fourth commandment. 'For in six days the Lord made heaven and earth, the sea, and all that in them is, and rested the seventh day: wherefore the Lord blessed the sabbath day and hallowed it' (Exod. 20:11). This means that the sequence for man of six days of labour and one day of rest is patterned after the sequence which God

followed in the grand scheme of his creative work. God created in six successive days and he rested on the seventh. That is the exemplar for man. In this connection there are a few questions to be asked and the questions contain their answers. Has God's work of creation ceased to be relevant to us? Has the fact that he created, not in one grand fiat but in the space of six days, become irrelevant? Is not the fact of creation basic to all Christian thinking? The biblical writers should be our monitors in this. How frequently the God of Christian faith and piety is identified by the inspired writers as the God who made the world and all things therein! More specifically, has the fact that God rested on the seventh day ceased to be relevant? God is not now creating; he is resting from his creative work. The sequence of six days of creative work and the seventh of rest is an irreversible fact in the transcendent sphere of God's relation to this universe which he has made. And now to the most pointed question of all: has the divine example become obsolete? Can we think of the exemplar established by God's working and resting as ever ceasing to be the pattern for man's conduct in the ordinances of labour and rest?

3. *The Sabbath commandment is comprised in the decalogue.* The fourth commandment is not an appendix to the decalogue, nor is it an application of the decalogue, nor is it an application of the decalogue to the temporary conditions and circumstances of Israel. There were ordinances in Israel, regulating the observance of the Sabbath, which were peculiar to the circumstances of the people of Israel at that time, and we have no warrant to believe that they are of permanent obligation. But the fourth commandment itself is an element of that basic law which was distinguished from all else in the Mosaic revelation by being inscribed on two tables of stone. The fourth commandment belongs to all that is distinctive and characteristic of that summary of human obligation set forth in the decalogue. It would require the most conclusive evidence to establish the thesis that the fourth command is in a different category from the other nine. That it finds its place among the ten words written by the finger of God upon tables of stone establishes for this commandment, and for the labour and rest it enjoins, a position equal to that of the third or the fifth or the seventh or the tenth.

4. *Our Lord has confirmed the relevance of the Sabbath institution.* 'The

sabbath was made for man, and not man for the sabbath. Wherefore the Son of man is Lord also of the sabbath' (Mark 2:27, 28). What the Lord is affirming is that the Sabbath has its place within the sphere of his messianic lordship and that he exercises lordship over the Sabbath because the Sabbath was made for man. Since he is Lord of the Sabbath it is his to guard it against those distortions and perversions with which Pharisaism had surrounded it and by which its truly beneficent purpose has been defeated. But he is also its Lord to guard and vindicate its permanent place within that messianic lordship which he exercises over all things—he is Lord of the Sabbath, too. And he is Lord of it, not for the purpose of depriving men of that inestimable benefit which the Sabbath bestows, but for the purpose of bringing to the fullest realization on behalf of men that beneficent design for which the Sabbath was instituted. If the Sabbath was made for man, and if Jesus is the Son of man to save man, surely the lordship which he exercises to that end is not to deprive man of that which was made for his good, but to seal to man that which the Sabbath institution involves. Jesus is Lord of the Sabbath—we dare not tamper with his authority and we dare not misconstrue the intent of his words.

For these four reasons we are compelled to conclude that the weekly Sabbath is embedded in that order which God has established for man as man. As an institution it antedated the fall of man and would have been, therefore, a feature of man's obedience in a perfect state of integrity and bliss. It antedated the promulgation of the ten commandments at Mount Sinai; the fourth commandment simply defined what was the already existing institution. The commandment finds its place within the summary of the rôle of life for man; it is not an appendix nor even a prologue. Our Lord himself confirms its permanent relevance; the Sabbath was made for man, and the Son of man, as the Saviour of men is its Lord. We must appreciate the cumulative force of these arguments. They mutually supplement and reinforce one another and they all converge to establish the principle that the weekly Sabbath is of perpetual obligation and application.

THE SANCTITY
The sanctity of the Sabbath resides in the command to keep it holy or

to sanctify it (Exodus 20:8); the sanctity is that which is involved in sanctifying it. There are two elements in the word 'sanctify'. It means, first of all, to set apart. If set apart it is distinguished from something else. This belongs to the sanctity of the seventh day. There are people who will say that every day is to them a sabbath, at least that every day is to them the Lord's day. This may seem very pious. It seems pious because there is an element of truth in the assertion that every day is the Lord's day. It is true that we ought to serve the Lord every day and every moment of every day. And our devotion to the Lord should not be one whit less at our weekly labours than in our worship in God's house on the Sabbath. We should dig or plough with as much devotion to the Lord as we pray or sing in the assembly of the saints. Whatsoever we do we are to do it to the Lord and to his glory. In this connection we should remember that the fourth commandment is the command-ment of labour as well as of rest. 'Six days shalt thou labour, and do all thy work' (Exod. 20:9).

But while it is true that we ought to serve the Lord every day and in all things we must not forget that there are different ways of serving God. We do not serve him by doing the same thing all the time. If we do that, we are either insane or notoriously perverse. There is a great variety in human vocation. If we neglect to observe that variation we shall soon pay the cost. One of the ways by which this variety is expressed and enjoined is to set apart every recurring seventh day. That is the divine institution. The recurring seventh day is different, and it is so by divine appointment. To obliterate this difference may appear pious. But it is piosity, not piety. It is not piety to be wiser than God; it is impiety of the darkest hue. The Sabbath day is different from every other day, and to obliterate this distinction either in thought or practice is to destroy what is of the essence of the institution.

The recognition of distinction is indispensable to observance. Too frequently among Christians, refraining from certain practices is merely a matter of custom. There is perchance adherence to honoured tradition, but it is the shell without the kernel. Truly, they do not do certain things, but this abstinence does not spring from a well-grounded sense of sanctity. And the consequence is that when solicitation or temptation to deviate from custom confronts them there is no recoil dictated by principle—they are the victims of circumstance. It needs to be under-lined that Sabbath observance soon becomes obsolete if it does not spring from the sense of sanctity generated and nourished in us by the recogni-tion that God has *set apart* one day in seven.

The second element in sanctity is that the difference which God has ordained is a difference of a specific kind. The Sabbath is set apart *to the Lord*—'the seventh day is the sabbath of the Lord thy God' (Exod. 20:10). It is 'a sabbath of rest to the Lord' (Exod. 35:2). The Sabbath rest does not mean inactivity. God's rest on the seventh day after six days of creative activity was not the rest of inactivity. Jesus said, 'My Father worketh until now, and I work' (John 5:17). And he said this in reference to this question of Sabbath observance. He justified the activity which the Jews had condemned, and he did this by appeal to the activity of the Father. God rested on the seventh day from his work of creation but he continued to be omnipresently active in the work of providence. Hence our rest of the Sabbath is not one of inaction, of idleness, far less of sloth. It is the rest of another kind of activity. It is indeed rest *from* the ordinary employments of the other six days. There is cessation from that activity and the labour it entails. But it is also rest *to* or rest *in*; it is rest *to* and rest *in* the Lord. That must mean the rest of activity in the specific worship of the Lord our God. There is release from the labours of the six days, but it is also release to the contempla-tion of the glory of God. Cessation from the labours of the week must itself have its source and ground in obedience to God, and the gratitude which is both the motive and fruit of such obedience will minister to the worship which is the specific employment of the Sabbath rest. This is just saying that rest from weekly labours and the exercises of specific worship are inseparable and they mutually condition one another. In a Sabbath of rest *to the Lord* we cannot have the one without the other.

This is the sanctity of the Sabbath institution—it is the sanctity of separateness and it is the sanctity of concentrated adoration of the glory of the Lord our God.

THE OBSERVANCE

It is sometimes said, and it is said by good men, that we do not now under this economy observe the Sabbath as strictly as was required of the people of Israel under the Old Testament. This statement of the case needs examination, and careful distinction must be made if we are to assess it properly. There is an element of truth in it. But there is also a good deal of error. It is true that certain regulations both preceptive and primitive, regulations which governed the observance of the Sabbath under the Mosaic law, do not apply to us under the New Testament. In Israel it was distinctly provided that they were not to kindle a fire throughout their habitations upon the Sabbath day (Exod. 35:3). It was also enacted that whosoever would do any work on the Sabbath would be put to death (Exod. 35:2).

Now there is no warrant for supposing that such regulatory provisions both prohibitive and punitive bind us under the New Testament. This is particularly apparent in the case of the capital punishment executed for Sabbath desecration in the matter of labour. If this is what is meant when it is said that observance is not as strict in its application to us as it was under the Mosaic law, then the contention should have to be granted. It must be said, however, that this would be a rather awkward and inaccurate way of expressing the distinction between the Mosaic economy and the New Testament economy in respect of Sabbath observance. For, recognizing to the fullest extent the discontinuance of certain regulatory provisions in the jurisprudence of Israel under the law of Moses, we may still ask quite insistently: What has this to do with the strictness of observance?

The force of this question can be made more obvious if we think of the regulatory provisions of the Mosaic law governing the observance of other commandments of the decalogue. There were regulations in connection with the other commandments, regulations which we have no warrant to believe apply to us under the New Testament. For example, in respect of the fifth commandment it was provided that the man who cursed father or mother was to be put to death (Exod. 21:17; Lev. 20:9). In respect of the seventh it was provided that the adulterer and the adulteress were to be put to death (Lev. 20:10). Now, however grievous these sins are, we do not believe that the sanction by which they were punished under the Mosaic law is applicable under the New Testament. Such provisions of the Mosaic law are so closely bound up with an economy which has passed away as to its observance, that we could hold to the continuance of these provisions no more than we could hold to the continuance of the Mosaic economy itself.

And so we come to the real point at issue: may it be said that we are free to observe less strictly the fifth and seventh commandments? The abolition of certain Mosaic provisions guarding and promoting the sanctity of these two commandments we must recognize. But has the sanctity of these commandments been in any way revoked or the strictness with which we observe them relaxed? The very thought is, of course, revolting. And every enlightened mind and tender conscience recoils from the suggestion. The fact is that the sanctity of these commandments is more clearly revealed and enforced in the New Testament than in the Old, and the depth and breadth of their application made more apparent. Is this not the burden of the Sermon on the Mount? And this is just another way of saying that the demands of strictness in the observance of these commandments are made more potent than they are in the Old. It is because this is the case, because the revelation of the sanctity of the commandments is more abundant and the illumining and sanctifying operations of the Holy Spirit more profuse, that the regulations guarding and promoting the observance of these commandments under the Old Testament have been abrogated. Hence the abolition of these regulations is coincident with the deeper understanding of the sanctity of the commandments. It is this same line of thought that must also be applied to the fourth commandment. Abolition of certain Mosaic regulations? Yes! But this in no way affects the sanctity of the commandment nor the strictness of observance that is the complement of that sanctity.

And so it is to confuse the question at issue to speak of observance under the present economy as less strict than under the Old. As in the case of the other commandments, it is the fulness of New Testament revelation and redemptive accomplishment that serves to confirm the sanctity of the Sabbath institution and the strictness of observance demanded of us. The only way whereby the logic of this conclusion could be controverted is by driving a wedge of sharp discrimination between the fourth commandment and the other nine. And this is a position which the proponents of less strict observance have not been successful in proving.

Sometimes appeal is made to what Jesus said on one occasion, 'It is lawful to do well on the sabbath days' (Matt. 12:12), and these words of our Lord are interpreted to mean that it is lawful to do on the Sabbath days everything that it is lawful or well for man to do. If that were the case, then it would be lawful to do on the Sabbath everything that man might lawfully do at any time, and there would be no necessary distinction between the activities on the day of rest and the activities of the six days of labour.

This word of Jesus was spoken in a context, and the context always determines the meaning of what is said. Jesus was vindicating and defending the doing of certain things on the Sabbath day. If we examine the context we shall find that the works defended and approved by him are not works of every conceivable kind; they are works which fall into certain categories. These categories are indeed very instructive—they are the categories of piety, necessity, and mercy. A work of piety, that is, work connected with the worship of the sanctuary, is in view when he says, 'Or have ye not read in the law, how that on the sabbath days the priests in the temple profane the sabbath, and are blameless?' (Matt. 12:5). A work of necessity is referred to when he says, 'Have ye not read what David did, when he was an hungred, and they that were with him; how he entered into the house of God, and did eat the shewbread, which was not lawful for him to eat, neither for them which were with him, but only for the priests?' (Matt. 12:3, 4). That is to say, dire necessity warranted the doing of something which under normal conditions would have been a culpable violation of divine prescription and restriction. And a work of mercy is in view when he says, 'What man shall there be among you, that shall have one sheep, and if it fall into a pit on the sabbath day, will he not lay hold on it, and lift it out?' (Matt. 12:11). It is this service of mercy which Jesus then in the most conspicuous way exemplified when he said to the man with the withered hand, 'Stretch forth thine hand. And he stretched it forth; and it was restored whole like as the other' (Matt. 12:13). It is in reference to such works of piety, necessity, and mercy that Jesus says, 'Wherefore it is lawful to do well on the sabbath days?', and, more specifically, it is in reference to the work of mercy illustrated by drawing a sheep out of a pit, and exemplified in the concrete situation by his own miracle of healing the man with the withered hand.

The occasion upon which Jesus spoke all these words was the criticism which the Pharisees brought against the disciples for satisfying their hunger by eating from the standing grain on the sabbath day. Jesus defended his disciples against this censoriousness, which arose, not from insight into the design of the Sabbath, but from the sophistry by which rabbinical tradition had perverted the Sabbath institution and had turned it into an instrument of oppression and hypocrisy.

It is true that we must guard against the encroachments which proceed from pharisaical imposition. This is self-righteousness and will-worship. It completely frustrates the divine design. The Sabbath was made for man and not man for the Sabbath. When we encumber the institutions of God with the accretions of our own invention we not only pervert his law but we impugn his wisdom and usurp his authority. We make ourselves lawgivers and forget that there is only one lawgiver. Not only the wisdom but the holiness of God is reflected in what he has not required, as well as in what he actually demands. If we add to his law then we suppose ourselves to be better and wiser than God. And that is the essence of impiety and lawlessness.

We must not, however, fall into the snare of libertinism because we want to avoid the charybdis of pharisaism. The opponents of Sabbath observance and of its complementary restrictions like to peddle the charge of pharisaism when efforts are made to preserve the Sabbath from desecration and to maintain its sanctity. We should not be disturbed by this type of vilification. Why should insistence upon Sabbath observance be pharisaical or legalistic? The question is: is it a divine ordinance? If it is, then adherence to it is not legalistic any more than adherence to the other commandments of God. Are we to be charged with legalism if we are meticulously honest? If we are jealous not to deprive our neighbour unjustly of one penny which is his, and are therefore meticulous in the details of money transactions, are we necessarily legalistic? Our Christianity is not worth much if we can knowingly and deliberately deprive our neighbour of one penny that belongs to him and not to us. Are we to be charged with legalism if we are scrupulously chaste and condemn the very suggestions or gesture of lewdness? How distorted our conception of the Christian ethic and of the demands of holiness has become if we associate concern for the details of integrity with pharisaism and legalism! 'He that is faithful in that which is least is faithful also in much: and he that is unjust in the least is unjust also in much' (Luke 16:10). Why then should insistence upon Sabbath observance be legalism and pharisaism? This charge can appear plausible only because our consciences have become insensitive to the demands of the sanctity which the ordinance entails. The charge really springs from failure to understand what is the liberty of the Christian man. The law of God is the royal law of liberty and liberty consists in being captive to the Word and law of God. All other liberty is not liberty but the thraldom of servitude to sin.

The law of God is summarily comprehended in the ten commandments. Underlying each commandment is a sanctity. Underlying the first is the sanctity of the being of God—there is none other but he. Underlying the second is the sanctity of the worship of God—he may be worshipped only in a way that is consonant with his spirituality and his holiness, and therefore only in the way which he has himself prescribed. Underlying the third is the sanctity of the name of God—the name of God expresses his glory and reverence for his being must carry with it reverence for his name. Underlying the fifth commandment is the sanctity of the parental relation, underlying the sixth the sanctity of life, underlying the seventh the sanctity of the source of life or of the instruments for the propagation of life, underlying the eighth the sanctity of property, underlying the ninth the sanctity of truth, underlying the tenth the sanctity of individual possession.

What then is the sanctity underlying the fourth commandment? It is the sanctity of every recurring seventh day as the day of rest to the Lord. Co-ordinate with this is also the sanctity of six days of labour and therefore the sanctity of the institution of labour. But the main emphasis rests upon the sanctity of each recurring seventh day. 'Remember the sabbath day to keep it holy.' It is not the sanctity simply of the seventh part of our time. That could be done in a variety of ways. It is the sanctity of each seventh day. And so the sanctity of the cycle and the sequence implied in the division of time into weeks is recognized and confirmed.

This ordinance rests upon the divine example. The cycle and sequence established for man in the division of time into weeks rests upon the sequence which God followed in the work of creation. We may speak of the Sabbath as the memorial of God's rest, the rest of delight and satisfaction in work accomplished. 'And God saw everything that he had made, and, behold, it was very good' (Gen. 1:31). In the Christian economy the Sabbath is the Lord's Day and therefore the memorial of the completion of a work of God greater than that of creation. It is the memorial of redemption completed by the resurrection of our Lord from the dead. It is altogether appropriate that the recurring seventh day of rest should now memorialize the rest from the labour involved in the working out of redemption upon which our Lord and Redeemer entered when he was raised from the dead by the exceeding greatness of the power of God.

But the Sabbath is not only a memorial of creation completed and redemption accomplished; it is also the promise of a glorious prospect, the foretaste of the Sabbath rest that remains for the people of God. It is the prospect of the grand finale to the whole of history, the Sabbath rest that is the promised sequel to the sum total of the toils and labours of history. 'We, according to his promise, look for new heavens and a new earth, wherein dwelleth righteousness' (2 Pet. 3:13). 'There remaineth therefore a sabbath-keeping for the people of God' (Heb. 4:9). The weekly Sabbath in the divinely established sequences of temporal history is the constant reminder to us of the beginning and the end. And for the people of God it is the foretaste of that eternal rest which was secured by redemption once for all accomplished and will be dispensed in redemption consummated. The perpetual relevance of the weekly Sabbath resides in the divine plan of history and of destiny, and with its perpetual relevance goes its perpetual obligation. Is it superfluous to be reminded of the words of the prophet? 'If thou turn away thy foot from the sabbath, from doing thy pleasure on my holy day; and call the sabbath a delight, the holy of the Lord, honourable; and shalt honour him, not doing thine own ways, nor finding thine own pleasure, nor speaking thine own words: then shalt thou delight thyself in the Lord; and I will cause thee to ride upon the high places of the earth, and feed thee with the heritage of Jacob thy father: for the mouth of the Lord hath spoken it' (Isa. 58:13, 14).

SELECT BIBLIOGRAPHY ON THE SABBATH

James Gilfillan: *The Sabbath Viewed in the Light of Reason, Revelation, and History*, 1861.

Daniel Wilson: *The Divine Authority and Perpetual Obligation of the Lord's Day*, 1830

A. E. Waffle: *The Lord's Day: its Universal and Perpetual Obligation*, 1885.

Thomas Torrens: *The Lord's Day Observance*, 1906.

Robert Cox: *Sabbath Laws and Sabbath Duties*, 1853.

Wilbur F. Crafts: *The Sabbath for Man*, 1885.

R. L. Dabney: *The Christian Sabbath*, 1882.

William B. Dana: *The Day for Rest and Worship*, 1911.

Norman C. Deck: *The Lord's Day or, The Sabbath: A Reply to the Seventh Day Adventists, c.* 1930

Eight Studies of the Lord's Day, 1885. (Author not given).

George Elliott: *The Abiding Sabbath*, 1884.

Paul Cotton: *From Sabbath to Sunday*, 1933.

John Holmes Agnew: *A Manual of the Christian Sabbath*, 1832.

L. W. Bacon & G. B. Bacon: *The Sabbath Question*, 1882.

James Orr: *The Sabbath*, 1886.

James A. Hessey: *Sunday: its Origin, History, and Present Obligation*, Bampton Lectures, 1860.

George Junkin: *Sabbatismos. A Discussion and Defence of the Lord's Day of Sacred Rest*, 1866.

R. H. Martin: *The Day. A Manual on the Christian Sabbath*, 1933.

James Macgregor: *The Sabbath Question, Historical, Scriptural, and Practical*, 1866.

G. A. Main: *The Sabbath in Divine Revelation and Human History*, 1928, (Seventh Day).

W. B. Trevelyan: *Sunday*, 1902.

Will C. Wood *ed.*: *Sabbath Essays*, 1880.

Samuel Walter Gamble: *Sunday, The True Sabbath of God*, 1900.

J. N. Andrews: *History of the Sabbath and First Day of the Week*, 1873.

Harmon Kingsbury: *The Sabbath: a Brief History of Laws, Petitions, Remonstrances and Reports etc.*, 1840.

J. D. Parker: *The Sabbath Transferred*, 1902.

William Milligan: *The Decalogue and the Lord's Day*, 1866.

Morris Fuller: *The Lord's Day or Christian Sunday: its Unity, History, Philosophy, and Perpetual Obligation*, 1883.

Micaiah Hill: *The Sabbath Made for Man: or, The Origin, History, and Principles of the Lord's Day*, 1857.

29

The Pattern of the Lord's Day[1]

IF we accept the witness of Scripture there can be no question that the weekly Sabbath finds its basis in and derives its sanction from the example of God himself. He created the heavens and the earth in six days and 'on the seventh day God ended his work which he had made; and he rested on the seventh day from all his work which he had made. And God blessed the seventh day, and sanctified it' (Gen. 2:2, 3). The fourth commandment in the decalogue sets forth the obligation resting upon man and it makes express appeal to this sanction. 'For in six days the Lord made heaven and earth, the sea, and all that in them is, and rested the seventh day: wherefore the Lord blessed the sabbath day, and hallowed it' (Exod. 20:11).

Many regard this sabbath institution as a shadow of things that were to come and, therefore, as an ordinance to be observed, it has passed away, because that of which it was a shadow has been realized in the full light of the new and better covenant. At this point suffice it to ask the question: Has the pattern of God's work and rest in creation ceased to be relevant? Is this pattern a *shadow* in the sense of those who espouse this position? The realm of our existence is that established by creation and maintained by God's providence. The new covenant has in no respect abrogated creation nor has it diminished its relevance. Creation both as action and product is as significant for us as it was for Israel under the old covenant. The refrain of Scripture in both Testaments is that the God of creation is the God of redemption in all stages of covenantal

[1] An address given at a meeting of the Lord's Day Observance Society and subsequently published by the Society.

disclosure and realization. This consideration is invested with greater significance when we bear in mind that the ultimate standard for us is likeness to God (cf. Matt. 5:48; 1 John 3:2, 3). And it is this likeness, in the sphere of our behaviour, that undergirds the demand for sabbath observance (Exod. 20:11; 31:17).

It is noteworthy that the sabbath commandment as given in Deuteronomy (Deut. 5:12–15) does not appeal to God's rest in creation as the reason for keeping the sabbath day. In this instance mention is made of something else. 'And remember that thou wast a servant in the land of Egypt, and that the Lord thy God brought thee out thence through a mighty hand and by a stretched out arm: therefore the Lord thy God commanded thee to keep the sabbath day' (Deut. 5:15). This cannot be understood as in any way annulling the sanction of Exodus 20:11; 31:17. Deuteronomy comprises what was the reiteration of the covenant made at Sinai. When the sabbath commandment is introduced Israel is reminded of the earlier promulgation: 'Keep the sabbath day to sanctify it, as the Lord thy God hath commanded thee' (Deut. 5:12). And we should observe that all the commandments have their redemptive sanction. The preface to all is: 'I am the Lord thy God which have brought thee out of the land of Egypt, out of the house of bondage' (Exod. 20:2; cf. Deut. 5:6). So what we find in Deuteronomy 5:15 in connection with the Sabbath is but the application of the preface to the specific duty enunciated in the fourth command. It is supplement to Exodus 20:11, not suspension. We have now an added reason for observing the Sabbath. This is full of meaning and we must linger to analyse and appreciate.

The deliverance from Egypt was redemption. 'Thou in thy mercy hast led forth the people which thou hast redeemed' (Exod. 15:13). It is more than any other event the redemption of the Old Testament. It is the analogue of the greater redemption accomplished by Christ. The sabbath commandment derives its sanction not only from God's rest in creation but also from redemption out of Egypt's bondage. This fact, that the Sabbath in Israel had a redemptive reference and sanction, bears directly upon the question of its relevance in the New Testament. The redemption from Egypt cannot be properly viewed except as the anticipation of the greater redemption wrought in the fulness of the time. Hence, if redemption from Egypt accorded sanction to the sabbath institution and provided reason for its observance, the same must apply to the greater redemption and apply in a way commensurate with the greater fulness and dimensions of the redemption secured by the death and resurrection of Christ. In other words, it is the fulness and richness of the new covenant that accord to the sabbath ordinance increased relevance, sanction, and blessing.

This redemptive reference explains and confirms three features of the New Testament.

I. THE RETROSPECTIVE REFERENCE

Jesus rose from the dead on the first day of the week (cf. Matt. 28:1; Mark 16:2, 9; Luke 24:1; John 20:1). For our present interest the important feature of the New Testament witness is that the first day of the week continued to have *distinctive religious significance* (cf. Acts 20:7; I Cor. 16:2). The only explanation of this fact is that the first day was the day of Jesus' resurrection and for that reason John calls it 'the Lord's day' (Rev. 1:10). The first day took on a memorial significance appropriate to the place the resurrection of Christ occupies in the accomplishment of redemption and in Jesus' *finished* work (cf. John 17:4), as also appropriate to the seal imparted by the repeated appearance to his disciples on that day (cf. Matt. 28:9; Luke 24:15–31, 36; John 20:19, 26). When Christ rose from the dead he was loosed from the pangs of death (cf. Acts 2:24), he entered upon life indestructible (cf. Rom. 5:10; 6:9, 10), became 'life-giving Spirit' (I Cor. 15:45), and brought 'life and immortality to light' (2 Tim. 1:10). In a word, he entered upon the rest of his redeeming work. All of this and much more resides in the emphasis which falls upon the resurrection as a pivotal event in the accomplishment of redemption. The other pivot is the death upon the cross. The sanctity belonging to the first day of the week as the Lord's day is the constant reminder of all that Jesus' resurrection involves. It is the memorial of the resurrection as the Lord's supper is of Jesus' death upon the tree. Inescapable, therefore, is the conclusion that the resurrection in its redemptive character yields its sanction to the sacredness of the first day of the week, just as deliverance from Egypt's bondage accorded its sanction to the sabbath institution of the old covenant. This is the rationale for regarding the Lord's day as the Christian Sabbath. It follows the line of thought which the Old Testament itself prescribes for us when it appeals to redemption as the reason for sabbath observance. The principle enunciated in Deuteronomy 5:15 receives its verification and application in the new covenant in the memorial of finalized redemption, the Lord's day.

II.   THE MANWARD REFERENCE

Under this caption we have in mind our Lord's saying: 'The sabbath was made for man, and not man for the sabbath: therefore the Son of man is Lord also of the sabbath' (Mark 2:27, 28).

The title our Lord uses to designate himself is one that belongs to him in his messianic identity, commission, and office. The lordship he claims is, therefore, redemptively conditioned; it is his lordship as Mediator and Saviour. As such, in accord with his own testimony, he is given all authority in heaven and earth (cf. John 3:35; Matt. 28:18). So every institution is brought within the scope of his lordship. Since he exercises this lordship in the interests of God's redemptive purpose, it is particularly true that institutions given for the good of man are brought within the scope of his lordship and made to serve the interests of the supreme good which redemption designs and guarantees. It is this governing thought that is applied in the text to the institution of the Sabbath. The accent falls upon the beneficent design of the Sabbath—it was made for man. 'Therefore the Son of man is Lord' of it.

When Jesus speaks of the *Sabbath*, he is specifying the institution defined by the fourth commandment, and he asserts his lordship over it in that precise character. There is not the slightest intimation of abrogation. For it is the Sabbath in that identity over which he claims to be Lord. Too frequently this text is adduced in support of an alleged relaxation of the requirements set forth in the commandment, as if Jesus on this ground were, in the exercise of his authority, defending his disciples for behaviour that went counter to Old Testament requirements. This totally misconstrues the situation in which the words were spoken. Jesus is defending his disciples against the charge of desecration brought by the Pharisees (cf. Mark 2:24). But in doing so he shows by appeal to the Old Testament itself (cf. Matt. 12:4, 5; Mark 2:25, 26) that the behaviour of the disciples was in accord with what the Old Testament sanctioned. It was not deviation from Old Testament requirements that our Lord was condoning, but deviation from pharisaical distortion. He was condemning the tyranny by which the sabbath institution had been made an instrument of oppression. And he did this by appeal to the true intent of the Sabbath as verified by Scripture itself.

Of special interest is the relation of the redemptive sanction of the fourth commandment to the claim of Jesus on this occasion. The lordship over the Sabbath is, as observed, redemptively conditioned and thus only within a redemptive design can his lordship of the Sabbath be understood. This is to say that the sabbath ordinance in its beneficent character comes to full expression within the realm of our Lord's mediatorial lordship. The Sabbath is not alien to redemption at the zenith of its realization and blessing. As made for man it continues to serve its great purpose in that administration that achieves the acme of covenantal grace. This Jesus' word seals to us—'the Son of man is Lord also of the sabbath'.

III.   THE PROSPECTIVE REFERENCE

'There remains therefore a sabbath-keeping for the people of God' (Heb. 4:9).

The context of this passage is all-important for its interpretation and for appreciation of its implications. At verse 4 there is quotation of Genesis 2:2: 'And God rested on the seventh day from all his works'. This, of course, refers to God's *own* rest. At verse 5 there is allusion to the rest of Canaan and quotation of Psalm 95:11 (cf. also vs. 3 and 3:11) in reference to the failure of too many to enter into it (cf. Psalm 95:10). The remarkable feature of verse 5, as of Psalm 95:11, is that this rest of Canaan is called God's rest ('my rest'). Why this characterization? It is not sufficient to say that it was the rest God provided. The proximity of reference to God's own rest in verse 4 requires more than the thought of mere provision by God. We cannot say less than that God calls it his rest because the rest of Canaan was patterned after God's rest—it partook of the character of God's rest. The same kind of identification appears in verse 10 with reference to the rest that remains for the people of God. 'For he that has entered into his rest, he also has ceased from his own works, as God did from his.' So the rest of Canaan and the rest that remains for the people of God are called God's rest because both partake of the character of God's own rest in resting from his creative work on the seventh day. Here is something highly germane to the present topic.

It is clear that the rest of Canaan and the rest that remains for the people of God are redemptive in character. Since they are patterned after God's rest in creation, this means that the redemptive takes on the character of that rest of God upon which the sabbath institution for man originally rested and from which it derived its sanction. We cannot but discover in this again the close relation between the creative and the redemptive in the sabbath ordinance and the coherence of Exodus 20:11 and Deuteronomy 5:15. We are reminded again that likeness to God governs man's obligation and is brought to its realization in the provisions of redemption. In the consummation of redemption the sabbath rest of God's people achieves conformity to the fullest extent. 'For he who has entered into his rest, he also has ceased from his own works, as God did from his' (cf. Rev. 14:13). The sabbath institution in all its aspects and application has this prospective reference; the whole movement of redemption will find its finale in the sabbath rest that remains. The weekly Sabbath is the promise, token, and foretaste of the consummated rest; it is also the earnest. The biblical philosophy of the Sabbath is such that to deny its perpetuity is to deprive the movement of redemption of one of its most precious strands.

Redemption has a past, a present, and a future. In the Sabbath as 'the Lord's day' all three are focused. In retrospect it is the memorial of our Lord's resurrection. In the present, with resurrection joy it fulfils its beneficent design by the lordship of the Son of man. As prospect, it is the promise of the inheritance of the saints. With varying degrees of understanding and application it is this perspective that dictated the observance of the Lord's day in Catholic, Protestant, and Reformed tradition. Shall we forfeit an institution so embedded in redemptive revelation and recognized as such in the history of the church of Christ? In the faith and for the honour of the Sabbath's Lord may we answer with a decisive, no! In devotion to him may we increasingly know the joy and blessing of the recurring day of rest and worship.

30

The Relevance of the Sabbath[1]

THE relevance of the fourth commandment is to be considered in respect of unbelievers and believers.

I. UNBELIEVERS

It is sometimes alleged that it is irrelevant, useless, and even improper to plead with unbelievers the obligation of Sabbath observance. This argument can be made very plausible. What is the use, it is claimed, of speaking of Sabbath observance to those who do not recognize God's claims upon them, who do not acknowledge the authority of God's Word, and have no commitment to Christ as Lord? In the indifference and ignorance so widespread, in the scorn so rampant respecting God's claims, we know only too well the reactions, sometimes of dismay, sometimes of rude hostility, sometimes of blank bewilderment, when we confront desecrators with the divine obligation and sanctions. And so it is easy to relieve ourselves of the unpleasant duty by pleading the futility and saying 'What's the use?'

It must be admitted that, in dealing with unbelievers and desecrators, much more is necessary than to plead the obligations of the Sabbath; and it is true that if this plea is isolated from the fundamental demands of the gospel grave misconception may be created and our witness greatly distorted.

The plea that it is wrong to urge Sabbath observance on unbelievers is invalid for several reasons:

1. Are we to say that it is improper or irrelevant to confront unbelievers

1 Taken from unpublished notes.

with the law of God, with the sin of transgression, and with the wages that accrue? Consider, in this connection, the other commandments. The argument rests upon the fallacy that the fourth commandment is in a different category, a fallacy that we may not theoretically profess but to which we have practically or indeed pragmatically succumbed.

2. By the law is the knowledge of sin. And once we recognize the fact of the Sabbath law the conviction of sin can come through this command. So the conviction which is the vestibule of faith may be induced in connection with the sin. Hence we are doing a great disservice to the gospel and to the souls of men when we exclude Sabbath desecration from the scope of reproof and condemnation.

Failure to observe the Sabbath law is a conspicuous manifestation of dispute with the authority and goodness of God.

3. Sustained emphasis upon the necessity of Sabbath observance, like emphasis upon other ordinances of God, is a restraining influence that prevents unbelievers from multiplying the transgression that reaps the judgment of God and accentuates the hardening in sin and insensitivity to the demands of God. It is both callous and cruel to allow men to go unchecked in the trespass that reaps damnation.

4. The observances which the Sabbath law enjoins are means of grace and therefore channels of salvation. Jealousy for the eternal interests of men will constrain us to plead with the ungodly that they cultivate these observances, to the end that being in Christ's way they may meet with Christ and become the partakers of his grace. While rightly placing in the forefront the obligations of the Sabbath ordinance, we must also remind men of its privileges, and appeal to all men, that only at the cost of everlasting peril may these privileges be ignored and trodden under foot.

5. The outward observance of the Sabbath promotes public order and makes for the preservation of our most cherished rights and liberties. Unrestrained violation of the commandments of God destroys the peace without which the social order and political order are impossible.

These reasons make the plea with which we are dealing not only fallacious but iniquitous, and shows how alien it is to the principles which govern the witness of the Church of Christ. It is not that we may be disposed to a theoretical espousal or defence of the argument in question. But we may be the victims of a way of thinking and practice that we do not overtly or theoretically profess.

II. BELIEVERS

When I speak of believers I have in mind all who entertain respect for the Sabbath institution and are characterized by observances in accord with its sanctity. There are several observations—

1. Sabbath observance is relevant only in the context of the whole counsel of God and of the sum total of Christian devotion. It is possible to make Sabbath-keeping, that is, abstinence from overt forms of desecration and attendance upon the exercises of worship, an instrument of the self-righteousness that is the arch-enemy of the Christian faith. This possibility is, I fear, too frequently an actuality. There are people who think that by these 'righteousnesses' they expect special favour from God and their religion consists to a large extent in these abstinences and exercises. They come under the indictment of God to Israel: 'Your new moons and your appointed feasts my soul hateth: they are a trouble unto me; I am weary to bear them' (Isa. 1:14). The Sabbath commandment must never be isolated from the law of God in its entirety, or from the gospel of redeeming, regenerating, and sanctifying grace. This is most relevantly pointed up in the Sabbath of the New Testament economy. It is the Lord's day, the memorial of Christ's resurrection, and if our Sabbaths are not sanctified by the recognition that the Son of man is Lord of the Sabbath, and by devotion to him as the Lord over all, then, however meticulous may be our abstinences and observances, they do not constitute Sabbath observance. They are an abomination to the Lord. The devoted Christian will be meticulous in abstinence and observance, but in the faith of, love to, and hope in, the Lord and Saviour Jesus Christ; and will be in accord with the Saviour's word: 'If ye love me, keep my commandments'.

2. The relevance of the Sabbath in respect of positive requirement. Even for believers there is the danger of negativism in the weariness of inactivity. The rest of the Sabbath is not idleness; it is activity in the sacred exercises of meditation, contemplation, and prayer. If we have this interest there is not a moment for weariness or boredom. The Sabbath day is not one minute too long for us. Is that not the Lord's

witness to the people of old, and even more relevantly to us? 'Call the sabbath a delight, the holy of the Lord, honourable . . . Then shalt thou delight thyself in the Lord' (Isa. 58:13, 14). God's own rest is not that of idleness or inactivity. It is that of joy and satisfaction in the works he has wrought. So must ours be.

If the Sabbath is the Lord's day, it ought to be suffused with the joy derived from and correspondent with the resurrection joy of the Lord. We should never fail to appreciate our Lord's own resurrection joy. Jesus came trailing the clouds of humiliation. We think of Gethsemane with its agonizing confession, its prayer of holy revulsion, and its bloody sweat; of Calvary with its cry of abandonment. Here are the lowest depths of humiliation, of incomparable agony. But then there is the sequel of resurrection exultation. 'Who for the joy that was set before him endured the cross . . . and is set down at the right hand of the throne of God' (Heb. 12:2). 'Ought not Christ to have suffered these things, and to enter into his glory?' (Luke 24:26). It is a morning without clouds, the morning of triumph, and therefore of triumphant joy. In this joy ours is begotten (cf. 1 Pet. 1:3).

Those jealous for the sanctity of the Lord's day are often accused of making or seeking to make the day one of gloom. There are two remarks respecting this charge. First, it is true that the observance has too frequently been conspicuously defective in respect of the joy that the day as the memorial of the resurrection should evoke. Why is it that so many in this category find the Sabbath a burden? Is it not because they know not the power and the joy of the resurrection? But, second, those who make the accusation confuse joy with jollity and jollification. The joy of which we are speaking now is a solemn, holy joy, and as such is a triumphant joy, filled with the raptures of adoration and praise. It stands in contrast with cold, hypocritical formalism and with secular jollity.

'This is the day that the Lord has made: we will rejoice and be glad in it' (Psa. 118:24).

The Church

31

The Church: Its Definition in Terms of 'Visible' and 'Invisible' Invalid

It has been common to make a sharp distinction between the church visible and the church invisible and with this distinction to apply definitions by which the differentiation can be maintained. This position calls for examination in the light of Scripture.

It may not be improper to speak of the church as characterized by attributes that are invisible or, in other words, to say that the church has invisible aspects. Various considerations readily come to mind. Only God knows completely and infallibly those who are his, those pre-destined to salvation and ultimately conformed to the image of his Son. The church cannot make a census of the elect nor of the regenerate. Again, the actions of God by which men are made members of the body of Christ are of such a character that they are imperceptible to men. The *fruits* are perceptible, but the actions are in the realm of the heart and spirit of man. We think, for example, of calling and regeneration. Furthermore, the people of God are so widely dispersed throughout the world that no person can bring the whole church, existing at even one time, within his purview. And then, who of men can know the whole company of 'the spirits of just men made perfect'? So from many angles our human limitations have to be recognized and these may be expressed by speaking of the church as invisible. At least the term 'invisible' has been used to draw attention to these obvious facts.

However, two reservations have to be made. The first is a question as to the felicity or even propriety of the term 'invisible' to give ex-pression to such considerations. There are liabilities that can be avoided if other terms are employed. The second is more than reservation. The distinction between the church visible and the church invisible is not well-grounded in terms of Scripture, and the abuses to which the distinction has been subjected require correction.

A rapid survey of New Testament usage will show how frequently the term 'church' designates what is visible. The church is the assembly or fellowship of the people of God, constituted by the call of God, a people formed for himself to show forth his praise and to bear witness to him in the performance of prescribed functions. The two instances in which our Lord used the term (Matt. 16:18; 18:17) make this clear. When Christ said to Peter: 'Upon this rock I will build my church', the investiture of the succeeding verse shows that the church is something to be administered upon earth. It is not an invisible entity but one in which ministry is exercised. And when in the execution of discipline, Jesus says: 'Tell it to the church' (Matt. 18:17), the church must be conceived of as the congregation to which information is to be conveyed.

As the copious evidence provided by the rest of the New Testament is examined we find this concept of the church exemplified again and again. We read of the church in Jerusalem and Antioch (Acts 8:1; 11:22; 11:26; 13:1; 15:3, 4, 22), the church at Ephesus (Acts 20:17, 28), the church at Corinth (1 Cor. 1:2; 2 Cor. 1:1), the church of the Thessalonians (1 Thess. 1:1), and even the church in a particular house (Rom. 16:5; 1 Cor. 16:19; Col. 4:15; Philem. 2). There is, obviously, in each case, reference to a group of believers united in the faith and fellowship of Christ, in a word, a congregation of the faithful. We should naturally expect that the New Testament would speak, therefore, of the *churches* of Christ. This is what we find repeatedly (cf. Acts 15:41; 16:5; Rom. 16:4; 1 Cor. 4:17; 7:17; 14:33, 34; 16:1; 2 Cor. 8:1; 11:8, 28; Gal. 1:21, 22; 1 Thess. 2:14; Rev. 1:4, 20; 2:7). Concrete as well as discrete visibility is involved. In several of these instances the plural is used to denote all the churches in a geographical area or even throughout the world. The latter is particularly apparent in the expression 'all the churches' (cf. Rom. 16:16; 1 Cor. 14:33; 2 Cor. 11:28) but it is implied in instances where 'all' does not occur (cf. 1 Cor. 11:16; 14:34). This means that the church universal, the church throughout the world, is not to be thought of apart from the particular components that make up the church universal, and, therefore, not apart from the visibility characterizing these components.

The question arises at this point: is there warrant for the use of the term 'church' in the singular to designate the 'churches' in their collective unity? The answer must be in the affirmative. It may be that in Acts 8:3—'Saul made havoc of the church'—the reference is to the church at Jerusalem (cf. 8:1) but, in view of his project to go to Damascus (cf. 9:1, 2), it is likely that 'the church' is considered more extensively. There can, however, be no question about the inclusive use in Acts 9:31. 'The church' refers to the whole of Judea and Samaria and Galilee and, therefore, to the *churches* in these provinces (cf. Gal. 1:22). And when Paul says that 'he persecuted the church of God' (Gal. 1:13; cf. Phil. 3:6) it is scarcely possible to think of the church restrictively. The generic reference of the term is patent in 1 Corinthians 12:28 (cf. Eph. 4:11, 12). The various offices and gifts specified cannot be contemplated as bestowed on anything less than the church universal, comprising all the churches of the saints. The parallel passage cited from Ephesians 4 speaks of the perfecting of the saints and the edification of the body of Christ and these must be considered inclusively. Then again, when Paul writes to Timothy and gives him instruction as to behaviour 'in the church of the living God, the pillar and ground of the truth' (1 Tim. 3:15), it is not simply to a particular church that this behaviour is relevant or the predications applicable, but to the whole church and, therefore, to all the churches of God, in this case called 'the church of the living God'.

It is particularly in the Epistle to the Ephesians that this generic and embracive use of the term 'church' appears. No restriction can apply to such propositions as these: God gave Christ 'to be head over all things to the church' (1:22), 'Christ is the head of the church' (5:23), 'Christ loved the church and gave himself for it' (5:25; cf. 3:10, 21; 5:24, 27, 29, 32; Col. 1:18, 24). These propositions indeed apply to each fellowship of the saints in its own individuality and they cannot have relevance in abstraction from the concrete manifestations of the body of Christ. But the fact is indisputable that to all collectively is applied the designation 'the church', and the whole company is considered in the broadest perspectives of Christ's design and accomplishment.

It might seem that in these latter passages the 'church invisible' is in view and that only to the church as such can the various properties belong. With reference to this inference there are several considerations:

1. Beyond doubt the reference in the term 'church' extends beyond the confines of this age and has its outreach to the age to come (cf. Eph. 3:21; 5:27). The church glorified is contemplated. But when this age gives place to the age to come and the whole body of Christ is perfected, we may not think of the church as invisible. It will be consummated in visibility.

2. Paul's doxology: 'To him be glory in the church and in Christ Jesus' (Eph. 3:21) cannot be regarded as having exclusive reference to the church as glorified; the church of which Paul speaks in 1 Corinthians 12:28 (cf. Eph. 1:22; 4:11) surely comes within the scope of that within which glory redounds to God.

3. When Paul affirms, 'Christ is the head of the church' (Eph. 5:23; cf. vs. 22; 1:22; Col. 1:18), this must apply to the church as administered upon earth, of which the apostle speaks elsewhere (cf. 2 Cor. 11:28; Eph. 4:11), and of which our Lord himself spoke (Matt. 16:18; 18:17).

4. The church as visible is subject to Christ (Eph. 5:24) and cannot be excluded from his dominion. The nourishing and cherishing that Christ imparts (Eph. 5:29) are activities wrought in the church visible by which it is maintained in accord with Christ's promise.

5. The church as an organized institution, endowed with the ministries of Christ's appointment, cannot be excluded from that through which *now* is made known to the principalities and powers in the heavenly places the manifold wisdom of God (Eph. 3:10).

These considerations suffice to show that it is impossible to dissociate the church visible from the relevance and application of the various propositions in these contexts. Hence, even in those passages in which the concept of the 'church invisible' might appear to be present, the case is rather that there is no evidence for the notion of the 'church' as an invisible entity distinct from the church visible. As noted earlier, there are those aspects pertaining to the church that may be characterized as invisible. But it is to 'the church' those aspects pertain, and 'the church' in the New Testament never appears as an invisible entity and therefore may never be *defined* in terms of invisibility. This is why, at an earlier point, the advisability of the use of the actual term 'invisible' has been questioned. It is a term that is liable to be loaded with the misconceptions inherent in the concept 'invisible church', and tends to support the abuses incident thereto. Other terms can more appropriately and safely be used to express these various aspects or attributes which have been characterized as invisible.

The thesis propounded is of deep practical significance. In our situation we have to contend with lamentable decline from the truth of the gospel and the institution of Christ within erstwhile Protestant denominations. For those within these denominations who are jealous for the gospel the responsibility becomes greatly accentuated. Too often, however, the fact and sense of corporate responsibility are suppressed if not overlooked. Sometimes resort is made to the thought of the 'church invisible'. In the absence of unity and fellowship in the denomination, comfort is derived from the unity and fellowship supposed to exist in the 'church invisible'. It is true that there is unity and fellowship in the body of Christ for all who are united to him, a fellowship that crosses denominational boundaries, and one the privileges and obligations of which are to be fully recognized and cultivated. The appreciation and cultivation of this fellowship, however, devolve upon all believers under all circumstances and cannot be regarded as a resort or substitute under the special conditions now being considered.

With respect to the comfort derived from the idea of the 'church invisible' a few things have to be said. The concept of the 'church invisible' is, to say the least, far too precarious upon which to build for the fulfilment of the obligation incumbent upon us to foster unity and fellowship in the church of God. Suffice it to ask: Where in the New Testament do we find the 'invisible church' as an institution in which we may exercise in any concrete and practical way the fellowship claimed?

When Paul enjoined upon believers all diligence 'to keep the unity of the Spirit in the bond of peace' (Eph. 4:3), he was surely thinking of the relations that obtain within the church in its visible character and expression (cf. Phil. 4:2). This is demonstrated by verse 7, for there the thought is the distribution and diversity of grace in the church. The charge he gives is for harmony in the unity of faith (cf. vs. 5). It should be apparent how alien to this obligation is escape to the idea of the 'church invisible'. It is to desert the practical for an outlet without warrant, and one that fails to provide the means for keeping 'the unity of the Spirit in the bond of peace'.

Strictly speaking, it is not proper to speak of the 'visible church'. According to Scripture we should speak of 'the church' and conceive of it as that visible entity that exists and functions in accord with the institution of Christ as its Head, the church that is the body of Christ indwelt and directed by the Holy Spirit, consisting of those sanctified in Christ Jesus and called to be saints, manifested in the congregations of the faithful, and finally the church glorious, holy and without blemish.

32

The Church: Its Identity, Functions and Resources

WHAT we are doing here this evening would have no propriety if it were not related to and promotive of the interests of the church of God. But what is the church? The building of stone, mortar, wood, or any other construction is not the church, and strictly, should not be identified by that designation. It is only as the place of meeting for the church of God that a building called a 'church building' has any meaning or propriety. The building is the meeting-house, and the church is the assembly, the congregation, the fellowship. So we may consider the three particulars specified in the title.

THE IDENTITY OF THE CHURCH

The church is not a denomination. A particular denomination may be the church and it is proper to say, for example, that the Free Church of Scotland is the church of God. But it may not be said that the church of God is the Free Church of Scotland. It may well be that, in a specified area, the only church of God is the congregation of the Free Church of Scotland. But how presumptuous and preposterous it would be to say that the church of Christ is the Free Church of Scotland! And the basic reason is that the orientation of our thinking would, in that case, be alien to what Scripture defines the church to be.

The church is the assembly of the covenant people of God, the congregation of believers, the household of God, the fellowship of the Holy Spirit, the body of Christ. It consists of men and women called by God the Father into the fellowship of his Son, sanctified in Christ Jesus, regenerated by his Spirit, and united in the faith and confession of

Christ Jesus as Lord and Saviour. Where there is such a communion gathered in Jesus' name, there is the church of God. And all throughout the world answering to this description constitute the church of God universal.

The church is an institution existing by God's action, maintained by his grace, and directed by his Spirit. As it exists by God's action, so it must be conducted in accord with his prescription. Its sphere of operation is defined by God himself and revealed to us in his Word.

It is all-important to bear in mind that the church of God is an institution. It may never be conceived of apart from the organization of the people of God in visible expression and in discharge of the ordinances instituted by Christ.

We are all liable to distortions and misconceptions. In reaction against sacerdotal views of the church, exemplified particularly in the Roman Catholic Church, it is understandable that Protestants should lapse into a depreciation of the place the church does occupy in the institution of Christ. Protest against a distortion of Christian doctrine is liable to engender an extreme in the opposite direction. It is imperative that we avoid any such extreme and, in reference to the church, we must fully appreciate its identity as the body of Christ. No characterization points up the wrong of underesteem more than does this one. We cannot think of Christ properly apart from the church. All the offices he exercises as head over all things, he exercises on behalf of the church. If we think of the church apart from Christ, or transfer to the church prerogatives that belong only to Christ, then we are guilty of idolatry. But if we think of Christ apart from the church, then we are guilty of a dismemberment that severs what God has joined together. We are divorcing Christ from his only bride. The central doctrine of the Christian faith should remind us of the evil of such divorce, for this doctrine is that 'Christ loved the church and gave himself up for it' (Eph. 5:25).

THE FUNCTIONS OF THE CHURCH

Since the church is a divine institution and Christ is its head, the functions are those prescribed by the head of the church and are, therefore, delimited. It is a travesty of the order God has established, for the church to go beyond its own sphere and arrogate prerogatives that are not its own. The temptation to do this ever lurks, and it may seem at times a necessity to fill up the gaps left by negligence on the part of other institutions, more specifically, negligence on the part of the family and the state. For this reason constant vigilance must be exercised to ensure that the church recognizes its province and rigidly adheres to the functions assigned by the head of the church and revealed to us in his Word. What are these functions?

1. *Worship.* It is imperative that this be given priority. When any other function is accorded priority, then the God-centred interest is displaced by the man-centred. Man's chief end is to glorify God. This governs all of life and it is exemplified in the church by the fact that worship is its principal function. The worship now in view is *specific,* and thus distinguished from the generic devotion that should characterize a believer in all his undertakings and commitments. It is also *corporate* and therefore distinct from the acts of specific worship in which individuals engage as individuals. And it is *prescribed* worship, the offering up of spiritual sacrifices and therefore indited and directed by the Holy Spirit. This regulative principle needs to be underlined. 'The acceptable way of worshipping the true God is instituted by himself, and so limited by his own revealed will, that he may not be worshipped according to the imaginations and devices of men, or the suggestions of Satan, under any visible representation, or any other way not prescribed in the Holy Scripture' (*Westminster Conf. of Faith,* XXI, i).

There are two aspects to worship, God's address to us and our response to this address. The former consists particularly in the reading and preaching of the Word, and the latter in adoration, reception, thanksgiving, and prayer.

In worship God is speaking to us. Do we prize this inestimable grace? The reading and preaching of the Word are the voice of God as truly as when the disciples heard the Father's witness to his own Son on the holy mount. The sense of high privilege accorded Peter, James, and John on that occasion is reflected in Peter's words: 'And this voice which came from heaven we heard, when we were with him in the holy mount' (2 Pet. 1:18). But the astounding feature of the apostle's teaching in this instance is the assessment of Scripture: 'We have also a more sure word of prophecy; whereunto ye do well that ye take heed, as unto a light that shineth in a dark place, until the day dawn, and the day star arise in your hearts' (2 Pet. 1:19). Scripture is continuously and abidingly the voice of God to us because, as 'borne by the Holy Spirit, men spake from God' (vs. 21). Our first response should be adoration, and adoration will elicit thanksgiving. Worship will then be characterized by the reverence that consists in a profound sense of the majesty of God, and we shall in our assemblies be constrained to exclaim: 'Surely the Lord is in this place . . . How dreadful is this place! this is none other but the house of God, and this is the gate of heaven' (Gen. 28:16, 17).

Prayer is an integral part of worship. Have we appreciated the efficacy of corporate prayer? We are familiar with Jesus' word: 'Where two or three are gathered together in my name, there am I in the midst of them' (Matt. 18:20). But have we noted the sequence in which this word occurs? Jesus is dealing with united prayer: 'Again, I say unto you, that if two of you shall agree on earth as touching any thing that they shall ask, it shall be done for them of my Father which is in heaven' (vs. 19). The assurance given to those gathered in Jesus' name is for the purpose of confirming the certainty of the Father's grace in fulfilling the requests of prayer offered in the unity of the Spirit and the bond of peace.

2. *Proclamation.* The proclamation in view now is distinct from the preaching of the Word which belongs to the worship of the church. Not all proclamation falls into the specific category of the corporate worship of the church. There are two activities that are particularly necessary to this proclamation.

The first is evangelism. It may not be assumed that the proclamation of the Word in the worship of the church is unevangelistic. All preaching has evangelistic application, and evangelistic emphasis should characterize the ministry of the Word in what is specifically the worship of the church. But there is also the evangelism that is outside and beyond the assembly of the saints for worship. It is the responsibility of all who confess the name of Jesus. Indeed it belongs to this confession. For a confession that does not bear witness to the saving power and claims of the Lord Jesus is one that belies its reality. There are, however, those who are officially set apart for the evangelization of the lost, and it needs to be stressed that this proclamation is the function of the church and should always be conducted under its auspices. Here we must catch the vision of the great commissions that repentance and remission of sins should be preached in Jesus' name unto all the nations (cf. Luke 24:47), and that nothing less than the discipling of all nations (cf. Matt. 28:19) is the demand of Jesus' lordship.

The second aspect of this proclamation is the declaration of the whole counsel of God as it bears upon every sphere of human activity. The church is not to discharge the functions of other institutions. It must not invade other spheres. But the church is charged to define the functions of these other institutions and the lines of demarcation by which their spheres are distinguished. It would be a travesty, for example, for the church to discharge the functions of the civil magistrate either locally or nationally. But the functions and duties of the civil magistrate do come within the scope of the church's proclamation in every respect in which the Word of God bears upon the proper discharge of these functions and responsibilities. When the civil authority trespasses the limits of its authority, it is the duty of the church to condemn such a violation. When laws are proposed or enacted that are contrary to the Word of God, it is the duty of the church in proclamation and in official pronouncement to oppose and condemn them. And it is also the obligation of the church to inculcate respect for and obedience to all enactments of civil authority that are the legitimate exercise of its function. It is misconception of what is involved in the proclamation of the whole counsel of God to suppose or plead that the church has no concern with the political sphere. The church is concerned with every sphere and is obligated to proclaim and inculcate the revealed will of God as it bears upon every department of life.

3. *Government*. Paul wrote to Timothy: 'These things write I unto thee, hoping to come unto thee shortly: but if I tarry long, that thou mayest know how thou oughtest to behave thyself in the house of God, which is the church of the living God, the pillar and ground of the truth' (1 Tim. 3:14, 15). No text evinces Paul's jealousy for proper government in the church more than this one. The considerations giving sanction to the necessity of right administration Paul specifies. The church is 'the house of God', 'the church of the living God', and 'the pillar and ground of the truth'. As exemplifying 'the truth' of which the church is the

pillar and ground, he proceeds to give us one of the most eloquent summaries in the New Testament, and this summary he calls 'the mystery of godliness' (vs. 16). The lessons are inescapable. Government and witness to the truth cannot be disjoined. Everything that interferes with good government impinges directly upon the truth of our Christian faith. Government is not a peripheral concern, nor does deviation from what is proper affect merely the periphery of sound doctrine. Deviation prejudices what is central, the mystery of godliness itself.

Our forebears knew this, and through struggles of blood and privation have left us the legacy of presbyterian government, government of the church by presbyters, not by a hierarchy and not by the civil authority. The church, they were zealous to maintain, is the body of Christ and Christ is its only head. My friends, prize your legacy and do not allow it to be compromised! It is the government by presbyters who exercise this function on a parity with one another, with no hierarchical domination or control. And beware of the subtle ways in which hierarchical aspirations are ready to assert themselves even within the presbyterian fold.

4. *Diaconal Ministry.* This is a ministry which to a large extent has ceased to be an arm of the church. Governmental measures have virtually deprived the church of its ministry in the sphere of charity. Regrettably the church has been too willing to have it so, and to have this responsibility wrested from its grasp. The church's witness to Christ has been correspondingly impaired and this means of communion neglected. Notwithstanding all provisions for the poor in the so-called welfare state, there is ample scope for the exercise of this ministry, and the church needs to be alerted to the needs, in some cases appalling, that exist in this area of Christian opportunity and obligation. How significant is the word of the apostle: 'But when James, Cephas, and John, who seemed to be pillars, perceived the grace that was given unto me, they gave to me and Barnabas the right hands of fellowship; that we should go unto the heathen, and they unto circumcision. Only they would that we should remember the poor; the same which I also was forward to do' (Gal. 2:9, 10).

THE RESOURCES OF THE CHURCH

What is the strength of the church of God? History has demonstrated how ineffective the church becomes when it relies on its own resources of wisdom and power. The strength of the church is in the realization of its own impotence. The apostle had to say: 'We are not sufficient of ourselves to think anything as of ourselves; but our sufficiency is of God' (2 Cor. 3:5). When we inquire as to the character of this sufficiency, what meets us is not simply the assurance of grace *sufficient*, however precious is such in itself. What meets us should overwhelm us with amazement. The expressions stagger us: 'Filled with all the fulness of God' (Eph. 3:19); 'the measure of the stature of the fulness of Christ' (Eph. 4:13). Who would dare to posit such resource? It would not have entered into the heart of man. But God has revealed this unto us by the Spirit. What then is 'the fulness of God' and 'the stature of the fulness of Christ'? The same Epistle supplies the answer: 'And hath put all things under his feet, and gave him to be the head over all things to the church, which is his body, the fulness of him that filleth all in all' (Eph. 1:22, 23). It is Christ who fills all in all. He 'ascended up far above all heavens, that he might fill all things' (Eph. 4:10). And in him also dwells the fulness: 'It pleased the Father that in him all the fulness should dwell' (Col. 1:19). How then can the church be the fulness of Christ? It is not because the church fills Christ. That would mean a reversal of the order involved in the church's dependence upon, and subjection to Christ as the head. The other passages are the index to the meaning (Eph. 3:19; 4:13). The church is the fulness of Christ because it is the recipient of the fulness that is in Christ; it is being filled from him and, therefore, filled unto all the fulness of God. Christ is the embodiment of all virtue —wisdom, truth, power, grace, love, mercy, peace, patience, longsuffering, goodness, righteousness. These are the resources of the church. For all these are his in his capacity as God-man and head of the church on behalf of the church. The church as his body is as intimately related to his offices and functions as his physical body is to his person. And the plenitude that is his as Saviour is bestowed upon the church. This was the witness of John: 'We beheld his glory, the glory as of the only begotten of the Father, full of grace and truth . . . And of his fulness have all we received, and grace for grace' (John 1:14, 16).

243

It is both the privilege and obligation of believers to appreciate more and more the complementation of Christ and the church. There is no need of ours, no demand arising from the high calling of God in Christ Jesus, no office involved in the service of Christ and the church, that is not supplied with grace for fulfilment out of the fulness that resides in Christ. It is an affront to Christ to doubt the superabundance of his resources on behalf of the church. The design entertained in loving the church and giving himself for it he will not fail to accomplish. He will 'present it to himself, a glorious church, not having spot or wrinkle, or any such thing . . . holy and without blemish' (Eph. 5:27).

33

The Church and Mission

A GREAT deal is being said today about the mission of the church, and the accent falls to such an extent upon mission that the function of the church is defined in terms of mission. It would be a total misunderstanding of Scripture, and of the New Testament in particular, to discount or even to underestimate the responsibility of the church in its mission to the nations. Was it not the commission of the Saviour on the eve of his departure from this world: 'Go ye therefore and disciple all the nations' (Matt. 28:19)? And no less important is the Saviour's word as recorded by Luke: 'Thus it is written, that Christ should suffer and rise from the dead on the third day, and that repentance and remission of sins should be preached in his name unto all the nations' (Luke 24:46, 47). As will be expanded later on, this is an all-important function of the church. But in order to place this responsibility in proper focus, it is necessary to have a biblical conception of the church. And it is just because this is not always entertained that the emphasis upon mission is so frequently a distortion of the concept of both church and mission.

What is the church? The basic idea of church in both the Old Testament and the New is assembly, the assembly of the covenant people of God, the people God formed for himself that they might set forth his praise. This Old Testament teaching is embedded in Peter's definition when he says: 'But ye are an elect race, a royal priesthood, a holy nation, a people for God's own possession, that ye may show forth the excellencies of him who called you out of darkness into his marvellous light: who in time past were no people, but are now the people of God: who had not obtained mercy, but now have obtained mercy' (1 Pet. 2:9, 10).

The central blessing of God's covenant with men is, in a variety of forms but to the same effect, 'I will be your God, and ye shall be my people', a blessing that attains the zenith of realization in 'the new Jerusalem' and 'the new heavens and the new earth' (Rev. 21:1–3). This concept of the church as the covenant people of God may be applied particularistically and generically, to the people of God in a particular house, or city, and to the people of God inclusively considered. Thus it is proper to speak of the *churches* of God throughout a province or throughout the world and of the church of God comprising all who are in the fellowship of God and of Christ (cf. for the latter, Matt. 16:18; Acts 8:3; 9:31; 1 Cor. 15:9; Gal. 1:13; Phil. 3:6). For our present purpose it is sufficient to understand that the relationship to God, the prerogatives and functions, the blessings and promises defining the church, belong to the local assembly and not merely to the church universal. The assembly of God's covenant people, wherever it exists, numerically small or great, is the church of God, purchased by Jesus' blood.

Co-ordinate with the idea that the church is the assembly of God's covenant people is the concept of the church as the household of God (Eph. 2:19), or, even more simply, the house of God (1 Tim. 3:15; Heb. 3:5, 6; 10:21; 1 Pet. 4:17). Since it is the house of God it is the place where God dwells and the people of God are; as Paul says, 'the habitation of God by the Spirit' (Eph. 2:22).

The church is the body of Christ. This designation must not be confused with the physical body of the Saviour formed in the virgin's womb, the body in which he suffered, the body laid in the tomb and in which he rose and ascended to heaven, the body in which he will be seen again when he comes the second time. In distinction from the body that was and is integral to our Lord's person subsequent to his conception in the virgin's womb, there is a figurative aspect to the designation. But this figurative use must not be allowed to obscure the intimacy and richness of the relationship to Christ expressed. The church and Christ are complementary—we may never think of the one apart from the other. And the union of Christ with the church is of an organism that exists on an immensely higher plane than any organic relationship with which we are acquainted in any other sphere of our experience. So intimate is this relationship that the church is the fulness of Christ in the sense that the church not only derives its life from Christ but has communicated to it the fulness of grace and virtue that resides in its plenitude in Christ.

When our thought of the church is governed by these concepts, we are compelled to recognize how God-centred and God-oriented must our conception of the church be. However important is the function of the church in its missionary outreach to the world, we can readily see how deflected becomes our perspective if we conceive of the church in terms of mission. As we give proper weight to the biblical teaching we discover that the church in origin, identity, and function is theocentrically conditioned. If we return to the passage in 1 Peter 2:9, 10 we find that as respects origin we are pointed to election—'an elect race', as respects identity to 'a holy nation, a people for his [God's] own possession', and as respects office and function to 'a royal priesthood' to show forth the praises of God and to 'offer up spiritual sacrifices acceptable to God through Jesus Christ' (1 Pet. 2:5). In the Old Testament the tabernacle was the focus of the assembly. There God met with his people and spoke to them; it was God's dwelling place with his people, the sanctuary of his presence, certified by the cloud of glory in the most holy place (cf. Exod. 29:42–46). These characteristics are not displaced or abrogated in the church of the New Testament. They reach rather the zenith of application and realization. Jesus is Immanuel, God with us, and as the Word become flesh he tabernacled among us and we beheld his glory (cf. John 1:14). The counterpart of the Old Testament institution and the continuity of both Testaments appear in our Lord's promise: 'Where two or three are gathered together in my name, there am I in the midst of them' (Matt. 18:20).

Thus, as the church is the assembly of God's people, the household of God, and the body of Christ, as living stones built up a spiritual house, to be a holy priesthood to offer up spiritual sacrifices, the central function in the worship of God. This is the only conclusion compatible with the God-oriented identity of the church. And this is the function to which the witness of both Testaments points. 'We are the circumcision who worship God by the Spirit [or worship by the Spirit of God] and rejoice in Christ Jesus' (Phil. 3:3).

It is impossible in the reading of the New Testament to overlook the place given to the edification of the saints. No passage is more instructive in this connection than Ephesians 4:11–16: 'And he gave some apostles, and some prophets, and some evangelists, and some pastors and teachers, for the perfecting of the saints unto the work of ministry, for the edification of the body of Christ', and so on. If the church is the fulness of Christ as the one who fills all in all, it is because the fulness that dwells in Christ is communicated. But it is not communicated automatically. It is communicated through ministry, and ministry is pre-eminently that of the Word of truth, of knowledge, of wisdom, of discernment. 'Let the word of Christ dwell in you richly, in all wisdom teaching and admonishing one another' (Col. 3:16). The stress that falls on doctrine or teaching is the index to this paramount concern, and only thus are we to understand the primacy accorded to prophecy in the exercise of the manifold gifts distributed by the Holy Spirit (cf. Eph. 4:11; 1 Cor. 12:28). 'He that prophesieth speaketh unto men to edification, and exhortation, and comfort.' 'He that speaketh in a tongue edifieth himself; but he that prophesieth edifieth the church' (1 Cor. 14:4). 'Yet in the church I had rather speak five words with my understanding, in order that I might teach others also, than ten thousand words in a tongue' (1 Cor. 14:19). It is in the light of this that the church is to be understood as 'the pillar and ground of the truth' (1 Tim. 3:15).

It is apparent that only in this context can the mission of the church be properly understood. That mission is a function of the church cannot be questioned. Already reference has been made to our Lord's commissions (Matt. 28:19; Luke 24:46, 47). It is necessary to take account also of Acts 1:8: 'But ye shall receive power . . . witnesses unto me . . . to the utmost part of the earth'. That the great commissions are not restricted to the original recipients is indicated by the promise appended in Matthew 28:20: 'Behold I am with you all the days unto the end of the age', as well as by the earlier statement that the gospel of the kingdom would be preached for a witness to all the nations 'and then shall the end come' (Matt. 24:14). The preaching is to continue to the end. Furthermore, since salvation is to be in effect to the end, and since it pleased God by the foolishness of the *preached* message to save them that believe, the preached message must continue to the consummation.

It is necessary now to focus attention upon the thesis that the church is the agent or instrument of mission, or, in other words, of evangelism. In Acts 13:1-4 we have an instructive lesson and example of this action on the part of the church. 'Now there were in the church that was in Antioch prophets and teachers . . . And as they were ministering to the Lord and fasting, the Holy Spirit said, Separate me Barnabas and Saul for the work whereunto I have called them. And when they had fasted and prayed and laid their hands on them, they sent them away.' They were designated by the Holy Spirit and they were sent forth by the Holy Spirit. But the action of the prophets and teachers was not super-fluous. Saul and Barnabas were set apart and sent away by the prophets and teachers after they had fasted, prayed, and laid their hands on them. Though these particular actions are referred to the prophets and teachers we cannot dissociate the actions from the church as a whole. The prophets and teachers were themselves in the church. In accordance with Ephesians 4:11 they were given to the church, and as servants of the church they acted on behalf of the whole church. Also, when Paul and Barnabas returned after this missionary journey, they gathered the church together and rehearsed all that God had done with them. It is surely this earlier pattern followed by the church at Antioch that Paul hopes will be adhered to by the church at Rome when, with his journey to Spain in view, he writes: 'Whenever I go to Spain . . . I hope . . . to be sent forth thither by you' (Rom. 15:24). He expects from the church at Rome a sending forth with commendation and blessing. Again when Paul was setting out on his second missionary journey from the same Antioch, he and Silas were committed by the brethren to the grace of God.

The purpose I have in view in recounting these details of the earliest missionary activity is to show how closely related evangelism is to the church of God and how the church sends forth the emissaries of the evangel. Paul could write to 'the church of the Thessalonians in God the Father and the Lord Jesus Christ', that 'from you sounded out the word of the Lord not only in Macedonia and Achaia, but in every place your faith which is toward God has gone forth' (1 Thess. 1:1, 8). It is of importance and urgency that this principle be asserted for two reasons in particular.

1. There is widespread failure in the conduct of missionary activity to

appreciate and apply this order. Far be it from us to impugn the sincerity and zeal of the promoters of many independent agencies for the promulgation of the gospel. And far be it from any of us to deny the fruits that have accrued from these evangelistic activities in the conversion of souls and the extension of the kingdom of God. But sincerity and zeal are not the criteria of propriety, nor is the conversion of souls the guarantee that the methods used have divine sanction. As in every sphere of activity related to the gospel, we need to examine our ways and reassess our enterprises in the light of the order which Scripture prescribes for us. And this is but to assert the will of him who gave the commission to disciple the nations and to bring every thought into captivity to his obedience. It is true that the organized church has oftentimes been apathetic and failed to carry out the demands of commission. But the remedy is not to abandon the church as the agent and instrument of mission, but to institute and pursue measures whereby all rightful and urgent zeal for evangelism can receive its outlet through the medium and in the solidarity of the church as the body of Christ. We must reject as monstrous blasphemy the tenet that the church is the extension of the incarnation, whether it be propounded in Roman Catholic form or in that of non-Roman communions. But we may not forget that the church is the body of Christ, and therefore that through which his witness is to be borne to the world. The church is the receptacle of Christ's fulness and declares his unsearchable riches.

2. The second reason for the assertion of this principle that the church is the agent of mission is that the church itself be aroused to its responsibility and vocation. Up to this point attention has been focused on the missionary activity of the more official ministry of the gospel. It is proper and necessary that this institution of Christ should be recognized and honoured. Paul and Barnabas were set apart. There are men set apart to labour in the Word and doctrine. Christ gave some evangelists and some pastors and teachers. There are particular offices in the church of Christ. How jealous the church should be that such should be equipped, called, and sent forth. 'Pray ye therefore the Lord of the harvest that he would send forth labourers into his harvest' (Matt. 9:38). The paucity of consecrated and endowed missionaries of the evangel is a commentary on the lethargy, coldness, indifference, lack of zeal on the

part of the church. Mission is the vocation of the church and if men are not forthcoming for the special office, judgment must begin at the house of God, and judgment, let us remember, to a large extent upon our prayerlessness. 'When Zion travailed she brought forth children' (Isa. 66:8).

But although the special office must be given due place and esteem, this is not the only aspect of the church's mission. The doctrine of the priesthood of all believers received appropriate recognition in the churches of the Reformation. But I fear that, in our reformed churches, the implications have been conspicuous by their neglect in the practical sphere. If there is the universal priesthood, there is also the universal prophethood. And herein lies the mission of the church.

In the New Testament we have an arresting example. 'And at that time there was a great persecution against the church that was at Jerusalem; and they were all scattered abroad throughout the regions of Judaea and Samaria, except the apostles . . . Therefore they that were scattered abroad went everywhere preaching the Word' (Acts 8:1, 4). It is not our interest now to discuss the extent of the dispersion of believers at Jerusalem. It has been thought that the dispersion applied to Hellenistic Jews. Our interest now concerns the fact that those scattered abroad went about preaching the Word, and from Acts 11:19-21 we learn that this activity extended to Antioch in Syria, which played so important a role in subsequent missionary expansion of the church. It would not be reasonable to restrict this preaching of the Word to the special offices of prophet, evangelist, and teacher, although from Acts 8:5ff. we must reckon with this more official ministry of the Word (cf. also Acts 13:1-4).

It is this evangelizing responsibility of the members of the church that we are so liable to neglect, and the indictments must be directed to multiple aspects of failure to bring to expression our profession, a failure that reflects on our conviction and devotion. No phase of evangelism is more indispensable to the spread of the gospel and to the building up of the church.

A disquieting departure from the New Testament institution at the present time is the opening of the office of the ministry to women. In this there is failure to recognize and maintain the line of distinction between the general office of believers and the special office of the ministry of the Word. There is not only ample scope, but an indispensable place for the activity of women in witness to the faith. It is here that women properly and necessarily perform the most effective service in the propagation of the gospel. Particularly does this obtain in witnessing to their own sex. There are here avenues of evangelism that are scarcely open to men. If women were alert to their opportunities and responsibilities in this realm of more personal witness and instruction, then not only would there be no plea on their part for entrance into the special office; there would be recoil from the suggestion.

In this failure on the part of men and women to understand and discharge responsibility and buy up opportunity, resides to a large extent the appalling spectacle that confronts us in the sphere of mission. At our doors and within our family circles is the call to mission. Our remissness springs from our lack of concern for the salvation of perishing souls, our lack of love, our lack of zeal for the claims of Christ and of his body the church, and finally our lack of jealousy for the glory of God. If fervour of spirit and the service of the Lord animate our hearts, then with the apostles we cannot but speak the things which we have seen and heard. And we may not be dismayed by the odds of unbelieving opposition and indifference. The gospel is the power of God unto salvation and his Word will not return unto him void. And he has put this treasure in earthen vessels that the excellency of the power may be of God and not of us.

34

The Relation of Church and State[1]

BOTH church and state are divine institutions. The state no more than the church owes its origin and authority to human expedient or contract. It is true, of course, that the form of government and the bounds within which a particular government wields its jurisdiction, may be and often have been determined by the will and consent of the governed. It is also true that the constitution and laws may be established by the vote of the people. But the institution of civil government is by divine ordination, and it is only because government has divine sanction that those who govern may exercise this authority and those who are governed submit to it. The civil magistrate is the minister of God and he is the minister of God for good.

Civil government has its own distinct sphere of operation and jurisdiction. This sphere is that of guarding, maintaining, and promoting justice, order, and peace. It is its function to prevent the encroachment upon, and to guard the exercise of the God-given liberties, rights, and privileges of the citizens, and it must provide against attempts to deprive the citizens of the opportunity to discharge their divine obligations. In maintaining and promoting these ends the civil magistrate is invested with the power of the sword to restrain evil, to punish evildoers, and to promote good (cf. Rom. 13:1–6; 1 Pet. 2:13, 14).

Since the civil magistrate is invested with this authority by God and is obliged by divine ordinance to discharge these functions, he is responsible to God, the one living and true God who alone has ordained him.

[1] Section two of a report prepared by a committee of the Orthodox Presbyterian Church.

The magistrate is, therefore, under obligation to discharge the office devolving upon him in accordance with the revealed will of God. The Bible is the supreme and infallible revelation of God's will and it is, therefore, the supreme and infallible rule in all departments of life. The civil magistrate is under obligation to recognize it as the infallible rule for the exercise of civil magistracy.

It must be recognized, however, that it is only within his own restricted sphere of authority that the civil magistrate, in his capacity as civil magistrate, is to apply the revelation of God's will as provided in Scripture. It is only to the extent to which the revelation of Scripture bears upon the functions discharged by the state and upon the performance of the office of the civil magistrate, that he, in the discharge of these functions, is bound to fulfil the demands of Scripture. If the civil magistrate should attempt, in his capacity as magistrate, to carry into effect the demands of Scripture which bear upon him in other capacities, or the demands of Scripture upon other institutions, he would immediately be guilty of violating his prerogatives and of contravening the requirements of Scripture.

The sphere of the church is distinct from that of the civil magistrate. Its sphere of operation has been defined in the first section of this report. What needs to be appreciated now is that its sphere is co-ordinate with that of the state. The church is not subordinate to the state, nor is the state subordinate to the church. They are both subordinate to God, and to Christ in his mediatorial dominion as head over all things to his body the church. Both church and state are under obligation to recognize this subordination, and the corresponding co-ordination of their respective spheres of operation in the divine institution. Each must maintain and assert its autonomy in reference to the other and preserve its freedom from intrusion on the part of the other. But while this diversity of function and of sphere must be recognized, guarded, and maintained, the larger unity within which this diversity exists must not be overlooked. The principle that defines this unity is the sovereignty of God, and the obligation emanating from it is the requirement that both church and state must promote the interests of the kingdom of God. It is only on the basis of such principles that any Christian conception of the relation of church and state can be developed.

To the church is committed the task of proclaiming the whole counsel of God and, therefore, the counsel of God as it bears upon the responsibility of all persons and institutions. While the church is not to discharge the functions of other institutions such as the state and the family, nevertheless it is charged to define what the functions of these institutions are, and the lines of demarcation by which they are distinguished. It is also charged to declare and inculcate the duties which devolve upon them. Consequently when the civil magistrate trespasses the limits of his authority, it is incumbent upon the church to expose and condemn such a violation of his authority. When laws are proposed or enacted which are contrary to the law of God, it is the duty of the church to oppose them and expose their iniquity. When the civil magistrate fails to exercise his God-given authority in the protection and promotion of the obligations, rights, and liberties of the citizens, the church has the right and duty to condemn such inaction, and by its proclamation of the counsel of God to confront the civil magistrate with his responsibility and promote the correction of such neglect. The functions of the civil magistrate, therefore, come within the scope of the church's proclamation in every respect in which the Word of God bears upon the proper or improper discharge of these functions, and it is only misconception of what is involved in the proclamation of the whole counsel of God that leads to the notion that the church has no concern with the political sphere.

When it is maintained that the church is concerned with civic affairs, is under obligation to examine political measures in the light of the Word of God, and is required to declare its judgments accordingly, the distinction between this activity on the part of the church and *political* activity must be recognized. To put the matter bluntly, the church is not to engage in *politics*. Its members must do so, but only in their capacity as citizens of the state, not as members of the church. The church is not to create or foster political parties or blocs. The proclamation of the church may indeed induce the members of the church and others to affiliate themselves, in their capacity as citizens, with one party rather than with another or, perhaps, to form a political party for the promotion of good politics. If the proclamation of the church is sound, the church has no need to be ashamed of the influence its proclamation exerts in this direction, nor does it need to be troubled by the charge that may be levelled against it to the effect that it is engaged in politics. In such circumstances the church must be prepared to pay the price for its faithful witness to the political implications of the message committed to it.

It might appear that this position regarding the duty of the church is inconsistent with the statement of the Westminster Confession, namely: 'Synods and councils are to handle or conclude nothing but that which is ecclesiastical: and are not to intermeddle with civil affairs, which concern the commonwealth, unless by way of humble petition in cases extraordinary; or, by way of advice, for satisfaction of conscience, if they be thereunto required by the civil magistrate' (chapter XXXI, section v). It may be that the conception of the right and duty of the church in reference to the functions of the civil magistrate and his discharge of, or failure to discharge, these functions, set forth in this report, goes beyond that envisaged by the framers of the Confession. If so, the Confessional statement does not make it necessary for us to resile from this conception. The Confession is not to be our supreme standard. But it is not apparent that there is an inconsistency.

Two observations need to be made. First, it should be remembered that the Confession defines the sphere of the magistrate's jurisdiction and it incorporates such a definition in what was intended to be the confession of the church (cf. especially chapter XXIII). The framers, therefore, considered it proper for the church to declare what the prerogatives of the civil magistrate are and what limitations circumscribe the sphere of his jurisdiction. It is surely implied that it is the right and duty of the church to declare from time to time what the applications and implications of such a definition of authority are. History has demonstrated how ready churches adopting the Confession were to resist arrogations and intrusions on the part of the state.

Second, the Confession says that 'synods and councils are to handle or conclude nothing but that which is ecclesiastical'. But to declare the whole counsel of God in reference to political matters, as well as other matters, is definitely an ecclesiastical function and was surely considered to be such by the framers of the Confession. Furthermore, the terms used by the Confession to designate the type of activity denied to synods and councils, namely, handling, or concluding, or intermeddling with 'civil affairs which concern the commonwealth', indicate that what is regarded as beyond the province of synods and councils is something quite different from proclamation of the whole counsel of God as it bears upon the conduct of civil affairs. The intermeddling prohibited can well be regarded as the kind of *political* activity which is not by any means accorded to the church in the thesis propounded in this report. The church is certainly not to be regarded as handling or concluding political affairs when it declares the religious and moral implications of political measures; it does not *determine* civil affairs, it simply propounds and defends the requirements of God's revealed will in reference to civil affairs. Finally, the Confession grants to synods and councils the right of 'humble petition in cases extraordinary' and of 'advice, for satisfaction of conscience, if they be thereunto required by the civil magistrate'. This provision contemplates direct appeal to the civil magistrate in reference to what is specifically commonwealth business, and goes further than the proclamation, in reference to political affairs, which the church in the discharge of its function may at all times perform.

The question remains: how is the church to proclaim the counsel of God as it bears upon civil affairs? It is obvious that there are two means, in particular, of proclaiming the Word of God, namely, the pulpit and the press. The church lives in the world and it lives within the domain of political entities. If it is to be faithful to its commission it must make its voice heard and felt in reference to public questions. The church may not supinely stand aside and ignore political corruption, for example, on the ground that to pronounce judgment on such issues is to intermeddle in politics. Political corruption is sin, it is public sin, and the church denies its vocation if it does not reprove it. When there is political revolution which contravenes the principles of God's Word and is directed against the kingdom of God, the church may not be an idle spectator on the ground that the powers that be are ordained of God. It must assess the revolution for what it is in the light of the Word of God and proclaim in pulpit and press what the judgment of the Word of God is. If political revolution is right; if it displaces usurpation and tyranny, and is in the interests of equity, the church may not refrain from expressing by like media the favourable judgment which the principles of the Word of God dictate.

It will happen, of course, in the imperfection which characterizes the church that there will be dissident voices. The judgments of men will differ. But this does not affect the principle that the official representatives of the church are under obligation to proclaim in Christ's name the judgment of his Word on all questions to which that Word is relevant, and such spokesmen ought to strive for unity of thought and expression in accordance with the Word of Christ. There ought to be in this matter, also, the unity of the Spirit in the bond of peace.

This proclamation may also take the form of corporate pronouncement. That is to say, the church may in its corporate capacity through its assemblies, whether provincial, national or international, make official pronouncement regarding the religious and moral implications of political measures or movements. In certain situations it is under obligation to do this for the instruction and warning of its own members and adherents as well as for the instruction of others, including those in whom is vested civil authority. Such pronouncements are for the purpose of proclaiming the Word of God and of vindicating God's authority in the issues involved. To deny that such a prerogative belongs to the church is to compromise on the universal relevance of the Word of God and on the testimony which the church must bear to the world.

It is necessary to be reminded that great caution and reserve must be exercised by the church in making pronouncements regarding political affairs. This caution is particularly necessary in connection with the pronouncements and resolutions of assemblies of the church. Hasty analyses and proclamations must be avoided, and great care must be exercised to ensure that pronouncements are in accord with and necessitated by the requirements of the Word of God. Too frequently the church has brought reproach upon the name of Christ, and has seriously curtailed its influence for good, by making pronouncements which are not supported by the requisite evidence or which are beyond the prerogative of the church. And the representatives of the church in the performance of their official ministrations must beware of turning the pulpit into a forum for the discussion of political questions, especially a forum for political partisanship. A lopsidedness prejudicial to the proclamation of the whole counsel of God is only too liable to characterize those who are alert to the religious and moral issues at stake in political trends and movements. Balance and moderation must be preserved here as elsewhere. But abuse, and the liability to abuse, do not rule out the obligation and the necessity of bringing the proclamation of God's Word to bear upon every department of life and, specifically, upon that department of life concerned with civil government.

35

Government in the Church of Christ

IT scarcely needs to be stated that in the institution of the New Testament those exercising the ruling function in the church of God are sometimes called elders and at other times bishops. In either case, the reference is to the same office, and the development whereby diocesan episcopacy has gained currency in the government of the church is without any warrant from Scripture and therefore can plead no sanction from the head of the church. It is quite apparent from Acts 20:17, 28 that the same persons are in view when in verse 17 they are called 'elders' and in verse 28 'bishops'. Again in Titus 1:5, 7 it is equally apparent that the same office-bearers are denominated elders in verse 5 and referred to by the name bishop in verse 7. Otherwise there would be no force or relevance to the statement in verse 7, 'For the bishop must be blameless as the steward of God.'

In reference to the topic in hand, there are four subjects with which we may profitably deal:

I. THE OFFICE OF ELDER

1. *Plurality*. Paul sent to Miletus and called the elders of the church and he enjoined Titus to ordain elders in every city. This, in itself, is a commonplace, but history has demonstrated that the implications are too frequently overlooked. The rule that is exercised in the church of God the elders execute in unison and on a parity with one another. In respect of ruling, there is no hegemony in the church of God. Within the presbyterian fold, the way in which this principle has been preju-

diced and sometimes well-nigh eliminated is by entertaining and giving practical effect to the notion that to the minister belongs a certain priority or superiority in the rule of the church. It needs therefore to be emphasized that in respect of rule the person who is called the minister has no more authority or jurisdiction than the ruling elder, and therefore no more responsibility devolves upon him than upon the elder.

The minister as a teaching elder has his own distinctive function, and exercises, by preaching and teaching, a peculiar prerogative in the church of God, but in ruling he is on a parity with the ruling elders. There are subtle temptations for both the minister and the ruling elder which point in the direction of discarding this principle and which, when succumbed to, violate its provisions. The temptation for the minister is to abuse the dignity which belongs to him as a minister of the Word and to extend that distinguishing prerogative into the sphere of government, so as to expect, if not claim for himself a certain hegemony in the matter of ruling. It is a temptation against which he must guard, and it is one to which the elders must be alert to lend no encouragement. The temptation for the ruling elder is to accord to the minister the hegemony he is only too ready to assume, and thus relinquish a good part of his responsibility in the exercise of government. Each elder must be aware of the parity that exists in the rule of the church, and therefore the parity of responsibility and obligation. It is a duty that must be stressed in our presbyterian circles, because its neglect has opened the door to a ministerial hierarchism that has been gravely detrimental not only to presbyterian polity but also to the pure witness of the gospel. There is a direct line of connection between every infringement upon proper government and the breakdown of witness to the truth itself (cf. I Tim. 3:15, 16).

2. *Oversight.* 'Take heed to yourselves and to all the flock, over which the Holy Spirit hath made you overseers' (Acts 20:28). There is, in the New Testament institution, such a thing as rule, regulation, government, oversight, administered by men who are endowed with certain gifts, called to exercise them, and invested by the Holy Spirit with authority to rule. While, on the one hand, the New Testament institution rules our diocesan episcopacy, on the other hand it proscribes rule by the people. In a word, the church, whether conceived of locally or

more ecumenically, does not rule itself. In that sense it is not a pure democracy. The elders are to rule.

It appears to me that there is grave failure to appreciate this fact even in our presbyterian churches. And it frequently appears in some such pattern of thought as the following. The elders are conceived of as simply the delegated representatives of the people and as exercising authority by delegation, hence by the will and sufferance of the people. When a majority of the congregation deems the policies and decisions of the elders contrary to their will or liking, then there is a simple solution—terminate the tenure of office by vote of the congregation. It is, of course, to be recognized that good presbyterian polity provides for the removal from office of those who prove incompetent or who exercise their office contrary to the institution of Christ. But this pattern of thought whereby elders are reckoned to be delegated representatives of the people is basically wrong. It is the Holy Spirit who has made them overseers, and they are delegated by the head of the church. It is the obligation of the people and the elders to recognize that the rule exercised by the latter is by delegation from Christ and to him they are responsible.

3. *Church*. It is within the church that oversight is exercised. There is here a fine and necessary distinction. While the oversight is over the church, it is not over something from which the elders themselves are excluded. Elders are not lords over God's heritage; they are themselves of the flock and are to be examples to it. The Scripture has a unique way of emphasizing unity and diversity, and in this instance, the diversity which resides in the rule exercised is kept in proper proportion by the reminder that the elders themselves also are subject to the rule which they exercise over others. Elders are members of the body of Christ and are subject to the very same kind of rule of which they are the administrators.

II. THE AGENT OF INVESTITURE

'The Holy Spirit hath made you overseers' (Acts 20:28). It is to be recognized that the Holy Spirit now does not act directly in the ordination of men to the eldership. In the institution of the church, there is the instrumentality of men. But the point to be stressed now is the fact that in and through that instrumentality there is the agency of the Holy Spirit. There are the following respects in which this truth is directly pertinent.

1. *Election to Office.* The congregation, in electing men to the office of elder, should elect only those whom they believe to be called by the Holy Spirit to perform this function. The Holy Spirit does not give any special revelation to the effect that certain men are called by him. The only way whereby the people may arrive at such a judgment is by the gifts and graces with which men are endowed. Nevertheless, the judgment they exercise on the basis of evidence available to them should in the last analysis be a judgment to the effect that the Holy Spirit and Christ as the Lord of the church have qualified these men for the office, and by the evidence of these gifts have placed upon them the imprimatur on the basis of which the people may elect. It is necessary for the people to be made cognizant of this fact, for too often election to this office is dictated by considerations which should never be given any weight in a matter of such moment to the church of Christ. After all, godliness is the prime requisite, but not all godly men are endowed with the gifts requisite to office in the church.

2. *Reception of Office.* Those who accept this office should do so only because they are themselves convinced that 'they are equipped and qualified by the Holy Spirit to discharge its functions. It is under the constraint of such a necessity that they consent to be set apart to the holy office. Here again there is a clamant need for prayerful and conscientious regard for the principle of divine investiture.

3. *Authority Exercised.* The man who is fitted by the Holy Spirit for the exercise of this authority is keenly sensitive to his own sin and infirmity. It is the sense of divine vocation and appointment that alone will impart the strength and confidence to exercise the jurisdiction which the office entails. When he is confronted by his own self-interrogation, or by challenge on the part of others, with the question: Why do you determine certain actions which so deeply affect the lives of others? he must be able to act in the conviction that the Holy Spirit has invested him with the right, and that back of his action lies the authority of Christ. How compromising has been the policy of presbyterial courts just because those determining these policies have not been animated and controlled by this conviction!

4. *Subjection to Authority*. It is the recognition of investiture by the Holy Spirit that warrants and requires subjection by the people. The principle that 'God alone is Lord of the conscience, and hath left it free from the doctrines and commandments of men which are, in any thing, contrary to his Word, or beside it, in matters of faith or worship' is inviolable; for there is one lawgiver. And the person sensitive to the lordship of Christ is alive to the demand, 'Call no man master upon earth, for one is your master, even Christ.' It will become for such a conscientious person a question: Am I surrendering my liberty, and the charter of that liberty, by subjection to rule administered by men? It is the conviction of this rule by men as the ordinance of God that alone constrains subjection, because it is subjection in the Lord.

III. THE INSTITUTION

What is in view under this caption is the institution of the church, 'the church of God which he hath purchased with his own blood' (Acts 20:28).

It has frequently been said that the church is 'the called-out ones', and it has been supposed that the etymology of the word for 'church' in the New Testament fixes this as the defining idea. It is true enough that those who are members of the church and of the body of Christ have been called effectually out of the world and translated from darkness into the kingdom of the Son of God's love. But there is no evidence to support the notion that the *church* is to be defined as the *called-out ones*. The biblical evidence will show that the idea is rather that of assembly or congregation. It would be more correct to say that the church is the *called-together ones*. The church is the congregation of the faithful, the communion of the saints, the fellowship of believers. As such it is an institution, an organization which has been constituted by Christ its head. The idea that the church consists of the *called-out ones* fails to take account of what is central, and one has reason to fear that it has ministered to the individualism which discards corporate responsibility and the necessity of maintaining purity and unity in the body of Christ.

The church is an institution or organization established by Christ, and it is to be regulated and conducted in accord with Christ's revealed will. In this connection, one of the notions it is most necessary to avoid, or, if need be, to correct, in connection with the government of the church, is the idea that the church is a voluntary organization or association. It is true that no one should be compelled by men to belong to the church. It is voluntary in that sense. But it is not a voluntary association in the sense that it prescribes its own aims and functions, devises its own constitution, and designs its own officers. The church is the church of God and of Christ, and its aims and functions are prescribed by its head, its constitution determined and its officers designed and appointed by him.

Perhaps no doctrine of the New Testament offers more sanctity to this fact than that the church is the body of Christ which he has purchased with his own blood. That which elders or bishops rule is the blood-purchased possession of Christ, that which cost the agony of Gethsemane and the blood of Calvary's accursed tree. It was that which was captive to sin, Satan, and death, and Christ redeemed it as his own precious possession. It is now his body, and he is the head. How shall we dare to handle that body, how shall we dare to direct its affairs, except as we can plead the authority of Christ? The church as the body of Christ is not to be ruled according to human wisdom and expediency but according to the prescriptions of him in whom are hid all the treasures of wisdom and knowledge.

IV. THE DUTIES

'Shepherd the church of God'; 'Shepherd the flock of God which is among you, not of constraint but willingly after a godly manner, nor yet for filthy lucre but of a ready mind, neither as lording it over those allotted to your charge but being ensamples to the flock' (Acts 20:28; 1 Peter 5:2, 3). In both cases, the thought is that of shepherding; it means much more than feeding. It implies all the tending that a shepherd accords to his sheep.

1. A shepherd keeps his flock from going astray. In practice this means instruction and warning. An elder must be apt to teach, fit to teach and ready to teach. He must be furnished with knowledge which enables him to teach, and able and eager to impart that knowledge to those who are under his care.

2. A shepherd goes after his sheep when they go astray. In practice this

means reproof and correction, in many cases the exercise of ecclesiastical discipline. If an elder watches over his charge with tender solicitude and love, he will in many cases prevent the necessity of public censure by the eldership as a court of the church, because his private instructions and admonitions will be corrective at the earlier stages of defection and deviation. How much of purity and peace would have been maintained in the church of Christ and will be maintained if elders are sensitive to the first steps of delinquency on the part of the people and bring the word of tender admonition and reproof to bear upon them before they reach the by-paths of open and censurable sin! A shepherd when he sees a sheep wandering does not wait until it reaches the well-nigh inaccessible precipices. The elder must do the same by the ministry of admonition and warning.

3. A shepherd protects his sheep from their enemies. Wolves enter in among the sheep. The wolves which harass the church of God are emissaries of false doctrine and of evil practice. Satan is never out of his diocese and his speciality is to destroy the pure witness and fellowship of the church of God. Perhaps there is no more ominous feature of members of the church than the lack of discernment; they can listen to what is good and true, and to what is bad and false, without discrimination. If we are to live in a world where the enemy is active and error rampant, we must be imbued with a good measure of the critical faculty, and here the elders in tending the flock must cultivate for themselves, and inculcate in the members of the church, that sensitivity to truth and right, so that they and the people will be able to detect the voice of the enemy. Jesus indeed said of his sheep, 'a stranger will they not follow, for they know not the voice of strangers' (John 10:5). But this discernment does not operate in a vacuum, and it does not act mechanically; it acts in the context of intelligent apprehension and understanding of the truth.

4. A shepherd leads his flock to the fold; he pours oil into their wounds and gives them pure water to quench their thirst. I would like to press home the necessity and the blessing of the ministry of consolation. We fail too often to calculate the extent to which the spirits of the people of God are wounded and broken. The factors creating such a state of heart and mind are many and diverse. It is one of the paramount functions of

the eldership to strengthen the weak hands and confirm the feeble knees, to say to them who are of a fearful heart, 'Be strong!' and to be the instruments of binding up the broken-hearted. In this connection I would mention specifically the sick, and the ministry of prayer in such instances. There is something of permanent relevance in the exhortation of James: 'Is any sick among you? let him call for the elders of the church, and let them pray over him, anointing him with oil in the name of the Lord' (James 5:14). We need not allow the difficulty that may arise in connection with the last clause to interfere with the obvious relevance of the earlier part of the verse nor of the promise annexed to the faithful compliance with this duty. We often fail to appreciate the blessing attendant upon this ministry of prayer, simply because our performance is so perfunctory and faithless. And we may not forget the spiritual blessing that so frequently accrues from the ministry of concerted prayer, when we repair to the bedsides of those who are laid low with affliction.

It may be retorted, is not this the Lord's own work? It is he alone who searches the heart and tries the reins of the children of men, and it is he who knows how to speak a word in season to him that is weary. Verily so! We may not arrogate to ourselves divine prerogatives. But the Lord uses men as his instruments, and we may not abdicate our responsibility nor our opportunity simply because the Lord himself is the dispenser of grace.

In concluding, it is well to be reminded of the necessity of personal private devotion. It is possible to lose our own souls in preoccupation with the needs of others. Piety must first burn in the individuality of our own hearts and lives. We shall not be the faithful keepers of the vineyards of others if we have not kept our own. We may not say, of course, that the ministrations of those who do not themselves cultivate personal piety are useless. But we must say that it violates the proprieties governing Christ's church, and stultifies the fervour and effectiveness of our ministry, if we do not ourselves exemplify the godliness which we ostensibly seek to conserve and promote in others. Hence our discharge of government in the church of God must ever proceed out of a heart devoted to Christ, and our service must be offered as a sacrifice consecrated to him. Our labour in all its details must be conducted as in

36

The Biblical Basis
for Ecclesiastical Union

IN ecclesiastical union two denominational communions join in submitting to one common form of government. Since ecclesiastical jurisdiction includes the maintenance of spiritual discipline, unity in polity requires agreement in the standards of faith and worship which such discipline maintains. Hence unification in polity, when properly sought and achieved, involves also unity in faith, discipline, and worship.

As we take account of the diversity that exists between denominations, arising from differences of ethnic identity, cultural background, and historical circumstance, the most conclusive evidence derived from Scripture is required to support the position that the obliteration of denominational separateness is an obligation resting upon these Churches of Christ. The differences that exist often manifest the diversity which the church of Christ ought to exemplify and make for the enrichment of the church's total witness. If ecclesiastical union impairs this diversity, then it may be achieved at too great an expense, and tend to an impoverishment inconsistent with the witness to Christ which the church must bear.

Though the diversity which manifests itself in differentiating historical development might appear to make ecclesiastical union inadvisable or even perilous in certain cases, yet the biblical evidence in support of union[1]

---

[1] That is, the union of *some* Churches. The union here referred to has to do with a particular situation which existed in Canada in the early 1960's. This unpublished article was an address delivered in that situation, and the qualification—emphasized in the concluding sentence of the article—would be understood by the author's hearers.

is so plain that any argument to the contrary, however plausible, must be false.

THE ETHNIC UNIVERSALISM OF THE GOSPEL

In Christ Jesus there is now no longer Jew or Gentile, barbarian, Scythian, bond nor free (cf. Gal. 3:28; Col. 3:11). The New Testament does not suppose that the differences natural to individuals nor those arising from ethnic identity, cultural background, and historical circumstance are to be obliterated by the gospel. But it does mean that the unity in Christ transcends all diversity arising from language, race, culture, history. What is more, this unity embraces and utilizes all the diversity that is proper and that is created by God's providence. If we should maintain that the diversity is in any way incompatible with the unity of which the church is the expression, then we should be denying *that* unity which the ethnic universalism of the gospel implies. Implicit in the universalism of the gospel is the same kind of universalism in that which the gospel designs, the building up of Christ's church.

THE UNIVERSALISM OF THE APOSTOLIC CHURCH

The church of the apostolic days embraced all nations, and kindreds, and peoples, and tongues. There is no evidence in the New Testament for the diversification of distinct denominations, and anything tending to such diversification was condemned (cf. 1 Cor. 1:10-13). The emphasis falls upon the oneness of faith (cf. Eph. 4:5) and the oneness of the fellowship of the saints (cf. Eph. 4:2-4, 11-16; Phil. 2:2, 3; 4:2).

JESUS' PRAYER FOR UNITY (John 17:20, 21)

It is a travesty of this text, as of all others bearing upon the unity of the church, to think of the unity for which Christ prayed apart from unity of faith in the bond of truth. Verse 21 must not be dissociated from verse 20. To divorce the unity for which Christ prayed from all that is involved in believing upon him through the apostolic witness is to sunder what Christ placed together. Furthermore, the pattern Jesus provides in this prayer—'as thou, Father, art in me, and I in thee'— makes mockery of the application of this text when unity is divorced from the characterization which finds its analogy in trinitarian unity and harmony. But while these and other distortions of this text are to be shunned, the prayer of Jesus does bear upon our question in two respects.

1. The fragmentation and consequent lack of fellowship, harmony, and co-operation which appear on the ecclesiastical scene are a patent contradiction of the unity exemplified in that to which Jesus referred when he said, 'as thou, Father, art in me, and I in thee'.

2. The purpose stated in Jesus' prayer—'that the world may believe that thou hast sent me'—implies a manifestation observable by the world. Jesus prays for a visible unity that will bear witness to the world. The mysterious unity of believers with one another must come to visible expression so as to be instrumental in bringing conviction to the world.

THE UNITY OF THE BODY OF CHRIST

The church is the body of Christ and there is no schism in the body (cf. 1 Cor. 12:25). As in the human body, there is diversity in unity and unity in diversity (cf. 1 Cor. 12). The point to be stressed, however, is the unity. If there is unity it follows that this unity must express itself in all the functions which belong to the church. Since government in the church is an institution of Christ (cf. Rom. 12:8; 1 Cor. 12:28; 1 Tim. 5:17; Heb. 13:7; 1 Pet. 5:1, 2), this unity must be expressed in government. The necessary inference to be drawn is that the government should manifest the unity and be as embracive in respect of its functioning as the unity of which it is an expression. A concrete illustration of this principle is the decree of the Jerusalem council (Acts 15:28, 29; 16:4).

THE KINGDOM OF CHRIST

Christ is the head of the church. So ultimately there is the most concentrated unity of government in the church of Christ. He alone is King. Any infringement upon this sovereignty belonging to Christ is a violation of what is basic and central in the government of the church. It follows that all government in the church must adhere to the pattern of a cone which has its apex in Christ.

Christ also instituted the apostolate with authority delegated from him (Matt. 16:18, 19; cf. Jn. 20:21, 23; Eph. 2:19–22). This apostolic authority is exercised now only through the inscripturated Word. But in the sphere of delegated authority the apostolate is supreme and will continue to be so to the end of time. This is the way in which the Holy Spirit, as the vicar of Christ abiding in and with the church, exercises his function in accordance with Christ's promise. He seals the apostolic witness by his own testimony and illumines the people of God in the interpretation and application of the same.

Subordinately, however, in terms of Matt. 16:19, the hegemony of the apostolate is undeniable and it exemplifies the descending hierarchy which Christ has established.

There is also in the New Testament institution the delegated authority of the presbyterate, always subject to the apostolic institution, to the Holy Spirit who inspired the apostles (Jn. 16:13; 20:22), and ultimately to Christ as the King and head of the church, but nevertheless supreme in this sphere of government.

Since all office in the church of Christ can be fulfilled only by the gifts of the Spirit, this structural subordination of the government of the church to the rule of Christ functions in living reality as a fellowship of the one Spirit. Every one who has the Spirit of Christ is thereby called, as a good steward of the manifold grace of God, to minister his spiritual gifts to all the saints, so far as he is given opportunity. In particular, those whose gifts are for rule in the church must exercise such gifts in the communion of Christ and his church.

When these principles of gradation and communion are appreciated, and when co-ordinated with the other considerations already established, especially that of the unity of the body of Christ, we appear to be provided with a pattern that points to the necessity of making the presbyterate as inclusive as is consistent with loyalty to Christ and the faith of the gospel. In a word, we are pointed to the necessity of unity in government, a unity that is violated when Churches of Christ adhering to the faith in its purity and integrity are not thus united.

37

Corporate Responsibility[1]

THAT we sustain corporate relationships to one another scarcely needs to be demonstrated. We are not independent units, of ourselves existent and to ourselves sufficient. Each of us has a father and a mother, and probably most of us have brothers and sisters. We exist by and in filial relationship. It is possible that when we grow up to years of maturity we may isolate ourselves and become hermits. But it is only too apparent how abnormal is such a life and how impossible it would be for all to practise it even on a limited scale.

If there is corporate relationship there are two co-ordinate or correlative facts. First, there is corporate responsibility—we have obligations to discharge toward those who are thus related to us. This appears particularly in the family, and it is scarcely less apparent in the responsibilities to be discharged in the commonwealth to which we may belong or in which we have our domicile. Second, there are corporate entities which, as such, have responsibilities distinguishable from the strictly individual and personal responsibilities which belong to the persons comprised in these corporate entities. This kind of corporate responsibility is most easily recognized, perhaps, in connection with the state or commonwealth. It is obvious that the state has functions to perform which are not the functions of individuals as such, and which it would be wrong for individuals to arrogate to themselves. What travesties result when individuals take upon themselves the execution of functions

1 The substance of an address given to the students of Westminster Theological Seminary on December 6, 1951, and published in *The Presbyterian Guardian*, February 15, 1952.

which properly belong to the state! The state performs these functions through the agency of individuals, of course. But they are the agents of public function and not individuals acting on their own individual responsibility.

When these corporate entities properly and faithfully discharge the functions which belong to them, then due credit or approval accrues to them. When they are remiss in the performance of their tasks, they are worthy of condemnation. We may, therefore, speak of corporate credit in the case of faithfulness and corporate guilt in the case of delinquency.

When we are thinking of this corporate responsibility and credit and guilt which attach to the corporate entity as such, we must, however, make another distinction. The corporate entity does not exist apart from the individuals composing or comprised in that entity. In like manner the corporate credit or guilt, of which we have spoken, never exists in abstraction and cannot be conceived of as existing apart from the individuals who compose the entity. It is a corporate credit or guilt, as the case may be, which devolves upon the individuals, and therefore becomes, in one way or another, individual responsibility. Hence, while we must distinguish between strictly individual and personal responsibility, on the one hand, and corporate responsibility, on the other, this does not mean that corporate responsibility is not individual and personal. A distinction must be drawn and maintained, but not the kind of distinction which absolves the individual from responsibility in respect of the corporate responsibility which devolves upon him by reason of his corporate relationships. We might draw the distinction in terms of individual responsibility and corporate-individual responsibility. But in any case the corporate responsibility must devolve upon the individuals and become individualized in a way distinguishable from strictly individual responsibility, but not in a way that relieves the individual of responsibility.

This principle of corporate responsibility becomes particularly important for us as members of the church of Christ. That the church is a corporate entity lies on the face of the New Testament, for the church is the body of Christ. Christ is the head of this body and believers are members. No word advertises the closely-knit solidarity more clearly than that of Paul: 'And whether one member suffer, all the members suffer with it; or one member be honoured, all the members rejoice with it. Now ye are the body of Christ, and members in particular' (1 Cor. 12:26, 27). If the fallacy of individualism and independentism appears anywhere it is in connection with the church of Christ; at no point does the gravity of the abnormality and offence of individualism become more conspicuous than when it takes the form of discounting the unity and solidarity of Christ's body. We cannot abstract ourselves from the corporate relationship which inheres in the very notion of the church as the body of Christ, and we cannot abstract ourselves from the corporate responsibility which belongs to the church as a corporate entity. The corporate witness of the church is our witness and the corporate default of the church is our default. There are three respects in which this principle becomes of urgent and practical concern to us.

1. DENOMINATIONAL AFFILIATION

Ideally there ought to be only one Christian church throughout the whole world, the church of Christ, one in doctrine, one in worship, one in government, one in discipline. Romanists and Episcopalians have no monopoly of the formula 'one holy, catholic, and apostolic church'. It is inherent in the nature of orthodox Protestant confession that the church of Christ throughout the world *ought* to be one in doctrine, worship, government, and discipline. Division within the church arose from unfaithfulness to Christ and declension from the apostolic pattern. Everyone imbued with zeal for the honour of Christ must deplore the fragmentation which has marred the body of Christ and to a large extent dissipated its witness.

But, because of sin and error in their manifold ramifications and expressions, division has arisen and, in the circumstances, division has been mandatory for the preservation of a pure witness and the promotion of that unity which alone is worthy of the name, the unity of the Spirit in the bond of peace. Consequently there have emerged distinct denominations, and it is necessary that we associate ourselves with one of these. What needs to be particularly stressed is the necessity of giving the most thoughtful and earnest consideration to the question: To which branch of the church of Christ shall we belong? It is very easy for us to let heritage, and tradition decide this question for us. We have been born and bred in the fellowship of a certain communion. Our family belongs to it. Our friends and companions are there. Its ritual and forms and practices are second nature to us. The very church buildings are hallowed by long and precious associations. Why should we raise the question?

If we are to appreciate the corporate responsibility entailed in membership in the body of Christ, we must face the issue, and that simply because our corporate responsibility is most accentuated and intense at that point where our Christian communion is most intimate. It surely goes without saying that communion is most intimate in that branch of the church of Christ to which we belong. It is mandatory therefore that we affiliate ourselves with a branch of the church which is faithful to Christ in its corporate witness and which discharges those functions that devolve upon it as a corporate entity. We cannot consider our own individual witness to Christ as independent of the witness which is borne by the branch of the church to which we belong.

There is, indeed, no stereotyped formula which all of us can apply in the various situations in which we are placed by God's providence. And we must not take lightly the matter of severing our connection with one denomination and joining another. Sometimes we may run away from solemn responsibilities and opportunities by severing our ecclesiastical bonds. And if we belong to a church that is unfaithful we should do what we can to bring that unfaithfulness to an issue before we abruptly terminate our connection with it. Our corporate responsibility is most intense in that very communion in which we happen to be, and this responsibility requires the ministry of reproof and protest.

But while the question we face is not simple, nor the solution one that can be applied according to stereotyped pattern, yet we must face the implications of the principle that the corporate witness of the branch of the church to which we belong is also *our* witness. It is our witness because the corporate witness of a church never exists in abstraction, but only as it is expressed in the corporate-individual witness of its members. And this question we can evade no less than our own strictly individual witness. *There* hangs our witness to Christ as head and king and Lord of his church.

II. DENOMINATIONAL RESPONSIBILITY

Corporate responsibility not only makes it mandatory that we give earnest consideration to the question of our denominational affiliation, but also that we be deeply aware of and sensitive to the state and condition of that church to which we belong or with which we have affiliated ourselves. We can never take the position that we can segregate ourselves and bear witness in our own congregation, disregarding what may be happening in the denomination as a whole. This is the resort of too many in churches which have become unfaithful to Christ in their corporate witness. Good people and also ministers of the Word have settled down and consolidated themselves in the position that in the situation of widespread declension and apostasy it is their responsibility to do their utmost to preserve and promote orthodox faith and practice in their own local congregation. And they console themselves with the thought that their congregation maintains a witness to Christ and his gospel even though unbelief may abound throughout the denomination.

It is necessary to be faithful, first of all, in our local situation and it is there that individual and corporate responsibility is most accentuated. But it is to desert the corporate responsibility which we avow in our local situation if we do not apply it in the broader context of the church as a whole. This is the same evil of independentism and individualism as that by which we seek to isolate ourselves as individuals from our corporate relationships and responsibilities. Only, in this case, this individualism is applied to the local congregation rather than to the individual person.

This evil of concentrating our thought and interest and concern upon the local congregation appears, however, in orthodox denominations as well as heterodox. It is not only in opposing wrong that our corporate responsibility appears. It manifests itself also in the whole range of those functions which it is the responsibility of the church as a corporate entity to perform. Every member of the body of Christ must be alert to the corporate functions of the whole church. It is only in this way that the witness of the church can be maintained and furthered. Sometimes exclusive preoccupation with the work and witness of the local congregation may arise from the persuasion that the denomination is strictly orthodox in its work and witness and that we need not concern ourselves about it. Let the premise be true, the inference is false. The unity of the body of Christ is the principle which exposes its falsity, and experience has demonstrated that the sure road to decline and eventual heterodoxy is exclusive absorption with the work and witness of the local congregation. The whole denomination is a unit, and if one member suffers all the others suffer with it, if one member is honoured all the others rejoice with it. Such organic unity makes isolation of any kind impossible.

Let us then take our full share of the responsibilities that belong to us in the church of Christ and let us realize that only as each one of us is conscious of our relation to the whole shall we be sensitive to the demands of the honour of Christ and of the purity and unity of his body.

III. ECUMENICAL RELATIONSHIP

The corporate unity which belongs to the church of Christ is much broader than the unity which exists within the particular branch to which we belong. Our corporate relationship to our own denomination is, of course, the most intimate, and in that relationship our obligation is most intense. But the body of Christ is more embrasive than our denomination. The body of Christ comprises all Churches which can properly be esteemed Churches of Christ. Therefore, will we, nill we, our corporate responsibility extends beyond the branch of the church to which we belong, and our corporate witness is affected by the corporate witness of the whole church of Christ throughout the world.

This brings into acute focus the situation in which we are placed as members of the body of Christ. We sustain ecumenical relations and therefore we cannot absolve ourselves of responsibility in relation to the condition and state of the whole church of Christ. If we think of the error and wrong which exist within the bounds of the church of Christ, if we think of the abominations which are committed in Zion, if we remember how the love of many has waxed cold, we cannot self-complacently congratulate ourselves that we are entirely unrelated to these evils. They are evils which exist within the body of which we are members, and they must affect and infect us.

Perhaps we have sometimes wondered why the Christian witness, even in orthodox Churches, is so impotent, why godliness is at such a low ebb, why, when it ought to be a mighty torrent, it is but a trickle scarcely seen among the stones at the bottom of the river's channel. There are many reasons. But this is one of them—the declension and coldness in the church as a whole have affected and infected the whole body and this infection betrays itself in the low state of godliness in the individual members. There are many lessons to be learned. One of these requires special mention. It is that we should be aroused to earnest prayer and passion that God would arise and have mercy upon Zion, that the time to favour her, yea, the set time may speedily come, that the church of Christ throughout the whole world may be arrayed again in garments of glory and beauty, fair as the moon, clear as the sun, and terrible as an army with banners. Faith imbued with zeal for the honour of Christ and the glory of God will have no sympathy with the defeatism which is, after all, but disguised fatalism. He who is head over all things is head over all things to his body the church. He has all authority in heaven and in earth. And he is the Lord of the Spirit. Implicit in the prayer he taught his disciples to pray, 'thy will be done as in heaven so in earth', is the prayer that the whole earth should be filled with his praise. Nothing less is the measure of the believer's desire. 'And blessed be his glorious name for ever: and let the whole earth be filled with his glory.' May we not pray for the peace of Jerusalem— 'peace be within thy walls, and prosperity within thy palaces'. And who knows but the floodgates of reformation grace and power may be opened and we shall have occasion to say, 'When the Lord turned again the captivity of Zion, we were like them that dream. Then was our mouth filled with laughter, and our tongue with singing: then said they among the heathen, The Lord hath done great things for them. The Lord hath done great things for us; whereof we are glad.'

38

The Creedal Basis
of Union in the Church[1]

THE only infallible word we possess, and demanding for that reason unreserved and wholehearted commitment, is the Word of God deposited for us in the Scriptures. 'All Scripture is God-breathed' (2 Tim. 3:16). Whenever any humanly-framed document is accorded the place that Scripture occupies in the Christian faith then we have committed the sin of idolatry. For this attitude is akin to the sin of giving to a creature the worship that belongs only to God.

It is therefore understandable and worthy of respect that Christians should take the position 'No creed but Scripture', and should aver that if God intended any summary of faith to be the bond of fellowship among Christians and churches, he would have provided in the Scripture itself this form of sound words as the bond of communion. Furthermore it cannot be denied but we do have in the Scripture summary statements that comprise the most basic elements of our holy faith (cf. Eph. 4:4–6; Phil. 2:6–11; 1 Tim. 3:16). This contention is worthy of respect because underlying it is the recognition of the supreme and unique place of Scripture in the regulation of faith and the whole conduct of believers in their individual and collective witness. It is also worthy of respect because it often springs from a wholehearted reaction against the exaggerated veneration for humanly-composed creeds and the halo of sanctity placed around them, so that to question any of their statements is esteemed to be presumptuous, if not blasphemous.

1. *The Necessity of Creeds.* More deliberate and mature consideration

[1] The substance of an address given at the Leicester Ministers Conference, England, April 1965.

will, I submit, show the *necessity* of creedal confession and formulation and there are certain observations that may be stated:

1. There is the analogy of the preaching and teaching institution. In the Old Testament we have the example of Ezra and his colleagues who 'read in the book of the law distinctly, and gave the sense, and caused them to understand the reading' (Neh. 8:8). We are not to suppose that preaching and teaching consist in no more than the quotation and reiteration of passages of Scripture. These functions are aimed at giving the sense and causing the people to understand. Creedal formulation is but one way of giving the sense of Scripture in succinct form.

2. It is a fact of history that the church in the maintenance and defence of the faith found it necessary to formulate her faith in creedal statement in order to guard the faith against the incursions of error. Can it be denied that the Nicene Creed proved to be the bulwark against a heresy that would have removed the cornerstone of Christian confession? The most prolific period of creedal composition was the Reformation. And can we discount the fact that this activity was coincident with the greatest revival of faith since the days of the apostles? It was the fruit of this revival of faith and the expression of it.

3. In the acceptance of Scripture as the Word of God and the rule of faith and life, there is the incipient and basic creedal confession. Some statement must be made to this effect and to the exclusion of all other norms of faith and conduct. But why should creedal confession be restricted to the doctrine of Scripture? There are other doctrines just as essential as the doctrine of Scripture. Furthermore, in our situation today, it is not sufficient to affirm Scripture to be the Word of God, the infallible rule of faith, because such a confession in the esteem of many comports with a view of Scripture that denies the doctrine of Scripture that the evangelical maintains and that is set forth in the Scripture itself. Thus the basic confession must be elaborated to assert and defend that view of Scripture implicit in the confession that it is the Word of God.

4. It is apparent that the most basic contradictions of unbelief may coexist with a watertight doctrine of Scripture. An Arian view of Christ's person may be entertained by one affirming the most orthodox doctrine of Scripture. And thus, as already indicated, the bond of fellowship must be extended to include other aspects of the Christian

confession, and there is opened a wide area of Christian witness that a creed adequate to fellowship must comprise.

Having said these things respecting necessity, the next question we face is that of extent and nature.

2. *The Extent of Creedal Confession.* Certain preliminary negations must be taken for granted. It will not suffice for a confession to be merely catholic; it must be a protestant confession. It must be more than goes under the name of evangelical; neo-orthodoxy is excluded for many reasons but chiefly because it is incompatible with the basic confession, the doctrine of Scripture. Is it sufficient then to have a common denominator confession, general and broad enough to express the faith of all true evangelicals, but lacking in the specifics on which such evangelicals are divided?

There is a great deal of argument that may be advanced in support of this solution for the question of ecclesiastical fellowship. Perhaps the most potent is the analogy of several organizations whose sole purpose is the furtherance of the kingdom of God and the interests of the gospel, and whose statement of faith is brief but thoroughly biblical as far as it goes. On this basis persons of truly evangelical faith may unite for the promotion of worthy ends. I am not now questioning the propriety of such organizations nor of the restricted confessional basis which forms the bond of union and co-operation in the enterprises concerned. Many worthy objectives can be undertaken in association with others on the basis of a restricted statement of faith and purpose. It may then be said: Why not adopt the same pattern for ecclesiastical affiliation and union?

I submit that the analogy does not hold in the kind of union that the unity of the church as the body of Christ contemplates and demands. The reason for this is that there is a radical difference between these organizations and the church of God. It is the difference between a voluntary organization and the church. The church is not a voluntary organization; it is a divinely instituted organization of which Christ is the head, the assembly of the covenant people of God, the fellowship of the Spirit, and the body of Christ. The witness given to bear and the confession to be made is the whole counsel of God. There is no restriction that may properly be devised, proposed, or imposed. Its faith is the whole revealed counsel of God, and the functions assigned to it can be nothing less or more than those appointed by Christ. Faith and function are not selective but given by Christ.

This principle expressed in the phrase 'the whole counsel of God' leads us to a series of considerations. If our confession is the acceptance of Scripture as *in toto* the infallible Word of God, then our confession can be nothing less than the whole counsel of God revealed in that Word. The acceptance of Scripture would be mockery if it did not carry that implication, and on no other position can we proceed with our inquiry.

It is here, however, that we encounter divergence when we undertake to relate this commitment to creedal formulation. For there is difference as to what we conceive the whole counsel of God to be on those very specifics which admittedly call for creedal statement in the historical situation in which God has placed us. This is the divergence in the matter of interpretation of the inscripturated Word.

The infallible rule of the interpretation of Scripture is the Scripture itself. But there is no infallible interpretation of that rule and hence there has never been complete agreement in the church respecting every detail of interpretation and application. There has not even been such agreement on specifics which are cardinal in the Christian confession. And even when there is agreement on all cardinal specifics of doctrine, as was true to such an extent in the Westminster Assembly, nevertheless there were differences among the divines on certain points of doctrine, not to speak of those concerned with government and discipline. In one instance at least the Confession of Faith was drawn up in such terms that the division of judgment could not appear and each could enjoy his own sense, as George Gillespie stated. Thus it would be impossible to attempt a creedal formulation on all points of biblical preaching, and no branch of the church has ever attempted to do so. Creedal confession is not a commentary on the whole of Scripture nor is it a systematic theology. Therefore, although commitment to the whole counsel of God is implicit in the confession of Scripture as the Word of God, this counsel of God cannot be incorporated in all its details in creedal confession and formulation. There must in the nature of the case be limitation and restriction, and creedal statement must be content to deal with what is more central in this counsel of God and determinative of what it is in its essential character and distinctiveness. This is not as hopeless a criterion as might appear at first sight. Since there is in Scripture the consent of all the parts and the unity of the whole, there is what has been called the analogy of the faith, or in other words, a system of truth. Creedal statement can and should take account of this and formulate its creed accordingly. This is the principle that governed the representative creeds of the 16th-century Reformation.

There is another factor that must be taken into account. It is a fact of history that creedal confession expanded as the exigencies of controversy and the demands of reformation pressed home the necessity of development. We must not discount, may I repeat, the situation in history in which God has placed us. This would be retrogression. But, of greater moment, it would be dishonouring to the Holy Spirit who in the unfolding events of providence has been enlightening the church to the fuller understanding of his revealed counsel. To go back upon this development and resort to a more attenuated creedal affirmation is to discard the work of the Holy Spirit in the generations of Christian history.

In dealing with the content of creedal confession, however, the more perplexing question is still before us and haunts us: how are we to resolve the diversity of interpretation and conception pertaining to the cardinal aspects of God's counsel? Perhaps the most faithful way of answering the question is to become concrete and instance some of the specifics that cannot be waived in creedal confession.

3. *Specific Examples*. First, let us think of the doctrine of election. It must be admitted that election is a cardinal doctrine of the Word of God. The doctrine of salvation is surely paramount in our faith and therefore in any confession individual or collective. But election is fontal in the whole process of salvation. Now if election must enter into our confession it should be plain that we get nowhere in our confession if we merely affirm God's election of men and that ultimate salvation is co-extensive with election. So divergent are the views of election stated in these general terms, that for one entertaining one view another view is a denial of election, and his commitment to the whole counsel of God requires of him that, if election is to be embraced in the creed that is the symbol of his faith, this doctrine must be expressed in terms that will

exclude what he esteems to be a negation of the truth. The difference between the Barthian view and the Reformed orthodox position is a patent instance. But, in addition, the person of whom I am thinking believes that election is an act of sovereign grace and is determined by nothing other than the unconditioned good pleasure of God, and that, if it is determined by God's foresight of some autonomous decision of men, then the doctrine is so eviscerated that the essence of election as taught in Scripture is removed. That is to say, the Reformed Christian cannot permit his confession at this point to be acceptable to an avowed Arminian.

Let us think also of the Atonement. It is surely to be acknowledged that no tenet of the faith is more precious than the vicarious blood-shedding of the Son of God. Any position that impinges upon its nature as obedience, expiation, propitiation, reconciliation, and redemption undermines the whole doctrine of vicarious atonement. Among evangelicals there is open and avowed cleavage on the subject of extent. The proponents of universal atonement are jealous for most of the categories in terms of which the nature of the atonement is defined. But they are not aware of the implications of their position in respect of extent as it bears upon the cardinal aspect of the doctrine. If the atonement itself is universal and some of those for whom it was made finally perish, then the atonement does not save any, does not expiate the wrath of God for any, does not reconcile any to God, does not actually redeem any. This is the central issue: does the atonement effectively redeem? If universal atonement is to be consistently maintained, then the logical issue is universal salvation. This inference is not drawn, of course, by true evangelicals. But it is no less true that the extent and nature are so bound together that the person aware of this interrelationship cannot allow lack of definiteness in the enunciation of the doctrine of the atonement; for, in that event, he would fall short of what he believes to be the counsel of God on the central tenet of his faith.

The atonement and justification are closely related. Justification rests upon all the categories, but it is here that vicarious obedience comes to focal expression and application. It is what has been called the active obedience of Christ. Christ's obedience is the only righteousness reckoned by God to a sinner's account in justification. The biblical doctrine of justification is that the righteousness of God is brought to bear upon our situation, and that it is because a righteousness with divine properties becomes ours that we are made the righteousness of God in Christ and justified freely by his grace. This righteousness is contrasted not only with human unrighteousness but with human righteousness.

Let us also reflect on the doctrines of sin and grace. The Reformed believe that man is totally depraved until regenerated by saving grace (cf. Rom. 3:9ff.). The whole construction of the application of redemption is determined and conditioned by this view of man in his fallen state. The doctrines of calling, regeneration, and the origin of faith are radically affected by this estimate of man's sinfulness. No one can deny but that the proclamation of the gospel to the lost is conditioned by this assessment of man's depravity. So even evangelism is conceived of in very different terms from that entertained by those who do not share this estimate of man's helplessness. That the confession of the Reformed person can ignore all these aspects of what he believes, no sympathetic and conscientious person, whatever may be his own viewpoint, could expect or demand.

We thus see from these examples that the soteriological confession, from this ultimate foundation in God's sovereign election to its completion in the application in redemption, is not the confession of the Reformed believer unless it is characterized by the views of election, atonement, sin, and grace which have been set forth. And it is to annul the purpose of church confession to suppose that the confession can be stripped and attenuated, and that these features are to be sacrificed in the interest of a more inclusive ecclesiastical fellowship.

Although I have dealt with these doctrines from the standpoint of the Reformed person, it must be remembered that the person not holding this viewpoint is just as conscientiously and necessarily compelled to exclude these and other tenets from his creedal confession. The reason is that he does not consider these doctrines to be scriptural. They are, he thinks, logical deductions or refinements that pervert the simplicity of the gospel. They are beyond the counsel of God, and to go beyond is just as perilous as to fall short. We may not add to or take from the Word of God. We thus have an impasse that cannot be overcome. Though Reformed evangelicals and non-Reformed evangelicals may embrace one another in love, in the bond of fellowship with Christ, and co-operate in many activities that promote the kingdom of God and the interests of Christ's church, yet it is not feasible, and not feasible in terms of commitment to Christ and to the whole counsel of God, to unite in creedal confession as the bond and symbol of ecclesiastical communion. And when we consider the whole question on the secondary bases of practical workability, is it not the case that the basic divergences in doctrine become the occasion for disputes that frustrate the unity and dissolve the bond of peace which the church must maintain and display?

Historical

39

Reformation[1]

THE Reformation Translation Fellowship (R.T.F.) under whose auspices we are meeting, had in view, no doubt, the Reformation of the 16th and 17th centuries when the word *Reformation* was adopted to identify the kind of translation activity which it intended to undertake. It is a worthy objective, to maintain and revive appreciation of the Reformation, and to propagate in foreign lands in their own languages the literary product of the Reformation and literature faithful to Reformation principles. In these days of an ecumenical passion that blurs the lines of distinction between truth and error, it is well to keep before our minds the great grace bestowed upon the church and the world in the Reformation. We are so far removed from those centuries that we are too ready to underestimate or even forget the surpassing privilege that is ours in the Reformation heritage. I am not discounting the harbingers of the Reformation in the century or centuries preceding the 16th. But it was in the latter that what had been dawning in the preceding period reached the full light of gospel blessing and liberation. We need but think of the superstition that encompassed the church when Luther nailed his theses to the church door in Wittenberg, in order to catch some vision of the darkness that then began to be dispelled and of the glory that had begun to appear on the horizon. And we also need to think of what would have been our situation today, if God in just and holy judgment had withheld his grace and suffered this superstition, with its entail of implications, to continue and develop the system of

[1] An address given in Edinburgh in 1965 at the Annual Meeting of the Reformation Translation Fellowship.

iniquity that it represented. Think of what our situation would be without a Protestant Reformation. For, notwithstanding the restraint placed upon Rome by Protestant revolt, secession, and protest, she has proceeded to formulate as dogmas those tenets which bring to expression the genius for invention that has been the secret of her corruption and imposture. In the course of a century she has given the impostures of the immaculate conception, papal infallibility, and the assumption of the virgin.

We fail to accord to the Reformers our debt of gratitude when we cease to prize our heritage. Other men laboured and we have entered into their labours. But far greater is the sin of failing to give praise to God.

This heritage is not only one to be cherished; it is one to be propagated. The Reformation was the rediscovery of the revealed counsel of God on the most vital issues of the Christian faith. It might be summed up in the rediscovery of salvation by grace. But the Reformation was the reassertion of the whole counsel of God, to the refutation of error and display of the truth. *Sola gratia* and *sola scriptura* were its fundamental principles. By one line of logical connection or another, all Reformation doctrine and practice are dependent upon and traceable to these two principles. These principles need to be propagated with renewed zeal and zest.

Reformation, however, must not consist only in retrospect nor in the repristination of the legacy furnished by the Reformation of the 16th and 17th centuries. Reformation is a present duty. It is true that we cannot properly engage in the present task if we discard our moorings in the past. If we do not build upon the foundations laid in the Reformation principles, then, to say the least, there will be something naive about our present efforts and the product of them. But Reformation as a task here and now is complexioned by the different context in which we live. I feel certain that the R.T.F. is keenly alive to this demand, and it is to this present task it addresses itself. How does the demand affect us now? What does it have in view and what are the emphases this hour requires?

No doubt many who are imbued with a sense of need and address themselves to it would look at the situation from different perspectives and place in the forefront different emphases. To these various perspectives we should be sympathetic. The situation is complex and therefore demands a whole gamut of activities to meet this complexity. But I do submit that in respect of both faith and life no emphases have greater priority or urgency than the three I am going to mention.

First, there is *sola scriptura*. As indicated already, this was basic in the Reformation. From the standpoint of the controversy with Rome it is still central. If any other canon is permitted to regulate our polemic, then our witness has the seeds of compromise and of failure from the outset. The Word of God is the sword of the Spirit, and Scripture alone is the Word of God for us. It is impossible to refute Romish contentions or resist its inroads if we allow any other canon to be the criterion of faith. This is the weapon God has given and, let it be remembered, Scripture, because of its sufficiency, is adequate to every controversy and to every challenge if we interpret and apply it aright in the richness and fulness of its counsel. It is adequate for the refutation of every imposture that Rome has foisted upon the world and the church.

Reformation today is not only concerned with Rome. It is ours to deal with what had not entered into the minds of the Reformers. There are many aspects to the challenge which movements within Protestantism offer to us. I shall reflect, however, on only one. It is the divergence from historic Protestantism expressed in what may be called in general terms the dialectic theology of which Karl Barth is the best known exponent. It might seem that *sola scriptura* is not the issue here. For this theology, especially in the hands of its chief exponent, is insistent that the Bible is the Word of God. Formally, there is no dispute with the *sola scriptura* principle. However, it is precisely on this question that the issue has to be joined. It is on the question of *scriptura*. When we say Scripture, we mean Scripture, that which is committed to writing, the Word written, the Word inscripturated. This is what the dialectic theology denies, and denies with vehemence. The Bible is not, it says, the Word of God *written*, it is not itself revelatory Word. It witnesses to the Word of God or the vehicle by which the Word of God comes to us. On the contrary, the historic meaning of the formula is that Scripture is the Word of God and the only Word available to us, that we have in Scripture the deposit of what God speaks to us, that here and now we have the voice of God directed to us in verbal utterance, and nowhere else. It is of paramount concern for true faith and the life of faith that the implications of Scripture as the Word of God *written* be fully appreciated and proclaimed. For the instrument of Reformation is the proclamation of the whole counsel of God, and if we do not have that revealed counsel in Scripture as the deposit of God's revealed will, then we have no way of knowing what that counsel is, and no criterion by which we may test the truth or validity of what is proclaimed.

A great deal is being said nowadays about the necessity of relevance, and in certain circles it is being averred that the Scripture as it was understood by Christians in the first century is not relevant to modern man; that, conditioned as he is by the scientific world-view, it is impossible for him to accept the framework in which the New Testament is cast. It is not to be denied that the gospel proclaimed must be relevant, that it must be presented to men where they are, and meet their needs in the situations in which they find themselves. But one thing must be said. It is only by the proclamation of the whole counsel of God, particularly regarding sin, misery, and the judgment of God, that men will discover where they are and begin to assess their need. Much of the plea for relevance proceeds on the premise that what men assess as their need, and demand for the satisfaction of this need, is that to which the gospel must be adjusted. The result is that the solution proposed and the message proclaimed are accommodations to humanly conceived and framed demands. There is the basic fallacy that men apart from the conviction created and conditioned by law and gospel are able to know what their real situation and need are. It is God's judgment respecting sin and misery that must be brought to bear upon men where they are and where they find themselves. When this priority is not observed, then all presumed relevance is a distortion of the gospel—in our day in the hands of its leading exponent, Rudolf Bultmann, such a distortion as denies the central elements of the gospel, the vicarious expiatory blood-shedding of the Saviour and his bodily resurrection from the dead. We must unashamedly and uncompromisingly declare the whole counsel of God, so that men, in conviction, will be *made* relevant to the gospel. This is the relevance Reformation requires and it is the relevance Reformation will bring.

Second, co-ordinate with *sola scriptura* is the witness of the Holy Spirit. Though Scripture provides the whole content of faith and is the sole regulative principle, we must equally insist that the effectual operation of Scripture is dependent upon the Holy Spirit. Our persuasion of the divine origin, character, and authority of Scripture is from the inward work of the Holy Spirit in our hearts. But not only so. All effectual understanding and application is dependent upon his abiding presence and operation in the hearts and lives of men. The failures that have so frequently attended the efforts of the church arise from dishonour to the Holy Spirit. Have we duly appreciated the great truth that this is the age of Pentecost? The Holy Spirit was given on the day of Pentecost in worldwide activity in the fulness of his grace and power. Pentecost was an event co-ordinate with the death, resurrection, and ascension of Christ in the fulfilment of God's worldwide redemptive design. It was a once-for-all event not to be repeated. But it is also an event that has not been repealed in its significance for his abiding presence and activity in the church and in the world.

Here I submit is one of the great sins; we have not been sufficiently conscious of the Spirit's function and grace; we have failed to bring *sola gratia* to its consistent expression.

With the emphasis placed today upon relevance is the interest in communication. Far be it from us to resist the indictment that belongs to us in this respect. But with all the cultivation that effective communication requires, have we neglected what is the secret of effectual communication, the unction, demonstration, and power of the Holy Spirit?

Third, there is the indispensable emphasis upon prayer, prayer individually and collectively. Our dependence upon the Holy Spirit is correlative with *sola scriptura*; likewise prayer is correlative with our dependence upon the Holy Spirit. When the church is earnest and persevering in intercession then we have the promise, 'Before they call I will answer, and while they are yet speaking I will hear.' It is striking how the Lord himself in the days of his flesh enlisted the disciples in the ministry of prayer for labourers to be sent into the harvest. 'Pray ye therefore the Lord of the harvest that he will send forth labourers into his harvest.' 'I have set watchmen.'

Retrospect, duty, prospect!

Reformation in prospect! It is our duty to pray for and labour unto worldwide reformation, whatever may be the purpose of God in the unfolding of his redemptive plan for the world. If we are jealous and zealous for Christ's honour, for the crown rights of the Saviour, we cannot have lesser desire and passion than the worldwide extension and embrace of his Kingdom. But it is not only the duty, desire, and passion that we must entertain. There is also the promise.

It will be granted by all of us that no book in the Bible is more replete with the gospel than the Epistle to the Romans. There is, however, a feature of this Epistle often overlooked. It is the note of universalism appearing so frequently. It appears in the theme of the Epistle (Rom. 1:16, 17); it appears in the delineation of the final judgment (Rom. 2:4-16); it appears in the indictment upon sin and sinfulness (Rom. 3:9-23); it appears in the interpretation of the effects of Adam's sin (Rom. 5:12, 18). But it also appears in those chapters in which the apostle unfolds for us not distributive and all-inclusive universalism, but what we may call the redemptive philosophy of world history, chapters 9-11. They disclose to us in a way that is without parallel in the New Testament the ways in which God's diverse providences to Jew and Gentile react upon and interact with one another for the promotion of his saving designs. It is the restoration and reclamation of Israel as a people that may be said to be the leading theme in chapter 11. But if it is the central theme, there is another that clusters around it or, perhaps more accurately, is interwoven with it. And this theme is the unprecedented blessing for the Gentiles. 'If the trespass of them is the riches of the world, and their defeat the riches of the Gentiles, how much more their fulness.' (11:12). 'For if the casting away of them is the reconciliation of the world, what shall the receiving of them be but life from the dead?' (11:15). 'Hardening in part hath befallen Israel until the fulness of the Gentiles be come in, and so all Israel shall be saved' (11:25, 26).

Again, I submit that we have been too ready to succumb to a defeatism by which we fail to entertain any confident hope respecting the future prospects of the kingdom of God and of the church in this world. If the texts I have quoted, and others I have not quoted, are the

Word of God, they are words of promise and hope for unprecedented success for the gospel and for a transformation that measures to the proportion of life from the dead. Surely there is a convergence of the word of Scripture, the power of the Holy Spirit, and the fervent exercise of prayer upon the assurance given that, if the trespass of Israel is the riches of the world, how much more their fulness! Promise dictates prayer, and hope is the incentive to prayer. When we pray for the conversion and restoration of Israel, what Paul calls their fulness, their receiving, and their salvation, we are praying for that which will be, in God's saving programme and purpose, the signal for unprecedented extension of gospel blessing for the world. Reformation in prospect is the demand of Christ's honour; as promise it is the ground of hope.

40

The Crux of the Reformation

THE nailing of Luther's ninety-five theses to the Church door in Wittenberg on October 31st, 1517, was the event that more than any other event marks the inception of the movement called the Protestant Reformation. It is well that we should celebrate that event (cf. Psalm 77:11). Celebration can be devoid of any significant appreciation of what was involved in that movement. We can become partisan idolaters, for celebration may be little more than an expression of loyalty to certain traditions. If we are to honour God, our remembrance will proceed from profound gratitude to him for the light that shone in the midst of darkness, and for the emancipation that occurred when the Reformers were cut loose from shackles of superstition and idolatry.

What was the light that arose in darkness? What is the heritage the Reformation has bequeathed? The issues at stake were not questions removed from the deepest and highest interests of men. They were issues that concern the human soul in its relation to God and ultimate destiny. They were intensely religious. I am going to focus attention on two of these.

AUTHORITY

First and foremost is the issue of authority, the standard or rule by which we are to answer all religious questions. The ultimate answer to that question is that God is the authority. Rome does not deny that proposition. To say that God is the authority does not, however, answer our practical concern. For the question arises: how does the will of God come into relevant relation to us? How does the mind of

God come into contact with our mind, so that God's mind for us on the great issues of life may be known and become our mind? The answer is, revelation from God to us. Again Rome does not deny that proposition. The second Vatican Council declares that 'through divine revelation, God chose to show forth and communicate Himself and the eternal decisions of His will regarding the salvation of men' (Revelation, I, 6). But even this proposition does not meet our quest. For we have to ask the question: Where is this revelation? Where do we find it?

Here there is a decisive answer. We find it in Holy Scripture (cf. 2 Tim. 3:16), and we have gone a long way. We have revelation from God in our hands, concrete and intelligible. It should not be overlooked that Rome, at the Reformation and now, says the same of Holy Scripture. Vatican II has declared that 'the books of both the Old and New Testament in their entirety, with all their parts, are sacred and canonical, because having been written under the inspiration of the Holy Spirit . . . they have God as their author and have been handed on as such to the Church.'

'Therefore, since everything asserted by the inspired authors or sacred writers must be held to be asserted by the Holy Spirit, it follows that the books of Scripture must be acknowledged as teaching firmly, faithfully, and without error that truth which God wanted put into the sacred writings for the sake of our salvation' (Revelation, III, 11).

Yet there is the great divide and it appears at this precise point in our progression. Rome says there is another treasury of special revelation besides Holy Scripture, a treasury that is likewise from God and to be co-ordinated with Holy Scripture. It is what may be called oral tradition, sharply distinguished by the word 'oral' in contrast with 'written'. It means that there were revelations given by Christ and by the Holy Spirit that were not included in Scripture, but are handed on from generation to generation in the church and by the church, particularly in and by the bishops as the alleged successors of the apostles. Vatican II is particularly insistent on this co-ordination and on the magisterium of the church in reference to both.

'Hence there exist a close connexion and communication between sacred tradition and sacred Scripture. For both of them, flowing from the same divine well-spring, in a certain way merge into a unity and tend toward the same end. For sacred Scripture is the Word of God, inasmuch as it is consigned to writing under the inspiration of the divine Spirit. To the successors of the apostles, sacred tradition hands on in its full purity, God's word which was entrusted to the apostles by Christ the Lord and the Holy Spirit . . . Consequently it is not from sacred Scripture alone that the Church draws her certainty about everything that has been revealed. Therefore both sacred tradition and sacred Scripture are to be accepted and venerated with the same sense of devotion and reverence' (Revelation, II, 9). 'Sacred tradition and sacred Scripture form one sacred deposit of the word of God, which is committed to the Church' (Revelation II, 10).

The task of authentic interpretation of both has been entrusted exclusively to the living, teaching office of the Church. Thus tradition, Scripture, and the teaching authority in the Church are so linked and joined together that one cannot stand without the other (cf. *ibid.*). Tradition develops because there is a progressive understanding and consensus in the Church. This is why in the Church of Rome we have such dogmas as the immaculate conception (1854), the infallibility of the pope (1870), and the assumption of the virgin (1950). Closely related to this claim to the teaching authority of the church is the primacy of the Roman Pontiff. The decrees of Vatican II are permeated with this claim. 'The sacred Council once again sets out . . . this doctrine of the institution, the perpetuity, the power and the nature of the sacred primacy of the Roman Pontiff and of his infallible magisterium' ('Dogmatic Constitution on the Church', III, 18). Though individual bishops do not enjoy infallibility yet 'when they agree on a single opinion to be held as definitive, they are proclaiming infallibly the teaching of Christ' (*ibid.*, III, 25).

'The divine Redeemer wanted his Church to be equipped with this infallibility in the definition of doctrine on faith and morals . . . In virtue of his office, the Roman Pontiff, head of the college of Bishops, enjoys this infallibility, when he makes a definitive pronouncement of doctrine on faith or morals, as the supreme pastor and teacher of all the faithful . . . His definitions deserve, in consequence, to be called unalterable of themselves, and not by reason of the Church's agreement; for they are delivered with the Holy Spirit's assistance, which was promised to him in the person of St. Peter. Consequently they stand in no need of approval on the part of others, and they admit of no appeal to another court . . . The infallibility promised to the Church exists also in the body of Bishops, when it exercises supreme magisterium in combination with Peter's successor. The assent of the Church can never fail to be given to these definitions' (*ibid.*).

Here we are not dealing with an academic question; it is one of intense religious concern. If I must listen to the voice of the Church as it comes to expression in the consensus of bishops, and particularly in definitive pronouncements of the Roman Pontiff, I must be assured that this voice is invested with divine authority. I must have assurance from God that this voice is his voice. I must have a word from him certifying to me that this is likewise his word. Where am I to find this assurance? To be most concrete, where am I to find God's own certification that the Pope's, the Roman Pontiff's definitive pronouncements of doctrine on faith and morals, are infallible and therefore binding me to faith and obedience?

I do find that the Lord Jesus said to Peter, 'On this rock I will build my church . . . And I will give thee the keys of the kingdom of heaven' (Matt. 16:18, 19). But I also find that Jesus breathed on the ten apostles and said: 'Receive ye the Holy Ghost: whose soever sins ye remit, they are remitted unto them; and whose soever sins ye retain, they are retained' (John 20:22, 23). So the binding and loosing referred to in the word addressed to Peter is not the exclusive prerogative of Peter. I also find that the church, as the household of God, is 'built upon the foundation of the apostles and prophets, Jesus Christ himself being the chief corner stone' (Eph. 2:20). I look in vain in the teaching of the New Testament, or in the practice of the apostolic church, for any primacy of Peter.

There is abundant evidence in the New Testament, and more particularly in the teaching of Jesus, for the authority vested in the apostles by delegation from Christ. And the legacy of the apostles, authoritative by the institution of Christ and by the inspiration of the Holy Spirit, we find in the books of the New Testament. But nowhere do we find that the apostles have successors invested with equivalent authority by delegation from Christ. Far less do we find any evidence for a successor to Peter in his supposed primacy.

What we do find in the claims of the Roman Catholic Church is a pretentious superstructure, based upon assumptions for which there is no evidence in the revelation God has given us. The consequence is a tyrannical distortion of what our Lord himself affirmed, and the Scriptures of the New Testament witness, respecting apostolic authority. The most recent pronouncements of Rome continue to reiterate and enforce the usurpations in respect of authority whereby the basic principles that God alone is the source of all authority, and his revealed will the norm, are made void in the magisterium of the Church, and most particularly in the supreme magisterium of the Roman Pontiff. It is the irony of this usurpation that in Roman claims we have the most blatant example of lording it over God's heritage in contravention of Peter's own inspired utterance: 'Neither as lording it over those committed to your charge, but becoming examples to the flock' (1 Pet. 5:3).

JUSTIFICATION

The second issue on which I am going to focus attention is that of justification. The basic religious question is: How can man be just with God? If man had never sinned the all-important question would have been: How can man be right with God? He would continue to be right with God by fulfilling the will of God perfectly. But the question takes on a radically different complexion with the entrance of sin. Man is wrong with God. And the question is: How can man *become* right with God? This was Luther's burning question. He found the answer in Paul's Epistles to the Romans and the Galatians, that we are justified by faith alone, through grace alone—'justified freely by his grace through the redemption that is in Christ Jesus' (Rom. 3:24); and 'being justified by faith we have peace with God' (Rom. 5:1).

It is to be acknowledged and appreciated that theologians of the Roman Catholic Church are giving a great deal of renewed attention to this subject, and there is a gratifying recognition that 'to justify' is 'to declare to be righteous', that it is a declarative act on God's part. But the central issue of the Reformation still remains. Rome still maintains and declares that justification consists in renovation and sanctification, and the decrees of the Council of Trent have not been retracted or repudiated. Even in the case of those theologians who admit that justification is declarative, the question still remains: on what ground does God justify? Is it on the basis of righteousness inwrought and outwrought, or on the basis of the righteousness of Christ wrought for us? The issue remains in all its poignancy. On what basis are we sinners justified before God and made heirs of eternal life? Is it righteousness infused by which we are made just, or righteousness imputed by which we are reckoned just? The issue concerns the heart of the gospel, the grand article of a standing or falling Church.

Renovation and sanctification are indispensable elements of the gospel, and justification must never be separated from regeneration and sanctification. But to make justification to consist in renovation and sanctification is to eliminate from the gospel that which meets our basic need as sinners, and answers the basic religious question: How can a sinner become just with God? The answer is that which makes the lame man leap as an hart and the tongue of the dumb sing. It is the proclamation that a sinner is accepted with God because he is clothed with a righteousness in which omniscience can find no spot and perfect holiness no blemish. Why so? It is the righteousness of God by faith of Jesus Christ (cf. Rom. 1:16, 17; 3:21, 22; 10:3; 2 Cor. 5:21; Phil. 3:9). This is not God's attribute of justice, but it is a God-righteousness, a righteousness with divine properties and qualities, contrasted not only with human unrighteousness but with human righteousness. And what this righteousness is, the apostle makes very clear. It is a free gift. 'For if by one man's offence death reigned by one; much more they which receive abundance of grace and of the gift of righteousness shall reign in life by one, Jesus Christ' (Rom. 5:17). 'For as by one man's disobedience many were made sinners, so by the obedience of one shall many be constituted righteous' (Rom. 5:19). 'Him who knew no sin he made to be sin for us, that we might be made the righteousness of God in him' (2 Cor. 5:21).

When Paul invokes God's anathema upon any who would preach a gospel other than that *he* preached (Gal. 1:8, 9), he used a term which means 'devoted to destruction'. It is a term weighted with imprecation. Why such language of passion? Paul was impassioned with the love of Christ and of Christ's gospel. To the core of his being he was persuaded that the heresy combated was aimed at the destruction of the gospel. It took the crown from the Redeemer's head. It is this same passion that must imbue us if we are worthy children of the Reformation. Central to the issue that raised the banner in 1517, and central to the issue with Rome still, is the gospel of a full, perfect, and irrevocable justification by free gift through faith in Jesus Christ, on the basis of a righteousness undefiled and undefilable, a righteousness in which omniscience finds no blemish, a righteousness of God, the righteousness of him who fulfilled all righteousness and was obedient unto death, even the death of the cross. It is this righteousness that prophets extolled. 'I will greatly rejoice in the Lord' (Isa. 61:10). 'Behold, the days come, saith the Lord, that I will raise unto David a righteous Branch . . . In his days Judah shall be saved, and Israel shall dwell safely: and this is his name whereby he shall be called, the Lord our righteousness' (Jer. 23:5, 6). It is in this righteousness that believers glory. 'Not having mine own righteousness, which is of the law, but that which is through the faith of Christ, the righteousness which is of God by faith' (Phil. 3:9).

41

Calvin as Theologian and Expositor[1]

IN assessing the place that John Calvin occupies in the history of the church and in the exposition of the Christian faith, there are two observations to be made at the outset. First, if we accord to Calvin a place of unique eminence, it is not to detract from others who by God's grace and enduement have adorned the church of Christ and enhanced the understanding of the inscripturated deposit of faith. God has endowed men in accord with his sovereign distribution of talent and grace, and we must humbly and gratefully recognize the contribution which each has been called to make to the building up of that body which will one day be presented faultless as the church glorious and glorified. Second, we must resist every tendency or disposition to a veneration that accords to men any of the deference or glory belonging only to God. This warning is not a platitude. We are only too liable, particularly on anniversary occasions, to indulge in the esteem that passes into adulation. And at all times we must remember that men, however great their stature, are still only men characterized by infirmity, earthen vessels into which God has put treasure, and our servants for Jesus' sake. There is no finality to Calvin's work. We can properly appreciate the work of men only when we bring to our evaluation the critical judgment that is based upon and instructed by the infallible Word of God.

As we think of Calvin we must think, first of all, of his greatest work, *The Institutes of the Christian Religion*. Over a quarter century, until this

---

1 The Annual Lecture of The Evangelical Library, London, 1964.

treatise reached its definitive form in 1559, he expended his greatest powers in the revision and expansion of this his masterpiece. The *Institutes* is the representative treatise of the Reformation. It was this work that gave to the Protestant Church the systematic presentation of Christian doctrine and the apologetic defence of Protestant faith indispensable to the polemic being conducted with Rome and to protection of the Reformation movement against those extremes and excesses invariably attendant upon liberation from tyranny. It was the *Institutes* that turned the battle to the gate. In Warfield's words: 'In the immense upheaval of the Reformation movement, the foundations of the faith seemed to many to be broken up, and the most important questions to be set adrift; extravagances of all sorts sprang up on every side; and we can scarcely wonder that a feeling of uneasiness was abroad, and men were asking with concern for some firm standing-ground for their feet. It was Calvin's 'Institutes' which, with its calm, clear, positive exposition of the evangelical faith on the irrefragable authority of the Holy Scriptures, gave stability to wavering minds, and confidence to sinking hearts, and placed upon the lips of all a brilliant apology, in the face of the calumnies of the enemies of the Reformation'.[1]

We have not done justice to Calvin, however, until we compass the whole range of theology. He is *par excellence* the theologian of the Christian church. Joseph Scaliger (1540-1609), himself a professor of theology at Geneva after Calvin's death and one of the most erudite of his time, exclaimed of Calvin: '*solus inter theologos Calvinus*'. The editors of the Brunswick edition of Calvin's works have not exaggerated when they say: 'For if Luther was supremely great as a man, Zwingli second to none as a Christian citizen, Melanchthon rightly designated the most learned of teachers, Calvin may justly be called the prince and standard-bearer of theologians'.[2] Or again in B. B. Warfield's words: 'What Thucydides is among Greek, or Gibbon among eighteenth-century English historians, what Plato is among philosophers, or the Iliad among epics, or Shakespeare among dramatists, that Calvin's 'Institutes' is among theological treatises'.[3] In the last century no one in

[1] *Calvin and Calvinism*, 1931, p. 373.
[2] *Calvini Opera*, I, 1863, p. IX.
[3] *op. cit.*, p. 374.

the British Isles was more competent than William Cunningham in the field of historical theology, and his verdict is: 'The "Institutio" of Calvin is the most important work in the history of theological science, that which is more than any other creditable to its author, and has exerted directly or indirectly the greatest and most beneficial influence upon the opinions of intelligent men on theological subjects'.[1]

If we ask the question as to the reasons for this assessment there is the paramount consideration that, in the words of William Cunningham, 'he is the greatest and best theologian who has most accurately apprehended the meaning of the statements of Scripture,—who, by comparing and combining them, has most fully and correctly brought out the whole mind of God on all the topics on which the Scriptures give us information,—who classifies and digests the truths of Scripture in the way best fitted to commend them to the apprehension and acceptance of men,—and who can most clearly and forcibly bring out their scriptural evidence, and most skilfully and effectively defend them against the assaults of adversaries'.[2] All of this Calvin fulfilled, and therein lies the secret of his pre-eminence.

I make bold to say, however, that the perennial and universal eminence belonging to Calvin must find its explanation in other additional factors, implied to some extent in Cunningham's summation of criteria, but, nevertheless, requiring expansion and supplementation. The first of these factors I am constrained to mention and place in the forefront is that feature which accords to Calvin's major treatise its perpetual up-to-dateness. It is true that Calvin was a man of his age and, therefore, all his writings bear the stamp of the period in the development of theological thought to which he belonged. This fact must always be taken into account in interpreting Calvin's views on various doctrines. It is unscientific in terms of theology to wrest statements from their historical context and apply them without discrimination to an entirely different historical context in which issues are precipitated that never arose in Calvin's mind or in the mind of his contemporaries.

But though Calvin was a man of his age the fact remains that he was to a remarkable extent, and to an extent not equalled by any other, a

1 *The Reformers and the Theology of the Reformation*, 1866, p. 295.
2 *op. cit.*, p. 296.

man of every subsequent generation. Why? Every careful reader of Calvin, especially of his *Institutes,* detects what may be called his biblico-theological method in contradistinction from the more scholastic method characteristic of his predecessors in the medieval tradition and of many of his successors in the Protestant tradition. This does not mean that Calvin is not systematic. He was a humanist before he was a reformer. And logic in argumentation and in the sequence and arrangement of his topics is manifest on every page. To use Reuss's terms, there is 'the admirable disposition of his material, the force and validity of his reasoning in dogmatics, the acuteness and subtlety of his mind'.[1] But it is the biblically oriented and biblically conditioned way in which the biblical material is treated that makes Calvin's presentation abidingly and irresistibly relevant to the Scripture itself. It is this character unencumbered by patterns extraneous to the Scripture itself, a character pervasively maintained, that ensures for his exposition the quality of up-to-dateness consonant with the permanent relevance of the Scripture as the living and abiding Word of the living and abiding God.

The second factor that contributes to this permanent significance of Calvin's work is what becomes evident on cursory examination. Calvin was the exegete of the Reformation and in the first rank of biblical exegetes of all time. The canons that guided his work as a commentator are well stated by himself in the dedicatory preface to his first undertaking as an expositor of books of the Bible, the Epistle to the Romans (1540). To Simon Grynaeus he begins by saying: 'I remember that three years ago we had a friendly discussion about the best way of interpreting Scripture. The plan which you particularly favoured was also the one which at that time I preferred to any others. Both of us felt that lucid brevity constituted the particular virtue of an interpreter. Since it is almost his only task to unfold the mind of the writer whom he has undertaken to expound, he misses his mark, or at least strays outside his limits, by the extent to which he leads his readers away from the meaning of his author. Our desire, therefore, was that someone might be found, out of the number of those who have at the present day proposed to further the cause of theology in this kind of task, who would not only study to be comprehensible, but also try not to detain

[1] *op. cit.,* p. IX.

his readers too much with long and wordy commentaries'.[1] In a letter
to Peter Viret, dated May 19, 1540 he writes: 'Capito, in his lectures,
has some things which may be of much use to you in the illustration of
Isaiah. But as he does not dictate any part to his hearers, and has not yet
reached beyond the fourteenth chapter, his assistance cannot at present
much help you. Zwingli, although he is not wanting in a fit and ready
exposition, yet, because he takes too much liberty, often wanders far
from the meaning of the Prophet. Luther is not so particular as to
propriety of expression or the historical accuracy; he is satisfied when
he can draw some it from fruitful doctrine. No one, as I think, has
hitherto more diligently applied himself to this pursuit than Œcolampa-
dius, who has not always, however, reached the full scope or meaning'.[2]

In exposition of Scripture there are few faults more exasperating than
that of reciting a mass of opinions in which the aim of elucidating the
text is lost sight of, and the mind of the reader is bewildered rather than
instructed. It is to Calvin's own words we may turn to illustrate his
determination to spare himself and his readers this liability. To Bucer
Calvin accorded the highest commendation. Referring to his commentary, he says that 'no one in our time has been more precise or
diligent in interpreting scripture'.[3] Yet he proceeds: 'Bucer is too
verbose to be read quickly by those who have other matters to deal
with, and too profound to be easily understood by less intelligent and
attentive readers. Whatever the subject with which he is dealing, so
many subjects are suggested to him by his incredible and vigorous
fertility of mind, that he does not know how to stop writing'.[4] Perhaps
no statement respecting his method and aims excels that in his Epistle
Dedicatory to the exposition of the twelve minor prophets, dated
January 26, 1559, 'If God has endued me with any aptness for the
interpretation of Scripture, I am fully persuaded that I have faithfully
and carefully endeavoured to exclude from it all barren refinements,
however plausible and fitted to please the ear, and to preserve genuine

1 *The Epistle of Paul the Apostle to the Romans*, English translation by Ross Mackenzie,
Edinburgh, 1961, p. 1.
2 *Letters of John Calvin*, English Translation, I, p. 164.
3 *Romans*, op. cit., p. 2.
4 *Ibid.*, p. 3.

simplicity, adapted solidly to edify the children of God, who, being not content with the shell, wish to penetrate to the kernel'.[1]

What must always impress the appreciative reader is the reverence with which Calvin approaches and deals with the Scripture. He is never forgetful that it is the Word of God. He writes again in the Epistle Dedicatory to his first commentary: 'Such veneration we ought indeed to entertain for the Word of God, that we ought not to pervert it in the least degree by varying expositions; for its majesty is diminished, I know not how much, especially when not expounded with great discretion and with great sobriety. And if it be deemed a great wickedness to contaminate anything that is dedicated to God, he surely cannot be endured, who, with impure, or even with unprepared hands, will handle that very thing, which of all things is the most sacred on earth. It is therefore an audacity, closely allied to a sacrilege, rashly to turn Scripture in any way we please, and to indulge our fancies as in sport; which has been done by many in former times.'[2] Here at the outset of his work as a commentator, he has not only indicated his breach with the tradition of allegorical interpretation, but he has inveighed against it as sacrilege. Unfortunately the indulgence of fancy against which Calvin protested is not a vice merely of the past. It is one that still persists to mar the purity and sobriety of pulpit ministration within the Protestant fold. Too frequently ingenious imagination has been substituted for the blood, sweat, toil, and tears of careful and reverent exposition; and the free rein of imagination has produced a pattern of spiritualizing that betrays its kinship with the allegorizing tradition which Calvin indicted as 'audacity, closely allied to a sacrilege'. In the Reformation period Calvin's commentaries are the prime example of emancipation from a hermeneutic that made it possible to turn Scripture in any way men pleased. It is more than surprising that heirs of the Reformation, priding themselves on the heritage of the Reformers, should show so little affinity with the guiding principles of the Reformation hermeneutic of which Calvin's commentaries are the superb example. May I be permitted to say, and say it with emphasis, that the Reformed expositor who is not in the habit of perusing Calvin's commentaries or, in any

[1] *Commentaries on the Twelve Minor Prophets*, Grand Rapids, 1950, pp. xviiif.
[2] *Romans*, Grand Rapids, 1947, p. xxvii.

case, is not imbued with the principles of interpretation they exemplify, is not worthy of his own claims and profession as an heir of the Reformation of the sixteenth century.

A third factor, and this leads me to my concluding observation respecting Calvin as theologian and expositor, is that by God's grace Calvin united in an eminent degree, a degree unsurpassed in the history of the church since the apostolic age, piety and learning. Any theologian is unfitted for his task unless he knows the power of the redemption of which Holy Scripture is the revelation. Without question, great contributions can be made and have been made to knowledge by men who do not know this power. But it is a travesty for a man not knowing the power of God's Word as the living and abiding voice of God to claim to be an expositor of it. This is but to say that the Scriptures cannot be properly interpreted and their truth formulated without the illumination and sealing witness of the Holy Spirit. Calvin has quite properly been called the theologian of the Holy Spirit. This is why Calvin's writings, and particularly his masterpiece, are suffused with the warmth of personal and practical devotion. Theology that does not promote encounter with the living God, and encounter with him as Father, Son, and Holy Spirit, in the unity that belongs to them in the mystery of the Trinity and in the particularity of relationship which each person sustains to us in the economy of salvation, is not Christian theology. Early in the *Institutes* we read: 'Indeed we shall not say that, properly speaking, God is known where there is no religion or piety'.[1] And then in the same chapter we find the definition of piety, exemplified in Calvin himself and as a pervasive attitude brought to expression in all of his expository and theological work: 'Here then is pure and genuine religion: it is faith so joined with an earnest fear of God that this fear also embraces willing reverence, and carries with it legitimate worship such as is prescribed in the law'.[2] The *Institutio* is not only the masterpiece of Christian theology; it is a devotional classic. It is theology, therefore, shot through with the warmth of ardent devotion.

[1] *Inst.* I, ii, 1, Eng. Trans. by F. L. Battles, Philadelphia, 1950, p. 39.
[2] *Inst.* I, ii, 2.

42

A Notable Tercentenary[1]

JULY 1, 1943, is a date that marks one of the most notable tercentenaries in the history of the Christian church. It was three hundred years ago on July 1, 1643, that the Westminster Assembly of Divines convened at Westminster, London, England.

That Assembly would have been a notable event even apart from the work that it produced in the four or five years that followed. The circumstances under which it was called and under which it met would have made it significant. But it is the work of the Assembly throughout the years that followed that makes this particular date of such lasting importance. It was the Westminster Assembly that gave to us some of our most priceless possessions, for it gave us the Westminster Confession of Faith and the Larger and Shorter Catechisms. Language fails to assess the blessing that God in his sovereign providence and grace bestowed upon his church through these statements of the Christian faith. The influence exerted by them is beyond all human calculation. We should indeed be remiss if we did not make this tercentenary the occasion for grateful remembrance of God's inestimable favour. Other men laboured and we have entered into their labours. Truly the lines are fallen unto us in pleasant places and we have a goodly heritage.

The Westminster Confession of Faith, and Larger and Shorter Catechisms are the flower and fruit of some fifteen centuries of creedal or confessional formulation of the Christian faith. This is just saying that the Westminster divines, when they sat at Westminster in the fifth decade of the seventeenth century, were the heirs of the labours of God's

[1] *The Presbyterian Guardian,* June 10, 1943.

servants for fifteen centuries as these servants of God had striven to set forth the truth of the Christian faith and guard it against error and distortion. The Westminster Assembly did not abstract itself from the history of the church but willingly and gratefully recognized itself as the debtor to all the wisdom and light that God in his providence had caused to be deposited in the expositions and formulations of the past.

More particularly, the Westminster divines were the heirs of all the other evangelical creeds of the Reformation period. The Reformation of the sixteenth and seventeenth centuries was peculiarly prolific in the production of confessions of faith. It was an age of ardent and polemic faith and the framing of creeds or confessions was the natural result. Nearly all of these creeds are notable and valuable exhibitions of Christian truth, and not a few of them are of priceless value. Many of them are to this day the accepted creedal symbols of the faith of the Protestant churches.

It is noteworthy, however, that the Westminster Confession and Catechisms are the last in the series of the great Reformation creeds. This fact of chronology is itself of great significance. The rich repertory of Protestant confessional statement covering more than a hundred years lay open before them. It was their happy lot to compare, to sift, to select and to evaluate in the full light of more than a century of faithful and devoted labour on the part of others. But perhaps of even greater significance is the fact that no other Protestant or Reformed Confession had brought to bear upon its composition such a combination of devotion, care and erudition as was exhibited in the work of the Westminster Assembly.

The Westminster Confession and Catechisms are, therefore, the mature fruit of the whole movement of creed-formation throughout fifteen centuries of Christian history, and, in particular, they are the crown of the greatest age of confessional exposition, the Protestant Reformation. No other similar documents have concentrated in them, and formulated with such precision, so much of the truth embodied in the Christian revelation.

This estimate of the Westminster standards might seem to accord to them a place so high that dishonour is paid to the Word of God, the

Scriptures. Indeed the accusation has sometimes been made that, when we thus appraise the Westminster standards and appeal to them, we are placing the Confession and Catechisms in the place of the Bible. Such an accusation, to say the very least, is due to gross misunderstanding. It goes without saying that the Bible is the supreme standard of faith. The Bible alone is the Word of God, the only infallible rule of faith and practice. The Westminster Confession and Catechisms have no normative character or authority in and of themselves. Their whole value resides in the conformity of their teaching with the Word of God, the Scriptures of the Old and New Testaments. The only reason why we give to them so high an appraisal is that they, more than any other similar documents in the history of the Christian church, set forth in precise and well-guarded language the truth of God revealed in the Holy Scriptures. They are, indeed, human documents. In that they differ absolutely from the Bible. They should never be regarded as sacrosanct. The Westminster divines were not infallible and they were not inspired as were the writers of Holy Scripture. The teaching of the Confession and Catechisms must always be subjected to the scrutiny of the Word of God. If we ever regard them as in themselves sacrosanct and authoritative, then we have committed idolatry and have fallen into the error of the Church of Rome.

But the reason why the Confession and Catechisms should be so highly honoured is that, to an amazing extent, their teaching does stand the scrutiny of the Word of God. They bear the marks of human infirmity and fallibility, but no other statements framed by men so adequately express the confession of Christian belief. For this reason they have been the Confessions of faith of some of the most faithful churches upon earth since the Reformation.

Every branch of the visible church must confess its faith both as testimony to the Lord and as the bond of fellowship among believers. It is surely to be expected that the church will confess its faith in the form that is most adequate and competent. When Presbyterian and Reformed churches adopt these Westminster standards as the symbols and confessions of their faith, they are but using the instruments with which God in his providence has furnished the church for proclaiming, inculcating and preserving the truth revealed in the Word of God; they are but using these means for maintaining the purity of the church and they are but ensuring that the bonds of fellowship be those of well-proven soundness and stability. Let us prove all things; but let us also hold fast that which is good.

43

The Importance and Relevance of the Westminster Confession

THE Westminster Assembly was called by ordinance of both Houses of Parliament and met for the first time on July 1, 1643. Nearly all the sessions were held in the Jerusalem Chamber in Westminster Abbey.

The first work which the Assembly undertook was the revision of the Thirty-Nine Articles of the Church of England. On October 12, 1643, when the Assembly was engaged in the revision of the sixteenth Article, there came an order from both Houses of Parliament to treat of such discipline and government as would be most agreeable to God's Word, and most apt to procure and preserve the peace of the Church at home and nearer agreement with the Church of Scotland and other Reformed Churches abroad, and also to treat of a directory for worship. It was in pursuance of this order that the Assembly prepared what are known as 'The Form of Presbyterial Church Government' and 'The Directory for the Public Worship of God'.

On August 20, 1644, a committee was appointed by the Assembly to prepare matter for a Confession of Faith. A great deal of the attention of the Assembly was devoted to this Confession during the years 1645 and 1646. It was not until December 4, 1646, that the text of the Confession was completed and presented to both Houses of Parliament as the 'humble advice' of the divines. This did not, however, include the proof texts. These were not presented to the Houses until April 29, 1647.

The amount of work and time expended on the Confession of Faith will stagger us in these days of haste and alleged activism. But the influence exerted all over the world by the Confession can only be understood in the light of the diligent care and prayerful devotion exercised in its composition.

The Westminster Confession is the last of the great Reformation creeds. We should expect, therefore, that it would exhibit distinctive features. The Westminster Assembly had the advantage of more than a century of Protestant creedal formulation. Reformed theology had by the 1640's attained to a maturity that could not be expected a hundred or even seventy-five years earlier. Controversies had developed in the interval between the death of Calvin, for example, and the Westminster Assembly, that compelled theologians to give to Reformed doctrine fuller and more precise definition. In many circles today there is the tendency to depreciate, if not deplore, the finesse of theological definition which the Confession exemplifies. This is an attitude to be deprecated. A growing faith grounded in the perfection and finality of Scripture requires increasing particularity and cannot consist with the generalities that make room for error. No creed of the Christian Church is comparable to that of Westminster in respect of the skill with which the fruits of fifteen centuries of Christian thought have been preserved, and at the same time examined anew and clarified in the light of that fuller understanding of God's Word which the Holy Spirit has imparted.

The Westminster Confession was the work of devoted men and the fruit of painstaking, consecrated labour. But it was still the work of fallible men. For that reason it must not be esteemed as sacrosanct and placed in the same category as the Bible. The latter is the only infallible rule of faith and life. The framers of the Confession were careful to remind us of this. 'All synods or councils, since the Apostles' times, whether general or particular, may err; and many have erred. Therefore they are not to be made the rule of faith, or practice; but to be used as a help in both' (XXXI, iv). It is not superfluous to take note of this reminder. We are still under the necessity of avoiding the Romish error. One of the most eloquent statements of the Confession is that of I, vi: 'The whole counsel of God concerning all things necessary for his own glory, man's salvation, faith and life, is either expressly set down in Scripture, or by good and necessary consequence may be deduced from Scripture: unto which nothing at any time is to be added, whether by new revelations of the Spirit, or traditions of men'.

In the category to which the Confession belongs, it has no peer. No chapter in the Confession evinces this assessment more than that which the framers chose for good and obvious reasons to place at the beginning —'Of the Holy Scripture'. In the whole field of formulation respecting the doctrine of Scripture nothing is comparable to that which we find in these ten sections. With the most recent deviations from biblical doctrine in mind, it is as if this chapter had been drawn up but yesterday in order to controvert them. Section i, for example, is so carefully constructed that, if chronology were forgotten, we might think that what is being guarded is the doctrine that Scripture itself is the revelatory Word of God in opposition to the present-day dialectical theology which regards it as merely the witness to revelation. When the Confession says, 'Therefore it pleased the Lord . . . to commit the same wholly unto writing', what is in view as committed wholly to writing is *God's self-revelation* and *the declaration of his will unto his church.* And so in the next section we find that Holy Scripture is stated to be synonymous with, or defined in terms of 'the Word of God written'.

Again, the distinction drawn so clearly between the ground upon which the *authority* of Scripture rests (section iv) and the way by which this authority is attested to us (section v) is one exactly framed to meet a current error. Those influenced by this error who aver that the Confession teaches that the authority of Scripture is derived from the 'inward work of the Holy Spirit bearing witness by and with the Word in our hearts' (section v) have failed to pay attention to what is elementary in the sequence of these two sections. The authority rests upon the fact that God is the author of Scripture; it is *our* full persuasion and assurance that is derived from the internal testimony of the Spirit. The Confession could not have been more explicit in setting forth this distinction. Thereby it has given direction for all proper thinking on the question of authority.

One of the most controversial chapters in the Confession is the third, 'Of God's Eternal Decree'. The development of this chapter and the finesse of formulation are masterful. There are three subjects dealt with, the decree of God in its cosmic dimensions, the decree of God as it respects men and angels, and the decree of God as it respects men. In connection with the first, the all-inclusiveness of the decree, embracing sin itself, is asserted, but with equal emphasis also that 'God is not the author of sin, nor is violence offered to the will of the creatures' (section i). In connection with angels and men, the statement most offensive to critics is that some are 'foreordained to everlasting death' (section iii). What is too frequently overlooked is that this statement, as it has respect to men, is explicated more fully in section vii. Here the doctrine, often called that of reprobation, is analyzed as to its elements in a way unsurpassed in the whole compass of theological literature. Nowhere else in so few words is this delicate topic handled with such meticulous care and discrimination. The concluding section (viii) places the 'high mystery of predestination' in proper perspective in relation to human responsibility and the comfort to be derived from it for all those who sincerely obey the gospel. Sovereign election of grace is not alien to the gospel. It is a tenet of the gospel, and the fount from which the gospel flows, as well as the guarantee that the gospel will not fail of its purpose.

All true theology is realistic; it takes the data of revelation and the facts of life seriously. At no point does a theology governed by sentiment rather than by facts quibble with the teaching of Scripture more than on the subject of sin. The Confession is not afraid to enunciate the doctrine of total depravity, and thus it says unequivocally that by original corruption 'we are utterly indisposed, disabled, and made opposite to all good, and wholly inclined to all evil' (VI, iv). Less than this is not a true transcript of the biblical teaching that there is none that doeth good, no, not even one, that the imagination of the thought of man's heart is only evil continually, and that the carnal mind is enmity against God. The severity of the Scripture's indictment, reflected in the Confessional teaching, is complemental to the radical concept of grace which the Confession entertains. However necessary it is to be true to the data of Scripture and the facts of life on the doctrine of depravity, this would only seal despair, were it not that grace is as thorough as sin is total. Herein lies the grandeur of sovereign grace. 'Those of mankind that are predestinated unto life, God, before the foundation of the world was laid, according to His eternal and immutable purpose, and the secret counsel and good pleasure of His will, hath chosen, in Christ, unto everlasting glory, out of his mere free grace and love' (III, v).

It is this theme of sovereign grace and love that the Confession pursues and unfolds in its various aspects. One of the most remarkable chapters for fulness of doctrine and condensation of expression is 'Of Christ the Mediator' (VIII). The whole doctrine of the person of Christ, of his finished work and continued ministry is set forth. If we are thinking of Chalcedon and the doctrine then formulated, nothing is more adequate or succinct than 'that two whole, perfect, and distinct natures, the Godhead and the manhood, were inseparably joined together in one person, without conversion, composition, or confusion' (VIII, ii). If we are thinking of the atonement in both its nature and design, what in so few words could be more inclusive than: 'The Lord Jesus, by his perfect obedience, and sacrifice of himself, which he, through the eternal Spirit, once offered up unto God, hath fully satisfied the justice of his Father; and purchased, not only reconciliation, but an everlasting inheritance in the kingdom of heaven, for all those whom the Father hath given unto him'? (VIII, v).

When the Confession deals with the application of redemption, it is noteworthy how the various topics are arranged. It sets forth first the phases which are the actions of God—Calling, Justification, Adoption, Sanctification (X–XIII)—and then those which are concerned with human response—Faith, Repentance, Good Works, Perseverance, Assurance of Grace (XIV–XXIII). Undoubtedly, the consideration that salvation is of the Lord and that all saving response in men is the fruit of God's grace dictated this order. It is consonant with the pervasive emphasis upon the sovereignty of grace.

That the application should be regarded as having its inception in effectual calling should not be overlooked. This is where Scripture places it, and it is rightly conceived of as an efficacious translation out of a state of sin and death into one of grace and salvation by Jesus Christ. Calling is not to be defined in terms of human response. The latter is the *answer* to the call. This perspective in the Confession needs to be appreciated—effectual calling is an act of God and of God alone. There is, however, one shortcoming in the definition the Confession provides. Calling is specifically the action of God the Father and this accent does not appear in the Confession.

In the two Catechisms produced by the Westminster Assembly, it is striking to observe how large a proportion is devoted to the exposition of the ten commandments. This shows how jealous the divines were in the matter of the Christian life. A similar proportion is not devoted to the law of God in the Confession. But the emphasis is proportionate to what a Confession should incorporate. It is well to note what is said about good works (XVI), the law of God (XIX), Christian liberty (XX), the Sabbath day (XXI), marriage and divorce (XXIV). Grace has often been turned into license. No creed guards against this distortion more than the Confession of the Westminster Assembly. Grace pure and sovereign is the theme throughout. But grace is unto holiness, and it confirms and enhances human responsibility. 'The moral law doth for ever bind all, as well justified persons as others, to the obedience thereof. . . . Neither doth Christ, in the gospel, any way dissolve, but much strengthen this obligation' (XIX, v).

In days of increasing encroachment upon the liberties which are God-given, the charter of liberty needs again to be resounded: 'God alone is Lord of the conscience, and hath left it free from the doctrines and commandments of men which are, in any thing, contrary to his Word, or beside it, in matters of faith or worship' (XX, ii). And when the church thinks that the modes of worship are a matter of human discretion, we need to be recalled to the regulative principle that 'the acceptable way of worshipping the true God is instituted by himself, and so limited by his own revealed will, that he may not be worshipped according to the imaginations and devices of men, or the suggestions of Satan, under any visible representation, or any other way not prescribed in the holy Scripture' (XXI, i). Or, when the sacred ties of matrimony are lightly regarded and even desecrated, what could be more relevant than the principles and restrictions enunciated in chapter XXIV?

The flabby sentimentality so widespread is not hospitable to the rigour and vigour of a document like the Confession. Its system of truth and way of life do not comport with current patterns of thought and behaviour. This is the reason for the collapse of the religious and moral standards which our Christian faith represents. It is folly to think that we can retain or reclaim Christian culture on any lower level than that which the Westminster Assembly defined. Christian thought may never be stagnant. When it ceases to be progressive, it declines. But we do not make progress by discarding our heritage. We build upon it or, more accurately, we grow from it.

Oftentimes it is pleaded that the Christian message must be adapted to the modern man. It is true that the message must be proclaimed to modern man, and to modern man in the context in which he lives and in language he can understand. But it is much more true and important to plead that modern man must be adapted to the gospel. It is not true that the doctrine of the Confession is irrelevant to the modern man. It is indeed meaningless to him until he listens to it. But when a man today becomes earnest about the Christian faith, when he gives heed to Scripture as the Word of God, when he faces up to the challenge of unbelieving ways of thought and life and demands the answer which Christianity provides, he cannot rest with anything less than the consistency and vigour which the Confession exemplifies. Unbelief is potent and subtle, and the believer requires the truth of God in its fullest expression if he is to be furnished to faithful witness and confession.

Issues in the
Contemporary World

44

The Significance of the Doctrine of Creation

NOTHING is more basic and determinative in shaping our thought than is our conception of God. The thought that does not begin with God and move towards him is essentially godless and therefore ungodly.

It might seem that the doctrine of creation is only remotely or, at least, secondarily involved in our conception of God. It is true that God is self-existent and self-sufficient. He is not dependent upon creation, and the act of creation did not change his being and internal necessary relations. Creation did not add anything to his eternal and inherent perfections. It might therefore be plausibly argued that our conception of God is not determined by that which God has created, and that our conception of God is independent of the view of creation we entertain. Let us not prejudice our view of God, it might be said, by introducing concepts of creation, since creation is really extraneous to the being, perfections and internal relations of the eternally blessed, self-subsistent and self-sufficient Godhead.

The fallacy of this line of argument is that we are speaking now of *our* conception of God. We are not self-existent and self-sufficient beings, existing in abstraction from creation, and viewing God in his eternal being and independence by some kind of super-intuition and perception. We are dependent beings, and it is only by creation and in the context of creation that we think and entertain a conception of God. When *we* think, and particularly when we think of God, we think as beings conditioned by creation. In other words, when *we* think of God we cannot think of God aright without thinking of our relation to him.

Even if the thought of our relation to him is not in the forefront of consciousness at a particular time, it must always be in the immediate background conditioning our whole attitude in thinking of him. To be quite specific, any thought of God by us must be conditioned by a profound apprehension of his transcendent majesty and glory; in a word, that he is God and that there is none else beside him. Our thought must always be determined by the fear of God. Reverence is the very soul of true thought, and worship is its invariable result. But why reverence and worship? Simply because he is God and we are his creatures. So far then as *we* are concerned, we can never think of God without thinking of God as God and of ourselves as his creatures. In other words, the thought of creation, the thought of our dependence upon God, is implicated in any true thought *we* entertain with respect to God. Without the concept of creation, then, we cannot think even one right thought of God. Hence the significance of creation for our conception of God and therefore for the Christian position.

There are, however, other respects in which the doctrine of creation basically affects our conception of God. Not only does our relation to God affect our thought of God, and must always condition our thought of him; it also affects our thought of the relation to God of the world in which we live. We live in space and time, and it is foolish to try to abstract ourselves from the conditions of space and time. They condition our thought as well as ourselves. Whence are they? Do they condition God? Our very relation to them compels us to ask: What is their relation to God? Obviously if they are aspects of his being they immediately determine our conception of God. And if they are not, whence came they, or whence are they?

We can readily see how germane is the first word of the Scripture, that God created the heavens and the earth, and the commentary of the Psalmist, 'By the word of the Lord were the heavens made, and all the host of them by the breath of his mouth'. All that which exists distinct from God himself owes its origin to the sovereign will and fiat of God. The whole of reality distinct from God himself is dependent upon God and dependent upon him because he caused it to be. The doctrine of creation affects the sole eternity and universal sovereignty of God. If anything that exists exists apart from the creative will of God, then we must posit something alongside of God and independent of him, and then we have adopted a dualism that cuts athwart the sole eternity, sole self-existence and universal sovereignty of God. And this means that he is not God.

Our topic is the significance of creation for our Christian position, and more is involved in the Christian position than our conception of God. We may now ask: How does the doctrine of creation affect our *faith*. It needs no proof to affirm that the Christian position is one of faith in God. The Christian position is one of Christian *faith*. The Christian redemption contemplates communion with God and without faith it is impossible to please him.

The faith of the Christian religion is the faith of God's redemptive grace, and redemption has no meaning apart from sin. Sin and redemption therefore set the points for the describing of the orbit within which, or in relation to which, Christian faith has meaning. How does creation affect these two points?

Creation means that all things owe their origin and existence to the will and fiat of God. Since God is just in all his ways and holy in all his works, this implies the inherent goodness of creation. It is not without profound meaning that it is written, 'And God saw everything that he had made, and behold, it was very good'. In no form did evil inhere in creation. Evil in all its forms, and particularly in the specific form that we call sin, originated subsequent to creation, that is, after God had finished all his works which he created and made. Two negatives follow from this: first, that evil and sin are not eternal; second, that sin and evil were not resident in God's created handiwork. Sin had an origin, and it originated subsequent to creation. Man, in particular, was created in the image of God and therefore replete with that which is the opposite of sin, namely, knowledge, righteousness and holiness. For sin as sin, for sin as guilt, man is responsible, and man alone is responsible. When viewed either seminally or actually it cannot be referred to divine authorship. On any other position it is impossible to maintain a doctrine of sin as the contradiction of the divine will and perfection.

For if we suppose that sin is something *necessarily* emanating from an entity that existed independently of God and outside of man, then at least man is not responsible. With the implications of such a supposition for God we have already dealt. If we suppose that sin is something necessarily arising from the constitution of man, then it is something belonging to the constitution of man, either because God in forming man was compelled to form man that way, or because God freely made man that way. On the first alternative we may shield God's responsibility at the expense of his sovereign power. On the second alternative God is directly responsible for making man with an evil constitution. But, on either alternative, man is not responsible: he is the helpless victim of the nature with which he is endowed. Human responsibility is removed, and with responsibility goes guilt, and with guilt goes sin!

We can see, then, how indispensable to the doctrine of human sin is the doctrine of creation. Creation was in its whole extent very good, and sin was not a necessity arising from that creation nor a necessity arising from the nature with which man was endowed. It originated as a free movement of defection and apostasy within man's own bosom.

How does creation affect the other focal point in Christian faith, namely, redemption? Redemption saves from and annuls sin, and sin is the contradiction of the divine will and perfection. Ultimately sin is the one and only thing in God's universe that is recalcitrant with reference to God. It is the one thing that is opposite to him. Other evils may in a sense be said to be opposite to him also. But all other evils are derivative from sin and they are the result of the reaction of the divine holiness to sin. So we may say that sin is the one and only thing in which contradiction to God inheres. Yet it is sin that redemption overcomes and destroys. Redemption cannot be defined as anything less than the making an end of sin and its evil consequences.

Now if God is to overcome sin it must be within the realm of God's government, that is to say, within the realm in which he exercises such absolute sway that he can deal effectively with it. If we do not hold a pure doctrine of creation, then we have opened the door for the positing of the existence of something that exists independently of God, and therefore of something outside the realm of his government. In that moment we have posited the existence of a realm that is unamenable to his absolute sway, and therefore a realm within which sin may be impervious to his redeeming power. We can see therefore the stake that redemption has in the fact of creation. Sin is not something that exists outside the universe that has come to be by God's omnipotent fiat and sovereign will.

It should not surprise us therefore that the Epistle to the Hebrews, conceiving of faith as projection into an unseen and hoped-for realm, should co-ordinate the faith, indeed identify the faith, by which believers in all ages were accepted by God, by which they lived the life of righteousness and by which they attained to the promise of an eternal inheritance, with the very faith by which we believe that the worlds were framed by the Word of God, so that things which are seen were not made of things which do appear.

Finally, the doctrine of creation affects our teleology, our philosophy of the end of all things. Nothing is more essential to, and determinative of the Christian position than that the end of all things is the glory of God. 'Of him, and through him, and to him, are all things: to whom be glory for ever. Amen' (Rom. 11:36). All things have their beginning and their end in God. The relevancy of creation to this truth is apparent. In the words of Revelation 4:11, 'Worthy art thou, our Lord and our God, to receive the glory and the honour and the power: for thou didst create all things, and because of thy will they were, and were created'.

45

The Relevance of the Historical

A GREAT deal is being said today about the necessity of relevance. It is alleged that Christianity, as it was understood by Christians in the first century, is not relevant to modern man; that modern man, conditioned as he is by the scientific world-view, cannot accept the framework in which the New Testament is cast, and that the gospel that will challenge him and meet him where he is conceptually and practically, is one bereft of this framework and greatly modified in its message and demand. It is not to be denied that the gospel proclaimed must be relevant, that it must be presented to men where they are, and meet their needs in the situations in which they find themselves. But one thing must be said. It is only by the proclamation of the whole counsel of God, particularly regarding sin, misery, and judgment, that men will discover where they are and begin to assess their need. Much of the plea for relevance proceeds on the premise that what men assess as their need, and demand for the satisfaction of this need, is that to which the gospel is to be adjusted. The result is that the solution proposed and the message proclaimed are accommodations to humanly conceived and articulated demands. There is the basic fallacy that men, apart from the conviction conditioned and created by law and gospel, are able to know what their real situation and need are. It is God's judgment respecting sin and misery that must be brought to bear upon men where they are and where they find themselves. When this priority is not observed, then all presumed relevance is a distortion of the gospel, and in our day such distortion as denies the central elements of New Testament Christianity.

The gospel is the glad tidings of salvation, and, while salvation is always to something that far transcends anything that our human situation could dictate, it is also salvation, first of all, from sin in its guilt, condemnation, corruption, and misery. Have we sufficiently pondered the great lesson of our Lord's promise that, when the Spirit of truth would come, he would convict the world of sin, of righteousness, and of judgment? In a gathering of this sort I am not bringing an indictment against the theoretical beliefs of any in this assembly. But I am asking the question with some concern and urgency: have we really grasped the implications of the word of our Lord just referred to? Theoretically we grant that all preaching of the gospel must be by the commission and endowment of the Holy Spirit. But the order Christ observed is not revoked. 'When he the Spirit of truth is come, he will convict the world of sin.'

The gospel in our day, as in any day, is the gospel that comes into a world of sin and misery.

Theologically speaking, at least, the most influential movements within Protestantism deny the historical character of what is recorded for us in Genesis 3. And we risk all reputation for scholarship and hope of being worthy of theological respect, if we maintain the historical authenticity of this chapter. Genesis 3, men say, is myth or legend, not history but story, portraying what happens to all men, but not a once-for-all series of events with abiding implications by virtue of the relations that Adam as the first man sustained to all men. Adam is every man; we are all Adam; we all sin as Adam sinned.

This might appear to be an effective way of maintaining, notwithstanding the denial of the historicity of Genesis 3, the fact that all have sinned. To unsuspecting evangelicals it becomes an appealing apologetic for the universality of sinfulness. But a little examination will show the fallacy.

1. It is not true that all sinned as Adam. There is a radical difference between Adam and posterity. We all come into the world as sinners. Adam and Eve did not. If we are all Adam, then two positions basic to the Bible's view of man are denied—the imputation to us of Adam's sin, and the doctrine of original sin. The beginning of *our* sinfulness was not by voluntary defection and transgression, as in the case of Adam, but by

divinely constituted solidarity with Adam in his sin. And original sin, means that we are *by nature* dead in trespasses and sins, not by acquisition as in the case of Adam and Eve.

We are dealing with the gospel in our day, and dealing with sin as that in relation to which alone the gospel has meaning. The whole question of Adam and of the record in Genesis 3 is basic. If we adopt the dialectical approach and interpretation, then we have failed to assess the human situation in sin to which the gospel is addressed. There is a fundamental error in our construction of the existential, and, deflected by this error, we cannot bring the gospel in the marvel of its grace to bear upon the real truth of sin in its gravity and depth. In reality it is the failure of relevance. For as the preachers of the gospel encounter the sinfulness of men, whether it be in the squalor and wretchedness of what we call the slums or in the façade of complacency of the opulent suburbs, the only explanation of the tangle of iniquity and the web of misery is the doctrine of original sin which Genesis 3 in the context of the biblical interpretation alone provides. 'The judgment was from one' (Rom. 5:16).

Let me expand this point one step further. As we face up to the human situation, as we are truly existential, there is but one indictment that adequately measures up to what we find in our contact with humanity. And, as we search our own hearts and honestly scrutinize our lives, there is but one indictment that we can bring. It is that of total depravity. I cannot untangle the iniquity of my own heart and I cannot rationalize it. 'The heart is deceitful above all things and desperately wicked; who can know it?' And as I turn to the grosser or more refined manifestations of iniquity in the church and in the world, there is but one verdict that describes it. 'The mind of the flesh is enmity against God' (Rom. 8:7). This verdict must indeed be applied in the concrete, to the endless forms in which iniquity manifests itself. But the verdict of Scripture cannot be stated in truer or more relevant terms. If we think we have to qualify it in order to make it more acceptable or intelligible to the modern mind, then we are trifling with God's verdict and with the form of sound words exemplifying the principle of verbal inspiration, 'not in words taught of human wisdom but in words taught of the Spirit' (1 Cor. 2:13). We are abdicating our vocation as messengers of the evangel unless the gospel we preach is one directed to depravity defined in these precise terms.

If the gospel is, first of all, one of salvation from sin in its guilt, defilement, misery, and power, it must have at its centre provision for sin in just these terms. And if the gospel is to meet us where we are, not in terms of our conception but in terms of God's judgment, it must be a gospel of God's doing, of God's action, of God's action with reference to his own judgment upon sin. Once I, a sinner, have accepted God's verdict, once God's Word has found me where I am and conviction has come to correspond with reality, it is useless to tell me that I must be crucified to the world and the world crucified to me, however much this demand may be enforced by the example of Jesus of Nazareth. I say it is useless, because it is not anything that I do in the realm of my experience, not even what I do in the moment of the noblest and most critical decision that meets my situation in sin. Nothing less than the message of what *God* has done, of what God did definitively with reference to his judgment upon my sin, can bring one ray of light and hope into my guilt, condemnation, alienation, curse, servitude, and misery. In reality no confidence to draw nigh in the assurance of faith can be engendered in the hearts of men except as there is to some extent the apprehension of what God has done once for all to meet the exigency of our sin and of our separation from God.

It is here that we are in contact with the fatal denial of the gospel in current Protestantism. What I have in mind now, in respect of the gospel, is the significance of the historical, and the undermining of the same in the theology of the present. If the only message that meets the need created by our sin is the message of what God has done in reference to his own judgment upon sin, then it must be what God has done in the realm that is as truly, as strictly, as critically historical as is our sinful situation and the judgment of God upon it. Here, brethren, is the glory and the grandeur of the gospel.

Let us think for a few moments of the incarnation. This doctrine is that the eternal Son of God, pre-existent from eternity, came into this world and became man. He who was above history, the Creator of history, became subject to history and to its conditions, not by ceasing to be what he was, but by becoming what he was not; by being begotten

333

of the Holy Spirit and conceived of the virgin at a definite point in time. If we possessed all the data, this point could be fixed in the calendar as precisely as any other event. It was a once-for-all event, an event not above history but in history, not repeatable and not retractable. The uniqueness is bound up with its historical factuality. This advises us that history has profound significance in the accomplishment of God's re-demptive will. 'When the fulness of the time was come, God sent forth his Son' (Gal. 4:4). In this historicity is already beginning to break upon our horizon the character of the gospel. History is invested with pro-found significance in redemptive accomplishment. The grand mystery of godliness is itself the harbinger of light and hope.

Let us now think for a few moments of the cross of Christ. It is impossible to eliminate from the witness of the New Testament the note of finality attached to the cross of Christ. Whether it be the testimony of our Lord that he came to give his life a ransom, that he should suffer and rise from the dead the third day, or that of Paul that Christ died for our sins, that he reconciled us to God by his blood, or of John that he redeemed us to God by his blood, or of Peter that he bore our sins in his own body upon the tree, it all points to that which comes to its most explicit expression in the Epistle to the Hebrews, that Christ was once offered to bear the sins of many, that once in the consummation of the ages hath he been manifested to put away sin by the sacrifice of himself, that having made purgation of sins he sat down at the right hand of the Majesty on high. It is this event, certified as event by its once-for-allness, certified as a finished event by the sequel of diametric-ally different character, certified as an historically dated event by the fact that the whole of redemptive history moves to this climax as some-thing belonging to the fulness of time, the consummating time; an event interpreted for us as God reconciling the world to himself, as redeeming us by Jesus' blood, as the making of purgation for sins, as propitiation for our sins and therefore interpreted as God's definitive action with reference to his own judgment upon sin—it is this event in the message of proclamation that meets me and you and all men to whom it comes, in the situation which God's verdict pronounces to be ours. No other message has relevance to the human crisis in that which defines it most basically and existentially. This event is relevant, and its proclamation the sound of the jubilee trumpet, precisely because the great event proclaimed was something that God did in history as concrete and datable as that in which we find ourselves. And it is because Christ vicariously bore sin and condemnation and wrought for our redemption what was unique, without parallel and incapable of parallel, unrepeated and unrepeatable, that we may as ambassadors on behalf of Christ and as of God beseech men to be reconciled to God, an exhortation which in reality means 'accept the message of God's once-for-all reconciling action and enter into the status which God's action has constituted and established'.

The interpretation that the cross of Christ is something exemplified, verified, and repeated when we are crucified to the world and the world crucified to us, is a complete perversion of the gospel and of the Pauline text (Gal. 6:14) in particular. It is true that through the cross of Christ we become crucified to the world, but only when the cross of Christ is perceived to be that once-for-all act of redemption, propitiation, and reconciliation, in which God has definitively dealt with his own judgment upon sin and executed judgment upon the god of this world. It is by the constraint of this marvel of God's grace proclaimed to us in the message of reconciliation that we are crucified to the world. Just as the epitome of the world is self-righteousness, it is in the supreme manifestation of grace in Christ's cross that self-righteousness receives its death blow.

Permit me to go a little further in delineating the significance of history in gospel accomplishment and message. The flat, unequivocal denial of the resurrection of Christ rests upon an assumption that is fundamentally sound. It is that resurrection, if there had been such, means bodily, physical reanimation; that the corpse of Jesus laid in the tomb revived, rose from the tomb, and was reunited with the spirit that had departed in the event of death. This is the only conception of resurrection that measures up to the New Testament definition. It is much less misleading to deny the fact and possibility, than to maintain a view of resurrection that denies its bodily, physical character.

What the gospel demands is the resurrection of Jesus from the dead on 'the third day', on 'the first day of the week'. Here again the historical is as integral as in the incarnation and the cross of Christ. In the witness of Jesus himself, both before his crucifixion and after his resurrection, and in the witness of the apostles, the conjunction of the death and resurrection proclaims the great lesson not simply of historic continuity between Christ crucified and the apostolic message (κήρυγμα), but between Jesus crucified and the risen Saviour, and this continuity as the only ground of the conjunction in the apostolic proclamation. It is this lesson that is so eloquently inscribed on Peter's climax on the day of Pentecost: 'This one, being delivered by the determinate counsel and foreknowledge of God, ye through the hand of lawless men have crucified and slain, whom God raised up, having loosed the pangs of death, inasmuch as it was not possible that he should be holden of it. . . . Therefore let all the house of Israel know assuredly that this same Jesus whom ye have crucified God hath made both Lord and Christ' (Acts 2:23, 24, 36). It is the stupendous fact of the identity of the crucified Jesus and the exalted Lord.

What is it that makes the gospel the message of power? How is it that the kingdom of God is power? How is it that the gospel comes into the guilt and degradation and misery of our sinful situation, and raises men and women from the mire and sets their feet upon a rock; takes them from the dunghill, and makes them princes and princesses in the city of God? It is not because the early church made the crucified Jesus the Christ of the kērygma. It is because the fact of the resurrection con-stituted the apostolic message. It is because the apostles and others were the witnesses of the exceeding greatness of the power of God, when he raised up Jesus from the dead and set him at his own right hand, that they proclaimed Jesus as Lord.

Allow me to bring this to the focus of its relevance as a historic fact. It is precisely because the resurrection of Jesus from the dead took place in all the concreteness of datable, calendar history, in history that is as concrete, factual, and phenomenal as the situation in which we men find ourselves in the desperation of our sin, and misery, and death, that it is the power of God to us. The resurrection must be history to be relevant to us. God came into our history and wrought with the exceed-ing greatness of his power, and, because Jesus now lives in the realm constituted by this resurrection power, in the glory his resurrection inaugurated and the ascension completed, proclamation is not in word only but in demonstration of the Spirit and of power, and faith rests not upon the wisdom of men but on the power of God.

One of the ways in which the temper of our day shows the antithesis of unbelief is the hopeless nihilism of its prospect. Death casts the pall of impenetrable darkness over the minds of men. Through fear of death they are all their lifetime subject to bondage. They do not have hope. The enigma of death makes life a pilgrimage into meaningless destiny. When Paul brings one of the sections of the Epistle to the Romans to a conclusion he says: 'But the God of hope fill you with all joy and peace in believing, to the end that you may abound in hope in the power of the Holy Spirit' (Rom. 15:13). The temper is one of total contrast. Joy, peace, hope! No, not merely! It is *abounding* joy, peace, and hope, for Jesus' resurrection has transformed the whole complexion of life, of perspective, of outlook, of destiny.

It is again eloquent of the unbreakable conjunction of Jesus' death and resurrection that the Epistle to the Hebrews should tell us that Jesus partook of blood and flesh 'in order that through death he might bring to nought him that had the power of death, that is the devil, and deliver them who by fear of death were all their lifetime subject to bondage' (Heb. 2:14, 15); and that Peter should write: 'Blessed be the God and Father of our Lord Jesus Christ, who, according to his abundant mercy, hath begotten us again to a living hope through the resurrection of Jesus Christ from the dead' (1 Peter 1:3).

The promise has been fulfilled: 'O death I will be thy plagues. O grave I will be thy destruction' (Hos. 13:14), Christ is the first that should rise from the dead. He is the firstfruits. And it is the event of the first Lord's day in its historic and factual concreteness that alone can be relevant for us in the reality of death and in the consummating event that will abolish it. 'Then will be brought to pass the saying that is written, Death has been swallowed up in victory. O death where is thy victory? O death where is thy sting?' (1 Cor. 15:54, 55). And this hope we may have 'as the anchor of the soul both sure and steadfast and which entereth within the veil, whither the forerunner is for us entered, even Jesus, made an high priest for ever after the order of Melchizedek' (Heb. 6:19, 20).

Finally, permit me to relate this subject of the historical to that which lies close to our interest, the authority and finality of Holy Scripture. The Scripture is a collection of books completed nearly nineteen centuries ago and written over a period of some fifteen hundred years. Why should such a collection have the authority of finality? I have attempted to bring to the forefront the centrality of the incarnation, death, resurrection, ascension, and coming again of Jesus as the Son of God. It is what is pivotal in this complex of events that grounds and vindicates the finality of Scripture. Familiarity is too liable to obscure the significance of what occurred some two thousand years ago. Something astounding occurred, something without precedent, without parallel, without repetition. It was one unique, incomparable event. It was the coming of the Son of God in human flesh into this world of sin and death. Our minds stagger when we think of the marvel of this condescension and conjunction, the God-man combining all the attributes of deity and all the attributes of humanity in one person, and as the God-man condescending to the lowest depths of humiliation conceivable. The whole history of redemptive revelation prior to his coming was the prologue. The focal point of Old Testament revelation was messianic prophecy. Old Testament Scripture is the inscripturated deposit of the revelation given in anticipation of Christ's coming, and New Testament Scripture is the deposit of that revelation of which Christ himself is the embodiment. There is no antithesis between Christ as the personal Word and the whole Scripture as the inscripturated Word. It is by virtue of what Christ supremely and astoundingly was and is, that Scripture possesses its finality and authority. And it is because Scripture is the deposit of God's revealed will that we can have any knowledge of, or access to Christ in his identity as the Word made flesh.

This is why Scripture possesses its finality and authority. The whole of Scripture is related to the incomparable events of the coming into the world of the Son of God, of the revelation that he is, of the work he accomplished, and of the redemption he wrought. Since there is no repetition of that complex of events, since the heavens must receive the exalted Christ until the times of the restitution of all things, the Scripture partakes of the finality that is correspondent with the finality of this complex of events, in a word the finality of Christ himself. Now once in the consummation of the ages has Christ been manifested. So now once in the same consummation of the ages has revelation taken its complete and final form until Christ will come again and revelation will be resumed in the manifestation of his glory.

46

William Barclay and the Virgin Birth

In four recent issues of *The British Weekly*[1] Dr. William Barclay has dealt with the subject of the Virgin Birth. There are several features of Dr. Barclay's treatment which demand examination and refutation if the interests of the evidence bearing upon the Virgin Birth and the interests of our Christian faith relating to the same are to be maintained. I am going to focus attention upon one of these features. I am going to do so because this one contention of Barclay's, if correct, makes all further debate unnecessary. The Virgin Birth would be a travesty inconsistent with what is central in the faith of the Incarnation.

Dr. Barclay, after discussing certain difficulties which he alleges to be 'comparatively unimportant', proceeds to deal with the great difficulty, as he thinks, into which the doctrine of the Virgin Birth really runs. 'The great difficulty', he says, 'is its impact upon the belief in the incarnation. If the Virgin Birth is a literal fact, then the conclusion is quite inescapable that Jesus came into the world in a way that is different from that in which every other man comes into the world, and that . . . we can no longer hold to his full manhood and his full humanity. . . . The supreme problem of the doctrine of the Virgin Birth is that . . . it leaves us with a Jesus who is half-and-between, neither fully divine nor yet fully human'.[2]

There are several observations which the analysis of this position demands.

[1] January 17, 24, 31 and February 7, 1963.
[2] *The British Weekly*, Jan. 31, p.8.

1. Even if it were granted for the sake of the argument that the Virgin Birth would impinge upon the full manhood of Christ, how would this interfere with his full deity? Has the line of demarcation between deity and humanity become so blurred that what is supposed to diminish the latter also diminishes the former? One is compelled to suspect a conception of deity that really denies the doctrine of the Incarnation of the Son of God.

2. To Dr. Barclay's statement, 'If there is one thing to which all the New Testament writers hold, it is the full and complete humanity of Jesus', we entirely accede. There is no dispute here. But we must bear in mind with equal tenacity the absolute uniqueness of the person of Christ. He is the eternal Son of God who *became* incarnate in human nature. He is the God-man, not ceasing to be what he eternally was but having become what he was not. Any other doctrine of the Incarnation is a denial of Jesus. He alone is God-man. So there is this inerasable distinction between him and us men. It is this absolute uniqueness that constitutes him the Saviour and his work one of salvation. Any toning down at this point undermines what is central in the Christian faith and his supreme example would be bereft of its true character. The Incarnation is the stupendous fact that God in the person of the Son became man; it is supernatural throughout. Since the person is supernatural the fact of the supernatural is never suspended. With this fact of the supernatural the Virgin Birth is completely congruous. The attempt to eliminate the supernatural at the point of his begetting in the virgin's womb, in order that he may be assimilated thereby to us men, can arise only from a pattern of thought that is not oriented to the uniqueness of Jesus' person and to the stupendous reality of the Incarnation.

3. Dr. Barclay uses the argument that the Virgin Birth 'impinges on the simple idea of Jesus as our example', for then he would have 'entered into life with an advantage which is denied to all other men'. I am assuming that Dr. Barclay maintains the sinlessness of Jesus. That appears to be implied in the same article from which the quotations have been taken. In any event the sinlessness of our Lord is basic to every aspect of his relation to us. On the question at hand it is *the* 'advantage' supremely indispensable to the example that he is. To argue, therefore, that 'advantage' must be excluded in order to make his example relevant, directly

impinges upon the incomparable 'advantage' that makes his example supremely relevant. Jesus was tempted in all points like as we are, yet without sin. It is his sinlessness that gave to his temptations their peculiar poignancy and to his high-priestly feeling of our infirmities power and efficacy (cf. Heb. 4:14, 15).

But the implications of Barclay's argument are even more perilous. Jesus is the Saviour and he does not save by his example. The latter would be of no avail other than to damn us by contrast if he had not saved us from our sins. Here 'advantage' is a beggarly term to use. For it is not advantage but inimitable distinctiveness that makes Jesus precious. And it is only as our faith in him is conditioned by that in which he incomparably differs, that his example can constrain our love and emulation.

4. On Dr. Barclay's assumptions the Holy Spirit was uniquely and especially operative in the birth of Jesus, even if we suppose that the Virgin Birth were not a literal fact.[1] Suffice it to ask: How does this affect the alleged argument of 'advantage'? Does this not make such a difference that 'advantage' must be posited in any case? Here I am but pleading an *ad hominem* argument. But it surely points up the inconsistency at which Dr. Barclay arrives.

5. In his concluding article Dr. Barclay says: 'We are not here tied to any one interpretation of this story. If we choose to take it literally and physically . . . we may certainly do so'. This may seem generous. It is a deceptive generosity. It is one that Dr. Barclay has no right to offer if the argument with which we are now concerned is valid. For if the Virgin Birth would impinge upon the full manhood of Jesus and 'leave us with an incomplete incarnation'[2] then there is no alternative but to reject the Virgin Birth. There is no place for equivocation. The humanity of Jesus and the reality of the Incarnation may not be prejudiced, and if the Virgin Birth does impinge on these there is no option. Let us be out-and-out on these matters. No service is rendered to our faith nor honour to Christ by double talk. Dr. Barclay has entered the lists in propounding an argument which, if correct, makes the doctrine of the Virgin Birth a travesty of our faith. What shall we then say of his

[1] *cf. ibid.*, Feb. 7, p. 8.
[2] *ibid.*, Jan. 31, p. 8.

342

verdict: 'There are no grounds for controversy here'.[1] Dr. Barclay's contention demands controversy. It is at the point of his major argument that the issue must be joined.

[1] *ibid.*, Feb. 7, p. 8.

47

God and the War[1]

THE topic on which I dwell is 'God and the War.' The question would very naturally and perhaps urgently arise, does God have anything to do with this war? War is, to say the least, a ghastly evil. I did not say, war is wrong. The waging of war is often highly necessary and even dutiful. For a sovereign state or federation of sovereign states the waging of war is oftentimes the only resort that remains, to guard the paths of justice, to promote the interests of God-given liberty and, paradoxical as it may seem, to conserve the blessing of true peace. The waging of war upon just and necessary occasion is no more wrong than is the execution of just judgment upon the violators of civil righteousness within a particular municipality or nation. But war is a ghastly evil in that it is always the consequence of sin.

As never before in the lifetime of the oldest of us we are confronted with the barbarities and brutalities of which corrupt human nature is capable. We witness tyranny, oppression, cruelty, suffering, the destruction of precious life and property. As we think of all this, there appears to be such foolishness and absurdity to it all, not to speak of the iniquity that lies behind the whole tragedy of turmoil and devastation. Can God have anything to do with such a spectacle of waste and destruction? Surely he is of purer eyes than to behold evil and he cannot look upon sin.

It is possible that our minds are not controlled by the thought of God's holiness. Perhaps our minds are controlled by an evolutionary philosophy, and we are incurable optimists. These ordeals are, we may be disposed to say, but the birthpangs of a better day. The evolutionary

[1] *National Republic Magazine*, Washington, D.C., December 1942 and January 1943.

process proceeds through conflict and suffering, and the greater the struggle the greater hope we should entertain for the ultimate result. In the past we became too complacent towards things as they were, too complacent towards the obsolete or the obsolescent. It is necessary by the law of progress that the upheaval be all the more radical and even painful, in order that we may shake off the scales or the chains that have clogged us in the past and step forward into the vistas and achievements of a new order.

But perhaps our minds *are controlled* by the thought of the holiness of God and, if so, our answer to the question may be that it is more honouring to the one living and true God to say that this war is entirely of man's making and that God has nothing whatsoever to do with it. We perhaps think that it is beneath the dignity and majesty that are his to be in any way related to so wretched and despicable a thing as war with its entail of untold enmities and miseries.

Perhaps we might try to shield the integrity of God by supposing that the world has simply got out of hand, and that God is not able to cope with the perversity of human nature. He is doing the best he can with a bad situation, and like our good selves he deserves our warm sympathy and support.

Or again, perhaps we entertain a more noble conception of the power of God and say that he has just left the world to go its own way. He has been pouring out the bowels of entreaty, he has been striving with men. But they have not been responsive to his pleadings and warnings. Men have proved themselves hard-hearted, stiff-necked and rebellious. In holy retribution he has withdrawn his hand and, as a sad spectator, leaves men to their own resources. He allows the world for a time to reel and stagger in the wisdom that is folly. And so he has no active providence in this war. His relation to it is one of bare permission.

All of these attempts to philosophize with respect to the rationale of the present conflict may be well-meaning. Indeed some distorted element of truth, twisted from its proper orientation, shifted from its proper context, inheres in each of these attempts. For if any system were entirely devoid of plausibility, devoid of any approximation to reality, it is not likely that it would have much appeal to any large proportion of men.

The question however recurs: Are these the answers of truth? Are they the answers of God's wisdom as deposited in his Word? Are they the answers of the Christian revelation?

When the question is thus qualified the answer simply is that it will not do to say that God has nothing to do with this war. It will not do to say simply that God allows or permits this war. For the Scripture says, 'Shall there be evil in a city and the Lord hath not done it?' (Amos 3:6). 'I am the Lord, and there is none else, there is no God beside me: I girded thee, though thou hast not known me: that they may know from the rising of the sun, and from the west, that there is none beside me. I am the Lord, and there is none else. I form the light, and create darkness: I make peace, and create evil: I the Lord do all these things' (Isa. 45:5–7). 'Surely as I have thought, so shall it come to pass; and as I have purposed, so shall it stand' (Isa. 14:24). All things come to pass by God's ordination and in his providence. We are faced with the inescapable truth that the whole of history in its broadest extent and minutest detail is the unrolling of the plan devised from eternity and accomplished by him of whom and through whom and to whom are all things. If our thought is guided by the Christian revelation we are shut up to the recognition that it is no honour to God to say that he has nothing to do with this war, nor that he occupies with reference to it the position of offended but sad spectator.

What then is the meaning of this war, as that meaning may be derived from the Biblical revelation? When we say *meaning* we are not presuming to claim that we in our puny finitude, and particularly we sinners in our sinful ignorance, are able to survey all the counsel of the Eternal as it is embodied in the events of history. God's way is in the sea and his path in the great waters. His footsteps are not known. Clouds and darkness are round about him. 'Canst thou by searching find out God? Canst thou find out the Almighty unto perfection?' (Job 11:7). How little a portion do we know of his secret counsel! But we do know in part, and God has not left us to wander in total darkness with respect to the mystery of his providence and the purpose of his will.

There are at least five propositions that may be elicited from the Scriptures with respect to the meaning of this war. If viewed from the standpoint of revelation they may be called reasons. If viewed from the standpoint of our responsibility they may be called lessons.

1. *This war is an evil consequent upon sin.* It is one of the logical issues of sin. 'From whence come wars and fightings among you? Come they not hence, even of your lusts that war in your members?' (James 4:1). We cannot deal with the topic *God and the War* unless we first propound the topic *Man and the War.* The sinful cause and occasion of war is the lust of the flesh, the lust of the eye, and the pride of life.

It is, no doubt, impossible for us to diagnose all the affections, motives, volitions, acts and purposes that have converged upon one another, that have interacted with one another, and that in unison bear the onus of responsibility for the gigantic catastrophe that has now befallen the world. We must recognize that a complex movement having its root far back in history, a complex movement of sinful impulse, ambition and action that only the all-seeing eye of God can fully view and diagnose, lies back of, and comes to fruition in, this present conflict.

While we are not able to survey that movement in all its factors and in their various interactions, nevertheless we cannot but recognize the broad features of that movement. It should be far from me, loyal as I trust I am to the cause being fought by the United States, Great Britain, China and other members of the United Nations, to disavow the responsibility that rests upon the nation of which I am a grateful citizen, and upon the nation of which I am a grateful resident. But whatever of responsibility rests upon us for failures of the past, and however much we must bow in shame and humility for the sins committed in our national capacities, we must not allow our judgment to be blinded to the stark spectre that stalks before us in the crime and barbarity of the Axis nations. It surely must be said that Nazi Germany has been the main perpetrator of wrong in plunging the world into the holocaust that is now upon us. And why did Germany descend to such acts of iniquitous aggression? We cannot explain it on any other ground than that the moral fibre of the German people had undergone some radical deterioration. There must have been an eclipse of those moral principles that guide just and humane treatment of fellow men. And when we say moral eclipse, we must not dissociate that eclipse from its religious source and basis. This source we must find in departure from the one living and true God, and such departure, in a country like Germany at least, means departure from the gospel of our Lord and Saviour Jesus Christ.

We do not need any profound knowledge of history to be able to discover the source of this departure, and therefore the source of the moral and spiritual débâcle witnessed in that religion of blood and race and soil embodied in the ideology of Nazi Germany. This source is found in the naturalistic and destructive criticism of our Christian faith that found a ready home and active sponsorship in German soil. This war is the logical issue of that religion of blood and soil embraced by German Nazism, and that religion is the logical outcome of that pseudo-Christianity that is based upon the denial of the divine authority and finality of Holy Scripture as the infallible Word of God. That is the diagnosis which, I am making bold to say, is the root cause of the onslaught on decency, justice, liberty, mercy and truth we have witnessed in the Nazi aggression.

But this indictment is a humiliating one for us. It is only too obvious that that same pseudo-Christianity, and that same godless religion that is its child, have found in our nations hospitable entertainment and sponsorship. It may not have produced in our nations the same notorious fruits that have been manifest in Nazi Germany. We should be thankful that some respect for truth and justice has survived among us. Yet the very same phenomenon is with us and prevalent among us. Let us painfully know that the virus that has produced in the Nazi regime those atrocities we severely condemn is a virus that we also have fostered and cultivated. It is the virus of a pseudo-Christianity that has denied the very foundations upon which the Christian faith rests.

The roots of these crimes reside in our fallen nature. For that corruption there is but one cure—the gospel of the grace of God. In this pseudo-Christianity we have the denial of that which is our only salvation from the corruption that issues in just such barbarous acts of tyranny, oppression and destruction as have confronted us in the avalanche of Nazi power. 'The earth also was corrupt before God, and the earth was filled with violence' (Gen. 6:11). This is *Man and the War*.

2. *This war is divine retribution for sin.* We may think lightly of sin, we

may be indifferent to it. But not so God. Sin is the contradiction of his glory, the contradiction of that law that is the reflex of his holy nature. And so 'the wrath of God is revealed from heaven against all ungodliness and unrighteousness of men, who hold the truth in unrighteousness' (Rom. 1:18).

It is, of course, true that God does not execute all his wrath in this world. But it is a settled datum of history, as recorded in the Scripture and abundantly corroborated by subsequent history, that when iniquity abounds the Lord rises up out of his place to punish the inhabitants of the world for their iniquity. He did this in the case of the Old World by destroying men from off the face of the ground. He did this in the case of Sodom and Gomorrha by destroying them with fire and brimstone. The divine philosophy of history forces us to the conclusion that in this present conflict we must discern the rod of the divine anger and the staff of the divine indignation.

We rightly regard with the utmost disapprobation the unspeakable iniquities committed by the Axis nations. We think of treachery and deceit, treachery that baffles our ability adequately to depict its true character—our minds immediately travel to Pearl Harbour! We think of tyranny and ruthless persecution—Nazi oppression of Jews and Christians in Germany and in the conquered states of Europe is the very acme of this iniquity! And if we are looking for the most classic example of the inexpressibly mean and contemptible we find it in the actions of Mussolini and of the Fascist regime in Italy. We can say that these are incarnations of blatant wickedness.

There often surges up in our minds the question: Why, if God is the God of justice, if by him actions are weighed, does he not forthwith destroy such perpetrators of iniquity from off the face of the earth? We are disposed to reiterate the plaint and question of the prophet, 'Righteous art thou, O Lord, when I plead with thee: yet let me talk with thee of thy judgments: wherefore doth the way of the wicked prosper? Wherefore are all they happy that deal very treacherously? Thou hast planted them, yea, they have taken root: they grow, yea, they bring forth fruit: thou art near in their mouth, and far from their reins' (Jeremiah 12:1, 2). Or perhaps we reiterate the questions of the psalmist when we, like him, observe the prosperity of the wicked. 'How doth

God know? and is there knowledge in the Most High?' (Psalm 73 : 11).

If our minds are imbued with the principles of the divine government as set forth in the Scriptures and as exemplified in history, we cannot escape the application to Germany, Italy and Japan of the word of God through Isaiah the prophet, 'O Assyrian, the rod of mine anger, and the staff in their hand is mine indignation. I will send him against an hypocritical nation, and against the people of my wrath will I give him a charge, to take the spoil, and to take the prey, and to tread them down like the mire of the streets' (Isaiah 10:5, 6).

Assyria was not more righteous than Israel, and Assyria did not set out on its campaign of conquest and destruction with the motive and intention of executing the dictates of divine retribution upon Israel. Oh no! For Isaiah continues, 'Howbeit he meaneth not so, neither doth his heart think so; but it is in his heart to destroy and cut off nations not a few' (vs. 7). Assyria's purpose did not coincide with God's purpose and neither does the purpose of the Axis nations with which we are now at war. Nevertheless, their campaign as the campaign of Assyria fulfils in the grand strategy of God's plan the purpose of holy retribution and judgment. We cannot diagnose the meaning of the crisis that is upon us nor derive the appropriate lessons from it unless we see in large letters the writing of divine displeasure upon us for *our* sins.

It is true that in due time the divine judgment will be executed also upon the instruments of this judgment upon us. Again, as in the case of Assyria, 'Wherefore it shall come to pass, that when the Lord hath performed his whole work upon Mount Zion and on Jerusalem, I will punish the fruit of the stout heart of the king of Assyria, and the glory of his high looks' (Isaiah 10:12). 'Therefore shall the Lord, the Lord of hosts, send among his fat ones leanness, and under his glory he shall kindle a burning like the burning of a fire' (vs. 16). But the greater iniquity of the instrument of judgment, and the greater judgment that will in due time be executed upon that instrument, must not blind us to the iniquity that is the ground for the divine anger against us. God is punishing us for our iniquity, let us therefore in submissiveness and humility hear the rod and him who has appointed it: When we stagger let us know that we stagger under the staff of God's righteous indignation.

3. *This war is the divine call to repentance.* 'When thy judgments are in the earth, the inhabitants of the world will learn righteousness' (Isa. 26:9).

Naturally we all long for the date when the bells of a victorious armistice or peace will begin to toll. We naturally think of days approximating those of the past. We think in terms of economic stability and comfort, and we perhaps pray for the early cessation of hostilities. But surely we have learned that there is something more important and precious than peace. Why have we gone to war? Is it not because we have deemed something more precious than peace? We must read the text again—'the inhabitants of the world will learn righteousness'. That is the lesson of *God and the War* that bears upon us with more practical moment than anything else. It is the lesson that we have been loath to learn, the lesson of individual and national repentance. I do not think I am unduly pessimistic if I say that the signs have not been pointing in the direction of penitence and humility. We have had much humiliation, but have we put on humility as a garment? Have we acquainted ourselves with the alarming prevalence of sexual immorality and of marital infidelity? Have we followed the history of the divorce courts, the facility with which divorce may be secured, and the frequency with which divorce is sought and granted? Have we witnessed the appalling increase in profanity, a tendency given impetus, deplorable to relate, by the example of some who occupy positions of high public trust? Have we taken cognizance of the lamentable increase in desecration of the Sabbath? Have we not rather heard or read the proclamation from the highest seat of government of a seven-day week, when God has said, 'Six days shalt thou labour, and do all thy work: but the seventh day is the Sabbath of the Lord thy God' (Exod. 20:9, 10)? Have we not heard, in the terms of a pernicious antithesis, that this war is to be won in the workshop and not in the church? Can we fail to discern that the economic and educational systems of this country are very largely devised and conducted in systematic disregard of the authority and will of God? Our defiance has surely reached Babel proportions when we think that in the interests of defending our civil and religious liberties we can dispense with the laws which God has ordained. For the laws of God are the only basis and guarantee of true liberty and true worship.

Our minds are very liable in these times to be blinded by a certain kind of panic. We quite properly desire and set our minds upon the preservation of our national liberties and integrity and, in order to that end, upon the defeat of those enemies that are arrayed against us. But in preoccupation with that end we are too prone to that panic that blinds our vision of the kingdom of God and his righteousness. I would not set up a false antithesis. But we should remember that no temporal catastrophe can be as bad as the strengthening of the bands of godlessness. I am not saying that it is necessary for us to undergo ultimate defeat in order to learn righteousness. May God forbid that this should be the case. But it would be better for us to suffer the humiliation of defeat, if thereby we should learn righteousness, than to be crowned with sweeping military victory if thereby we are to be confirmed in the ways of ungodliness. 'Seek ye first the kingdom of God, and his righteousness' (Matt. 6:33). 'The kingdom of God is not meat and drink; but righteousness, and peace, and joy in the Holy Ghost' (Rom. 14:17). Let us ever remember the sovereign prerogatives of God's kingdom and even in the pursuance of a life-and-death military conflict let us learn to think even then in terms of the kingdom of him who is the 'King eternal, immortal, invisible, the only God' (1 Tim. 1:17). 'If my people, which are called by my name, shall humble themselves, and pray, and seek my face, and turn from their wicked ways; then will I hear from heaven, and will forgive their sin, and will heal their land' (2 Chron. 7:14).

4. *The perfecting of Christ's body, the church, is being promoted by this war.* The whole of history is the unfolding of God's purpose. But we must also remember that all authority in heaven and in earth has been committed unto Christ. He is head over all things, and he is head over all things to his body, the church. It is with respect to him that the Lord says, 'Yet have I set my king upon my holy hill of Zion.' 'Ask of me, and I shall give thee the nations for thine inheritance, and the uttermost parts of the earth for thy possession' (Psalm 2:6, 8). He is head over all things and is ordering all affairs in order to promote the welfare of his bride, the apple of his eye. 'All things work together for good to them that love God, to them who are the called according to his purpose' (Rom. 8:28).

We quite properly view with dismay and even horror the way in which true and faithful believers are downtrodden and persecuted in many parts of the world. We cannot but view with the keenest alarm the way in which the enemies of the gospel have been successful in frustrating the efforts of the true church to propagate the gospel, and the jeopardy into which the cause of evangelization throughout the world has been cast. We should cry from the depths of distress and real solicitude, 'Lord, how long shall the wicked, how long shall the wicked triumph?' (Psalm 94:3). And we should with grief reiterate the complaint of the psalmist, 'O God, the heathen are come into thine inheritance; thy holy temple have they defiled; they have laid Jerusalem on heaps' (Psalm 79.1). The false optimism of indifference to, or escape from, the realities of current history should have no place in our outlook. The extinction of the true church is inherent in the philosophy of Nazi Germany and pagan Japan. Here we have a religious philosophy at work that is the antithesis of the Christian faith.

But as we confront the grim realities of the present situation we must not forget the reality of the situation that is more ultimate, the situation created by the transcendent kingship of our Lord and Saviour Jesus Christ as the king and head of the church. Through all the upheavals, sufferings, tribulations, persecutions and even executions of God's people, there runs an invincible purpose that cannot fail of execution, the completion of the whole body of Christ, in line with the word of the apostle, 'I would ye should understand, brethren, that the things which happened . . . have fallen out rather unto the furtherance of the gospel' (Phil. 1:12). These sufferings fill up that which is behind of the afflictions of Christ, to the end of furthering the great purpose that Christ had in view in coming into the world, and of bringing that purpose to its consummation in the glorification of a countless multitude whom no man can number out of every nation and kindred and people and tongue. It cannot fail to be true, 'These are they which came out of great tribulation, and have washed their robes, and made them white in the blood of the Lamb' (Rev. 7:14).

Let not our certitude and peace be disturbed. Christ sits as king and he must reign until all his enemies shall have been made his footstool. He will not leave off until he will bring forth the headstone of this living temple with shoutings, crying, 'Grace, grace unto it'. 'The hands of

Zerubbabel have laid the foundation of this house; his hands shall also finish it' (Zech. 4:9).

5. *The war vindicates God's sovereignty*. It is an inexpressible comfort in these days of upheaval and turmoil to know that all events, great and small, are embraced in God's sovereign providence. He has not resigned the reins of government. Present history is not moving toward chaos. It is moving in the grand drama of God's plan and purpose to the accomplishment of his holy designs and to the vindication of his glory.

Before the avalanche of totalitarian human government, many professing Christians are capitulating and many have also enlisted in the unholy crusade of taking 'counsel together, against the Lord, and against his anointed, saying, Let us break their bands asunder, and cast away their cords from us' (Psa. 2:2, 3). With respect to the true church of God they have said, 'Come, and let us cut them off from being a nation; that the name of Israel may be no more in remembrance' (Psa. 83:4). We must be reminded in such a situation that in this universe there is only one totalitarian government, and that men must assume in it the place of humble submission and obedience. 'The Lord reigneth; let the people tremble; he sitteth between the cherubim; let the earth be moved. The Lord is great in Zion; and he is high above all the people' (Psa. 99:1, 2). 'Be still, and know that I am God. I will be exalted among the nations, I will be exalted in the earth' (Psa. 46:10). All history is under God's governance and is moving towards his tribunal where every infraction upon truth and deviation from justice will receive its final adjustment and adjudication. 'He cometh to judge the earth: with righteousness shall he judge the world, and the people with equity' (Psa. 98:9). It is here that the believer finds solace, for it is the secret place of the Most High and the shadow of the Almighty. Through all the disquieting events of our history there runs the sovereign and holy purpose of the Lord God omnipotent. And even though clouds and darkness are round about him, justice and judgment are the habitation of his throne. He fulfils his righteous purpose through the unrighteous wills of wicked men.

We must assert, and take refuge in, the absolute sovereignty of the eternal God, the absolute sovereignty of him who is the God and Father of our Lord Jesus Christ, and with equal universality the mediatorial sovereignty of the Lord Jesus Christ, the God-man, the incarnate Son, the Saviour-King, the King of kings, and Lord of lords. In the words of the prophet let us say to ourselves and others, 'Enter into the rock, and hide thee in the dust, for fear of the Lord, and for the glory of his majesty. The lofty looks of man shall be humbled, and the haughtiness of men shall be bowed down, and the Lord alone shall be exalted in that day' (Isa. 2:10, 11).

48

The Christian World Order[1]

By the term, *The Christian World Order*, I take it that what is meant is a world order that in all its aspects and spheres is Christian, an order so conformed to the principles of Christianity, and so pervaded by the forces that are operative in Christianity, that the whole of life will be brought into willing captivity to the obedience of Christ.

Are we justified in entertaining the conception of Christian world order? Or, at least, are we justified in entertaining such an order as an ideal towards which we should work and strive? Do we have any assurance that such a world order is attainable? And, if we have no assurance that it is attainable, are we not mocking ourselves and others by framing the conception and, particularly, by working towards the achievement of it? Should we not rather descend from the clouds and deal with more practical and sensible matters?

We shall have to acknowledge frankly that we do not have the right from God's Word to believe that a Christian world order in the purity and completeness of its conception will be realized on this side of that great and momentous event towards which the history of this world is moving, namely, the appearing of the glory of the great God and our Saviour Jesus Christ, the visible glorious advent of the Lord himself. For a Christian world order, in the *purity* and *completeness* of its conception, is a world order that has brought to complete and perfect fruition the redemptive, regenerative and restorative forces that are embodied in the Christian redemption and revelation. Such an order would mean the complete elimination of sin and of all its effects, and the

[1] *The Presbyterian Guardian*, October 10, 1943.

full attainment of righteousness and holiness. To whatever school of eschatological persuasion we belong, we cannot believe that such an order will antedate the advent of the Lord.

It is true that the postmillenarian believes that before Christ comes the world will become Christian. But even the most consistent supernaturalistic postmillenarian cannot hold that, even in that period of unprecedented prosperity for the kingdom of God upon earth which he posits as antedating the Lord's coming, the world order will be so completely conformed to the divine will that all sin will be eradicated and righteousness and holiness be all-pervasive. He, with other supernaturalists, believes that such an order will have to wait for the new heavens and the new earth wherein dwelleth righteousness (2 Pet. 3:13). A Christian world order, if the word 'Christian' is applied with consistency, means an order in which the principle of redemption and restoration is brought to its complete and all-pervasive expression and fruition.

So a Christian world order, in the purity and completeness of its conception, will not antedate that manifestation of power and glory when Christ will come again without sin unto salvation, when he will bring to naught all rule and all authority and power, and when all his enemies shall have been made his footstool.

Our dilemma would seem to be indeed perplexing. If we have to wait for the supernatural forces that Christ's advent will bring in its train before the order of absolute right and holiness will be ushered in, is there any sense in speaking of a Christian world order except as an eschatological hope? Particularly and most practically, is there good sense in working towards the establishment of a Christian order when we know that, in the completeness of its conception, it is not attainable in what we generally call this life?

We must be bold to say that the Christian revelation does not allow us to do anything less than to formulate and work towards a Christian world order in the life that we now live. It is not difficult to demonstrate the validity and even necessity of this thesis.

The standard of thought and the rule of conduct for us are divine obligation. The rule and standard for us are the irreducible claims and demands of the divine sovereignty, and these irreducible claims are that the sovereignty of God and of his Christ be recognized and applied in the whole range of life, of interest, of vocation and of activity. That is just saying that the demands of the divine sovereignty make it impossible for us to evade the obligation to strive with all our heart and soul and strength and mind for the establishment of an order that will bring to realization all the demands of God's majesty, authority, supremacy and kingship. And this, in a word, is simply the full fruition of the kingdom of God, wherever we are, and in the whole compass of thought, word and action.

But, since we have fallen, and since the only way now whereby the claims of the divine sovereignty can even begin to be realized within the compass of our responsibilities is through the redemptive and mediatorial work of Christ, then there rests upon us, with like universal and unrelaxed stringency, the obligation to bring to bear upon the whole compass of life the supernatural and redemptive forces that are inherent in the Christian redemption and revelation. And this is just saying that the ideal and goal imposed upon us by the kingship and kingdom of our Lord and Saviour Jesus Christ is nothing less than Christian world order. To recede from this conception and aim is to abandon what is implied in the prayer Christ taught his disciples to pray, 'Thy kingdom come, Thy will be done in earth, as it is in heaven' (Matt. 6:10). And it is to renounce what is overtly expressed in the words of the apostle, 'For though we walk in the flesh, we do not war after the flesh: (for the weapons of our warfare are not carnal, but mighty through God to the pulling down of strongholds;) casting down imaginations, and every high thing that exalteth itself against the knowledge of God, and *bringing into captivity every thought to the obedience of Christ*' (2 Cor. 10:3–5).

WHAT IS THE CHRISTIAN ORDER?

To the concrete question of what constitutes Christian world order, we may now address ourselves. It is necessary at the outset to premise any discussion of this practical question upon the fact of human sin and depravity. Any attempt to erect Christian order upon the ruins of human depravity must end in dismal failure. Indeed, it would be an inherent contradiction. For Christian order is order that is Christian and, if Christian, it rests upon the supernatural and redemptive foundations of Christianity. Christian order is order brought into existence by the deliverance from sin and evil wrought by redemption and regeneration. The principles and forces that must be at the basis and centre of Christian order in any of its forms must be the principles and forces of God's regenerative and sanctifying grace. Any idealism or reconstruction that proceeds upon a programme that is congenial to fallen human nature, or that is readily adjustable to the impulses and passions and principles of fallen human nature, has denied the very genius of Christian order.

There is, therefore, something drastic about the transformation that Christian order effects. This is why we are so reluctant to entertain a Christian programme of procedure in some of the most practical spheres, such as those of education and industry. We are so often content to have a few amendments and corrections that give a Christian veneer to certain institutions. Without question these corrections may have, to a certain extent, a salutary influence, but these amendments do not change the basically non-Christian character of the principles and methods by which these institutions or orders operate. The Christian principle as applied to every order is radical and revolutionary in the true sense of these words, radical and revolutionary because it is organically regenerative. It deals not by half-measures nor by indirection, but by honest, thoroughgoing effectiveness, with the reality of human sin and with the all-pervasive corruption it has brought in its train.

THREE DIVINE INSTITUTIONS

What then is this order that Christianity contemplates? There are three basic divine institutions in human society—the family, the church and the state. All of these institutions are social in character; in each of them there is a plurality of individuals. That plurality, it is true, may sometimes be the minimum of plurality. The family, for example, is constituted first of all by two individuals. But in each case there is plurality. This is such an elementary, obvious fact that it may seem puerile to mention it. But, elementary though it be, the implications for Christian order are of profound importance. When we say that these basic institutions comprise a plurality of individuals, we must not forget that it is a plurality of *individuals*, and we must not overlook the importance of each individual in his singularity. This has too often been the bane of social theories and movements. The individual is the ultimate unit in every social organism and organization, and Christianity never over-looks the individual person.

In dealing with Christian world order there is no concept with which Christianity has furnished us that is more expressive and comprehensive than that of the kingdom of God, and it was none other than our Lord himself who said, 'Except a man be born again, he cannot see the kingdom of God' (John 3:3), 'Except a man be born of water and of the Spirit, he cannot enter into the kingdom of God' (John 3:5), 'Except ye be converted, and become as little children, ye shall not enter into the kingdom of heaven' (Matt. 18:3). The kingdom of God begins its reconstruction with the individual. It never submerges the individual in the social mass. It never suppresses or blurs the needs, the interests, the obligations and the destinies of the individual in his relations to God or to men. Christian world order in its zeal to renovate and reconstruct the orders of society must ensure that the needs of the individual are fully met and his interests fully guarded and promoted.

THE FAMILY

It is, nevertheless, true that when we are dealing with *order* we have principally to do with the organization of individual persons. The first is the family; it is the fundamental ordinance of divine institution. The family existed prior to the fall. God said, 'It is not good that the man should be alone; I will make him an help meet for him' (Gen. 2:18). Implanted in the very nature of man is the necessity for, and the instincts towards, family life. But sin has brought ruin into the family institution. And perhaps no instinct has been more abused and no sanctity more desecrated than the instinct that is related to, and the sanctity that finds its basis in, that ordinance of marriage with which the family begins. The history of this world is strewn with the wrecks caused by the abuse and distortion of the sex impulse.

The family is the primary social ordinance. When sin wreaks its havoc here, when the sanctities that guard and ennoble family life are desecrated, and when family honour is laid in the dust, then all social order is out of joint and degradation reigns supreme in every realm.

The history of our generation and the commanding facts of developments in science, economics, and politics, the exigencies arising from the close interdependence of all nations, are compelling us to give more attention to the question of world order than ever before in the history of our era. We are all aware of the urgent concern that the leading statesmen of all countries are entertaining with respect to this question. As Christians we are compelled to face the responsibility of Christian world order. Let us not camouflage the issue. Until the family, the basic social institution, the institution through which also the individual as the ultimate unit of society is brought into being and through which he receives the heritage, the nurture and the training that will fit him for every social responsibility and function—until the family is redeemed from its sin, whether it be the sin of coarse immorality or the sin of refined godlessness, and until it is renewed and rehabilitated by the grace of God, it is a moral, psychological and social impossibility for Christian world order to be instituted.

'Husbands, love your wives, even as Christ also loved the church, and gave himself for it' (Eph. 5:25). 'Wives, submit yourselves unto your own husbands, as unto the Lord' (Eph. 5:22). 'Children, obey your parents in the Lord: for this is right. Honour thy father and mother; which is the first commandment with promise; that it may be well with thee, and thou mayest live long on the earth. And, ye fathers, provoke not your children to wrath: but bring them up in the nurture and admonition of the Lord' (Eph. 6:1–4). 'But fornication, and all uncleanness, or covetousness, let it not be once named among you, as becometh saints' (Eph. 5:3). These are the affections, instincts, and principles that must regulate marital and family life, and only then can any Christian foundation be laid for that social organization that can be called Christian. The Christian programme is radical, and we see how grave the responsibility and colossal the task when we face the dismal fact that the rarity of the Christian family makes it as precious as diamonds.

THE CHURCH

The second basic divine institution is the church, the visible church. It might seem that, since the church is an ordinance of redemption and pre-eminently the institution of God's redemptive grace, since it is the company of the faithful, renovation and reconstruction would not have to be applied to the church as to the individual and to the family. It might seem, rather, that from the church would radiate the influences and forces of renovation. But alas! we have to deplore the fact that the professing church has to a lamentable extent become the habitation of dragons and the scene of abominations. If the church had been unfalteringly faithful to the principle of its origin, constitution, witness and operation, then the situation would simply be that it should have to continue to unfold and apply with ever-increasing perseverance the principles upon which it rests. But the sad fact of our situation today is that judgment must begin at the house of God and the church must have applied to it the same radical, revolutionary and reconstructive principles and forces which we have already found to be indispensable to Christian world order.

The church is the church of Christ. It is subject to him, derives its faith from him, owes obedience to him, performs the functions prescribed by him, restricts itself to the sphere appointed by him and advances his glory. Faith, testimony, worship, government—these four words sum up the function of the church. It is faith absolutely faithful to the Word of God. It is worship in accordance with the prescriptions of his will. It is government directed by the ecclesiastical order instituted by Christ and his apostles. It is testimony to the whole counsel of God to all nations and kindreds and peoples and tongues.

Truly it is not the function of the church to put Christian world order into effect. The church must occupy its own sphere of operation and limit itself severely to that sphere appointed to it by Christ. When the church attempts to become totalitarian then it has violated Christian order. But it is the function of the church to establish and promote Christian order within its own divinely instituted domain, and it *is* the function of the church to *proclaim* the world order to which God's sovereignty and Christ's headship obligate in every sphere.

O how crushing is the shame that rests upon the church! Christian world order is an impossibility when the institution that is pre-eminently the instrument of testimony to Christ is itself the chamber of abominations. It is surely mockery and hypocrisy for the church to point the way when she herself has committed whoredom in the sanctuary of God.

Judgment must begin at the house of God, judgment that will issue in purification of faith, of testimony, of worship, and of government. Purified and renewed, sound in faith, steadfast in testimony, pure in worship and faithful in government, the church will become the channel of redeeming light and grace to a world lost and staggering in the confusion that the rejection of the counsel of the King of kings has brought upon it. 'O that thou hadst hearkened to my commandments! then had thy peace been as a river, and thy righteousness as the waves of the sea' (Isa. 48:18). When the church puts on her garments of glory and beauty, then under the captaincy of him who is Faithful and True, the King of kings and Lord of lords, she will go forth, fair as the moon, clear as the sun and terrible as an army with banners. Then it will be said again, 'In Judah is God known: his name is great in Israel. In Salem also is his tabernacle, and his dwelling place in Zion. There brake he the arrows of the bow, the shield, and the sword, and the battle. Thou art more glorious and excellent than the mountains of prey' (Psalm 76:1–4). Humiliating indeed is our reproach. But by God's grace and Christ's power, how glorious our vocation and responsibility!

THE STATE

The state is the third basic divine institution. It might be thought that, while the redemptive and regenerative forces of Christianity have an obvious bearing upon the individual, the family and the church, yet the state cannot be regarded as coming in any direct way under the demands and influences of the Christian revelation. The state has to do with civil order, the preservation and promotion of civil righteousness, liberty and peace. It will be said that the civil magistrate in the discharge of his official functions has no religious obligations and therefore should not and cannot be regulated in the discharge of his office by the Christian revelation; in other words, that the Bible is not the rule of conduct for the civil magistrate as it is for the individual, for the family and for the church.

This position embraces a strange mixture of truth and error. There is truth in this position insofar as it recognizes the limits of civil authority. Civil authority is not totalitarian. Civil authority must never trespass into the sphere of the family, or of the church, and it must guard the God-given rights and prerogatives of the individual. If the distinction of spheres is once blurred or obliterated, then good order is impossible and Christian principles are negated.

It is also true that those in whom is vested the right of civil government must exercise that government in accordance with the laws of the commonwealth. If they are not able to do this in accordance with conscience, then they must abdicate their office or seek by the constitutional means provided by the commonwealth to change those laws. Especially is this the case with believers who recognize that their supreme obligation is to God and to Christ.

But a fatal element of error inheres in this position, if it is thought that the Christian revelation, the Bible, does not come to the civil authority with a demand for obedience to its direction and precept as stringent and inescapable as it does to the individual, to the family and to the church. The thesis we must propound as over against such a conception of the relation of the Bible to civil authority is that the Bible is the only infallible rule of conduct for the civil magistrate in the discharge of his magistracy, just as it is the only infallible rule in other spheres of human activity.

God alone is sovereign. His authority alone is absolute and universal. All men and spheres are subject to God. The civil magistrate derives his authority from God. Apart from divine institution and sanction, civil government has no right to exist. 'The powers that be are ordained of God' (Rom. 13:1). Since civil government derives its authority from God, it is responsible to God and therefore obligated to conduct its affairs in accordance with God's will. The infallible revelation of his will God has deposited in the Scriptures. It will surely be granted that there is much in the Scriptures that has to do with the conduct of civil government. And this simply means that the Word of God bears upon civil authority with all the stringency that belongs to God's Word.

Furthermore, the Word of God reveals that Christ is head over all things, that he has been given all authority in heaven and in earth. The civil magistrate is under obligation to acknowledge this headship and therefore to conduct his affairs, not only in subjection to the sovereignty of God, but also in subjection to the mediatorial sovereignty of Christ, and must therefore obey his will as it is revealed for the discharge of that authority which the civil magistrate exercises in subjection to Christ. Christian world order embraces the state. Otherwise there would be no Christian *world order*.

To recede from this position or to abandon it, either as conception or as goal, is to reject in principle the sovereignty of God and of his Christ. The goal fixed for us by the Christian revelation is nothing less than a Christian state as well as Christian individuals, Christian families and a Christian church. And this just means that the obligation and task arising from Christ's kingship and headship are that civil government, within its own well-defined and restricted sphere, must in its constitution and in its legislative and executive functions recognize and obey the authority of God and of his Christ and thus bring all of its functions and actions into accord with the revealed will of God as contained in his Word. We thus see how radical and reconstructive is a philosophy of Christian world order, if we are to face that conception frankly and address ourselves to the responsibility it entails.

It is, of course, true that all of life is not exhausted by the family, the church and the state. These, however, are the basic divine institutes of society. A Christian world order will embrace every department of life —industry, agriculture, education, recreation. But since these institutions are basic, it is inevitable that the Christianizing of every other department of life will proceed apace with the Christianizing of these basic institutions.

When we contemplate such stupendous responsibility as that arising from the sovereignty of God and of Christ's supreme kingship and lordship, we may well be crushed by the sense of our own insufficiency. How weak we are and how formidable are the enemies of God and of his kingdom! Who is sufficient for these things? We are indeed totally insufficient and the task is overpowering.

But this overpowering sense of our weakness and inability is no reason for faintheartedness. It is rather the very condition of true faith and perseverance. The responsibility is ours: it is stupendously great. The insufficiency is ours: it is complete. But the power is God's. The grace is of God. The promise is his. 'Thou hast a mighty arm: strong is thy hand, and high is thy right hand. Justice and judgment are the habitation of thy throne: mercy and truth shall go before thy face' (Psalm 89:13, 14). How necessary it is to remember that Christ has spoiled principalities and powers, triumphing over them in his death, and that he is now exalted far above all principality and power and might and dominion and every name that is named, not only in this world but also in that to come! Being by the right hand of God exalted and having received the promise of the Father, he hath sent forth the Holy Spirit. We must do honour to Christ and to his kingly authority and might. We must also do honour to the Holy Spirit who convicts the world of sin, of righteousness and of judgment. We have not only an almighty advocate in heaven at the right hand of God, but also an almighty advocate upon earth. How puny and helpless are the powers of evil when they are set over against the irresistible grace and power of him who is himself God, possessing with the Father and the Son the totality of Godhood, the Spirit of the Father and of the Son! And how shameful and vile is our faintheartedness and unbelief! 'Greater is he that is in you, than he that is in the world' (1 John 4:4). It is the peculiar prerogative of the Holy Spirit to take of the things of Christ and show them unto us. It is his to glorify Christ. Let us lay hold upon the promise, 'If ye then, being evil, know how to give good gifts unto your children: how much more shall your heavenly Father give the Holy Spirit to them that ask him!' (Luke 11:13), and let us in his strength go forth to claim every realm for him who must reign until all his enemies shall have been made his footstool.

49

Christian Education[1]

Any one who is alive to and reflects upon our social responsibilities knows how colossal and complex an undertaking is the education of youth. The evils which the educational enterprise encounters are manifold and there is no uniformity in the problems arising. They vary from decade to decade and from place to place, indeed also from individual to individual.

The topic of Christian education may be approached from the angle of an evil of which I fear too few are aware, but one that is the bane of education at all levels. It is the bane of fragmentation. By fragmentation I mean that the pupil is not provided with what imparts a sense of unity, of wholeness, of correlation. This may most properly be called the need for, and aim of, *integration*. There is ground for suspicion that this directing principle is frequently absent and, therefore, those responsible for education at all levels need to address themselves to this question for self-assessment.

Perhaps the most germane example of the thesis that integration is a paramount concern of education is the place that education occupies in the fostering and development of character. It is not to be questioned that culture, however highly cultivated, has failed of its chief end if it contributes to the promotion of evil rather than that of good. The more highly educated the boy or girl becomes, the more dangerous the education acquired becomes if it is brought into the service of wrong-doing. It is easy to take the position that the fostering and cultivating of

[1] An address given in Dingwall, Ross-shire, in January 1973.

good character is not the concern of the school, that this is the function of the home and of the church. Admittedly, the home and the church are basically responsible, and it is also obvious that when the home and the church neglect this culture or are even remiss in imparting it, then the school is faced with a well-nigh impossible task. But it is apparent how devastating to the best influences exerted by the home and church will be the influence of the school if it pretends to be neutral on moral issues, or if the teaching of the school is alien to the ethical principles inculcated by home or church or both. And as it concerns integration, how chaotic for the pupil if opposing ethical norms are fostered in the same school. We know only too well to what depraved human nature inclines.

Underlying the plea for integration and co-ordination in education is the need for a unified world-view, a common conception of reality. If there is basic divergence in reference to world-view there cannot possibly be integration in education. It is here that our present topic becomes relevant and mandatory. Primarily there must be the acknowledgement that the Christian faith is ultimate for thought and outlook, that the Scriptures of the Old and New Testaments are the Word of God, the infallible rule of faith and practice, and that for us now special revelation from God comes to us only in these Scriptures. And I submit that on any other premise our Christian faith cannot be maintained, defended, and promoted. In Christ we have the supreme revelation of God. He is God incarnate, the effulgence of God's glory and the express image of his being, the image of the invisible God, and the focus of revelation. But this in no way displaces or prejudices the finality of Scripture, because only in Scripture do we have the revelation that he is, and only through Scripture do we come into saving contact with him.

Now if the biblical revelation is ultimate for thought, outlook, and practice, we must readily see the implications for education. We have found that education must aim at integration, and that this integration must rest upon and proceed from a philosophy, a world view, an integrated conception of reality. The Christian, unless he is afflicted with intellectual schizophrenia, derives his integration and his world view from the Christian faith, and this means from the Christian revelation.

namely, Holy Scripture. To use other terms, every thought is brought into captivity to Christ and therefore to the revelation of which Christ is the focus. And the Christian teacher abandons his or her faith at the point of vocation in life if he or she fails to bring this integration to bear upon the education conducted. In a word, education must be Christian. And this means far more than that the teacher conducts himself or herself as a Christian; it means that the subject matter of the classroom must derive its interpreting principles from the Christian revelation.

It is not difficult to illustrate how this orientation comes to expression and conditions the character of the instruction. No tenet is more basic in our Christian faith than the doctrine of creation, that God created the heavens and the earth. This is the answer to the 'Whence?' of our world and of the universe. How indispensable to education from the earliest years, even before the child arrives at school age, is the word of Gen. 1:1: 'In the beginning God created the heavens and the earth.' That God made the world and all things is close to the first, if not the first, element of nursery instruction, and it is a capital mistake to think that this concept diminishes in relevance as education advances. No question is more urgent than that of whence. Whence our environment? Whence the universe in which we live? Correlative is the doctrine of God's providence, that not only did God make the world but that also he sustains it by his power and directs it by his wisdom, and that, as we have derived our being from him, in him we live and move and have our being.

We are painfully aware of the extent to which aimlessness, frustration, and despair have gripped our generation. Life is, for so many devoid of meaning or intelligible purpose. Are we to suppose that our schools have no responsibility? It is fully admitted that the family and the church bear a large share of the default creating this situation. But unless the school fosters the fear of the Lord as the beginning of knowledge and of wisdom, the influence of the home and of the church, even when it is to a high degree exemplary, tends to be negated, and it is common knowledge and experience that in many cases the school has undermined what home and church have sought to establish and develop.

On the other hand, it is to the credit of teachers and of schools that, when home and church have gone by default, certain teachers and schools have done the greatest service in filling the vacuum which this default has left in the culture of the pupils.

I have made reference to creation by God and to his all-sustaining and directing providence as basic to the world view which the Christian revelation provides and therefore indispensable to the integration which a biblically oriented education will furnish. There is another aspect of the Christian revelation that is fundamental to this same objective. Education is concerned with human beings. But what is man? More properly, who is man? Education, apart from any conception of man as to his distinguishing identity, purpose, and destiny, is inconceivable. Many teachers may not be intelligently aware of the theory that underlies their teaching practice. But theory there must be. If it is not determined by conscious reflection on the part of the teacher, it has been shaped by tradition, or by the training the teacher received, or by the educational system in which the teacher plays a part. If education is to be Christian, it must be based upon and conducted in terms of the Christian view of man. If not, it is not Christian, and if not Christian it is alien and opposed to Christian interests. What is man? What is his distinct identity and office? Here the Christian faith is unequivocal. The whence of man is, with all other things, the creative action of God. But what is his identity? It is this, that man was made in the image of God. It is not that the image of God is in man. Man is in the image of God, man *is* the image of God. This is his definition and his definition involves his function and purpose. Further expansion of this subject cannot be undertaken now. But the implications for education are bound to be obvious. Perhaps the observation of paramount importance is that education is hereby placed in an entirely different perspective by reason of the dignity belonging to the being of man and the corresponding responsibility devolving upon those concerned with the culture of that being. To put it pointedly, education is concerned not with entities but with persons who are the image of God, persons with respect to whom this is most ultimate that they are made in the image of God. If and when teachers become imbued with this conception, then their vocation comes to be viewed in an entirely different perspective.

When the Westminster Assembly placed at the head of its Shorter Catechism the question: 'What is man's chief end?' and gave the answer:

'Man's chief end is to glorify God, and to enjoy him for ever', it was giving, not only the keynote of a sound theology, it was enunciating a foundation principle of sound pedagogy. If boys and girls, young men and young women, are in the image of God, if that is their identity, their chief end cannot be anything less than to glorify God and to enjoy him. And education that is destitute of this objective, or has allowed it to suffer eclipse has lost its direction. That the glory of God and the enjoyment of him is the goal of all life, is surely an axiom of Christian profession. If education is the preparation for more mature and competent life, it cannot be any exception.

If education is to be conducted in terms of the viewpoint provided by the Christian faith, then to ignore what is central in the Christian faith would be impossible; for to ignore what is central would nullify the Christian character of the education. What is central? It is redemption, and redemption presupposes the need for redemption—sin in its guilt, defilement, and power. Education is not directed to boys and girls, men and women who are unafflicted by the depravity and liabilities of sin. It is directed to those who are natively in rebellion against God. The essence of sin is to be against God and against our fellow human beings. This is its extreme gravity and the judgment of God is correspondingly extreme. If we fail to take account of our definition as human beings, that we are made in the image of God, then education misses its chief end, as noted earlier. But it is the fact that man is in the image of God that makes sin so serious and, consequently, makes all the more indispensable the religious instruction that is specifically Christian, that is to say, the religious instruction centred in the realities of sin and redemption. All of this is implicit in the terms 'Christian Education'. If it is Christian, it is Christo-centric and thus must find its focus in all that is involved in the person and work of the Lord and Saviour Jesus Christ as Redeemer and Lord. There is no common denominator religion that meets the human situation in its sin and judgment. Only the provisions of God's grace in the Son of his love meet our need. And to withhold from pupils the elements of the Christian faith is not only to conceal from them the realities of life but also to deprive them of the only means of meeting the exigencies and crises of life and of fulfilling the great end of their existence. To put it bluntly, it is to damn them to godlessness.

The thesis I have been propounding is not that of religious education in schools, and not simply that of Christian education in schools. The thesis does imply the latter. But there may be Christian education in schools and yet the education may not be Christian. And the reason is that the subjects which are the main business of the school curriculum are not taught from the standpoint of the world view derived from the Christian revelation. Christianity gives us a world view; it enunciates principles which underlie all our thinking if we are Christian; it prescribes the governing conceptions in terms of which we are to interpret reality. Christianity is not something tacked on to our world view; it is itself a world view. And the central features of our Christian faith are conditioned by, and in turn condition, that world view.

Two examples will suffice, the teaching of history and science.

History is the unfolding of God's plan in the world he created, the world he sustains by his power, and directs in wisdom, justice and grace. In the words of the Reformer, John Calvin: 'While the turbulent state of the world deprives us of our judgment, God by the pure light of his justice and wisdom regulates all these commotions in the most exact order and directs them to their proper end' (*Inst.* I, xvii, 1). It is not that we can scan the hidden purposes of God or fathom the depths of his counsel. His way is in the sea and his path in the great waters; his footsteps are not known. But how important for life to know that history is not the product of aimless fate, but that God's counsel stands and he will do all his pleasure! The grandeur of God's sovereignty must govern our view of history, and no greater service can be rendered by the school than to ensure that children and youth become imbued with this conception. By the same token it is tragedy if we fail.

In respect of science, there are two principles that have to be borne in mind. The first is that the pursuit is in fulfilment of God's mandate to subdue the earth and therefore to bring its resources into the service of man. This should impress upon us the dignity of the vocation, the vocation of scientific research. This is the Christian attitude and it is not too early for pupils at the primary school to be imbued with this attitude as their teachers seek to demonstrate the wonders and treasures of the world in which they live and from which they derive their sustenance. The second principle is that 'the highest aim of scientific investigation', to use borrowed words, is 'to glorify God by bringing to light the wonders which God fabricated into the structure of this marvellous world and the universe of which it is a part' (G. H. Girod in *Torch and Trumpet*, Sept. 1967, p. 4). Is not the highest aim that we should be constrained to exclaim at every stage of scientific progress: 'O Lord, how manifold are thy works! in wisdom hast thou made them all: the earth is full of thy riches' (Psalm 104:24)! It is readily seen how radically different the classroom becomes when these two principles govern the thought of the teacher and are therefore communicated to the pupils of his charge. And let it not be forgotten that no other orientation is compatible with the world-view our Christian faith provides and demands.

It is plausible to maintain that, although the implications of the Christian faith have a close bearing upon the teaching of history, for example, yet in the teaching of languages, in arithmetic, and mathematics there could not be any difference between the secular school and the Christian school. Are we to suppose that there is a Christian Latin as distinct from non-Christian, a Christian arithmetic as distinct from non-Christian? This is not the contention of those espousing the cause of Christian education and it is misunderstanding and misrepresentation to suppose or aver that it is. But the implications of the Christian faith have, nevertheless, the most intimate bearing on instruction concerned with such subjects.

Let us take, for example, the subject of language. It is a platitude to say that language is a most interesting phenomenon. But I submit that it is not a platitude to say that it is an astounding phenomenon. I also submit that there is a lamentable hiatus in the teaching of language if this feature is not impressed upon the student. For this hiatus neglects what supplies the highest motivation and incentive to language culture. The point here is: why does man speak? Why is there for man the privilege of such diversified and enriching communication? The reason is that God speaks, and man speaks because he is made in the image of God. And the same principle applies to writing as the recording of speech. This is the foundation of Christian education as it is concerned with language and literature.

Or again, let us think of mathematics. It is not that there is Christian and non-Christian mathematics. But in the Christian school mathematics